BIBLE CHARACTERS

Jeremy & Sheila Dare

Date : Nov 1975

BIBLE CHARACTERS

ALEXANDER WHYTE, D.D.

VOLUME ONE

OLD TESTAMENT

MARSHALL, MORGAN & SCOTT
London

MARSHALL MORGAN, AND SCOTT
BLUNDELL HOUSE
GOODWOOD ROAD
LONDON SE14 6BL

Two Volume Edition 1952
Reprinted 1953
Reprinted 1956
Reprinted 1958
Reprinted 1959
Reprinted 1962
Reprinted 1964
One Volume Edition 1967
This Edition 1972

ISBN 0 551 05138 8

PRINTED IN GREAT BRITAIN BY
LOWE AND BRYDONE (PRINTERS) LTD., LONDON

VOLUME ONE

THE OLD TESTAMENT

An account of the world in this
one single view as God's world.

—Butler

CONTENTS—PART ONE

FIRST SERIES

Adam to Achan

SECOND SERIES

Gideon to Absalom

THIRD SERIES

Ahithophel to Nehemiah

BIOGRAPHICAL NOTE

Alexander Whyte was born in the Southmuir of Kirriemuir, Angus, on 13 January, 1836, and died in London on 6 January, 1921. His career therefore covered the greater part of the nineteenth century; and as his biographer says, " it was no ordinary life which began in a two-roomed Forfarshire cottage in the decade of the Reform Bill, when the Ten Years' Conflict in Scotland and the Oxford Movement in England were changing the face of the religious world; and which reached its quiet close in Hampstead amid the menacing ground-swell which followed the storm of the Great War ". Though he followed with ardent interest all the public events of those 80 years, being at heart a strong Gladstonian, he never allowed anything but his duty to the pulpit and the congregation to claim his real attention. The result was, to quote his biographer once more, that " the pulpit was his throne "; and, as everyone knew, he made his name as " Whyte of Free St. George's ". His method was to devote a long morning, usually from 8 o'clock till 2 in the afternoon, to work at his desk; and it was in these hours that all his pulpit work was prepared. From his earliest years he turned his face towards the Church; and it is on record that, when he was employed as a small boy by a farmer near Kirriemuir to herd the cattle, the farmer's wife, seeing the cattle straying into the growing corn, came out " raging him " with the words, " I dinna ken fat ye're gaen to dae, or foo in the hale warld ye'll ever earn an honest living ". The delinquent appears to have met this onslaught calmly—" What wad ye think if ae day I was to wag my pow in a poopit?"

Whyte's message was directed straight to heart and conscience; and he was wont to say that theology and the strife of contending schools were not for him. To follow in the steps of The Master and to lead his flock in the same path would fill all the working day " and the night too, for that matter ". Yet " sermon ", in the ordinary sense of that forbidding word, was no true name for the message he delivered. He could be solemn and awe-inspiring when needed; but the path of his argument was lit by flashes of humour, more often than not derived from the homeliest source. The seed-bed of his word was the Bible, Old and New Testament alike, watered and enriched by Bishop Butler, William Law, The Shorter Catechism and the *Pilgrim's Progress.* And the modern generation may well be reminded that his Commentary on the Shorter Catechism was long a minor—some would say a major —classic in the religious reading of Scotland.

Whyte had his reward for his undeviating attention to the pulpit of Free St. George's and to his Sunday Evening Class for men, in world-wide recognition of his well-nigh unique service to mind and conscience. How that reward was earned, readers of this book may learn for themselves. But, it is not inappropriate to recall here the words written by his eldest son soon after Whyte's death thirty years ago :–

"He was sent as the messenger of the Church to rally the Highlands after the shock of the judgment of the House of Lords (1905). Never have I heard him deliver an appeal so powerful in its simplicity, so racy in its manner, so moving in its effect. His theme was always the same: that the Church was greater than the Law by which it had been smitten, and that the mission of the Church was greater than the Church itself. With an infinite variety of illustration, drawn from Scripture, from Bunyan, from the daily paper, and from the hillsides and lochs that spread their coloured panorama like a vast amphitheatre round his open-air pulpit, he delivered a message which his own congregation in Edinburgh was hardly ever privileged to hear. During the Highland tour of 1905 the power and freedom of his address exceeded anything before or since. It was a spoken word *in excelsis,* and could hardly be transferred to the written page.

"The tour covered seven counties, by rail, motor, and wagonette; starting out at 8 o'clock in the morning, stopping about 11 at a wayside church or to meet a vast concourse on a heathered hillside, moving on again, an hour later, to lunch with a selected body of ministers who came in from all parts to greet him; and pressing on again to repeat twice before sunset the experiences of the morning. He was in his seventieth year, yet neither in body nor in spirit did he show signs of fatigue. No great political leader ever underwent a greater strain in popular work, or was received with greater devotion. I remember, before we had proceeded far on the tour, he used to say to me every morning, 'Now, Fred, you have heard all this before: you had better go off and fish; you can come back in the evening, and we shall see whether your basket is better than mine'. It was remarkable that, though he was really delivering the same message on each occasion, it never emerged from his ardent mind twice in the same form."

LONDON
1952.

SIR FREDERICK WHYTE.

First Series

ADAM TO ACHAN

I

ADAM

LET US MAKE MAN
IN OUR IMAGE

In the wise and good providence of Almighty God a new and an entrancing light has been cast in our day on the origin of the earth and on the early ages of mankind. A noble succession of ministers and interpreters of nature has been raised up in these later generations who, by the labours they have undertaken, and by the methods they have followed, have been enabled to make discoveries that had not entered the mind of man to imagine in former ages. Up till our day far more was known about the way and process of our redemption than about the way and process of our creation. But it will be in the complete and harmonious combination of these two kinds of knowledge, divine revelation and human science, that we shall come to a perfect man, in which the whole body of knowledge and faith and love shall be fitly joined together and compacted by that which every joint supplieth.

Magnificent as have been the services of such men as Herschel, and Faraday, and Lyell, and Darwin, and Spencer, at the same time their magnificent services have lain far more in the regions of matter and motion than in the mind and the heart of man. It is enough for any man, or for any school of men, to be enabled to take us back to the first beginnings of this present system of things, when as yet our earth was without form and void, and to lead us up step after step, age after age, till we open our eyes on this wonderful world as it now is. To one of His servants God gives the talents of revelation and inspiration, and to another the talents of observation, and experiment, and discovery, and the exposition of discovery—to each one of His servants separately as He will. And to each several steward and servant of His, according to his faithfulness to the talents committed to him, his Master at His coming will say, 'Well done!' And it is surely a kind of forecast and foretaste of that "Well done!"—the warm exclamation of wonder and of worship that rises out of our enlarged minds and exalted hearts as we lay down *The Outlines of Astronomy, The Principles of Geology, The Origin of Species, The First Principles,* and suchlike books. At the same time, at their best, those ministers and interpreters of nature do not satisfy their readers. Even in their own rich and well-worked fields they do not satisfy all their readers. Even after they have led us so far up on the shining path of scientific truth, we feel sure that there are still sources and paths and fields of light, as well as shadows and belts and whole worlds of darkness, over which we have been hurried, and into which we have not been led or let look. We feel not unlike that famous philosopher of our day who divined that there must surely be a serious disturbance somewhere in the order and stability of the solar system that no astronomy had as yet discovered, acknowledged, or attempted to account for. As we are carried away by the spell of the great writers on evolution, we feel all the time that, after all has been told, there is still something unrecognised and undescribed from which we suffer the most disturbing and injurious influences. All the time we feel in ourselves a backward, sideward, downward, perverse pull under which we reel and stagger continually; it is an experience that makes us wiser than all our teachers in some of the most obscure, but at the same time some of the most certain matters of mankind and their spiritual history. Speaking for myself, as I read the great books of our modern scientific men with a delight and an advantage I cannot put enough words upon, I always miss in them—in them all, and in the best of them all—a matter of more importance to me than all else that they tell me. For, all the time I am reading their fascinating discoveries and speculations, I still feel in myself a disturbance, a disorder, a disharmony and a positive dislocation from the moral, and even from the material, order of the universe around me and above me: a disorder and a dislocation that my scientific teachers neither acknowledge nor leave room for its acknowledgment or redress. That is magnificent! That is noble! That is divine! I exclaim as I read. But when I come to the end of my reading—Is that all? I ask. I am compelled by all my experience and all my observation to ask, Is that all? Is that your very last word to me? Then, if that is all, I must still go in search of a philosophy of nature and of man that understands me, and accounts for me, and has, if so be, a more comprehensive, a more scientific, a more profound, and a more consoling message to me. In one word, and to speak out the whole of my disappointment and complaint in one word, What about SIN? What is SIN? When and where did SIN enter in the evolution of the human race and seize in this deadly way on the human heart? Why do you all so avoid and shut your eyes to SIN? And, still more, what about JESUS CHRIST? Why do I find nothing in your best text books about HIM who was WITHOUT SIN? About Him who is more to me, and to so many more of your best readers, than all Nature, and all her suns, and systems, and laws, and processes put together? Far more. For He has carried both our understanding and our imagination and our heart so absolutely captive that we cannot read with our whole heart the best book you have written because His name is not in it. WHO and WHAT is HE, we insist, who has leapt at a bound above all law and all order of matter and of mind, and of cosmic and ethic evolution, and has taken His stand of holiness at the head of the human race? Schools of science, schools of morals, schools of philosophy, ministers and interpreters of nature and of man, what is SIN? and what think ye of CHRIST?

Bishop Butler has taught us, and that with an impressiveness we can never forget, that knowledge at its best is not our proper happiness. With all his immense weight Butler has impressed upon us that our proper province is virtue and religion, life and manners; the science of improving the temper and making the heart better. This is the field assigned us to cultivate, he exclaims, and how much it has lain neglected is indeed astonishing! And thus it is that Moses, so to call him, with two or three splendid strokes, passes over all that which so fascinates and absorbs our modern men of science, and takes up mankind at that point when they have the image and likeness of God completely and perfectly stamped upon them. Nor does Moses delay long, even upon that, but, after one great and fruitful word upon that, he passes on to take up at more length, in his own wonderful way, and in answerable style, the temptation and the fall of Adam and of all Adam's offspring. 'The Scripture begins,' says Butler, 'with an account of God's creation of the world, in order to ascertain who He is concerning whose providences, commands, promises, and threatenings this sacred book all along treats, the Maker and Proprietor of the world, He whose creatures we are—the God of Nature. Revelation, indeed, considers the common affairs of this world, and what is going on in it, as a mere scene of distraction, and cannot be supposed to give any account of this wild scene for its own sake. This earth, our habitation, has everywhere the appearance of being a ruin, and revelation comes in on the supposition that this world is in a ruined state.' Thus Butler. And Moses begins his priceless contribution to that revelation by telling us what, without him, would have remained a dreadful mystery to us—that is to say, he tells us how man was made upright, and how he fell from that estate wherein he was created by sinning against God. It is a fashion with the prevailing philosophy of our day to decry and contemn the old, orthodox, and fruitful argument from final causes; but I shall continue, in this matter also, to follow Bishop Butler, to me by far the deepest and the wisest philosopher the world has ever seen. Now Moses, long before Butler, is clear and sure as to the final cause of our creation. In his opening pages, Moses, after his royal manner, lets us hear the Maker of all things taking counsel with Himself concerning His end and object in the creation of man. "Let us make man in our image, after our likeness.' And then, from this and from many other Scriptures, we learn that the image and likeness of God is love: love, knowledge, righteousness, and true holiness, with dominion over the creatures.

Now, the multiplication and the increase of the image of God is an altogether worthy reason, adequate explanation, and final cause for the creation of this world, and for all the processes, preparations, and providences through which this world has passed. Love amply accounts for and explains and justifies it all —God's love to man, and then man's love to God and to his neighbour. All of God's wisdom and power that was expended on this world, and on Adam its possessor and its priest, was all to find its reward and its return in a world replenished with a race of creatures who were to be such partakers of the divine nature that they would live for ever and grow for ever in the love, in the holy fellowship, in the blessed service, and in the full enjoyment of God. That was why God made man. That was why God prepared such a home for man as this world in Adam's day was, and still in our day is. The Garden of Eden in Moses, delightful as it is, is but a dim, a faded, and colourless picture of what God had prepared for them that were to walk with Him in that garden, and were to tell Him, as they walked with Him, how much they loved Him who had planted it. But all the time, as Thomas Goodwin says, the true Garden of Eden was in the gardener's own heart. And his blessed task was set to Adam in his own heart. And what more blessed task could have been set by God to man than to till, and water, and dress, and keep, and reap his own heart for God? And that the serpent came in all his malignity and subtlety and sowed tares in that mystical garden—that should only have given God's son and servant an embraced opportunity and an occasion of all joy to show to God and to the serpent, to heaven to hell, how much he loved and feared God for all that God had done for him. But, how it went with Adam and with Eve, and with the Garden of Eden, and with Cain and Abel their children, Moses tells us in his sad history. And then, by the time he takes his pen in hand to tell us all this, Moses himself has been banished out of Canaan for his sin, and is waiting for death in the wilderness. And thus it is that he dips his pen in such an inkhorn of tears, and describes to us with such sympathy, and in such sad words, that aboriginal mystery of iniquity—the temptation, the fall, and the expulsion of Adam from Eden. And then Moses adds in a psalm which he indites more immediately concerning himself the well-known words: 'Thou turnest man to destruction; and sayest, Return, ye children of men. For we are consumed by Thine anger, and by Thy wrath are we troubled. Thou hast set our iniquities before Thee, our secret sins in the light of Thy countenance. Who knoweth the power of Thine anger? Even according to Thy fear, so is Thy wrath. Return, O Lord, how long? And let it repent Thee concerning Thy servants. Make us glad according to the days wherein Thou hast afflicted us, and the years wherein we have seen evil.'

In one of William Law's finest dialogues Theophilus asks his pupil Humanus how he would set about convincing a man of his fallen estate. And Humanus answers to this effect: Man is a poor, miserable, weak, vain, distressed, corrupt, depraved, selfish, self-tormenting, perishing creature. And this world is a sad mixture of false good and real evil; a widespread scene of all sorts of trials, vexations, and miseries, all arising from the frame and nature and condition both of man and the world. This is the sure and infallible proof of the fall of man. The fall of man is not a thing to be learnt from any history whatsoever, but shows itself everywhere and every day and in every man with as much clearness as we see the sun. My first attempt, therefore, upon any man, to convince him of Adam's fall as the ground of Christ's redemption, should be an attempt to do that for him which affliction, disappointment, sickness, pain, and the approach of death have a natural tendency to do; that is, to convince him of the vanity, poverty, and misery of his life and condition in this world. I would appeal at first to nothing but his own nature and condition in this world to demonstrate this capital truth of Holy Scripture that all mankind lie in a fallen state. Humanus says that the mere approach of death is enough to bring any man to his senses. And so it is. Death is the great debater. Death does not bandy words. Death comes to us with overwhelming proofs of our fall in his hands. There is no browbeating or perplexing of Death. Your smart replies and unanswerable arguments will not stagger Death. All your shafts are quenched like tow before the bosses of his buckler. Now, Death made his first approach to this world in that hour of Adam and Eve's first temptation. God's own fatherly and forewarning words first uttered the dreadful name of Death. O, if Adam had only believed God about sin and death! O, if he had only stopped his ears against the father of lies! O, if he could only have foretasted guilt and remorse and agony of conscience as he was led up to the tree! O, if he could only at that fatal moment have foreseen that coming garden where the Son of God Himself lay among the dark olive-trees recoiling from sin and death in a sweat of blood! O, if he could only have seen spread out before him all the death-beds of all his children on the earth, and all the beds of their second death in hell! O Adam and Eve in Eden, and still under the tree of temptation, look before it is too late; look on through the endless ages at the unutterable woes that you are working! 'Ye shall not eat of it, neither shall ye touch it, lest ye die.'

An Egyptian Father has said somewhere that while the four evangelists supply the wool, yet it is Paul who weaves the web. And what Paul does in this respect for Matthew, and Mark, and Luke, and John, he does at the same time for Moses, and David, and Isaiah. Moses, indeed, supplies the history, but it is Paul, that prince of the apostles, who takes us down into the philosophy, as we say, of that history. As we go on speaking about this and that man of science, and this and that book of science and of the philosophy of science, the unlettered people who hear us are tempted to envy us our time and our talents and our books. But they need not. Really, if they knew it, they need not. For, as long as they have Moses and Paul, the Book of Genesis and the Epistle to the Romans, they need envy no man. Thomas à Kempis used to say that his idea of perfect rest and perfect happiness was 'to sit with a little book in a little nook'. Now, with these two little books of Moses and of Paul, and with another little epistle or two of Paul's added, those who are otherwise quite unlettered men will soon become wiser men than many of their teachers. The most unlearned and ignorant man among us has sin in himself; and he has Christ, if not yet in himself also, then in his Bible, and thus in his offer; and with both sin and Christ in his heart, and with Paul on sin and on Christ in his hand, the most unlettered man is already a man of the truest and the deepest science, and a philosopher of the first water. For it is just those two men, Adam and Christ, with their sin and their righteousness, that so stumble and so throw out our evolutionists; and it is in his handling of those two men, and of that which we have of those two men alone, that Paul shows his matchless philosophic power. Those two stumbling-stones on which so many false philosophies have been ground to powder are the very foundation-stones, corner-stones, and cope-stones of Paul's immortal school and far-shining temple of truth.

In every epistle of his the apostle's immediate, supreme, and alone subject is Jesus Christ. Paul has not a moment of his time, nor a corner of his mind, nor a beat of his heart, nor a stroke of his pen for any other person, great or small, but Jesus Christ. And Paul is in the very heat and at the very heart of one of his greatest chapters on Jesus Christ, and on the atonement that we sinners of mankind have received through Jesus Christ, when, if I may say so, the very sweep and grasp of Paul's mind, the very philosophical necessity of Paul's great intellect, all compel him to go back and take up Adam into his great argument and great gospel. The passage is one of the most profound and magnificent even in his profound and magnificent epistles. It runs thus: 'Wherefore, as by one man sin entered into the world, and death by sin, therefore, as by the offence of one judgment came upon all men to condemnation, even so by the righteousness of one the free gift came upon all men unto justification of life. For as by one man's disobedience many were made sinners, so by the obedience of one shall many be made righteous.' To Paul's so comprehensive mind, so far-sweeping imagination, and so righteousness-hungry heart, Adam and Christ are the two poles upon whom this whole world of human life revolves. As the best expositor of Paul I know of anywhere says, Adam and Jesus Christ, to Paul's heaven-soaring eye, stand out before God with all other men 'hanging at their girdles.' And it is in his evolution, illustration, and enforcement of this great truth that Paul brings in, and makes so familiar to us those peculiarly Pauline and polar terms—law and grace, faith and works, condemnation and justification, enmity and peace, alienation and reconciliation, imputation and sanctification, sin and holiness, the flesh and the Spirit, eternal life and eternal death, and such-like. On all these Scripture subjects the Westminster Catechisms supply us with Paul's doctrines in a nutshell; as will again be seen and acknowledged when theology shall have recovered herself from her temporary lapse into mere Bibliography, and when Bible history shall have again become Bible doctrine and a Bible life.

And then, just as the full truth about the atonement led the apostle back from Christ to Adam, so in another epistle of his, the resurrection of Christ, and the resurrection of all those who have fallen asleep in Christ, leads Paul back again to Adam in this way. 'For since by man came death, by man came also the resurrection of the dead. For as in Adam all die, even so in Christ shall all be made alive. And so it is written, The first man Adam was made a living soul; the last Adam was made a quickening spirit. The first man is of the earth, earthy; the second man is the Lord from heaven,' The 'second man' and the 'last Adam' are most happy names and most illustrious titles of Paul's bold invention for his Master, our Lord and Saviour Jesus Christ. Which glorious Man is called the Second Adam, says Theophilus, as having in His generation that very perfection which the first Adam had in his creation. And because He is to do all that for us by a birth of grace, which we should have had by a birth of nature from Adam, had kept his first estate of sinless perfection.

Praise to the Holiest in the height,
   And in the depth be praise;
In all His words most wonderful,
   Most sure in all His ways.
O loving wisdom of our God!
   When all was sin and shame,
A second Adam to the fight
   And to the rescue came.

Now, what say you, Academicus, to all that?

II

EVE

ADAM WAS FIRST FORMED, THEN EVE

According to Moses, and taking Moses as he has come down to us, Eve, the mother of mankind, was, so to speak, an afterthought of her Maker. And it is surely something remarkable that four of the devoutest, boldest, and most original writers that have ever lived have taken and have gone out upon the same view. The creation of this world was the work of love, for God is Love. God so loved the very thought of this world that He created it and made it the exquisitely lovely world that we read of in Moses. But love is full of afterthoughts, of new ideas, and of still better intentions and performances. And thus it is that Moses is very bold to write as if God in His growing love for this world had found out a still better way of peopling this world than the way He had at first intended—had finished, indeed, and had pronounced very good. A new kind of love; a love such as even heaven itself had never seen nor tasted anything like it; a love sweet, warm, tender, wistful, helpful, fruitful; a love full of a 'nice and subtle happiness ';—the mutual love of man and woman,—took our Maker's heart completely captive as a still better way of replenishing earth with its children than even that noble and wonderful way by which heaven had been replenished with its angels. And thus it is that Moses, in his second chapter, lets us see our Maker coming back to earth; lets us hear Him finding fault with His first work in Adam, very good as it was; and lets us watch Him re-touching His work, till He takes Eve out of Adam and gives her back to Adam a woman to be his married wife, to be an help meet for him, and to be the mother of his children. So Moses in Genesis. And then, Plato in his *Symposium* teaches his Greeks the same thing: that man cannot live alone, that love is the true and only good of man, and that the best love of earth is but a foretaste and an assurance of the love of heaven. And then, Jacob Behmen has a doctrine all his own of the origin of woman; of the sphere and the functions of sex in this life, as well as of its absence from the life to come: a doctrine to enter on which would lead us too far away from our proper work to-night. Suffice it to say that for philosophical depth, for speculative power, for imaginative suggestiveness, and for spiritual beauty there is nothing better in Moses the Hebrew Plato, or in Plato the Attic Moses, than Behmen's doctrine of Adam and Eve. Behmen's reading of Moses leads him to believe that there must have been something of the nature of a stumble, if not an actual fall, in Adam while yet he was alone in Eden. Adam, at his own and alone creation, was pronounced to be 'very good.' There must therefore, Behmen holds, have been some sort of slip or lapse from his original righteousness and obedience and blessedness before his Maker would have said of Adam that he was now in a condition that was 'not good.' And thus it was that Eve was created to 'help' Adam to recover himself, and to establish himself in paradise, and in the favour and fellowship and service of his Maker. 'It is not good that man should be left alone. This shows us,' says Jacob Behmen's best English interpreter, 'that Adam had somehow altered his first state and had brought some beginnings of evil into it, and had made that not to be good which God at one time had seen to be very good. And, therefore, as a less evil, and to prevent a greater, God divided—ii. 21—the first perfect human nature into two parts, into a male and a female creature; and this, as you will see by-and-by, was a wonderful instance of the love and the care of God toward our new humanity. Adam was at first the total humanity in one creature, who should, in that state of perfection, have brought forth his own likeness out of himself in such purity of love and in such divine power as he himself had been brought forth by God. But Adam stood no longer in the perfection of his first estate as the image and the likeness of God. The first step, therefore, towards the redemption and recovery of Adam beginning to fall was to take Eve out of him, that he might have a second trial and probation in paradise; in which, if he failed, an effectual Redeemer might then arise out of the seed of the woman. Oh! my friends, what a wonderful procedure is there to be seen in the Divine Providence, always turning all evil, as soon as it appears, into a further display and an opening of new wonders of the wisdom and the love of God!' But you will start up as if you had been stung by the old serpent himself, and will angrily demand of me—Do I believe all that? My confident and overbearing friend, I neither believe it nor disbelieve it; for I do not know. But I believe about the first Adam, as I believe about the Second, that had it all been written even the world itself could not have contained the books. And the longer I live and listen and learn, the more slow I become of saying that I disbelieve anything that men like Moses hint at, and that men like Plato and Behmen and Law speak out: all three, all four, men whose shoe latchet neither you nor I are worthy to unloose. But, as Bishop Martensen quotes: 'The time has not yet come, and our language has not yet acquired the requisite purity, clearness, and depth to permit us to speak freely, and without, in some respect or other, provoking misunderstanding, upon a subject in which the deepest enigma of human existence is concentrated.'

But listen, and without interrupting him, to Moses on Eve, the mother of mankind. 'And the Lord God said, It is not good that the man should be alone; I will make him an help meet for him. And the Lord God made a woman, and brought her unto the man. Now the serpent was more subtle than any beast of the field which the Lord God had made. And the serpent said to the woman, Ye shall not surely die. And when the woman saw that the tree was good for food, and that it was pleasant to the eyes, and a tree to be desired to make one wise, she took of the fruit thereof, and did eat, and gave to her husband with her, and he did eat. And the eyes of them both were opened.' Eve gave to Adam that day, and Adam took at Eve's hand, what was not hers to give nor his to take. And any woman who gives to any man what is not hers to give nor his to take, their eyes, too, will be opened!

> Out of my sight, thou serpent! That name best
> Befits thee with him leagued, thyself as false
> And hateful; nothing wants, but that thy shape,
> Like his, and colour serpentine may show
> Thy inward fraud, to warn all creatures from thee
> Henceforth . . . Hate hard by lust.

O Eve, Eve! fatal mother of so many fatal daughters since! Would God thou hadst resisted the devil for thyself, for thy husband, and for us thy hapless children! O Eve, Eve, mother of all flesh! 'And the Lord God called unto Adam and said unto him, Where art thou? And he said, I heard Thy voice in the garden, and I was afraid, and I hid myself because I was naked. Who told thee that thou wast naked? And the man said, The woman Thou gavest me to be with me, she gave me of the tree, and I did eat. I was alone, and Thou broughtest this woman to me. I rejoiced over her with singing. I blessed Thee for her. I took her to my heart. I said, This is now bone of my bone and flesh of my flesh. And the Lord God said to the woman, Woman, what is this that thou hast done? So He drove out the man; and He placed at the east of the garden of Eden cherubim and a flaming sword which turned every way, to keep the way of the tree of life.'

After the mystics, Milton is by far the best commentator on Moses. Masculine, massive, majestic, magnificent, melodious Milton! Hear Moses, then, on Eve, our much deceived, much failing, hapless mother, and then hear Milton.

MOSES

And the Lord God said, It is not good that the man should be alone: I will make him an help meet for him.

MILTON

> —I, ere thou spak'st,
> Knew it not good for Man to be alone. . .
> What next I bring shall please thee, be assured
> Thy likeness, thy fit help, thy other self,
> Thy wish exactly to thy heart's desire.

MOSES

And the Lord God made a woman, and brought her to the man. And Adam said, Therefore shall a man leave his father and his mother, and shall cleave unto his wife.

MILTON

Under His forming hands a creature grew,
Manlike, but different sex, so lovely fair,
That what seem'd fair in all the world, seem'd now
Mean, or in her summ'd up, in her contain'd
And in her looks, which from that time infused
Sweetness into my heart, unfelt before,
And into all things from her air inspired
The spirit of love and amorous delight.
On she came,
Led by her Heavenly Maker, though unseen,
And guided by His voice; nor uninform'd
Of nuptial sanctity, and marriage rites:
Grace was in all her steps, heaven in her eye,
In every gesture dignity and love.

Hail wedded love, mysterious law, true source
Of human offspring. By thee,
Founded in reason, loyal, just, and pure,
Relations dear, and all the charities
Of father, son, and brother first were known.
Perpetual fountain of domestic sweets.
Here Love his golden shaft employs, here lights
His constant lamp, and waves his purple wings.
Sleep on, blest pair!

MOSES

Now the serpent was more subtle than any beast which the Lord God had made.

MILTON

—I now must change
These notes to tragic; foul distrust, and breach
Disloyal on the part of man, revolt,
And disobedience: on the part of Heav'n
Now alienated, distance and distaste,
Anger and just rebuke: sad task, yet argument
Not less but more heroic than the wrath
Of stern Achilles.

MOSES

And she took of the fruit thereof and did eat, and gave also to her husband with her, and he did eat.

MILTON

Earth felt the wound, and Nature from her seat
Sighing through all her work gave signs of woe,
That all was lost.
Earth trembled from her entrails, as again
In pangs, and Nature gave a second groan;
Sky lower'd, and muttering thunder, some sad drops
Wept at completing of the mortal sin
Original.

MOSES

And the man said, The woman whom Thou gavest to be with me, she gave me of the tree, and I did eat.

MILTON

To whom the Sovran Presence thus replied,
Was she thy God, that her thou didst obey
Before His voice, or was she made thy guide
Superior, or but equal, that to her
Thou didst resign thy manhood, and the place
Wherein God set thee? Adorn'd
She was indeed, and lovely to attract
Thy love, not thy subjection.

MOSES

And unto Adam He said, In the sweat of thy face shalt thou eat thy bread.

MILTON

Idleness had been worse;
My labour will sustain me.
So spoke our father penitent.
To whom thus also th' angel last replied:
—Only add
Deeds to thy knowledge answerable, and faith,
Add virtue, patience, temperance, add love,
By name to come called charity, the soul
Of all the rest; then thou wilt not be loath
To leave this Paradise, but shalt possess
A Paradise within thee happier far.
He ended, and they both descend the hill;
The world was all before them, where to choose
Their place of rest, and Providence their guide;
They hand in hand, with wand'ring steps and slow,
Through Eden took their solitary wav.

Great minded Milton! 'The great number of books and

papers of amusement, which, of one kind or another, daily come in one's way have in part occasioned, and most perfectly fall in with, and humour, our idle way of reading and considering things. By this means, time even in solitude is happily got rid of without the pain of attention; neither is any part of it more put to the account of idleness, one can scarce forbear saying, or spent with less thought, than great part of that which is spent in reading.' Thus Butler. Let Moses and Milton and Butler be more read.

But it is high time to turn to Paul, who is a far greater authority and commentator on Moses than Plato, or Behmen, or Milton, or Law. Now, Paul does not say very much about Eve, but what he does say has in it all his characteristic strength, straightforwardness, and evangelical consolation. Adam was the protoplast, says Paul to Timothy, quoting the expression from the wisdom of Solomon. Adam was first formed, then Eve. And Adam was not deceived, but the woman being deceived was in the transgression. 'Of the woman,' says the son of Sirach in his tremendous attack on women, 'came the beginning of sin, and through her we all die.' How it might have been with us to-day if the serpent had tried his flattery and his lies on Adam we do not know, and we need not ask. Only, let the truth be told. The devil, as a matter of fact, never spake to Adam at all. He approached Eve with his glozing words. He succeeded with Eve, and then Eve succeeded with Adam. Flattery led the woman astray. And then love led the man astray. The man could not refuse what the woman offered. 'The woman was deceived,' says Bengel, 'the man was persuaded.' And, because Eve was first in the transgression, Moses put certain special punishments upon her in his day, and Paul put certain other humiliations, repressions, and submissions in his day. God, in Moses, laid on Eve that day

> The pleasing punishment that women bear;

as, also, that her desire should be to her husband, and that he should rule over her. O husbands of women! O young men, to whom is their desire! God help all such women! And, if their desire must so be, let us pray and labour at our tempers and at our characters, at our appetites and at our inclinations, lest their desire be their everlasting loss. 'With my soul have I desired Thee, O God, in the night. Delight thyself also in the Lord, and He will give thee the desires of thine heart. Because he hath set his love upon Me, therefore will I deliver him; I will set him on high, because he hath known My name. With long life will I satisfy him, and I will show him My salvation. As for me, I will behold Thy face in righteousness: I shall be satisfied, when I awake, with Thy likeness.'

That emancipation of women which they owe to Jesus Christ had not had time to work itself fully out in Paul's day. And thus it is that we read in Paul's first Epistle to Timothy that the women are to learn in silence with all subjection, and that they are not to usurp authority, but are always to be in silence.

> To whom thus Eve with sad demeanour meek:
> Ill worthy I such title should belong
> To me transgressor, who for thee ordain'd
> A help, become thy snare; to me reproach
> Rather belongs, distrust and all dispraise.
> So spake, so wished, much humbled Eve.

'Let the women learn in silence,' and, 'I suffer not a woman to teach her husband, but to be in silence.' Yes; truth and beauty, Apostle Paul. But who is to be her husband? Who is to fill up the silence? All women would be proud to sit in silence if their husbands were like the husbands in Timothy's diocese; that is to say, if they would but speak out in the silence. And would speak out wisely, and advisedly, and lovingly, and always well. And, once in every woman's life she does sit as silent and as teachable as Paul himself would have her sit. When God takes her by the hand and brings her to the man for whom He has made her, then she for a season puts on the ornament of a meek and a quiet spirit. 'Even as Sara obeyed Abraham, calling him lord: whose daughters ye are, as long as ye do well, and are not afraid with any amazement. Likewise, ye husbands, dwell with them according to knowledge, giving honour unto the wife, as unto the weaker vessel, and as being heirs together of the grace of life, that your prayers be not hindered.'

'Notwithstanding, she shall be saved in The Child-bearing, if they continue in faith and charity and holiness with sobriety.' I am glad to see that the Revised Version leans to the mystical and evangelical interpretation of Paul's 'childbearing.' For, as Bishop Ellicott says, nothing could be more cold and jejune than the usual interpretation. And Paul is the last man be to cold and jejune on such a subject. Yes, I will believe with the learned revisers, and with some of our deepest interpreters, that Paul has the Seed of the Woman in the eye of his mind in this passage, and that he looks back with deep pity and love on his hapless mother Eve; and then, after her, on all women and on all mothers, and sees them all saved, with Eve and with Mary, by the Man that Mary got from the Lord, if they abide and continue in faith, in love, in holiness, and in sober-mindedness.

III

CAIN

I HAVE GOTTEN A MAN FROM THE LORD

CAIN'S mother mistook Cain for Christ. As soon as Eve saw her first-born son she no longer remembered the anguish. What a joyful woman Eve was that day! For, what a new thing in the earth was that first child in the arms of that first mother! Just look at the divine gift. Look at his eyes. Look at his hands. Look at his sweet little feet. Count his fingers. Count too. his toes. See the lovely dimple in the little man's right hand. What a child! And all out of his own mother's bosom. And all his father's son. Adam's son. A second Adam. A new man all to themselves to keep for their own. Look at him taking his first step. Hear him essaying his first syllable; the first time he says, Mother! and the first time he tries to say, Father! The Garden of Eden, with all its flowers and fruits, was forgotten and forgiven from the day that heaven came down to earth; from the day on which Eve got her first-born son from the Lord God. Nor, if you think of it, is it at all to be wondered at that little Cain's happy mother mistook him for Jesus Christ. Put yourself back into her place. Eve had brought banishment from Eden on her husband and on herself by listening to the father of lies. But the Lord God had come down to Eve in her terrible distress, and, beginning His book of promises with His best promise, had promised to her that the seed of the woman should bruise the serpent's head, and should thus redeem and undo all the evil that she had brought on herself and on her husband. And here, already, blessed be God, is the promised seed! And that, too, sent in such a sweet, heart-satisfying, and heavenly way! A man from God in her own arms! Why, Eve would have been a cold-blooded, hard-hearted atheist if she had not so hailed the birth of her first-born son. She would have made God a liar unless she had said, This is our God: for we have waited upon Him and we have gotten a man from Him. And yet, with all that, it was not so to be. As we know now, Cain was not to be the Christ. No. The angel Gabriel was not sent to Adam and Eve. The Angel of the Annunciation who stands in the presence of God passed by Eve, and Sarah, and Rachel, and Hannah, and Elizabeth, and all the other mothers in Israel, and came to a virgin espoused to a man whose name was Joseph. And the angel came in unto her, and said, Hail, thou that art highly favoured, the Lord is with thee: blessed art thou among women. And Mary said, My soul doth magnify the Lord.

And then, Cain and Abel as children together,—till their mother's cup ran over. With what motherly love that first mother watched the two little brothers as they played together. Look at them planting a garden in their sport, and putting men and women of clay in the garden and calling the man a father and the woman a mother. Till, tired of their garden and its ever-falling fathers and mothers, the two little angels went off hand in hand to go and meet their own returning father. And then, with a child in each hand, Adam came home to Eve, saying, Surely these same shall comfort us concerning our work and toil of our hands, because of the ground which the Lord hath cursed.

'And in process of time Abel became a keeper of sheep, but Cain, like his father, became a tiller of the ground. And Cain brought of the fruits of the ground an offering unto the Lord. And Abel, he also brought of the firstlings of his flock and of the fat thereof. And the Lord had respect to Abel and to his offering; but unto Cain and to his offering the Lord had not respect. And Cain was very wroth and his countenance fell. And the Lord said to Cain, Why art thou wroth, and why is thy countenance fallen? If thou doest well, shalt thou not be accepted? and if thou doest not well, sin lieth at the door.' Look at the seventh verse of the fourth chapter of Genesis, and you will see in that verse, and for the first time in the Bible, that terrible word SIN. That word, the most awful word ever uttered in heaven or earth or hell—SIN! John Milton is our best commentator on Moses. But Milton's description of SIN is far too dreadful for me to repeat here. Read it yourselves. Read the second book of *Paradise Lost*, and you will see SIN with her father and her son both standing beside her. And read, and read, and read over and over again Moses and Milton and yourself till you both see and feel both SIN and her father and her son all in yourself. Moses and Milton write for grown-up men, and not for babes who are still on their unskilful milk, as most men and women are.

Envy came to its full maturity all at once in Cain. Some sinful passions have taken time and environment to spring up and to mature to their full fruit in the human heart and in human life.

But envy, the wickedest, the deadliest, and the most detestable of all our sinful passions, came to a perfect man all at once. Eve's first-born son envied his brother Abel. Cain envied Abel because of his goodness, and because his goodness had found him acceptance and praise of God. And is his envy and hate of his brother's goodness and acceptance Cain rose up and slew his brother. Envy, surely, even in the end of the world, can no further go than that. I defy the wickedest heart in this house tonight to improve upon the way of Cain. And yet let us not be too sure. Let us look yet closer at Cain; and, all the time, let us keep our eye upon ourselves and see.

Cain envied Abel. He envied his brother, his only brother, his trustful, confiding, affectionate brother, his brother who worshipped him, and who would have given him his altar, and his lamb, and his fire from heaven, and all that he had if Cain would but have laid aside his gloom and taken it all. But no; Cain will not be beholden to his younger brother. Nothing will satisfy Cain now but one thing. A coal from hell has by this time so kindled hell in Cain's heart that all the rebukes and commands of Adam, and all the tears and embraces of Eve, and all the soft answers and submissions of Abel could not quench the wrath in Cain's evil eye, or take the fall out of his sunken countenance. Let the holy man here who has never had this same hell-fire in his heart at his brother, at his dearest and best and only friend on earth, at his old playfellow, at his present fellow-worshipper, let that happy man cast stones at this miserable wretch with murder in his heart at Abel his unsuspecting brother.

'Some sins in themselves, and by reason of several aggravations, are more heinous in the sight of God than others.' The offence was aggravated by the motive, says Bacon in one place. And so it was with Cain's offence. For his motive was envy of his brother's goodness, and of the acceptance and the praise that his brother's growing goodness was every day bringing him from the Lord. 'The Lord had respect unto Abel, and to his offspring.' That was all. But that was quite enough to kindle all hell in Cain's evil heart. And let our brother worship God alongside of our altar also, and let him find more acceptance with God and with man than we find; let him be better gifted of God and better placed by God; more approved of God and of God's people than we are, and you will soon see Cain. Praise the talents, the industry, the achievements of our very best and dearest friend, and it is gall and wormwood to us. But blame him, belittle him, detract from him, pooh-pooh and sneer at him, and we will embrace you, for you have put marrow into our dead bones, you have given wine to him that was of a heavy heart. Praise a neighbouring minister's prayer, or his preaching, or his pastoral activity at another minister's table, and you will upset both him and his listening house for days and for years to come. Of the six sins that are said to forerun the sin against the Holy Ghost, the fourth in the fatal order is "envy at another's grace." Take care, then, how you gad about with a tongue in your head that no man can tame, and tempt good men and women toward that sin which shall never be forgiven them.

"And Cain talked with Abel his brother; and it came to pass, when they were in the field, that Cain rose up against Abel his brother, and slew him." Abel might have escaped his end, and might have saved his brother, if he had not been so easy, so innocent, and so unsuspecting. If he had even attended to his dog at his heel he would have seen that there was something wrong somewhere that morning. For Cain had not shut his eyes all last night. Cain could not sleep all last night. He had been up and out and all about all night like a ghost. His face was fallen in. His eyes were green and black. Abel's dog growled and barked at Cain as if he had been a vagabond already. Abel had never seen a corpse, else Cain's face that day was like nothing in the world so much as the face of one of our corpses in its coffin. Nor did Cain talk like his usual self that morning. He stammered as he talked. He talked about things he had never, that Abel remembered, talked about before. Were it not that perfect innocence is so blind and so deaf, Abel would have found opportunity and would have turned home again that fatal morning. And even had Abel asked what Cain had against him that morning, Cain might have admitted fierce anger, or some other evil feeling at something or other, but he would never have admitted envy. No man from that day to this has ever admitted envy. To every other wickedness confession has often been made; but did you ever confess envy? or did you ever have envy confessed to you? No, never. I wonder, do the confessors in the confessional get at envy? If they do in the darkness and through the bitter brass, then there is something to be said for that heart-racking and sin-extorting system. No. Only by the stone, only by the dagger, only by the pistol, only by the cup, only by the bitten back and the slandered name is envy ever found out. In his noble answer to Tilken's abominable libel Jacob Behmen says, "We, poor children of Eve, no longer walk together in the love of God; but, full of passion, we envy, vilify, dishonour, and denounce one another, wishing to one another death and all kinds of evil; we enjoy, as we enjoy nothing else, each other's loss and pain and misery."

"And the Lord said unto Cain, Where is Abel thy brother?" The Lord asked at Cain what He knew quite well, in order that Cain might know that the Lord knew. But, instead of telling the Lord and Adam and Eve where Abel was buried, and instead of crying all his days ever after to the Lord, Deliver me from blood-guiltiness, Cain gave to the Lord the brazen-faced answer, Am I my brother's keeper? "And the Lord said, What is this that thou hast done? A fugitive and a vagabond shalt thou be in the earth." And not Cain, and all unarrested murderers only. We are all fugitives and vagabonds in the earth. We all are, or we ought to be. For the voice of our brother's blood cries to God against us. And, one day, we shall all be arrested and arraigned on that very same charge before the judgment-seat of Christ; unless, indeed, we surrender ourselves before that seat is set. "For this is the message that we have heard of Him, that we should love one another. Not as Cain, who was of that wicked one, and slew his brother. He that loveth not his brother abideth in death. Whosoever hateth his brother is a murderer; and ye know that no murderer hath eternal life abiding in him." It was an old superstition that a murdered man's body began to run warm blood again as soon and as often as its murderer was brought near it. And in this way they used to discover who the real murderer was. Now, just suppose that that was indeed a natural or a supernatural law in the age of the world and in the land in which we live,—how many men still living would begin to be all over with blood in your presence? The man sitting next you at this moment would be like a murdered corpse. The preacher now standing before you; your mother's son; the very wife of your bosom, when she does not flatter and fawn upon you; your own son; your dearest friend. Yes; you would then be what Cain all his days was, and all men finding you would slay you. They would not know, they would be horrified at what it meant, when their throats began to run blood as they passed you on the street, or as you talked with them in the field, or as you sat eating and drinking with them at your table, or at their table, or at the Lord's table. But you know. And you know their names. Let their names, then, be heard of God in your closet every day and every night, lest they be proclaimed from the housetops to your everlasting confusion and condemnation at the last day.

And Cain went out from the presence of the Lord, and Cain wandered up and down a fugitive and a vagabond, thinking every bush an officer, till a child was born to him in his banishment. Dr. Delitzsch, that old evangelical exegete who is so much at home among all those Old Testament men, tells us that Cain called his child by a name such as the rich man in hell might have called his child by if an heir had been born to him in his place of torment. For Cain said, Let his name be called Enoch, for God hath sent His angel to dip the tip of his finger in water to cool my tongue. And little Enoch and his mother somewhat lifted the curse off Cain, and somewhat quieted and rested Cain's vagabond heart. And Cain builded a city and called it Enoch, after his son, for he said, Here will I rest and dwell and hide myself, for God hath refreshed me and hath revived me with my wife and children. And, with that, Cain the murderer of Abel passes out of our knowledge. But let us hope and believe that the presence of the Lord came and dwelt in that city of Cain and his wife and children, according to the splendid psalm —"O Lord, Thou hast searched me and known me. Whither shall I go from Thy Spirit? or whither shall I flee from Thy presence? If I make my bed in hell, behold, Thou art there. If I take the wings of the morning and dwell in the uttermost parts of the sea, even there shall Thy hand lead me and Thy right hand shall hold me."

Now, since all this was written for our warning, and for our learning—come, all envious-minded men and women, come with me, and let us offer to God the envious-minded man's prayer. We have never confessed envy to man, but God knows our hearts. "O dear God, never suffer the devil to rub his vilest leprosy of envy upon me. Never let me have the affections of the desperate and the damned. Let it not be ill with me when it is well with others. Let me have Thy Holy Spirit to promote my brother's good, and to give Thee thanks for all his prosperity and praise. Never censuring his actions curstly, nor detracting from his praises spitefully, nor upbraiding his infelicities maliciously, but pleased with all things that Thou doest or givest. That we may all join together in the communion of saints, both here and hereafter, in grace and in glory, through Jesus Christ our Lord. Amen."

IV

ABEL

THE BLOOD OF SPRINKLING

Righteous Abel would have silenced his own accusing blood if he only could. When Cain suddenly struck him down, dying Abel took all the blame on himself. As long as he could speak Abel excused his brother, and sought to be reconciled to his brother. He put himself in the wrong and his brother in the right. He saw, now, when it was too late, how he had grieved and vexed and offended his brother. He had not thought about his brother. He had not put himself into his brother's place. He had not looked at things with his brother's eyes. He had been glad, and he had let his gladness too much appear, when his own offerings were respected and his brother's despised. Forgive me, O my God! Forgive me, O my brother! was Abel's last prayer. Whatever dead Abel's blood may have cried, I feel sure what dying Abel himself cried. Lord, lay not this blow to my brother's charge, he cried. And when Abel had said that again and again he fell asleep.

If Cain had only done the exact opposite of what he immediately did as soon as he had buried Abel; if he had only determined in spite of it all still to abide in the land of Eden; if he had only kept himself in the presence of the Lord, and had not allowed himself to go out from the presence of the Lord; if he had only laid the foundations of his city beside Abel's grave, then Abel's prayer for his brother would have been heard, and Abel's blood from that day would have begun to speak almost like the blood of Christ itself. Had Cain all his after days prevented the dawning of the morning that he might offer unceasing sacrifices beside his brother's grave; had he risen from his bed at midnight till, being in an agony, his sweat was as it were great drops of blood falling to the ground on Abel's grave; then Cain would have been a pattern that in him God might first show forth all long-suffering to those who should after Cain believe to life everlasting. And if you would but determine to learn to-night of Cain and Abel; if you would but keep at home and dwell in the presence of your past sin, and in the presence of the Lord; if you would but build your house, and if God would but prepare your table, in the presence of your enemies; now that Christ's atoning blood has taken the place of Abel's accusing blood; now that Christ's peace-speaking blood is every day and every night being sprinkled from heaven upon His and other men's murderers,—you would even yet escape being a fugitive and a vagabond on the earth, and would be made a fellow-citizen with the saints, and of the household of God.

Where, then, is Abel thy brother? Answer that on the spot. Where hast thou hid him? Say on the spot, Lord, come with me and I will shew Thee. Go back often to Abel's grave. Go back continually to your past life. Go back to your school days. Go back to your college days. Go back to your first office, your first shop, your first workshop. Recall your first friend. Pass before your eyes the first young man, the first young woman, you were intimate with. Call up the long-mouldered corpse of your first affection, your first passion, your first love, your first lust. Give instances. Give names; and ask if God has another case like yours in all His Book. Face full in the face that monstrous folly; that word, that act, that makes you blush scarlet and turn in your seat to think of it. They are turning on their beds in hell at this moment for far less. Go back to that farmhouse in the country, to that hamlet up among the hills, out of which you were so glad to escape from the presence of the Lord, and from the place of your sin, and get away to hide yourself in the great city. See how one ghost awakens another ghost till they come up an army of the ghosts of dead men and dead women against you. Men and women now dead, and in their own places. Men and women also still alive, but dead to you,—would God they were! Men and women who, when they, or their children, or only their spoken or written names pass before you, make you wish they were dead—they or you. Go back, I say. In God's name, in God's strength, go back! Take time, and go back. Take trouble, and go back. Take pains, and go back. Do not grudge time and trouble and pains. You will be well paid for all your time and trouble in humiliation, in remorse, and in godly sorrow. Even if you took, what Cain, it is to be feared, did not take—even if you took one whole hour every night alone with your past life, it would not be mis-spent time. Redeem the time. Redeem it, and you will be justified for so doing long before the great white throne is set. No; one whole hour every twenty-four hours of your present life would not be too much time to give to go over your past life. I undertake that if you will go home, and shut your door, and begin with such an hour to-night, you will not fall asleep in your chair. Why are you so pushed for time to repent? Why is retrospection the only thing that you have no time for, and always push it into a corner? Is it because you are not your brother's keeper? Is it because no grey head has ever gone down to a grave that your hands dug? Is it because no young man's faith, and no young woman's trust, and no unsuspecting friend's good name has ever been shaken, or deceived, or pulled down and murdered by you? Have your hands been always so washed in innocency? Are there no tears against you in God's bottle, and no names in His book? God takes care and account not of murdered lives only, but also of murdered names and reputations. How many men and women have we all struck at with that sharp razor, an envious, malicious, murderous tongue? Work at your consciences, you children of God, till they are as quick to detect, to record, and to recollect an unkind, unjust, unhandsome, slighting, detracting, belittling, sneering word, or look, or shrug, as they are to keep you in mind of a foul blow in a field, and a far-back grave in a wood. It would lay some high heads here low enough this night if the graves of all the good names and reputations they have had a hand in murdering were to suddenly open around them. All good men, all men of God, keep a whole churchyard of such graves ever open before them. And, if you do not, whatever you may think you are, and whatever other men may think you are, Christ, your angry Judge, knows what you are.

There are no ministers here, but there are a good many divinity students who will too soon be ministers. Will they listen and let me speak a word or two to them on the blood of Abel? One word which I have purchased a right to speak. Alas! alas! We are called and ordained to be our brother's keeper long before any one has taken us and shown us the way to keep ourselves. And with what result? With what result let our communion-rolls and our visiting-books answer. If any minister would be shut up and determined to preach nothing else and nothing ever but the peace-speaking blood of Christ, let him read every night in his communion-roll, in his young communicants' class list, and in his pastoral visitation-book. *That* name, *that* name, *that* name, that *family* of names! Where are the owners of all these names? What account can I give of them? If they are not here to-night, where are they? Why are they not here, and why are they where they are? What a preacher Paul must have been, and what a pastor, and supported and seconded by what a staff of elders, since he was able to say to his assembled kirk-session in Ephesus that he was clear of the blood of all his people! What mornings to his tent-making, and to his sermons, and to his epistles; and what afternoons and evenings to humility, and to tears, and to temptations, both publicly and from house to house! Like Samuel Rutherford, and long before his day, always at his books, always among his people, always at their sick-beds, always catechising their children, always preaching and always praying. No, I know no reading so humbling, so condemning, so killing to us ministers as our communion-roll. We ministers must always appear before our people, and before God, clothed from head to foot with humility, with a rope upon our heads, and with nothing in our hands or in our mouths but the cross of Christ and the blood of Christ, that speaketh better things than that of Abel.

The blood of Christ! O my brethren, what blood the blood of Christ must be! What wonderful, what wonder-working blood! What amazing blood! How can even the blood of Christ atone for, and make amends to God and man for, all our envy, and malice, and murder of men's bodies, souls, and reputations? The more I think of that—I do not know, I cannot tell, I cannot imagine. And then, not atonement and amends only, not bare pardon for all the past only, but eternal life, and all that leads up to eternal life, and all that eternal life is and contains. For the Holy Ghost also is the purchase of Christ's blood, a new heart also, and a whole lifetime of the means of grace. The Bible also, the Sabbath day, the Lord's table, a minister after God's own heart, deep, divine, unsearchable providences, a peaceful death-bed, a happy resurrection morning, a place at the right hand of the Judge, an open acknowledgment and acquittal on the day of judgment, "Come, ye blessed of My Father," and then a mansion with our own name in blood upon its door-post and its lintel to all eternity! Yes; precious blood indeed! What blood that must be that can so outcry and drown silent in its depths all the accusing cries that are even now going up to God all behind me and all around me! I feel that I would need a whole Redeemer and all His redeeming blood to myself. But, then, after that fountain filled with blood has drowned in the depths of the sea all the accusations that my sinful life has raised against me, that same blood will still flow for you and will do the same service for you. And the blood of Christ is the same blood yesterday, to-day, and for ever. For after it has spoken better things than that of Abel to you and to me, it will still abide and will still do the same service to our children and to their children, till a multitude that no man can number have washed their robes and made them white in the blood of the Lamb. No wonder that Paul called that blood not the blood of Christ only, but the blood of God.

V
ENOCH

AND ENOCH WALKED WITH GOD: AND HE WAS NOT; FOR GOD TOOK HIM

WHEN a reader of the Bible first steps across the borders of the Bible, and, for love of the Bible, begins to read the ancient books that lie around and beneath the Bible, he comes sometimes upon a real treasure, but more often upon a heap of rubbish. When a reader of the Bible first hears of The Book of Enoch, taking Coleridge's excellent advice, he sells his bed to buy that book. Enoch walked with God, he says to himself. I have the whole Bible in my hands, all written, he says to himself, by men all of whom so walked, but let me get all the books of all such men, before I have either time or money for any other manner of man or any other kind of book. But when, after long looking for it, he at last holds The Book of Enoch in his hand, it is with what a disappointment! For one thing, he soon sees that he has been deceived and imposed upon. Enoch! He has not read the first chapter of the book till it is as clear as day to him that Enoch never saw the book that goes under his ancient name; and besides, it is simply impossible that any man who had ever walked with God as Enoch walked could have written a single chapter of such an inflated and fantastic book. In four verses of his own Bible—in two verses in the Old Testament, and in two verses in the New Testament—there is more truth and more beauty and more guidance how he is to walk with God, than there is in all the hundred and eight chapters of the so-called Book of Enoch taken together. Still, our Bible scholars must work on in rubbish-heaps like The Bible of Enoch, if only for the sake of the chips and the filings of the Bible that are sometimes to be found there. But unless you are a Bible scholar, and are able to get good out of a book that returns but a far-off echo of your Bible, you will spend your time and your money far better than by spending either on The Book of Enoch. "And Enoch walked with God; and he was not, for God took him." There is substance there for him who knows what substance is, and there is style there for him who knows what style is. And that is but one single verse out of a whole Bible full of such substance and such style.

This, then, is the book of the generations of Adam. "Adam

begat a son in his likeness, after his image, and called his name Seth. And Adam lived after he had begotten Seth, he begat sons and daughters, and he died. And Seth lived, and died. And Enos lived, and died. And Cainan lived, and died. And Mahalaleel lived, and died. And Jared lived, and begat Enoch. And Jared lived after he begat Enoch, and begat sons and daughters, and he died. And Enoch begat Methuselah. And Enoch walked with God after he begat Methuselah, and begat sons and daughters. And Enoch walked with God; and he was not, for God took him." What is that? Let us go back upon that. Let us ponder all that passage over again. Adam and all his sons, after they had begotten sons and daughters, died. But of Enoch, the seventh from Adam, we read very differently. Adam, and Seth, and Enos, and Cainan, and Mahalaleel, and Jared all lived, they simply lived on, after they had had children born to them, and then died. But Enoch walked with God after his first child was born. As much surely as to say—could anything be said with more plainness?—that it was only after his first child was born to him that Enoch really and truly began to walk with God. Fathers and mothers, young fathers and young mothers, fathers and mothers whose first child has just been born, and no more—seize your opportunity. Let not another day pass. Begin to-day. Begin to-night. It is late, if not yet too late, with the most of us: but it is not yet too late with you. Take Enoch for your father. Take him for your patron patriarch. Take him for your example. Follow him in his blessed footsteps in his family life. It was his first son that made Enoch a saint. As soon as he saw his first child in his image, and in his arms, Enoch became from that day a new man. All men begin to walk for a short season with God when their first child is born; only Enoch, alone almost of all men, held on as he had begun. Enoch's heart ran over to God when his first child was born; and his tender, noble, princely heart never went back from that day from God, never grew cold again, never grew hard again, and never again forgot or neglected God. And as child followed child, Enoch, their father, grew more and more in grace with the growth of his house, till at the last he was not, for God took him. What an inheritance of blessed memories Enoch's children must have had! We all have fathers and mothers with God, for God has taken them; but, unless it was Elijah's children, no man's children ever looked up to heaven with such wondering and worshipping eyes as Enoch's children looked. My father! my father! The chariot of Israel, and the horsemen thereof!

Enoch, the wisest and the happiest of men, began his religious life where most men have not yet come to at the end of their religious life. He began by believing that God IS. With us, with all that we can do, we but attain to occasional hopes and confused convictions that perhaps God IS. We do not, indeed, even at our worst, in as many words deny that God IS. But scarce one in a thousand of our actions is performed, scarce one in a thousand of our words is spoken, on the pure and clear and sure ground that God IS. At our best we believe in a languor and in a dream that God is away out somewhere in the universe. We call Him "infinite" in our catechisms and in our creeds, in our psalms and in our prayers, not thinking what we are saying, and then we go away and live as if He were infinitely far away from us and from this whole world. Only, after death, when at last death comes, we fear that, somewhere and somehow, we shall see God. But Enoch never saw death, because he ever saw God. Enoch never died. Enoch did not need to die. Death could do nothing for Enoch. Death was neither friend nor enemy, first nor last, to Enoch. Death was not appointed for men like Enoch. As Dr. Herrick has it in his *Heretics of Yesterday,* Enoch was the first recorded mystic. "The first mystic of whom we have any record was Enoch, and the four words which furnish us with his whole biography is the best definition we have of true spiritual mysticism,—Enoch walked with God." You are an orthodox theologian when you take pen and ink and subscribe with your hand that God IS. But you become a mystical theologian and a spiritual man who you begin to believe with your whole heart that God is beside you, and within you, and is nowhere else for you but in your own heart. Commonplace men see now and then a skirt of God, and catch now and then a broken ray, a scintilla, as a mystic would say, of God glory; but Enoch walked with God up and down the land of Eden, as a man walketh with his friend. God was in Enoch's heart. "He looked within and saw God mirrored there." Enoch, from the day that his little child was born, felt God shed abroad in his heart. He entered every new morning into his own heart to walk there with God. He walked abroad every morning with his child in his arms, and with his God in his heart. Enoch so entered and so dwelt with God in his own heart, that God could not endure to loan him to this world any longer. When I first heard tell that there was a Book of Enoch, did I not promise myself a great treat! What an autobiography that must be! I wonder, will Enoch enter into particulars, I said to myself, and will he give instances, and tell in plain pedestrian words, giving chapter and verse, and step after step, just as I can understand it and imitate it, how he, Enoch, walked with God: really, and on his own solid feet, and on this solid earth, how he walked with God? But when I made an effort and got the book, what was I in every chapter introduced to and made to walk with, but cherubim and seraphim, principalities and powers, angels and devils, seven holy ones, and four holy ones, and three holy ones; behemoth and leviathan; wild camels, wild boars, wild dogs; eagles and elephants and foxes; giant men and siren women—till I rose up and put Enoch in my shelf and took down William Law. Took William Law to my heart and read in him for the thousandth time his two golden chapters showing, How all orders and all ranks of men and women of all ages are obliged to devote themselves to God; as, also, How great devotion to God fills our lives with the greatest peace happiness that can be enjoyed in this world. Till, like everybody who takes up William Law, I could not lay him down till I had come to his concluding chapter, "Of the excellency and greatness of a devout spirit." And then, when I turned the last page, and came to the printer's name, I felt like that member of my young men's class who told me that he read Law slowly and grudgingly, counting the pages every now and then, lest he should come too soon to the end. Yes, Dr. Herrick, you are right; Enoch was the first mystic, and his biography is written in as few words as would have pleased the arch-mystics themselves. Enoch, the true and genuine Enoch, never wrote a book, far less The Book of Enoch. But he did for us what very few books know anything about, he walked with God, and so sets us on thinking what walking with God might mean. My brethren, I am not making play with solemn words, nor am I practising upon you when I say it—walking with God is both the most difficult thing and the most easy thing in all the world. It is so difficult as to be found positively an impossibility by most men; while to one man here and there among men it is as easy to him as breathing is, as easy as eating is when he is hungry, and as drinking is when he is thirsty. Suppose you had exhorted Cain to begin to walk with God from the day that he murdered Abel—it would have taken nothing short of a miracle to make the murderer do it. A miracle could have made him do it, but it would have been a miracle. But suppose, on the other hand, that Enoch had for any cause fallen out of step with God for a single day, what a weary and heavy-laden man you would have had in Enoch that night! But, not to wander so far from home, how few of us ourselves ever entered into our own hearts, where alone God walks with men. God dwelleth not in temples made with hands, nor walketh on the pavement that leads up to such temples. Your first step in the direction of God is not taken when you put on your Sabbath clothes and walk demurely into your pew. No; but it is taken when you put on humility upon your proud heart, and fill your hot heart full of meekness, and resignation, and quietness, and contrition, and a broken, heavenly, holy heart. To hold your peace when you are reproved is a direct and sure step toward God. To be silent when you suffer wrong—God takes at that great moment a great step of His toward you. To let a slight, an insult, a blow, a scoff, a sneer fall on your head like an excellent oil, and on your heart like your true desert—with that man will I dwell, says the God of Israel in His prophet. Every step you take out of an angry heart and into a meek heart; out of envy and into admiration and honour; out of ill-will and into good-will;—on the spot your heavenly Father seeth you and loveth you, and sayeth to His angels, Hast thou considered My new servant? Enoch, on the day his first child was born, just began to lay aside all malice, and all guile, and hypocrisies, and envies, and all evil-speakings, and as a new-born babe desired the sincere milk of the word that he might grow thereby. He just began to live in the Spirit before the dispensation of the Spirit, and walked in the Spirit even before the Spirit was as yet given. And though his family, and his friends, and his enemies did not know so much as the very name of the fruit of the Spirit, they all ate and drank that fruit in Enoch's walk and conversation; for the fruit of the Spirit is love, joy, peace, long-suffering, gentleness, goodness, faith, meekness, temperance, and such like.

Are any of you, my brethren, in your secret heart, in continual fear of death? Are you, though no one knows it, all your lifetime subject to that terrible bondage? Well, Enoch of all the Bible characters is the best of them all for you. For Enoch was translated that he should not see death. Begin then to-night, and as long as you are left on the earth a living man with Enoch. Walk with God. Walk with Him into whose presence death never comes, and in whose whole kingdom no grave is ever dug. You have neglected God until to-night. But you are not yet dead. Your body is still warm and free and your own. Your soul is still in this church this Sabbath night. You are not yet in hell. God has not yet in anger said, Cut that cumberer down! Instead of that, He is still waiting to be gracious to you. Begin, then, to walk all the rest of your life on earth with God. And, if you are not to have your name added to the names of Enoch and Elijah; if you are not to be translated; if you are not to remain and to be alive when Christ comes; even so, your death, if it must be, will only be a circumstance in your walk with God. It will only be a striking and a never-to-be-forgotten incident and experience to you. It will only be a new departure, the opening up of a new prospect, and your first entrance on that which God hath prepared for them that love Him. If you will only walk close enough with Enoch and with Enoch's God you will never really taste death. You will not know where you are. Is it past? you will ask in astonishment. Am I really gone over Jordan? And it will all be because you importuned so often on earth, and said, and would not be kept quiet from saying, O wretched man that I am! who shall deliver me from the body of this death? Behold, now, thy Deliverer for whom thou didst so often cry; behold, He has come at thy cry, and has come for thee out of Zion. O death, where is thy sting? O grave, where is thy victory? The sting of death is sin; and the strength of sin is the law. But thanks be to God which giveth us the victory through our Lord Jesus Christ.

VI

JUBAL

HE WAS THE FATHER OF ALL SUCH AS HANDLE THE HARP AND THE ORGAN

THE Bible has a way of its own of setting the solitary in families. Over and above, and sometimes entirely superseding the original and natural order of father and son, the Bible set up an intellectual, a moral, and a spiritual order of fatherhood and sonship. As, for instance, thus: In the natural order, according to the flesh, as the Bible would say, Adam was the father of Cain, and Cain was Adam's first-born son. But, in the moral order, Cain was Satan's first-born son. Cain was of his father the devil. The devil was a murderer from the beginning, and Cain took, at his deepest, of his father in hell, for he hated his brother in his heart till he fell upon his brother at an unawares in the field and slew him. Cain was of that wicked one and slew his brother. And that deep and quick principle of family life runs through the whole of the Bible till it comes to a head, and to its fullest and clearest and most commanding expression in the other direction, in that house in Israel when the Son of God stretches forth His hand toward His disciples, and says, Behold My mother and My brethren!

Now, Jubal would seem to have been a solitary man so far as sons and daughters were concerned. Jubal had a brother, Jabal: he was the father of such as dwell in tents, and of such as have cattle. But the Bible is silent as to any children begotten of his own body that Jubal had. The only children that Jubal had in his image and after his likeness were his harp and his organ. For children's shouts and laughter all up and down his solitary house Jubal had only now the sound of his harp and now the sound of his organ. Jubal took to inventing and perfecting his harp and his organ because he had no other children with whom to play and to whom to sing. Or, perhaps, it was that the melodious soul of Jubal was so hurt within him at the way that

> disproportion'd sin
> Jarr'd against nature's chime, and with harsh din
> Broke the fair music that all creatures made
> To their great Lord,

that at last he rose up and said, Go to, I will make melody to God with a stringed instrument and with a praise-breathing pipe if men and women will so forget God. And it was so. And Jubal did so. As for me and my house, Jubal said, we shall make melody in our hearts to God. And he made that melody along with those two children of his, till his harp and his organ were more to him than sons and daughters; far more than Cain and Abel were to Adam, and far more than Shem and Ham and Japheth were to Noah. These same, he said, as he knit a new string into his harp, and hollowed out a new pipe for his organ —these same shall comfort me concerning my work and the toil of my hands, because of the ground which the Lord hath cursed. And Jubal walked with God after he begat his harp and his organ. And Jubal lived and added string to string in his harp, and pipe to pipe in his organ, till God's angels came and took Jubal home to his harp of gold.

By the time of Moses and Aaron Jubal had a whole tribe to himself of sons and daughters in those melodious men and women who rose up and called him their very and true father, and blessed his honoured name. Do you suppose that Jubal's great name was ungratefully forgotten on the shore of the Red Sea that morning? Do you think it. Then Miriam, the prophetess, the sister of Aaron, took a timbrel in her hand, and all the women went out after her with timbrels and with dances. "Who is like unto Thee, O Lord, who is like unto Thee, glorious in holiness, fearful in praises, doing wonders?" And after the schools of the prophets arose in Israel, Jubal's name would be written in letters of gold upon the lintels and the door-posts of those ancient homes of religion and learning and art. "And Samuel kissed the Lord's anointed, and he said to the Lord's anointed, After that thou hast come to the hill of God it shall come to pass that thou shalt meet a company of prophets coming down from the high place, with a psaltery, and a tabret, and a pipe, and a harp before them, and they shall prophesy. And the Spirit of the Lord shall come upon thee, and thou shalt prophesy with them, and thou shalt be turned into another man." And still, if you would hear sacred music at its best, and see sacred spectacle at its best, do not go either to the Sistine chapel in Rome, or to the Bayreuth theatre in Bavaria, but come to the temple of Solomon, the house of the Lord at Jerusalem. If you would see Jubal's children in their multitudes and at their highest honours, come up to Jerusalem at one of the great feasts. And if you would never be a niggard again in your contributions to the worship of God, read over and over again the two Books of The Chronicles in your so musical Bible. "So when David was old and full of days, he made Solomon his son king over Israel. And he gathered all the princes of Israel, with the priests and the Levites. Now, the number of the Levites, man by man, was thirty and eight thousand. Of which, four thousand praised the Lord with the instruments which I made (said David) to praise therewith." And again, "He set the Levites in the house of the Lord with cymbals, with psalteries, and with harps, according to the commandment of David, and of Gad the king's seer, and Nathan the prophet, for so was the commandment of the Lord by His prophets. And the Levites stood with instruments of David, and the priests with the trumpets. Moreover, the king and the princes commanded the Levites to sing praises unto the Lord with the words of David, and of Asaph the seer; and they sang praises with gladness, and they bowed their heads and worshipped." The temple in Jerusalem was the earthly palace of Israel's heavenly King; and for riches, and for beauty, and for melody of voices, and for instruments of music God gave commandment that His earthly temple should be made as near to the pattern of His heavenly temple as the hands of His people Israel could make it. "Behold, bless ye the Lord, all ye servants of the Lord, which day and night stand before God in the house of the Lord. Lift up your hands in His sanctuary and bless the Lord. The Lord that made heaven and earth, bless thee out of Zion."

The experts in that kind of history tell us that all the evidence that is forthcoming goes to prove that the apostolic and post-apostolic churches did not make much use of musical instruments in public worship. And the reasons they give for that state of things—a state of things so unlike the Church in Israel in ancient times, and the Church Catholic in modern times—are such as these: The poverty of the people; their persecuted and unsettled condition; and the fact that all the musical instruments then attainable had become incurably tainted with the theatrical and other immortal associations of that dissolute day. But it is pointed out that, as time went on, and when the Christian faith and the Christian worship became the faith and the worship of the empire, then Jubal came back again; till, as we know, in some parts of Christendom to-day he takes up the whole time and performs the whole service. In the Life of St. Philip Neri, Dr. Newman's patron saint, there is a beautiful chapter on Music. It was written in dear old Philip's rule for his spiritual children that they should all study to rouse themselves to the contemplation of heavenly things by means of musical harmony. And we are told that the sweet old saint was profoundly convinced that there is in music and in song a mysterious and a mighty power to stir the heart with high and noble emotions; as also an especial fitness to raise the heart above time and sense to the love and pursuit of heavenly things. And it was his own exquisite sensitiveness to all harmony that gave him that extraordinary sweetness of expression, of speech, and of gesture which made him so dear to all.

As to the Reformers, we find Luther in his *Table Talk* full of his best heart-eloquence about music. "The fairest and most glorious gift of God," he exclaims, "is music. Kings and princes and great lords should give their support to music. Music is a discipline; it is an instructress; it makes people milder and gentler, more moral, and more reasonable." "Music," he says in another place, "is a fair and glorious gift of God, and takes its place next to theology. I would not part with my small skill in music for much." And yet again: "Music is a fair and sweet gift of God. Music has often given me new life, and inspired me with a desire to preach. Saint Augustine had a conscientious scruple about music. He was, however, a noble and a pious man, and if he lived now he would be on our side." As to the use of instrumental music in the services of the Church of England, it is most interesting and most instructive to find Taylor, with his resounding style, leaning, if anything, against it; while Hooker, with his magnificent sober-mindedness, stands up stoutly for it. Hooker, as his contention with the Puritans goes on, becomes all for instrumental music. That is to say, if Hooker can ever be said to be all for anything but height, and depth, and a superb sober-mindedness.

Those who, like St. Augustine, are noble and pious men, and who like him have a conscientious scruple about instrumental music, if they are determined to fight for their scruple, they will find an all-but-unanswerable arsenal of fighting materials in Jeremy Taylor. Yes, in Jeremy Taylor, of all men in the world. And lest they should not possess the incomparable preacher and debater, I will, in fairness to the truth, supply them with a stone or two for their sling out of that great genius. "The use of musical instruments," says Taylor in his *Ductor Dubitantium,* "may also add some little advantage to singing; but such instruments are more apt to change religion into airs and fancies, and to take off some of its simplicity. Organs are not so fitted as sermons and psalms are for edification. The music of instruments of itself does not make a man wiser; it does not instruct him in anything. At the same time, I cannot condemn it if it be employed as an aid to true psalmody. And yet, at its best, music must not be called so much as a circumstance of divine service, for that is the best that can be said even of the voice itself." And then the omnivorously bookish bishop goes on to fortify his cautious position out of all the apostolic fathers, as his way is. And his way is a right learned, able, and eloquent way, as you will see if you will buy or borrow his *Ductor Dubitantium,* and will redeem enough time to read it. Which you must all do before you root your mind and your heart and your will irrevocably either for or against instrumental music. Read the best that has been written both for and against every subject whatsoever, before you root your temper either for or against the subject in question. And if you are still deep in your reading when the debate is hot, and the votes are being canvassed for, just say to the canvasser that you are not yet half through your reading, and that he must go and enlist those whose reading is finished, and whose enlightened and enfranchised minds are ready for him. And if your too much reading holds you in from making a speech or even from recording a silent vote, you will have lost nothing. You know, and we all know, how you lost your temper, your self-command, and the respect and love of some of your fellow-worshippers, by the way you spoke so often and so long, and voted so ostentatiously, before you had begun to read, or to listen to those who had read, on a former occasion.

And then, reading, and listening to those who have read, and all,—before we either open our mouth on this question of music, or cast our vote, a little imagination rightly directed, a very little imagination, will save us from making fools of ourselves, and it will keep us back from offering to God the sacrifice of a fool. Just imagine Almighty God, with this universe of angels and men in His heart and on His hands, and engaged day and night in steering it into an everlasting harbour of harmony and peace, and truth, and wisdom, and love. Take in something of the magnificence and the wisdom and the love of God. And then imagine Him looking down and listening to one of our debates with all our passions in a flame as to whether we are to worship our Maker with a psalm or with a hymn or with a sentence; with an American organ, or with a real, home-built, and high-priced English organ; and, in another place, whether the line is to be given out by the precentor, or the whole psalm read once for all by the minister—and so on to an adjourned meeting on the question. Imagine Gabriel who stands before God, with twain of his burning wings covering his face, and with twain covering his feet, and with twain wherewith to fly—imagine that seraph, full to a flame of the majesty and the glory of God, looking down on the church of God on earth and seeing a minister of Jesus Christ sewing up the paraphrases with needle and thread on a Sabbath morning in terror and in anger lest a neighbour minister should come and give out, "O God of Bethel" to be sung to the God of Bethel; or " 'Twas on that night"; or, "How bright these glorious spirits shine." You have heard about the angels weeping, have you not? If you were where Jubal now is you would see their head waters over the way that we quarrel, fall out, and hate one another about our worship of God. Why, very Baal himself would be ashamed of such worshippers, with such ideas and with such passions as we have. The fly-god himself would cast us and our vain oblations out of his presence. "God is a Spirit, and they that worship Him must worship Him in spirit and in truth; for the Father seeketh such to worship Him." Only be at peace among yourselves, He says to us. Only give place to one another. Only be of one mind. Only please one another to edification, and you will best please Me. Only agree about it among yourselves first, and then come into My house with a psalm, or with a hymn, or with a spiritual song, or with a harp, or with an organ, or with what you will. Call in Jubal, My servant, to assist you, if you feel you need his assistance, and if you are unanimous in your call. Or, sit still as you are till you are unanimous, and let your neighbours call him in who are already unanimous. Only, My little children, have peace among yourselves, and love one another, and so shall ye be Mine accepted worshippers. "The sacrifices of God are a broken spirit: a broken and a contrite heart, O God, Thou wilt not despise. Whoso offereth praise glorifieth Me: and to him that ordereth his conversation aright will I shew the salvation of God."

VII

NOAH

MAKE THEE AN ARK

EVEN after the four full chapters that Moses gives to Noah, Peter in the New Testament makes a very important addition to our knowledge of Noah. "Noah the eighth person was a preacher of righteousness," adds the apostle. We have it in as many words from Moses himself, and he gives almost the half of one of his chapters to it, that Noah became a planter of vineyards and an owner of vineyards and a dealer with wine in his old age. But with only eight souls saved, and some of them scarcely saved, there was no evidence at all in Moses that the divine ordinance of preaching had been as yet set up on the earth, and much less that Noah was ordained to that office. Now, as a preacher myself I have a deep professional interest, as well as some other deep interests, in asking myself why it was that Noah was so signally unsuccessful as a preacher. Was it because it was righteousness that he preached? That may very well have been it; for so far as my own experience goes, righteousness is the one thing that our hearers will not have at our hands. All other kinds of preaching—polemical preaching, apologetical preaching, historical and biographical preaching, sacramental preaching, evangelical preaching—some of our people will welcome, and will indeed demand; but they will all agree in refusing and resenting the preaching of righteousness; the preaching of repentance and reformation; the preaching of conversation and conduct and character. No; they would not have it. Josephus supplements Moses and Second Peter, and tells us that Noah preached and pleaded with them to change their dispositions and their actions till he was afraid they would kill him. Of one thing we are sure, Noah did not discredit his preaching by his life, as so many of our preachers do. For Noah had this testimony as long as he was a preacher, that he walked with God. Thee, said the Lord to Noah in giving him his instructions about the ark—Thee only have I seen righteous before Me. My father's tutor, says the author of *The Decline and Fall of the Roman Empire,* believed all that he professed, and practised all that he enjoined. Could it have been that the preacher's sons and daughters undid all their father's preaching as soon as he had preached it? Physician, heal thyself, did his congregations call out to the preacher of righteousness as he came down from his pulpit and went home to his house? Yes, that would be it. I am almost sure that would be it. For one sinner still destroyeth much good. And we know that Noah had one son—he was his second son, Ham—who helped to bring down his father's grey hairs with sorrow to the grave. What way could a preacher of righteousness be expected to make with a son like his second son among his sons at home? No way at all. It was impossible. That, I feel almost certain, would be it.

I am not to ask you to enter with me into the theophanies of the flood, nor into the naval architecture of Noah and Moses, nor into the geology that emerged after the flood was over, nor into the longevity of Noah and the distribution of his sons. My one and sole aim with you is a practical aim. My one and sole remaining ambition in life is to preach righteousness. To preach righteousness,—the nature of it, the means to attain it, the terrible difficulty of attaining it, and the splendid reward it will be to him who at last attains it. To preach righteousness, and all matters connected with righteousness, first to myself, then to my sons, and then to my people. This one thing I do. And in this one light shall I ask you to look at Noah, and at his ark, and at his vineyards, and at his wine, and at Ham, his reprobate son.

Not only did Noah preach his best and his most earnest as the end drew near; not only Noah himself, but every tree that fell in the forest, and every plank that was laid in the ark; every axe-stroke and the echo of every hammer was a louder and ever louder call to the men of that corrupt and violent day to flee from the wrath to come. But, sad to say, the very men without whose help the ark would never have been built; the very men who felled the trees, and planed and laid the planks, and careened and caulked the seams of the finished ship—those very men failed to take a passage in that ship for themselves, for their wives and for their children. Many a skilled and high-paid carpenter, many a strong-limbed and grimy-faced black-smith, and many a finisher and decorator in woodwork and in iron, must have gnashed their teeth and cursed one another when they saw their children drowning all round them, and the ark shut, and borne up, and lifted up above the earth. But those carpenters and blacksmiths and finishers were wise men and their loss was salvation compared with many of those architects and builders and ornamenters of churches who compete with one another and undersell one another in our day. As also compared with all those publishers and printers and booksellers of Bibles, and all those precentors and choirs and organists, and all those elders and deacons and door-keepers, who are absolutely indispensable to the kingdom of God, but who are all the time themselves outside of it. The Gibeonites in Israel were hewers of wood and drawers of water to Israel; they dwelt in Israel, and had their victuals there, but they were all the time aliens from the commonwealth of Israel. And all Noah's own excellent sermons, all his pulpit appeals about righteousness, and all his crowds of congregations would not have kept his grey head above the rising waters that he had so often described in his sermons, had he not himself gone and done what the Lord commanded him to do. That is to say, had he not, not only prepared the ark, but had he not gone up into the ark, and asked the Lord to shut him in. We ministers may preach the very best of gospels to you, and yet at the end of our ministry be castaways ourselves. "What if I," wrote Rutherford to Lady Kenmure—"What if I, who can have a subscribed testimonial of many who shall stand at the right hand of the Judge, shall myself miss Christ's approval, and be set upon the left hand? There is such a beguile, and it befalleth many. What if it befall me, who have but too much art to cover my own soul and others with the flourish of ministerial, country holiness!" The next Sabbath after that on which Noah preached his last sermon on righteousness, sea monsters were already whelping and stabling in his pulpit.

There had never been such dry seasons since the memory of man. It seemed as if the whole earth would surely die of famine. All the time the ark was a-building the heavens were as brass and the earth as iron. Had Noah preached and prophesied that this terrible drought of rain would last till this generation repented of their corruptions and their violence, there would have been a perfect pentecost among them. Thousands would have turned to the Lord that very day. As it was, many was the day that the worst scoffers at the preachings were of the preacher's own household. Many was the Sabbath-day when Noah disappeared into the forest and fell on his face and prayed that he might have a sign from heaven. But still the branches broke into dust and ashes under him as he wrestled with God for even one little cloud in the sky. And all the chapt and blasted earth around him mocked at him and at his sermons and at his threatenings of a flood of water. But all he ever got for answer to his prayer in the wood was what he already knew, and, indeed, every hour of every day called to mind: "My Spirit shall not always strive with man. Make thee an ark of gopher wood!" Till Noah, moved with fear, returned to his place and worked with all his might for another six days preparing an ark to the saving of his house. The Lord is slow to wrath; slow to a proverb and to a jest. But we have His own warning for it that His Spirit will not always strive with man. Not so much as a man's hand of cloud had been seen for weeks and for months in the west. But no sooner was the ark finished and Noah was shut in, than God arose and gave the signal. And the stormy wind that fulfils His pleasure struck the ark that moment like a park of artillery. And not the ark only, but the whole creation shook, and shuddered, and groaned, and travailed with the wrath of God. The firmament fell in sunder in the twinkling of an eye, and the waters which were below the firmament leaped up to meet the waters which were above the firmament. And the waters prevailed exceedingly upon the earth, and all the high hills that were under the whole heaven were covered. And Noah only remained alive, and they that were with him in the ark.

There has never been anything again on the face of this earth like that ark for the next hundred and fifty days. And there will never be anything like it again till the day of judgment. Such was the wrath of God, and such was the horror and the suspense, the roaring of the storm without, the roaring of the brute beasts within, and the overwhelming fear. There is only one thing that outdoes that ark on this earth, and that is the heart of every regenerate man. No; that is too much to say; not of every regenerate man, but only of that man among the regenerate who has been taken deep down into the noble and saving knowledge of his own heart. With God's judgments against him and against his sin all around him! with his past sin and his present sinfulness finding him out a thousand times every day, knocking at his door, calling in at his window, dogging his steps; with his soul reeling and staggering within him like a drunken man, and with earth and hell let loose within him—that rocking, reeling, midnight ark is a predestinated picture of the soul of every deeply true and deeply exercised saint. Not of sham saints, and not of saints on the surface, but of every son and daughter of fallen Adam who is truly being made in their heart of hearts, and in the divine nature, the sons and daughters of the Lord Almighty, the Lord All-Holy. And most of all are the hearts of God's great saints like that ark in the wild beasts that made that ark hideous to sit in, to eat and drink in, and to sleep and worship in for the next hundred and fifty days and nights. All the evil beasts that ever roared and ravened for their prey were in that ark; each one after his kind. Apes and peacocks were there also, and sparrows and magpies; snakes also, and vipers, and adders. Dogs with their vomit, and sows with their mire. As the blessed Behmen has it about himself: A man's soul is sometimes like a wolf, sometimes like a dog, sometimes like a lion, sometimes like a serpent—subtle, venomous, and slanderous; sometimes like a toad—poisonous, and so on; till my soul, says that singularly subtle and singularly saintly man, is a cage of cruel and unclean birds. And not Behmen's soul only, but yours and mine, if we really know anything at all about the matter in hand. Those wild beasts are all there till God in His great pity opens the windows of heaven over us and says to us: O thou afflicted, tossed with tempests, and not comforted. This is as the waters of Noah unto Me. The mountains shall depart and the hills be removed, but My kindness shall not depart from thee, neither shall the covenant of My peace be removed, saith the Lord that hath mercy on thee. This is the heritage of the Lord; and their righteousness is of Me, saith the Lord.

How did Noah and his household occupy themselves during the whole of that long and dreary voyage? They had no chess and no cards; no old newspapers and no sensational novels. I have no idea how the rest of the family occupied themselves; but I can tell you to a certainty what Noah did. I have no books, said Jacob Behman, but I have myself. And Noah had himself all those hundred and fifty days and nights. Himself, and Ham, and the woman who had gone down at his door with Ham's name on her drowning lips. He had Shem also, and Japheth, and their wives, and their mother. And if all the romances that ever were written had been on board, and all the games with which men and women have murdered time since time began, do you think that Noah would have had either time or taste for them? What do you think? Do you think he would? There is no way of killing time like prayer. If you would be at the end of your longest voyage before you know where you are, walk with God on the deck of the vessel. Tell Him every day about your children. Tell Him their names. Describe their opening characters to Him. Confide to Him your fears about them. And if one of them has gone astray, or is beginning to go astray, you will have enough in him alone to keep you alone with God for, say, one hour every day. I warrant you the wettest ground under the ark was as dry as tinder before Noah's eyes were dry. They all feared to ask their father why he wept as he walked with God, for they all knew quite well that it was for them that he so walked and so wept.

"And the sons of Noah that went forth of the ark were Shem, Ham, and Japheth." There will be plenty of men that will go forth of earth and into heaven with all Ham's evil memories, and more. But from the north pole to the south pole, and from the rising to the setting of the sun in the new heavens and the new earth, there will not be so much as one man found there with Ham's still lewd, still hard, and still impenitent heart.

VIII

HAM

AND HAM SAW HIS FATHER, AND HE TOLD HIS TWO BROTHERS WITHOUT

THERE was an old vagabond, to vice industrious, among the builders of the ark. He had for long been far too withered for anything to be called work; and he got his weekly wages just for sitting over the pots of pitch and keeping the fires burning beneath them. That old man's heart was as black as his hands. It was of him that God had said that it grieved and humbled Him at His heart that He had ever made man. The black asphalt itself was whiteness itself beside that old reprobate's heart and life. Now Ham, Noah's second son, was never away from that deep hollow out of which the preparing pitch boiled and smoked. All day down among the slime-pits, and all night out among the sultry woods—wherever you heard Ham's loud laugh, be sure that lewd old man was either singing a song there or telling a story. All the time the ark was a-building, and for long before that, Ham had been making himself vile under the old pitch-boiler's instructions and examples. Ham's old instructor and examplar had gone down quick to hell as soon as the ark was finished and shut in. But, by that time, Ham could walk alone. Dante came upon his old schoolmaster in hell when he was being led through hell on his way to heaven; and so did Ham when he went to his own place. But that was not yet. Ham was not vile enough yet. His day of grace had not come to an end yet. His bed in hell was not all made yet. He had more grey heads to bring down to the grave first. He had to break his old father's heart first. As he will soon now do, if you will wait a moment. Ham had been born out of due time. Ham had not been born and brought up in his true and proper place. Ham should have been born and bred in Sodom and Gomorrah. Not the ark, lifted up above the waters of the flood, but the midnight streets of the cities of the plain were Ham's proper place. The pairs of the unclean beasts that Ham attended to with his brothers were clean and chaste creatures of God compared with Ham. For Ham could neither feed those brute beasts, nor bed them, nor look at them, nor think about them without sin. More than one of those abused beasts will be brought forward at the day of judgment to bear testimony against one of their former masters. From a little boy Noah's second son had been a filthy dreamer. The best and the holiest words his father could speak had an unclean sense to his son. Every vessel in the ark and every instrument held an unclean association for Ham. Within all those steaming walls the only truly brute beast was Noah's second son. Sensuality takes a most tremendous revenge on the sensual sinner. What an inexpiable curse is a defiled mind! Well might Bishop Andrewes pray every night of the week for all his life, and that too, with sweat and tears, that his transgressions might not be retained upon him as his punishment. It would be ill to imagine a worse punishment than an imagination steeped in sin. "O!" cries Dr. Newman, "the inconceivable evil of sensuality!" "If you once begin to think about forbidden things," says Cicero, "you will never be able to think about anything else."

It is not in as many words in Moses, but I have read it elsewhere, that there was a woman who clung to the door of the ark which was in the side thereof; and the woman cried and prayed. Ham! she cried. Ham, my husband! she cried. Ham, my destroyer! Preacher of righteousness! she cried, open thy door! Where is thy God? Open thy door and I will believe. Throw out thy son Ham to me, and I will take him to hell in my arms! Is there a woman within these walls, or are they all she-wolves? as she dashed her head against the shut door. Mother of Ham! Wife of Ham! Sisters of Ham! she cried. My mother's blood is on his skirts. My own blood is on his hands! Cursed be Ham! And the ark shook under her words and her blows. And Ham, Noah's second son, listened in the darkness and through the seams of pitch. And then he kneeled in prayer and in thanksgiving, and he blessed the God of his fathers that she had gone down, and that the waters still prevailed.

Why do the sons of our preachers of righteousness so often go wrong? you will often hear it asked. I do not know that they do. But, even if they did, I would not wonder. Familiarity, and near neighbourhood, to some orders of mind, naturally breed contempt. And then, our preachers are so busy. Composing so many sermons; holding together, by hook or by crook, so many straggling congregations; fighting, now this battle and now that in church and in state; and worst of all, with all that, sitting down to write a book. As good almost kill a man as kill a good book, said a great man, who was much better at making a good book than he was at bringing up a good child. But what a bitter mockery it must be, especially to a minister, to hear his books called good on every hand and bought by the thousand, and then, soon after, to see his sons and his daughters neglected, grown up, and gone astray! To me there is one specially awful word in Bishop Andrewes' *Devotions*. Words like that word always make me hide my Andrewes out of sight. "What a strange person Keble is! There is Law's *Serious Call*—instead of leaving it about to do people good, I see he reads it, and puts it out of the way, hiding it in a drawer." The word I refer to may not make you hide your Andrewes out of sight. Words differ and grow awful or otherwise as the people differ who employ them. "I have neglected Thee, O God!" That, to me, is the awful word. We speak of parents neglecting their children. But we, your ministers, above all other men, neglect God, and that in nothing more than in the way we neglect our children. After the clean beasts and the beasts that are not clean shall have witnessed against Ham, and before Ham is taken away, he will be taken and questioned and made to tell how busy his father was, day and night, all these years, preaching righteousness and building the ark. Everybody all around knew what went on among the slime-pits by day and among the warm woods by night,—everybody but the preacher of righteousness. Ham will tell—you will all hear him telling—how his father worked, in season and out of season, at the work of God. Concerning Noah standing on His right hand the angry Judge will interrogate Ham standing on His left hand. Did My servant here, thy father, ever restrain thee from making thyself vile? Did he, or did he not? Speak to Me the truth. And Ham will swear to it, and will say before the great white throne this: My father is innocent of me, Ham will say. My father never knew me. My vileness is all my own. No man ever had a father like my father. O Noah, my father, my father! Ham will cry.

All this time, as Ham will witness, Noah knew nothing of all that we know now. Noah was as innocent of the knowledge of his second son's past life as he still is of what will come to light at the last day. And thus it was that, as soon as the preacher of righteousness stepped out of the ark, he did exactly what we could have told you he would do. Noah went forth, and his sons and his wife, and his sons' wives with him. And Noah builded an altar unto the Lord, and the Lord smelled a sweet savour, and said, While the earth remaineth, seedtime and harvest, and cold and heat, and summer and winter, and day and night shall not cease. And now, with all that has passed, what a Noah you will surely see! Come, all you fathers who have come through trouble, and you will see here how you are to walk with a perfect heart before your house at home. What a father Noah will be, and what a husband, and what a husbandman! If we had come through a hundredth part of Noah's terrible experience; and then had found a hundredth part of Noah's grace at God's hand; we, too, would have said, As for me and my house, we shall walk with a perfect heart and shall serve the Lord. And God spake unto Noah, and to his sons with him, saying, And I, behold, I establish My covenant with you, and with your seed after you. And the bow shall be in the cloud, and I will look upon it that I may remember My everlasting covenant. And the sons of Noah that went forth of the ark were Shem, Ham, and Japheth; and Ham is the father of Canaan.

In his beautiful sermon on "The World's Benefactors," Dr. Newman asks, "Who, for example, was the first cultivator of corn? Who first tamed and domesticated the animals whose strength we use and whom we make our food? Or who first discovered the medicinal herbs which, from the earliest times, have been our resource against disease? If it was mortal man who first looked through the animal and vegetable worlds, and discriminated between the useful and the worthless, his name is unknown to the millions whom he has benefited." Only, Noah's name is quite well known to the millions he has benefited; as, also, to the millions he has cursed and destroyed. Corn and wine, the Bible always says. The first farmer who sowed, and reaped, and threshed, and ground, and baked corn, we do not know his name. But we have Noah's name now open before us; it was he who first planted a vineyard and manufactured its grapes into intoxicating drink. Millions every day bless the day he did it, and pledge his name for doing it; while other millions curse the day. And which of these cries goes up best before God another day will declare. Only, if you would read and remember your Bible before you eat and drink, you would know better how to eat and how to drink so as to do all to the glory of God, and against that day. And it is surely significant, with an immense and an eloquent significance, that the Bible tells us that the first vine-dresser at his first vintage was found in a state such as Ham and Shem and Japheth found their father. It would be at the time of harvest and ingathering. Or, perhaps, it was a birthday feast—the birthday feast of his first son, or it might be of his second son. Or, to make another guess where we do not know, perhaps it was the anniversary of the laying of the keel of the ark; or of the shutting-to of the door of the ark; or of the day when the tops of the mountains were seen; or of the day when the dove came into the window of the ark with an olive-leaf in her mouth plucked off. It was certainly some such glad and exalted day as one of these. Come, my sons, said the old saint over his wine; come, let us eat and drink to-day and be merry. The fathers are full of far-fetched explanations and apologies for Noah. One will have it that, admitting the drunkenness, still Noah was all the time innocent; it was the unusually strong wine that did it. It was the too-heady wine that was alone to blame. Another will have it that Noah did not know this new drink he had stumbled on from milk. And yet another, that the whole history is a mysticism, and that the preacher of righteousness was only drunk in a figure. But the Bible does not mince matters; nor does it waste words even on Noah. In the Bible the "saints are lowered that the world may rise."

Now, who of all Noah's household should happen to come in at that evil moment but Ham; and he, too, flown with insolence and with his father's wine. But, blessed be the Lord God of Shem; and God from that hour shall surely enlarge Japheth. How, still, it humbles and chastens such sons as Noah's first and third sons to see their parents' imperfections—their father's faults at table, and their mother's follies everywhere. Shem's and Japheth's respect and reverence all remained. Their love for their father and their honour for him were not any less, but were much more, after the noble and beautiful service they did him that day. Only, ever after that terrible day, with what watchfulness did those two brothers go out and come in! With what wistfulness did they look at their father as he ate and drank! With what solicitude, and with what prayer, and not for their father only, did Shem and Japheth lie down at night and rise up in the morning! It brought Noah, and Shem, and Ham, and Japheth back again to Moses' mind when he received and read and transcribed the Fifth Commandment on Mount Sinai: Honour thy father and thy mother, and that thy days may be long upon the land which the Lord thy God giveth thee.

It is easy for those who are standing on the shore to shout their counsels to those who are sinking in the sea. It is easy for those who are in cold blood to tell a man in hot blood how he should behave himself. And it is easy for us sitting here, with all our passions at our heels for the moment, to moralise over the preacher of righteousness when he awoke from his wine. At the same time, it is only by laying such sudden and ungovernable outbursts as his was to heart that we shall ever learn how to hold ourselves in when we are mad with anger at our children. I have more understanding, says the psalmist, than all my teachers; for Thy testimonies are my meditation. I understand more than the ancients, because I keep Thy precepts. Now, if David's hot anger against Absalom or Solomon had come upon him when he was in that mind, and had he remembered ancient Noah and his wakening from his wine, what would David have done? With the Holy Spirit not taken away from him, David would have recollected his former falls, and he would have retreated back upon his own fifty-first psalm. He would have taken Absalom, whom he so much loved, and the angry father and the exasperating son would have kneeled down together, and then David would have said, with weeping, Who can bring a clean thing out of an unclean? Wash me thoroughly from mine iniquity. Purge me with hyssop. Then will I teach transgressors Thy way! And Ham himself would have fallen on his father's neck, and would have said, I am not worthy to be called thy son! Fathers and mothers, when our children are overtaken again in a fault, instead of cursing them and striking at them, and casting them out of doors as Noah did, let us say to ourselves that we have only begotten our children in our own image. Let us then, for that is the best time to do it—let us take them, and go with them, and beseech God to melt them, and change them, and alter them, and make them not our sons and daughters any more, but His own. And see if He will not do it. See if He will not deliver them over again to us with these words, Take them and bring them up for Me, and I will give thee thy wages. "If a father is intemperate," says William Law, "if he swears and converses foolishly with his friends, let him not wonder that his children cannot be made virtuous. For there is nothing that teaches to any purpose but our ordinary temper, our common life and conversation; and almost all people will be such as those amongst whom they were born and bred. If a father would pray every day to God to inspire his children with true piety, great humility, and strict temperance, what could be more likely to make the father himself become exemplary in these virtues? How naturally would he grow ashamed of wanting such virtues as he thought necessary for his children."

Now, all we here are the sons and daughters of one or other of Noah's three sons. By those three men were all the nations of the earth divided after the flood. And we are the sons of Ham, if we are his sons, by this.—When every imagination of our heart is defiled. When we are in lewd company. When we have enjoyment over an unclean song, an unclean story, or an unclean newspaper report. When we steal a lewd book and take it to our room with us at night. When we hide away an impure picture in our drawer, where Keble hid the *Serious Call*. When we report our neighbour's shame. When we tell our companion not to repeat it; but when we would burst if we did not repeat it. When we rush to pen and ink to advertise abroad some fall or some fault of our brother. When we feel that we have lost something when his fault is explained, or palliated, or covered and forgotten, and when he is set on his feet again. Ham's sons and daughters have not all black hands and black faces. Many of them have their hands and their faces as white as a life of cosmetics and idleness can whiten them. While, all the time, Ham holds their black hearts. My brethren, let us henceforth begin to be the sons and daughters of Shem and Japheth. Let us refuse to look at, or to be told about, anything that exposes, not our own father or son or brother only, but all other men's fathers, and mothers, and sons, and brothers. Let us keep our eyes shut to the sight of it, and our ears shut to the sound of it. Let us insist on looking on the best, the most blameless, and the most serviceable side of our neighbour. Let us think of Noah as a preacher of righteousness; as the builder of the ark; as elected, protected, and delivered by God; and as, with all his falls, all the time in God's sure covenant of peace, and under God's rainbow and God's oath. And when he is overtaken in a fault, ye that are spiritual restore such an one in the spirit of meekness, lest thou also be tempted. Some one has called the Apostle Paul the first perfect Christian gentleman. I shall always after this think of Shem and Japheth as Paul's Old Testament forerunners in that excellent, beautiful, and noble character.

IX

NIMROD

THEREFORE IS THE NAME OF IT CALLED BABEL

NIMROD was Noah's great-grandson through Ham; and he was a mighty hunter. He was the father, as William Law has it, of all those English gentlemen who take their delight in running foxes and hares out of breath. With one drop of his ink, and with one stroke of his pen, Moses tells us a great deal about Nimrod; and, the masterly writer that he is, Moses leaves still more to our imagination. 'And Cush begat Nimrod; he began to be a mighty one in the earth. He was a mighty hunter before the Lord; wherefore it is said, Even as Nimrod the mighty hunter before the Lord.' Nimrod's name, you will see, was a proverb in Israel down even to the day that Moses composed this book. Dante, also, Moses' equal in condensation and in force, lets us see that vast, vague, looming, swelling, gibbering giant in this thirty-first Inferno. His shoulders, his breast, his arms, his ribs,—Dante is amazed at the cloudy glimpse he gets of Ham's grandson down among the gloomy pits. O senseless spirit! shouts Virgil at the giant. And then to his charge:

Nimrod is this,
Through whose ill-counsel in the world no more
One tongue prevails. But pass we on, nor waste
Our words; for so each language is to him,
And his to others, understood by none.

Matthew Henry, still the prince of commentators for the common people, says that Nimrod, no doubt, did great good by his hunting instinct at the beginning of his career. He would put his people under deep obligation by ridding them of the wild beasts that infested those early lands. But then, as time went on, and as Nimrod's ambition grew, he would seem to have taken to hunting men instead of beasts. Great conquerors, after all, are but great hunters before the Lord. Alexander himself, the Great, as we call him, is to Daniel but a great pushing he-goat. And from that Nimrod was led on to build cities with walls, and towers, and barracks, and fortresses. Note of Nimrod's ambition, says our sagacious commentator, that it was boundless, expensive, restless, over-bold, and blasphemous.

Archbishop Whately thinks that the whole story of the building of the Tower of Babel, the confounding of the speech of the builders, and their consequent disruption and dispersion, north, south, east, and west, is a veiled history of a great outbreak of religious controversy in that early and eastern day. The archbishop does not pretend to have discovered just what the great controversy was all about; probably the whole thing would be unintelligible to us. But, on the whole, he thinks it must have been some dispute connected with the worship of God. In 1849 there was much less freedom allowed in the Church of England for such speculations than there is in our day; and thus it was that Dr. Whately had to come out about the Tower of Babel in one of the foreign tongues of Babel, and behind the veil of anonymity. A living writer in the same church looks on the Tower of Babel as a 'sublime emblem'; and Landor makes Isaac Barrow and Isaac Newton talk together in his noble English about that Tower as if it had been, at the top at least, the first astronomical observatory of those Babylonian fathers of that queen of the sciences. But we come back from all these, not uninstructive speculations in their way, to the powerfully written passage before us, in which so much is told us in such small space. 'Go to, let us go down, and there confound their language, that they may not understand one another's speech.'

Philo Judæus, the father of allegorical interpretation, has a beautiful tract entitled *The Confusion of Languages*. But Jacob Behmen, Philo's Teutonic son, far outstrips his Hebrew father in the depth, pungency, directness, and boldness of his interpretations and his applications. Babel, to Philo, is the soul of man; the confounded, confused, and scattered-abroad soul of man; and in his confused and scattered treatise we stumble on not a few things that are both wise and deep and beautiful. To Behmen, Babel is all that it is to Philo, with this characteristic addition, that Behmen's books are full of contemporaneous examples and illustrations of the Babel-like confusion that had come already to the Reformed Church of his day. Babel, to Behmen, is full of the controversies, verbal orthodoxies and heterodoxies, misunderstandings, misconstructions, and heart hatreds of the mighty hunters of his day. Babel, 'philosophically taken,' was to Philo the sum total of the passions of the soul let loose on the individual; evangelically taken, to Behmen, Babel was all those passions let loose also on the body of Christ. It is not easy and plain for any one of us to put our finger on our own Babel, says Behmen. For we are all working at the building of that Tower: we are all too much given over to words and to names, to sects and to parties, to men and to churches. Words rule us, and things lose all power over us. Names master us and tyrannise over us. Let every man enter into himself, and he will be sure to find a whole Tower of Babel, with all its consequences, standing in his own mind and in his own heart continually. The only possible escape from that Tower and its confoundings and confusions is to get clean away from the letter which killeth, and to go down into the spirit which giveth liberty and life. Leave off all disputations and all divisive words and names, and begin thy life again with God and with love alone. As Paul was not to be absolutely ignorant of everything but Christ and Him crucified all the time that he was to know nothing else, so Behmen is not to deny, nor forswear, or for ever forget the Lutheran catechisms and confessions of his day; only, he is to go beneath them all to the ground out of which they all spring, and above them all to the light and the air in which they all live and grow. And then he hopes to return to them with a love and a light and a life and a freedom that verbal Babel knows nothing of. Arguments, controversies, debates, disputes, even when they are true and needful, have always something of Babel in them; and they who must engage in them will have need of another and a better life outside of them, beneath them, and above them, as Jacob Behmen had.

And thus to come home, and to take current controversy among ourselves: political, religious, and, indeed, all kinds of controversy; if you will look well to it you will soon see why the name of it all is to be called Babel. All true moralists, all true logicians, all true teachers of rhetoric, unite to tell us and to testify to us that we all deceive and damage both ourselves and our neighbours and the truth every day by our words; by our misuse and our abuse of words. Words, indeed, are both the instrument and the vehicle of all thought and all intercourse. We cannot think, any more than we can speak or write, without words. But, unless we are early and well-taught, and unless we continually watch and teach ourselves, we shall become the complete slaves of our own instruments, and our carriages shall run away with us continually. 'Words are wise men's counters; wise men do but reckon by them; but they are the money of fools.' To prove that and to illustrate that, I had collected and arranged a table of wise men's counters and fools' moneys, and had intended to take in that table here. But I have departed from that intention. I have departed from that intention lest some of you should go off upon a word, and leave the proper and full lesson unlearned. It will be far better that each man who is intent on his own deliverance and improvement, should make up such a table of political, theological, scientific, and social controversialisms for himself, and out of his own conversation, and should, as Socrates would have taught him, ask himself, cross-question himself even, as to what he means by them when he uses them. Let us get into the truly intellectual, truly moral, and truly religious habit of asking ourselves, and insisting on an answer from ourselves. What is that name, nickname, by-word, that I am casting abroad about my brother so loudly and so loosely? What is the original root of it in language, and in me? What does it connote, as the schools say, first in my own mind, and then in its true content, and then in my hearer's or reader's capacity? Is is fair to use such a name and nickname? Is it just? Is it true? Would I like such and such names and nicknames to be attached to me by those who are opposed to me? It is very annoying, and, indeed, exasperating, to be pulled up in that way when our eloquence and our indignation and our denunciation are in full flood. But truth, love, goodness, godliness, are to be achieved by no man on easier terms. As Behmen would say, Babel is to be escaped in no other way. And, since Behmen is so full and so good, as I think, on Babel, and since he himself has been so much the victim of Babel—more almost than any man I know—let me show you once more the kind of thing that has made me love him: and, almost to say of him, as Dr. Newman says of Thomas Scott, that he owes him his own soul. I do not owe my soul to Behmen, or to any of his school; but I owe some lessons in my soul's deliverance and purification that I would be a cold-hearted creature if I did not on all hands acknowledge and share with you. A true Christian, says Teutonicus in his *Regeneration*, a Christian who is born anew into the Spirit of Christ, has less and less mind to contend and strive about matters of religion. He has enough to do within himself. A true Christian is really of no church. He can dwell surrounded by all the churches. He can even enter them all, and take part in all their services, without being bound up with any one of them. He has but one creed, which is, Christ in him. If men would but as fervently seek after love and righteousness as they do after disputatious matters, we should soon all be the children of one Father; and there would be no matters left to dispute about. If we did not know half so many contrary doctrines, and were more like little children; if we only had more good-will to those who hold the contrary doctrine, the contrariness would soon give way, and we would all be of one mind. Ungodly ministers go about sowing abroad contentions, reproaches, misconstructions; and, then, ungodly people catch all these up and make an ungodly religion out of them, and bring forth fruit accordingly. They despise, revile, slander, and misrepresent one another, till Babel, and all its sins and miseries, is again falling on us and burying us. What, asks Freher at himself and at the Spirit of his Master—what is an honest, simple Christian to do amidst such a variety of sects and contentions? He is to keep out of them; and he is to thank God that he has neither the call, nor the talent, nor the temptation to enter into them. He is to keep his heart clean and sweet to all men, and hot and bitter only at himself. No man's persuasion justifies me in hating him. And if I hate his persuasion too much, if I give up too much of my passion to hating any man's persuasion, I will soon end in hating myself. I must hate that only which hinders me myself from being a new creature in Christ Jesus. Therefore is the name of all controversy called Babel by the great mystics, the great masters of the life and love in the soul.

X

TERAH

AND TERAH TOOK ABRAM HIS SON TO GO INTO THE LAND OF CANAAN

THE first Jew was a Gentile. The first Hebrew was a heathen. The father of the faithful himself was, to begin with, a child of wrath even as others. To no man on the face of the earth had it been said as yet that to him and to his seed pertained the adoption, and the glory, and the covenants, and the giving of the law, and the service of God, and the promises. Why, we may well wonder, why was the covenant of life so long in coming in, and taking effect? Why,—since God will have all men to be saved, and to come unto the knowledge of the truth,—why were all the families of the earth not embraced in the covenant of life at once? Why was that new covenant not made with Adam, the father of us all? There would surely have been a fine fitness had Adam been our father in the covenant of grace as well as in the covenant of works. Now, why was he not? It may have been because he had made such a fatal breakdown in his first covenant. Or, it may have been because he had never taken that tremendous breakdown sufficiently home to heart. Neither the greatest sanctity nor the greatest service is forfeited by the truly and sufficiently penitent man. And it must surely have been that Adam lost the fatherhood of all penitent, believing, and holy men by the lack of depth and intensity and endurance in his repentance. Abel, Adam's second son, would have made a most excellent covenant-head. And, almost to a certainty, we, to-day, would have been called the children of faithful and acceptable Abel but for his brother's envy, and but for that foul and fatal blow in the field. Enoch, in the lack of Abel, would have made a model Abraham. How Enoch would have walked with God in Ur of the Chaldees, and in Haran, and in Canaan, and in Egypt, and back again in Canaan, confessing, all the time, that he was a stranger and a pilgrim with God on the earth! How Enoch would have told and would have taught his children after him that without faith it is impossible to please God! How he would have gone before them and shown them the way to come to God, believing that He IS, and that He is a rewarder of them that diligently seek Him! But the divine will was in a strait betwixt two in Enoch's case. Enoch was sorely needed on earth, indeed; but his own desire to depart, taken together with God's desire to have Enoch with Him, carried the day; which carriage, for Enoch, at any rate, was far better. Noah, we would have boldly said, was expressly made for the faithful place, and the place for him. For by faith Noah, being warned of God of things not seen as yet, moved with fear, prepared an ark to the saving of his house; by the which he condemned the world, and became heir of the righteousness which is by faith. And then, Noah was a preacher of righteousness to boot. But, instead of the faithful, Noah lived to become the father of all those who drown all their covenants of faith and of works alike, both with God and with man, in the wine-fat. All this time, then, all this disappointed and postponed time, the angel of the covenant had been passing unceasingly from land to land, and from nation to nation, and from tongue to tongue seeking for some of Adam's sons who should be found worthy to take up the calling and election of God; till, at last, the star came and stood over the house of Terah, on the other side of the flood. Now, this Terah, in his inherited and invincible ignorance, served other gods, and he had brought up Abram, his so devout son, to the same service. But those two Gentile men, father and son, served their Gentile gods with such truly Jewish service that God was constrained to wink at their unwilling ignorance. The God of all grace graciously accepted Terah and Abram for their love and for their obedience to the light that lighteth every man that cometh into the world. And thus it was that the true God raised up Abram the son of Terah, that righteous man from the east, and called him to his foot, gave the nations before him, and made him rule over kings. And thus it was also that Abram's second greatest son put Abram his father into his great catholic sermon on Mars hill, and said this about Abram: God, he said, that made the world, hath made of one blood all nations of men, that they should seek the Lord, if haply they might feel after Him and find Him, though He be not far from every one of us. For in Him we live and move and have our being; for we also are His offspring. To Him that hath shall be given, is an absolute and a universal law and rule with the God of righteousness. And thus it was that He said to Abram, the son of Terah, in Ur of the Chaldees: Well done, good and faithful servant. Because thou hast been faithful over a few things, I will make thee ruler over many things. Get thee out of thy country, and from thy kindred, and from thy father's house, into a land that I will show thee.

It would have been entirely true to nature, and it would have been a most beautiful and a very fine lesson to all the families of the earth, had the divine call come to Terah, the father, and had Terah taken Abram, and had the son set out with the father to go together to the land of promise. But it is above and beyond nature, and it is a still nobler and a still more sublime sight, to see the call coming to the son, and then to see the father submitting himself to that call; entirely and immediately accepting it; and setting out under his chosen son to act upon that call and to follow it out. I can easily imagine a thousand suspicions, and rebukes, and remonstrances, and threatenings that Terah might have addressed to his son Abram when he first communicated the vision and the voice to his Chaldean father. It would be no imagination to repeat to you some of Terah's refusals, and remonstrances, and indictments, and protestations, and punishments. We have heard them, or the like of them, a thousand times. We have heard them as often as the same heaven opened and the same voice spoke to the young intellectual and spiritual emigrants of our New Testament day. But not one word of such stagnation, stubborn, unbelieving speeches came out of the mouth of Abram's noble father. Far from that. Nay, I know not that we would ever have had Abram, or would ever have heard his name, unless his humble-hearted, youthful-hearted, brave-hearted and believing-hearted old father had taken his chosen son by the hand, and his chosen son's wife, and had said, Yes, my son Abram, and my daughter Sarai, yes, let us set out at once for the land of Canaan. Why Terah himself was not taken, and himself made the father of the faithful, we do not know; unless it was that he was to stand at the head of human history in a still nobler fatherhood and a still more honourable office. That is to say, to be the patron patriarch and first father of all humble-minded, open-minded, free-minded, and hospitable-minded old men all the world over. Yes, that was it. Terah was taken in Ur of the Chaldees, and was there made the type and the teacher of all those wise men of the east, and of the west, and of the north, and of the south: all the elect within the election, and without: all those men old in years, but whose eye is not dim, nor their intellectual nor their spiritual strength one iota abated. Terah is the Magian father of all those sweet, wise, beautiful souls who stand rooted in a green and genial age: all those in whom, though their outward man may perish, yet their inward man is renewed day by day. Terah, the father of Abram, is at the same time the father of all those statesmen, and churchmen, and theologians, and philosophers, as well as of all those many plain men among us, who to old age are still open to all divine visions and to all divine voices; to all new truth and to all new light; to all new departures in divine providence and in divine progress, and then to all new opportunities and all new duties. They are all Abram's brethren, and they all take of Terah, his father. All they whose living faith in the everliving God is such that they see and feel His heavenly life still quickening all existence, and His heavenly light still lighting all men in His living word, in His living church, in His living providences, and in the living souls of all His children. A teachable, tractable, pliable son is a fine sight to see, and such a son is the best blessing that any good father can have of God. But a still teachable, tractable, pliable-minded, genial-minded, hopeful-minded father is a still finer sight to see; a still rarer, nobler, and even more delightful sight to see. A father who reads his reading son's best books, and who sits at the feet of his student son's best teachers, and who walks arm in arm with his elect son away out of the worn-out past and away up into the land of promise—that is a father to descend from, and to be proud of above peers and princes. A father who unites a large and a sage experience to a free spirit of expectation, and enterprise, and hope, and steadfast faith, and full assurance. And, thank God, at every new vision and at every new voice of His we ever find such sons of Terah in the church and in the state, in the congregation and in the family, and a right honourable place they fill, and a right fruitful. Get thee out of thy country, and from thy kindred, and from thy father's house, into a land that I will show thee. And Terah took Abram his son and Sarai his daughter-in-law, his son Abram's wife, and he went forth with them from Ur of the Chaldees, to go into the land of Canaan. Let all our old and venerable men continue to take Terah for their first father till their flesh is given back to them like the flesh of a little child, and till their youth is renewed like the eagle's.

As it turned out, then, it was neither Adam, nor Abel, nor Enoch, nor Noah, nor Terah, but it was Abram, Terah's choicest son, who was installed of God into the fatherhood of all foreknown, predestinated, called, justified, and glorified men. But, with all his excellent natural qualities and abilities, and with all that Terah could teach his son,—and then, to crown all, when he took his staff in his hand and walked out of Ur not knowing whither he went,—with all that parental instruction and example, Abram still had, himself, great things both to undergo and to perform before he was ready to be made the father of a faithful seed. A great bereavement, a great disappointment, a great temptation, a great transgression, a great humiliation, and a great surrender of his rights—all these great experiences, and more than all these, had to be passed through, and their full fruits had to be reaped up into Abram's heart and life and character, before Abram could be trusted, could be counted on, as the foundation stone of the Old Testament Church; and before the patriarchs, and prophets, and psalmists, and kings of Israel could be built up upon him. I am the Almighty God; walk before Me and be thou perfect. But, like his far-off Son, Abram had first to be made perfect through suffering. And Abram's first baptism of suffering was not so much the leaving of his fatherland; it was much more the death of Terah his father and his fellow-traveller. Plato says that there is always a little child hidden away deep down in the very oldest man's heart. And Abram's heart was just the heart to have hidden away deep down in it Terah's little child. And that little child awoke in Abram's heart, and filled the tent and the camp with its cries and with its tears when Terah too soon gave up the ghost in Haran. As long as Abram had his father beside him and before him, faith, and love, and hope, and obedience were all easy to Abram. With a father like Terah to talk to, to pray and to praise with, and to walk arm in arm with at the head of the emigrant household, Abram's face shone like the sun as he turned his back on the land of his nativity. All that Abram really cared for came out of Chaldea with him. Terah, his venerable father; Sarai, his beautiful sister-wife; and Lot, his managing nephew; and under Lot's charge all his flocks and herds; and, above all, with this new amazing, divine hope and secret in his heart—with all that with him Abram walked with God, and was already perfect. But the sudden death of Terah made that happy Chaldean company to come to a standstill in Haran. It made Abram stand still. It changed the whole world to Abram. Abram's believing heart was absolutely buried in his believing father's grave in Haran. But such was the depth, and the sincerity, and the true piety of Abram's mourning for his father, that, by the time that the days of his mourning were accomplished, Abram's first faith in God had come back again to his dead heart. The call of God sounded more and more commanding in his mourning heart; till the promise became, even more than at the beginning, both a staff of God in his hand and a cordial of God in his heart. As a great psalmist-son of his sang of himself in after days in Israel—when Abram's father and mother forsook him, then the Lord took him up. All the same, the whole after way from Haran to Shechem was often a solitary and a steep way to Abram: a dim, a headless, and a leaderless way to Terah's pious and childlike son. At the same time, when Terah died in Haran, and when Abram took the old man's death to heart with such grief, with such resignation, with such an assured reliance upon the divine promise, and with such full assurance of God's grace, and truth, and power, and faithfulness, a great step was taken both to the land of promise, and to Abram's predestination as the father of all faithful men.

Abram's great bereavement was immediately followed by a great disappointment. The Lord thy God, so sang the call and the promise in Abram's hopeful heart—The Lord thy God bringeth thee into a good land, a land of brooks of water, of fountains and depths that spring out of valleys and hills; a land of wheat, and barley, and vines, and fig trees, and pomegranates; a land of oil, olive and honey; a land wherein thou shalt eat bread without scarceness, thou shalt not lack anything in it; a land whose stones are iron, and out of whose hills thou mayest dig brass. But no sooner had Abram begun to build an altar at Bethel; no sooner had he begun to lengthen his cords and to strengthen his stakes, than a terrible famine of all these things fell on the whole land. Till Lot only put words upon the terrible darkness that fell on Abram's overwhelmed heart when he upbraided Abram, and said, Would God we also had died in Haran! Would God we had listened to our kinsmen in Chaldea when they dissuaded us from this folly and from this wilderness!

The hands of the pitiful women have sodden their own children; they that did feed delicately are desolate in the streets; they that were brought up in scarlet embrace the dung-hill. We have drunken our water for money; our wood is sold to us. We have given the hand to Egypt, and to Assyria that we may have bread. No wonder that after such a sudden collapse of hope as that, Abram's faith completely gave way for a season. Sarai was all that Abram now had. She was the wife of his youth. She had come with him and she had stood beside him in all his losses and disappointments; and if he should lose Sarai in Egypt everything was lost. Say, I pray thee, that thou art my sister, that it may be well with me for thy sake, and my soul shall live because of thee. And Sarai was as weak as her husband was, and she fell into the same snare of unbelieving fear. Till the end of that sad business was that the Lord plagued Pharaoh and his house with great plagues because of Sarai, Abram's wife. And till Pharaoh called Abram and bitterly rebuked him. Were you ever bitterly rebuked for your sin by some one far beneath you in age, in knowledge, in experience, and in the calling and the grace of God? Did you ever taste that bitterest of all galls of seeing innocent men and women plagued for your sin? Then you will understand better than even Moses could tell you, what Abram felt as he saw the unoffending king of Egypt struck with plagues for Abram's falsehood and for Abram's deceit. It is not told in Moses, but I can well believe it, that nothing that ever happened to Abram so hastened forward his humility, his detachment from this world, and his heavenly-mindedness, as his fall in Egypt, and all its consequences to Pharaoh and to Pharaoh's household. What is this that thou hast done to me? Those who have these accusing words sounding in their ears from the reproaches of innocent and injured people, they will be shut up like their father Abram to that grace of which God so timeously and so fitly spake to Abram when He said to him: Fear not, Abram, for I am thy shield and thy salvation.

Jonathan Edwards, one of the purest and princeliest souls that ever were made perfect through suffering, has told all that fear God what God did for his soul. In intellect Edwards was one of the very greatest of the sons of men, and in holiness he was a seraph rather than a man. And to have from such a saint, and in his own words, what God from time to time did for his so exercised soul is a great gift to us out of the unsearchable riches of Christ. Well, Edwards testifies to the grace of God that immediately after every new season of great distress, great mortification, great humiliation. great self-discovery, and great contrition, there was always given him a corresponding period of great liberty, great enlargement, great detachment, great sweetness, great beauty, and great and ineffable delight. Till he testifies to all who fear God, and challenges us out of Hosea, saying to us: Come, let us return to the Lord our God: for He hath torn, and He will heal us; He hath smitten, and He will bind us up. His going forth is prepared as the morning; and He shall come to us as the rain, as the latter and former rain unto the earth. And so was it with Edward's first father in his re-migration out of Egypt back to Canaan. But if Pharaoh was sore plagued because of Abram's transgressions, then Lot, at any rate, had his advantage out of all that. As our magnificent New Testament commentary on the Old Testament has it, Abram came out of his trespass in Egypt more than ever a stranger and a pilgrim with God on the earth. He came back to Canaan very rich in cattle, in silver, and in gold. But, like all his mortified sons, his heart was no more in his riches. God makes men rich who do not care for riches, and He brings to poverty those who like Lot sell their souls for sheep and oxen. He hath filled, sang Mary, the hungry with good things, and the rich He hath sent empty away. Abram was filled with good things as he came back to Canaan, which had now recovered from her famine. As full as he could hold, and more. But Abram's heart was less and less in his cattle pens and in his money bags; and more and more his heart was in those promises that are never received in this life, but are kept for us in that city which hath foundations, whose builder and maker is God. In former days, in the days before Haran and Bethel, and especially in the days before Egypt, if the land had not been able to bear both Abram and Lot, Abram would have said to Lot, I will journey east to Jordan, where it is well watered like the garden of the Lord, and the rest of the land thou canst take after I have left it. But after Egypt, and all the other times and places that Abram has come through, he has no heart left for any such choice or any contention about cattle and sheep, and corn and wine. Let there be no strife, I pray thee, between me and thee, for we be brethren. In Edwards's experience Abram's mortifications and humiliations in Egypt and elsewhere had resulted in an amazing elevation, detachment, supremeness, and sweetness of soul. Till, without knowing it, on the heights above Bethel, Abram was made the father of Him who sat on those same heights long afterwards, and, remembering Abram, opened His mouth and taught His disciples, saying: Where your treasure is, there will your heart be also. Blessed are they which do hunger and thirst after righteousness, for they shall be filled. Seek ye first the kingdom of God, and His righteousness, and all these things shall be added unto you.

And now, as Terah and Abram were in all that, so are all their true children. We also are continually being called to go out, not knowing whither we go. We also are sojourners in a strange land. We also die in faith, not having received the promises. We also desire a better country, that is, an heavenly. And, O! how well it is with us if God is not ashamed to be called our God, and if He has prepared for us a city! Like Abraham in Ur, we are the sons of a father who hears our call, and who takes us by the hand and leads us on the way. Or it is otherwise, just as God in His deep wisdom and love wills it to be. But, fatherful or fatherless; with Terah for our father, or with God alone; still His call comes to us all to arise and come out with Him to a land that He will show us. Arise, He says to us, and go forward in faith, in obedience, in trust, and in a sure hope. The very progress of the years, were it nothing else, would be a continually renewed call to go forward, and to walk henceforth with God. From childhood, ere ever we are aware, we have migrated into youth. From youth we are soon ushered into manhood, and from one stage of manhood on into another; till, if we have God's blessing on us, we become old like Terah, with our eye not dim, nor our strength abated. Youth, man, married man, father, master, citizen, and so on. Maid, wife, mother, mistress, widow indeed, and so on. Migrating from one field of human life into another, and never leaving one field till we have reaped in its full harvest, and never entering upon a new field till we are prepared to plough it, and sow it, and reap it,—what a noble life we are called to lead on this earth, and all the time the pilgrims of God, and preparing ourselves for His city! What a noble education did divine providence pass Terah's son through, and with what profit to his mind, and heart, and temper, and whole moral character. His childhood spent in ancient Chaldea; his very crossing of the flood Euphrates on such an errand; the snows of Lebanon; the oaks of Bashan; Damascus; Salem; the Nile; the pyramids; the great temples; the famous schools and schoolmasters of Egypt, at whose feet Moses was to sit in after days,—all that, and much more that we neither know nor can imagine. What a noble education Terah's son was passed through of God. But not half so noble, not half so wonderful, not half so fruitful as our own. What were Babylon, and Nineveh, and Damascus, and Salem, and all Egypt, to this western world and to this nineteenth century after

Christ! What were all the science of Chaldea, and all the lore of Egypt, but the merest rudiments and first elements of that splendid sunshine of all manner of truth and opportunity which floods around us from our youth up! And as we are led on from school to school; and from author to author; and from preacher to preacher; and from one stage of intellectual and spiritual migration and growth to another; to what a stature, to what a breadth, and to what a height of faith, and knowledge, and love, and all manner of grace and truth may we not attain. Let us be up and doing. Let us open our eyes. Let us open our ears. Let us open our hearts. For thou, Israel, art My servant, Jacob whom I have chosen, the seed of Abraham my friend.

XI

ABRAHAM

ABRAHAM MY FRIEND

I DID not know before that God had ever needed a friend. I did not know, I could not have believed, that any mortal man could possibly have be-friended Almighty God. I need a friend. I need companionship. I need advice and counsel and correction. I need to be cheered and comforted. I often feel lonely. I often despond. I often miss my way of life. I often commit myself to rash, ill-considered, and irretrievable steps. I often hurt both myself and other men with me. And, therefore, I need near me a faithful friend. A friend to speak to me in time, and with wisdom, and with both sympathy and encouragement. A friend loveth at all times, and a brother is born for adversity. And there is a friend that sticketh closer than a brother. Faithful are the wounds of such a friend. Ointment and perfume rejoice the heart: so doth the sweetness of a man's friend by hearty counsel. Iron sharpeneth iron: and so doth a man sharpen the countenance of his friend. Bacon needed a friend. The principal fruit of friendship is the case and discharge of the fulness of the heart. You may take sarza to open the liver, steel to open the spleen, flower of sulphur for the lungs, castoreum for the brain; but no receipt openeth the heart but a true friend—a true friend to whom you may impart griefs, joys, fears, hopes, suspicions, counsels, and whatsoever lieth upon the heart to oppress it. And our own Edward Irving, a great student of Bacon, often sorely needed a wise friend, as we see in his sad life and read in his superb sermons. The great office of a friend is to try our thoughts by the measure of his judgments; to task the wholesomeness of our designs and purposes by the feelings of his heart; to protect us from the solitary and selfish part of our nature; to speak to and to call out those finer and better parts of our nature which the customs of this world stifle; and to open up to us a career worthy of our powers. "Now," adds the most eloquent of all our Presbyterian preachers, "as every man hath these four attributes—infirmity of judgment, selfishness of disposition, inactivity and inertness of nature, and adversity of fortune,—so every man needeth the help of a friend, and should do his endeavour to get one." For all these four attributes Solomon needed a friend, and Bacon, and Irving, and you, and I,—but, surely, not God. And yet it stands written out in more scriptures than one that Almighty God endeavoured to get a true friend in Abraham, and got one.

Now, of no mortal man but of Abraham alone does Almighty God ever speak and say, He was My friend. God employs many gracious, beautiful, and endearing names in speaking of the patriarchs, and prophets, and psalmists, and other saints of His in Israel; but it is of Abraham alone that God testifies to Israel and says, Thou art the seed of Abraham, My friend. Now, I wonder if we can get at what was in the Divine Mind, and at what He put into the prophet's mind in that so remarkable and unparalleled expression. Can we put our finger on anything in Abraham's life and say, Here, and here, and here, that wonderful man proved himself to be the friend of God? We have only a few short chapters to cover the long life of Abraham. I wonder shall we find enough in those chapters to satisfy us why Isaiah, and James, and then why both Jew and Mussulman and Christian, all unite in calling Abraham what they call no other man—the friend of God? Let us try.

Well then, we see this, to begin with, that God appeared and asked of Abram a service; a kind of service, and an amount and a degree of service, that He has never needed to ask the like of it again of any other man, if we except the Man Christ Jesus. God had for long—from the fall—been looking out for some man with mind enough and with heart enough to be made the father and the founder of a family into which He could send His Son. God promised His Son to Adam and Eve; but generations and generations had to pass before the fulness of time came. And all those successive generations had to be filled with all that with which our Bible is filled from Genesis to the

Gospels. And the foundations of all that had first to be laid in some elect, called, believing, obedient, godly-minded, heavenly-minded man. Only, where was the man to be found who had all the qualifications needful for this supreme post? The long-looked-for man was found at last in Abram, Terah's choice son, in Ur of the Chaldees. To Terah's son, first of all good men on the face of the earth, was God able to say, Get thee out of thy kindred; walk before Me, and be thou perfect. And Abram believed God. Abram believed God with such a depth, and with such a strength, and with such a promptitude, and with such a perseverance that by Abram's faith the foundations of the whole Church of God on earth and in heaven were laid in him. No doubt, the beginning and the middle and the end of that friendship was all in God. No doubt, Abram would have protested against, and would have repudiated the name of friend of God with fear and with shame. But that does not alter the fact. It is still God's way to impute to us what He does for us: and to reward us for what we let Him do in us. God works in us both to will and to do; but, at the same time, He holds that we work out our own salvation. And so it was in the beginning of His ways with Abraham. God chose Abraham, and called him, and blessed him. But at the same time, God always has made much of the fact that Abraham had the mind and the heart to do what he did both for God and for all the families of the earth. And that immense venture of faith and of love on the part of Abraham, to call it a venture, was so original, so unheard of, and so full of all the great qualities of a godly heart and a heavenly life, that Abraham has ever since been called, not only the father of the faithful, but also the foremost and topmost friend of God. You understand, then, and will take home the lesson. Abraham had the heart to choose, and to prefer, and to venture for God, and for the will and the call of God, before everything else in this world. Abraham immediately, unquestioningly, cheerfully, joyfully arose and went out to do and to be all that God had asked him to do and had promised him to be. Till, as Butler has it, God justified Abraham's taste, and supported his cause, and acknowledged and claimed him as His friend: him, and his seed after him.

Edward Irving says that it is part of the office and service of a true friend to call out, and to prepare a scope for those finer feelings of the heart which are chilled and driven back upon the heart in this cold, distrustful, selfish world. Now, if that is true, and if God's heart and our hearts are in the same image in that also; if His heart also is chilled and shut up within itself in this same selfish world; then Abraham's so pressing intercession for Sodom was the part of a true friend to God. Humanly speaking, Sodom and Gomorrah would have been destroyed, and God's heart which was so full of answer to intercessory prayer would never have been discovered, had it not been for Abraham's so friendly part performed that day both to God and to the doomed cities of the plain. And while Abraham was seeking first his own ends and the ends of the two cities in his persevering prayer, he was at the same time without knowing it serving God's greatest ends still more. For God's greatest ends always are that His great Name may be known; His great grace helped down and experienced; and His great heart drawn out to all its depth; and that, too, by persevering and importunate prayer. You are a good man's best friend when you provide him with, and press upon him, opportunity upon opportunity of doing good. And Abraham was the opportune and importunate friend of the Hearer of Prayer when he said, Peradventure, and peradventure, and peradventure, and peradventure, and again, peradventure, and when God in friendly answer reduced the price of Sodom from fifty righteous men to ten. And the Lord went His way as soon as He had left communing with Abraham; and Abraham returned to his place.

Honest Joseph Hall counts up ten trials of Abraham's faith and friendship through which God saw good to pass His friend. And the last of the ten was more terrible to Abraham than all the rest taken together. If any of you is a father, and has a son of your old age; a son of much faith and of much prayer on your part, and of much pure miracle on God's part; then add to that, that your only son is the one and only instrument and chosen vessel of all God's remaining promises to you: and then, that he lies at the point of death. I do not add that he is to die under your hand like Isaac. I only add that he is to die with your consent and surrender and approval. If any of you that is a father or a mother has, or has had, a child like that, then you are the seed of Abraham, the friend of God. For, how you lay all night on the earth before God. How you would neither eat bread nor drink water. How you pleaded and promised and protested; how you vowed and swore and despaired. Then you will know something of how God did tempt Abraham. I do not understand this dark dispensation of God—all the seed of Abraham are often compelled to say. All is dark as midnight to me. Why should my dear, pure, inoffensive, so indispensable, and so promising son be taken away from me in the bloom of his beautiful youth? But God knows. God gave him, and it is God's place to take him when He pleases. I do not understand it. But God's understanding is infinite and unfathomable, and He does nothing of caprice, or of arrogance, or of hard-heartedness, or of oversight, or of neglect. And, when I come to myself, and think of it, if I had ten sons, and all of them were Isaacs, I would build the ten altars with my own hand. In His will is my tranquillity of mind, and my strength of heart, and my submission, and my obedience—so all Abraham's seed are called on and are enabled to say.

Abraham withheld not Isaac from his Friend on one of the mountains of Moriah; and in the same country, two thousand years after, God was not to be outdone by Abraham in the seal of His friendship to Abraham and to his seed for ever. And the bare mention of that brings God, and His friendship to us and our friendship to Him, two thousand miles nearer us and two thousand miles more possible to us than Abraham's too splendid faith and too wonderful love. With all that has been said I have difficulty in believing what has been said. No; not exactly in believing it, but in what we call realising it. For all that we have read and heard in Abraham's history,—that any mortal man should be able to befriend Almighty God, still remains a very startling thing to say about Almighty God. But not about Jesus Christ. We could have befriended Him ourselves. And I think, nay, I feel sure, we would have done it too. Multitudes of men and women who were as weak and as evil and as unbelieving as we are, will be led out at the last day to receive the thanks of the Father because they befriended His friendless Son. The women of Galilee who ministered to Him of their substance will be brought forward; Martha will be brought forward, and the woman at the well; the owner of the ass's colt, and the owner of the upper room, and the owner of Gethsemane; Simon the Cyrenian also, who helped Him to carry His cross; the soldier also who gave Him some of his vinegar to drink; and Joseph of Arimathea, and Nicodemus, and the women with their spices, and the angel who rolled away the stone. O!—you start up and exclaim: O! if my lot had only been cast in Galilee, or in Samaria, or in Judea, or in Jerusalem! O! you cry, how you envy the men and women to whom the Father will say, Inasmuch as ye did it to Him, ye did it to Me! But, as you still cry that, this scripture comes up into mind. You will remember it when I repeat it: "Ye are My friends if ye do whatsoever I command you." And again: "Greater love hath no man than this, that a man lay down his life for his friends."

And again, in the same kind: "Henceforth I call you not servants, but I have called you friends." And then, to His Father, this: "Neither pray I for these alone, but for them also which shall believe on Me through their word." Well then, we do not need, we have no temptation now, to challenge the wisdom and the love that cast our lot two thousand years after Christ; as the same wisdom and love cast Abraham's lot two thousand years before Christ. Abraham believed the word of the Lord in his day; and if we believe in our day through the word of the disciples, then are we Abraham's seed, and need envy neither Abraham our father nor any of our brethren. Abraham laid down his life and the life of Isaac at the call of God. And Jesus Christ, Son of God, and Son of Abraham, laid down His life at the same call. But our call, our first call, is not yet to lay down our life, but to take Him as our Friend who has laid down His life for ours. Now, what do you all say to that? Are you His friends on that footing? A friend gives full scope to his friend's love and goodness. Have you given Jesus Christ full scope to His life and death for you? Has this Man laid down His life for you? He has, if you have ever asked Him to do it. He has, if you have ever come up to His cross and said over Him, He gave Himself here for me. He has, if you have ever said, I lay my sin and my death on Jesus Christ. Did it ever come to this terrible pass with you, your life or His? And how did that terrible pass end? When was it? Where was it? How long ago was it? When did it take place last? Has it taken place to-day? Is it taking place every day? Then you need envy neither Abraham nor any other man. Your day is the best of days for you. Your call is the best of calls for you. And you will be brought forward among the very first and the very best as that sinner who has adorned the doctrines of the death of Christ, and of the heart of God to sinners, as no other sinner has done from Abraham's day to the day of judgment. Does that amazing Man still stand offering me His death for me, and His living and everlasting friendship to boot? Then, this moment; then, in this house, and on the spot, I am His friend, and He is my friend.

All that is most commendable to speak, and most consoling to hear. It is very blessed to speak and to hear about Christ and His friendship to death in the sanctuary to-night; but it will all die out of our hearts in the shop, in the office, in the kitchen, in the drawing-room, and in the dining-room to-morrow. So it will. But, then, that is not all that our Lord says about how we are to make friends with Him, and to keep up that friendship. He is very practical and matter-of-fact in His friendship.

"Ye are My friends," he goes on to say, "if ye do whatsoever I command you." Well then, take the thing by the handle. Try that door. Strike up, and keep up, the friendship on that plain, pedestrian footing. You cannot attain to His cross, you complain. His blood is too remote, too transcendental, too, somehow, spiritual, and too altogether heavenly for you. I wonder at you. But let that pass. Try this commonplace way. Do this and that which He commands you to do, and you will be as much—ay, and more, His friend than if you preached and prayed and praised His blood and righteousness day and night, and did nothing else. Do this for one thing that He so pointedly commands. Shut your door to-night. And if you have no door to call your own, yet you have a heart with doors. Enter your heart, then, and pray to your Father, whose true temple is the praying man's heart. And see if He does not one day tell all the world who took His Son in earnest, and who did not. O, how easy on that footing is the friendship of God! O, how impossible it is to get past it! And then, do this to-morrow—to-morrow when the lights shall all be out in the church, and when the preacher's voice shall be silent, and when the Chaldeas and the Sodoms and the Egypts of this world shall have all men's choices and friendships—do this. God has the day prepared, and has filled it full for this purpose. All to-morrow love your enemies, and your rivals—that is to say, try to do it. Work at it. Enter into the strait gate of it. Bless them that curse you. Do good to them, and to their wives and children, who hate you, with, or without cause. Ye are My friends, says the Son of God, if ye do that. Then, again, if you are a father with a sick son, or a son in a sudden accident; or a son who has not succeeded at school, or at college, or in life; or a son who has brought grey hairs here and there upon you, till all men mark it. How you deal with that son of yours will prove, or will disprove, you a friend of God as much and as surely as if your name had been Abraham, and your son's name Isaac. Or, if God needs you or your son to go abroad on any mission of His, as He needed Abraham, then go. Be like noble old Terah, go half the way with your elect and expatriated son, till God arises out of His place and comes to meet you, and says to you—As sure as I live, all the land on which thou standest will I give to thee and to thy seed with thee, because thou hast not withheld thyself or thy son from Me. Or, if it is this. If there is a famine of bread and water where corn and wine had been promised and expected; or if the laughters and the shouts of baptized children are silent where they would have been as the voices of God's angels to you,—what then?

Then thy God will descend into thine heart, and He will ask: Am I not more to thee than sons and daughters? Is My love not better to thee than corn and wine? Am I, and My salvation, and that city of Mine which hath foundations, not more to be desired by thee than all else that I could give thee? Till you will find it in your bereaved and broken heart to say to Him henceforth and continually, Whom have I in heaven but Thee? And there is none upon earth that I desire beside Thee. My flesh and my heart faileth; but God is the strength of my heart, and my portion for ever.

XII

LOT

GOD DELIVERED JUST LOT

WE are still away up among the fathers and the founders of the great families of mankind. Terah was the father of all those old men among us whose day is not done, nor their eye dim, nor their natural force abated. Abraham was the father of the faithful. And Lot, his nephew, was the father of all such as are scarcely saved. Lot began his religious life very early in life, and he began it very well. Lot was singularly happy in having a grandfather like Terah, and an uncle like Abraham. And Lot himself must have had something very good about him to begin with, when he left all his youthful associates, both young men and young women, and set out he knew not whither. Only, the two best men on earth—they knew. They were going out of Chaldea; and if they would let him Lot would go with them. Now that same is all the religion that many of our own young men have still. And, in a way, and for some men, it is quite enough to begin with. All men are not gifted as Abraham was gifted. All men are not called as Abraham was called. All men are not made to lead. All men are not fitted to be explorers and pioneers in morals or in religion, any more than in science, or in art, or in business, or in public life. There are great, and powerful, and original, and epoch-making men; and then there are men who follow those great men, and who fill up what they find out and set agoing. And the most part of our young men cannot do a wiser or a better thing for a long time to come than just to follow their fathers and their other forerunners like Terah and Abraham. Had Lot just held on as he began; had he kept close to Abraham, and had he been content to share Abraham's prospects and prosperity and peace, Lot would have lived a pure and a happy life; he would have escaped many sorrows, and, instead of being scarcely saved; saved indeed, but saved with the fire and brimstone of Sodom and Gomorrah smouldering in his skirts; he would have gone down to a truly patriarchal grave, an elder of a good report and a father of a blameless name. All went well enough with Lot as long as he had the good sense, and the good feeling, and the good manners to know his proper place and to keep it. He left Chaldea and came to Haran with the Abrahamic emigration. He held a grandson's cord at Terah's grave, and he received his share of Terah's testament. When Abraham rose up and left Haran and entered the land of promise Lot went all the way with him. Wherever Abraham went, Lot went. Where Abraham built an altar, Lot either offered at that altar or he built another like it for himself. When the Lord spoke to Abraham, the uncle never hid from the nephew any word of the Lord that could either guide him in his behaviour or confirm him in his pilgrimage. When the terrible famine fell on Canaan, Abraham took Lot down to Egypt with him; and after the famine passed off, Lot returned to the land of promise with his chastened uncle.

I am not sure that Egypt had not been a sore temptation to Lot as well as to Abraham. Nay, I am quite sure, when I think of it, that it must have been. Mean-minded men, sordid-minded men, self-seeking men have constant temptations wherever they go. Wherever they go they carry their temptations with them. They manufacture temptations to themselves in every place and out of every thing. And Lot was not a high-minded man. With all his early opportunities, and with all his early promises, Lot was not, and never became, a high-minded man. We are never told all his life one large-hearted, or one noble-minded, or one single self-forgetful thing about Lot. Low-minded men see their opportunity in everything. Your stumble, your fall, your misfortune, your approaching age, your illness, your death—all is grist to the mill of the mean-minded man. And Abraham's fall in Egypt, and, especially, Abraham's fast-growing indifference to his fast-growing wealth, would be a secret delight to Lot. And then, that Abraham and Sarah with all their wealth had no son! Why, let Lot just wait on a few years and the whole of the immense family inheritance will be his. He will be the undisputed heir of Terah, and Abraham, and Sarah, and all. Lot is the father of all of you who are waiting for dead men's shoes. You all take of Lot who marry, and build, and borrow money on the strength of the rich man's old age, and that ageing woman's childlessness. True, there was that Eliezer of Damascus, and some other men who were deep in Abraham's confidence, and much trusted by him, —but blood is thicker than water, and Lot will live in hope.

It was Lot's highest interest to behave himself well before Abraham, and to do nothing that would lead Abraham to suspect his nephew's false and sordid heart. But sordid-heartedness like Lot's will not always hide. Lot struck what might well have been a fatal blow at his own dearest hopes with his own hand. And had Abraham not been a weak, old unworldly soul; had Abraham not borne all things, and believed all things, and hoped all things, and endured all things, Lot would soon have reaped as he had sown. But Abraham was what he was, and Lot had his profit out of that. Abraham had come up out of Egypt overwhelmed with shame and broken in his heart; and one result of all that was that he was overwhelmed with shame at his increasing prosperity also. Abraham, after Egypt, was the first father of all those who since his day have every day said, He hath not dealt with us after our sins, nor rewarded us according to our iniquities. Every new acre of pasture land, and every new well of water for his cattle, and every new time of stocktaking, only made Abraham confess himself more and more a stranger and a pilgrim with God on the earth. But not his nephew. Not Lot. Lot was fast becoming the father of all hard-faced, hard-hearted, close-fisted, money-loving men. And Lot's herdmen knew their master, took of him and studied how to please him. They removed the landmarks; they drew off the water; they picked constant quarrels with Abraham's patient herdmen, till the strife between the two camps was the scandal of the whole country round. But blessed are the peacemakers. Hear, then, what the first peacemaker in the Bible said, and go and say and do likewise, 'And Abraham took Lot and said to him, Let there be no strife, I pray thee, between me and thee, and between my herdmen and thy herdmen; for we be brethren. Is not the whole land before thee? Separate thyself, I pray thee, from me. If thou wilt take the left hand, then I will go to the right; or, if thou depart to the right hand, then I will go to the left.' And then hear this, and resolve never, all your days, under any offer, or opportunity, or temptation of any kind to do what miserable, mean-spirited Lot did. Just hear what he did. You would not believe it. 'And Lot lifted up his eyes and beheld all the plain of Jordan, that it was well watered everywhere, before the Lord destroyed Sodom and Gomorrah, even as the garden of the Lord, like the land of

Egypt as thou comest into Zoar. And Lot chose all the plain of Jordan, and Lot journeyed east, and Lot dwelled in the cities of the plain, and pitched his tents toward Sodom.' O my friends, labour to have a heart created within you that will make it simply impossible for you ever to do to anybody what Lot did that day to Abraham. What a man chooses, and how a man chooses, when opportunities and alternatives and choices are put before him—nothing more surely discovers a man than that. Abraham chose household peace; while Lot chose good pasture ground at the cost of disgrace, and shamelessness, and all unhandsomeness and ingratitude, and got Sodom to the boot of the bargain. Abraham, though the older man, and the man, moreover, with all the title-deeds to all the land of Canaan in his hands, put all that wholly aside and placed himself on an equality with his dependent nephew; placed himself under Lot, indeed, and give him his choice. One would have thought that if anything would have melted Lot's brazen face and made him blush and become a man, it would have been the nobility, the munificence, and the fine high-mindedness of his uncle. But Lot's heart was turned to stone. Till with his hard eyes Lot stood up and looked out the best land and the best water in all the country round, and drove his flocks down into it without a moment's hesitation, or a touch of remorse, or so much as a Thank you. Lot knew quite well both the name and the character of that city lying in the rain and sunshine below. He had often heard his uncle praying and plotting with God with all his might for Sodom. But Lot had no fear. Lot did not care. His cattle were already up to their bellies in the grass around Sodom, and that was heaven upon earth to Lot.

It is a time of most tremendous import when a young man is still choosing toward what city he is to pitch his tent for life. And how often our young men make their choice as if the history of Lot had never been written. Think, fathers; oh, think, mothers; think, young men, also, with so much at stake—think what the temptations and the dangers and the almost sure issues of this and that choice in life must be. All our trades, professions, occupations in life have, each one, its own perils and temptations and snares to the soul; as well as its own opportunities of gain, and honour, and praise, and service. The ministry, teaching, law, medicine, the army, political life, newspaper life, trade of all kinds, the money-market of all kinds, and so on. Open your eyes. Count the cost. Are you able? will you venture? Take that line of life which you are just about to choose. Take time over it. Look all round it. Imagine yourself done with it. Look at this man and that man who are done with it. Would you like to be like them? Study well the successes and the failures in that line of life. Read the thirteenth and the nineteenth chapters of Genesis, and then take those two chapters with you to your knees, and so make your choice. Look at your motives in making your choice. Look at its dangers, its temptations, and especially at its companionships. Look at the people you will have to part company with, and at the people among whom you will henceforth dwell, and then let the die be cast. Lot chose all the plain of Jordan, and pitched his tent toward Sodom.

Just when Lot is beginning to make the acquaintance of the men of Sodom, and is finding them, as he was sure he would find them, not so bad as they were reported; just as he was opening accounts for his tent and his camp with the merchants of Sodom, the Lord is hastening down to redress the wrong and to recognise and recompense Abraham. You put God in your debt as often as you do any handsome and unselfish thing; and, especially, anything in the pure interests of righteousness and peace. And it is wise and politic to put God in your debt now and then. For He always pays His debts sooner or later. And He always pays you with His gold for your paper, and with His usury to your uttermost farthing. And thus it is that we go on to read that the Lord said to Abraham, after that Lot was departed from him, 'Lift up now thine eyes, and look from the place where thou art, northward, and southward, and eastward, and westward. For all the land which thou seest, to thee will I give it, and to thy seed for ever. Arise, walk through the land, in the length of it and in the breadth of it, for to thee will I give it. Then Abraham removed his tent, and came and dwelt in the land of Mamre, and built there an altar to the Lord.' With all that, then, which is it to be with you? The plain of Jordan with Lot, or the plain of Mamre with Abraham? A family altar with the father of the faithful, or a seat at sunset in the gate of Sodom with Lot?

Lot was not long in getting a lesson that would have brought a less besotted sinner to his senses. The first war in the Bible broke out in the valley of the Jordan not very long after Lot had settled in Sodom. The war is known in ancient history as that of the four kings against five. Moses would have had no interest in that dim old dispute but for Lot. Lot, with all his great faults, nay, rather because of his great faults, gets chapter after chapter of Moses' precious space. Well, the upshot of that war was that the kings of Sodom and Gomorrah were defeated and fled, and Lot was taken prisoner with all his possessions, and was marched off in great haste up the Jordan and away to the mountains. But as Lot's guardian angel would have it, one of Lot's herdmen escaped; and how his heart would sink as he came near Abraham's encampment at Hebron! But to whom else could he go? His own conscience of the past bitterly upbraided him as he told Abraham the disaster; but Abraham had something else to do than to trample on a fallen man. In three crowded verses Moses tells his readers the result. Abraham fell upon the sleeping camp, and Lot was a free man next morning with all his goods. Now, you know yourselves how you return back again to your former life as soon as the strain of the tribulation is over. As the cruel kings hurried Lot up the Jordan with a rope round his neck, how that chastised saint vomited up Sodom and all her works, and how he cursed himself as the greatest fool in all the land of Canaan. You can all cast your stones of anger and scorn and astonishment at Lot; I cannot. Till you try to break loose from an old evil way, you will never believe me how impossible it is for you to do it.

All this time there must have been something far better in Lot than anything that Moses lets us see. To read Second Peter on Lot is far more comforting than to read Moses. For Peter tells us in his Second Epistle that, when God turned the cities of Sodom and Gomorrah into ashes, He delivered just Lot, vexed with the filthy conversation of the wicked. But, then, to read that only makes us stop and say and ask, Why did a man with a beginning like Lot, and with past experiences like Lot, why did he not rise up and leave a life, and a neighbourhood, and an occupation, and a companionship out of all which so much danger and so much vexation of soul continually sprang? The reason was that he had invested in Sodom, as our merchants would say. He had invested money, and he had embarked himself and his household in the land round Sodom, in the produce of Sodom, and in her splendid profits. And all the vexations that wrung his heart Lot could never make up his mind to be done with Sodom and Gomorrah for ever. I suppose there must be just men among ourselves who have chosen early in life, or who have inherited, or who have themselves built up a business, the partners in which, the questionable righteousness of which, nay, the not questionable unrighteousness of which, often vexes their hearts far more than we know or would believe. But to come out of that manufacture, that import, that export; to refund with usury those moneys; to rise up at the loss of thousands and thousands, nay, possibly at the loss of every penny a man possesses; to leave a splendidly paying business merely at the twinge of a secretly tortured conscience,—no man ever does it. Lot therefore is the father of all those men whose righteous souls are vexed with the life they are leading, but who keep on enduring the vexation. And Peter's New Testament point is this—that righteous men will go on enduring vexation like that of Lot till the Lord Himself rises up and comes down to deliver them. Lot's deliverance came through a catastrophe the sound of which and the smoke of which blows like opening hell into our eyes to this day. Just what God will have to do to deliver your soul and mine from the things that so endanger our souls and so vex them His time will tell. Only, this we may rely upon, that the Lord knoweth how to deliver the godly out of their temptations, and He will do it too, if He has to burn up all we possess with fire and brimstone from heaven. In that terrible day may His angels be near to lay hold of us!

XIII

SARAH

BUT SARAH WAS BARREN,
SHE HAD NO CHILD

'WHICH things are an allegory,' says the Apostle when he brings in Sarah and Hagar her handmaid into the fourth chapter of his Epistle to the Galatians. And no doubt, his first readers must have understood the Apostle's mystical argument and must have got the good they needed in their day out of his spiritual exposition. But if Paul had only been led to take up our text of to-night, and to treat Sarah and her childlessness as an allegory, what an evangelical argument, and what a fruitful and far-reaching application both the Galatian Church and all the churches ever after would have got! For, out of this little, parenthetical, hidden-away verse the whole of the succeeding eleven epoch-making chapters of Genesis immediately spring. Chaldea, and Canaan, and Egypt; Hagar and Ishmael; the promise of Isaac, and then the birth, the circumcision, the sacrifice, and the deliverance of Isaac; all the trials and all the triumphs of his father's and his mother's faith; all their falls; all their victories; all God's promises, and all His wonderful and adorable providences in their so exercised lives; all their attainments in truth and in obedience; and then, to crown all, the complete fulfilment of God's so long delayed promise—all that, and much more that has not been told—it all arose out of this, that Sarah had no child. 'It is an allegory,' says Bengel, 'when anything is said and another thing more excellent is signified.' And I cannot get it out of my heart that my text to-night, biographical reality, real historicity, and all, is somehow an allegory also. It will persist in my heart that Abraham is my faith in God's promise to me of the fruit of the Spirit in me; while childless Sarah, Abraham's married wife, is my still unfruitful heart. For I have some faith, but I have no love. I have not enough faith to make my love fruitful. My heart is as much without a spiritual seed as was Sarah's silent tent. I laugh at the idea, like Sarah behind her tent door. I say to myself, half in faith, half in fear, half in mockery at myself, Shall I ever have pleasure? Shall Christ ever be formed in me? Till I am sometimes, like poor Sarah in her sterile tent, driven desperate. Driven desperate, and reckless, and wild. Like Sarah, I fall into sore temptations between the Divine promise on the one hand, and my own evil heart on the other hand. Like her, also, I am driven to dangerous, and, sometimes, I fear, to positively sinful expedients, in my desolation and desperation. And, like Sarah, I involve and fatally injure other people also in my desperation. But still the great promise holds on its course, and is repeated, and enlarged, and enriched, and sealed; and still it is with me as it has been from the beginning. Till, as I believe, and am determined to go on believing—God help my unbelief! —God's promise to me also shall, in God's way and at God's time, be all fulfilled. And my heart also, like Abraham and Sarah, shall see of her travail and shall be satisfied. Yes. Had Paul, or even Philo; had Behmen, or Bunyan but taken up this text, and said, "Which things are an allegory," we would have had doctrine, and depth, and beauty, and assurance, and comfort to our heart's content.

But to come back to solid ground, and to speak no more about parables. As time went on, and as the hope of any possibility of her ever becoming a mother died out of Sarah's heart, she became absolutely desperate. Had meekness, and humility, and resignation, and the blotting-out of herself, but grown apace with her disappointment, that would have hid Sarah from all her temptations, and it would at the same time have hastened the lifting off of her cross. But her terrible cross had but inflamed and intensified her pride; it had but determined her to find some wild and wilful way for herself out of God's way and God's will. It was intolerable to Sarah to live on any longer such an embarrassment to her husband, such an evident obstacle to the prosperity of his house, and such an eyesore and jest to all the camp and to all the country around. And in the wildness of her pride Sarah determined to as good as slay herself, and to make it impossible for Abraham in his heart of hearts any longer to despise her. And thus it was that what looked like a perfect miracle of humility in Sarah, was really an act of exasperated pride. Sarah sacrificed herself on the cruellest altar on which any woman ever laid herself down; but the cords of the sacrifice were all the time the cords of a suicidal pride; till the sacrifice was both a great sin in the sight of God, a fatal injury to herself, to her husband, and to innocent generations yet unborn. What looks to all men's eyes like a martyr's devotion may all the time be but impatience, and petulance, and pride, and revenge. The outward act may sound heroic, while all the time cowardice and selfishness and exasperated pride may be at the bottom of it. To sacrifice yourself, therefore, is not enough. Your mind, your motive, your spirit, and your temper in making the sacrifice, that is everything. Sarah sacrificed herself to the last drop of a woman's blood; but all the time her heart was as high as heaven and as hot as hell both against God and against her husband also. 'Behold, now, the Lord hath restrained me; but there is my maid!'

You are a truly humble man when you are truly despised in your own eyes. But your humility has not stood its very last test till you are despised in our eyes also every day. The truest, humility is attained; the truest humility is ascertained, and certified, and sealed only by humiliations being heaped upon it from without; from above, from beneath, and from all around. And, had Sarah's humility been a true and a genuine humility; had her ostentatious sacrifice of herself not had its secret roots in a deep and a cruel pride; she would have opened her heart to all Hagar's contempt. Hagar's scorn would have been an excellent oil to Sarah's head, and she would thus have secured and hastened her own fruitfulness and motherhood. But Sarah of herself had run herself into a temptation too terrible for her to bear. Her humiliating childlessness was honour, and rest, and peace, and love compared with her uttermost and incessant misery now. 'My wrong be upon thee,' she assailed her husband, 'for I am despised in the eyes of my own maid!' My brethren, you must make up your mind to bear with what has sprung upon you out of your own past misdeeds. It is the least you can do to hold your peace, and to bear with meekness the hand of God. Your life all your days may henceforth be made bitter to you because of your past. But what would you have?

Would you have a peaceful, a free, an untrammelled, and a happy after-life out of a past life like yours? You cannot have it. Life is not built on that plan. God does not live in heaven and rule on earth on that principle. Or, if He does, the worse it will be for you in the long-run. Put it in words and look at it. Would you run yourself and other people into sin and guilt as suits you, and then would you wipe your mouth and walk off as a guileless and an innocent man? You cannot do it. And you need not try. Kiss the rod rather. Kiss the rod, and the hand that holds it. Say, It is the Lord. Say that though He should slay you, yet you will not complain. Say this; say it with Micah when he was in some such distress, say, 'I will bear the indignation of the Lord, because I have sinned against Him, until He plead my cause and execute judgment for me.' Cast out the bond-woman and her son! No, Sarah, you cannot do it. You may try to do it, but the angel of the Lord will bring Hagar and Ishmael back again upon you. You surely know Hagar, Sarah! She is your own handmaiden. But for you, you must remember, Hagar would have still been a pure, modest, obedient child. And if she and her unlawful son are thorns in your eyes, they are both thorns of your own planting. You bought Hagar in Egypt. You bribed her to leave her mother's house. You engaged to be a mother to her. You took her, and made her your tool; you debauched her, and then you would cast her out. And you did, and would do all this, in spite both of God and man. And now you would like to get back to where you were before your terrible trespass. You would fain have Hagar and her fatherless boy back in Egypt, and your tent in Canaan the abode of peace and love and honour it was at the beginning. No, Sarah, mother of so much mischief, you cannot have it. It cannot be. Shall not the Judge of all the earth do right?

Hagar had not come from Ur of the Chaldees with the immigration, neither had she been bought by Abraham in Canaan. Hagar, originally, was an Egyptian child. When Sarah was down in Egypt with her husband Abraham, young Hagar had been recommended to Sarah for a lady's maid. And Sarah had made trial of the girl in the place, and had been glad to find that she had all the talent and all the character she had been certificated to have. And though it looked a wild proposal that Hagar should leave her mother's house, and all the religion and civilisation of Egypt, to go to the savage land of the Philistines, yes, what a princess like Sarah had once set her heart upon, poor people like Hagar's parents could not oppose. Sarah was rich, and she had the imperious temper of riches. And, besides, Sarah, the sister of Abraham, was a favourite in Pharaoh's palace. Hagar's expatriation and banishment so far from home made her all the better a maid to Sarah. Hagar had no choice. She must please her mistress. She had no temptation or opportunity to do anything else. She was so far from home now that Sarah became both mistress and mother to the poor Egyptian girl. All went well, only too well, indeed, with Sarah and Hagar till Sarah's sin began to find her out. And when Sarah dealt hardly with Hagar she fled from the face of her mistress. Poor Hagar! Mother of so many miserable women in all lands and in all ages ever since. Hundreds of miles, weeks of wilderness, and of tears, and of bleeding feet, and of a bleeding heart from her mother's door. Afraid to face her mother. Terrified at the thought of her father. Spat upon and cast out of doors by her sisters and their husbands. Shall she kill her child? Shall she kill herself? Oh, why was I born? Oh, why did I ever come to this cursed land? Why did I ever take the wages of that wicked woman? Let the night perish on which she took me and led me up into her bed! Let darkness and the shadow of death stain it; let a cloud dwell upon it; let the gross darkness terrify it! Till she awakened and found herself with a well of water close beside her. 'Return to thy mistress. Submit thyself to thy mistress Not only to the good and gentle, but also to the froward,' said the angel at the well. And as she drank of the well she said, Beer-lahai-roi. Thou God seest me! Behold, that well still springs up in the wilderness of Shur; it is to be found on the road between Kadesh and Bered.

Beer-lahai-roi. Thou God seest me! Hagar, by reason of the extremity of her sorrow; by reason of the utter desolateness and brokenness of her heart; and by reason of the sovereign grace and abounding mercy of God—Hagar, I say, stands out before us in the very foremost rank of faith, and trust, and experience, and assurance. Hagar, to me, stands out among God's very electest saints. Hagar has only one or two who can stand beside her in her discovery of God, in her nearness to God, in her face-to-face fellowship with God, in the instructiveness, in the comfort, and in the hopefulness of her so close communion with God. Not Adam before his fall; not Enoch, who so pleased God; not Abraham at his call, or after offering his son; not Jacob at Bethel, nor Israel at the Jabbok; not Moses on the mount and in the cleft rock; not Isaiah in the temple, and not John in the spirit—not the best and the most blessed of them all was more blessed or better blessed than was Hagar the polluted outcast on her weeping way to Shur. The pure in heart shall see God.

And, what impurity Hagar had contracted of Sarah and Abraham she had washed away, her head waters and her eyes a fountain of tears, all the way from Abraham's tent door to that well in the wilderness. She had washed her polluted body and her scornful and revengeful heart with her penitential tears, till, by the time she came to the well, she was counted clean enough to see God. And she saw God at that wilderness-well with a clearness, and with an assurance, and with a rapture, and with a submission, and with an immediate obedience that all combine to lift up Hagar and to set Hagar beside, and even before, both her master and her mistress in the favour and in the fellowship of God. For, from that day on the way to Shur, all the days of Hagar's pilgrimage on earth, we still see Sarah and Abraham entreating Hagar with hardness till she drinks again and again of the well of God, and again and again has Almighty God given to her and to him as the heavenly Father of her fatherless son. In Thee, O God, the fatherless have always found mercy.

Now, in God's mercy, is there any Hagar here? Is there any outcast here? Is there any soul of man or woman ready to perish here? Who can tell who is here? Where would such be found if not here? Is not this the house of God? Does this house not stand on the wayside to Shur? Has this house not been Beer-lahai-roi to many who were in far greater straits, and under far greater guilt, than ever Hagar was? Many have said of this house, Thou God seest me! Many have come up to this house with a secret burden. Many have gone home from this house to take up their cast-off cross, and to endure to the end. Is there a motherless woman-child here? Is there a deceived, injured, cast-out sinner here? My sister, thy God is here. Thou hast been led of His angel in coming here. His well is here. He has dug that well for thee. Spring up, O well! And that is He Himself, His true and very Self, Who is now laying His hand on thy dishonoured and downcast head. That is His Holy Spirit who is now bringing these tears to thine eyes. That is His voice in thy heart, saying 'Hagar, Sarah's maid, whence comest thou, and whither wilt thou go?' Stoop down, Hagar, and drink and be refreshed and revived. Fall down and weep. Lift up thy heart and pray. Behold, Hagar, He is lifting thee up. He is washing thy feet. He is washing thy hands. He is washing with water and with blood thy heart. Think, Hagar, think. Believe, Hagar, believe. Admire, Hagar, and praise. For He is the same wonderful, wonderful, most wonderful God who met the first Hagar on her way back to her mother's disgraced and angry door. Wonderful is His name. He was in Egypt, He was in Canaan, He was in Mamre, and He appeared at Shur. He was there when thou wert born in thy mother's house in Scotland also. He swaddled thee, He girded thee, He called thee by thy name. The foolishness of thy youth was not hid from Him. He bore with thee, and still bore with thee. And when thy lovers had hold of thy deceived heart, He pitied thee, and had thoughts of love toward thee. And when thy lovers wearied of thee, and had served themselves of thee, then His time of love began with thee. When thou didst fall His hand held thee up. When thou hadst destroyed thyself He redeemed thee. He made thy sin bitter to thee. He made thy life a wilderness around thee. He made thy heart a wilderness within thee. He made this whole world flint to thy feet, and dust to thy mouth, and a very hell to thy cast-off heart. And when He had humbled thee, and tried thee, and utterly broken and silenced thee, He came near at the well of Shur to thee, and these, to His everlasting praise, were His words to thee, 'Fear not, for thou shalt not be confounded. For thy Maker is thy husband. For the Lord hath called thee as a woman forsaken and grieved in spirit. For a small moment have I forsaken thee, but with everlasting kindness will I have mercy upon thee, saith the Lord, thy Redeemer. O thou afflicted, tossed with tempest, and not comforted; no weapon that is formed against thee shall prosper, and every tongue that shall rise in judgment against thee shalt thou condemn. This is the heritage of the servants of the Lord, and their righteousness is of Me, saith the Lord.'

'Doubtless Thou art our Father, though Abraham be ignorant of us, and Israel acknowledge us not. Thou, O Lord, art our Father, our Redeemer. Thy name is from everlasting.'

XIV

ISAAC

ISAAC LOVED ESAU BECAUSE HE DID EAT OF HIS VENISON

THE patriarch Isaac presents but a pale appearance as he stands planted between two stately and so impressive personages as his father Abraham on the one hand, and his son Jacob on the other hand. Isaac, notwithstanding our familiarity with his name, has hitherto made very little impression on our minds. Were we suddenly asked what we remember about Isaac, the chances are that we would get very little further than that memorable day when Abraham took his only son, and bound him, and laid him on the altar, upon the wood. And, indeed, as we follow out the sad declension of Isaac's character to the end, it is forced upon us that it would have been well for Isaac, and for all connected with Isaac, that Abraham's uplifted hand had not been arrested by the angel of the Lord. Had Isaac died on his father's altar, an immense impression for good would have been made on all who ever heard of his submission and devotion; and, besides, the whole after-history of Israel, and of the nations around Israel, would have been far purer, far more peaceful, and every way far more happy. But all that is in the far future.

Isaac, like Noah and Lot before him, those two other shipwrecks of the best early promise, made a splendid start. In his early start in faith and in obedience, Isaac by a single bound at once out-distanced all who had gone before him. We are so taken up with Abraham's faith and surrender in the matter of Moriah, that we forgot the splendid part that Isaac must have performed in that terrible trial; that magnificent triumph of faith and submission. I do not wonder that the Church of Christ has all along persisted in seeing in Isaac an outstanding type of our Lord, and in making Mount Moriah a clear forecast of Gethsemane and of Calvary. For, when it came to the last agony beside the altar on that terrible hill-top—'Not my will, but thine be done," was wrung from Isaac's broken heart, just as long afterwards, and not far from the same spot, this same surrendering cry was wrung from the broken heart of our Lord. Josephus reports a remarkable dialogue that passed between Abraham and Isaac that day, in addition to the dialogue that Moses reports. As soon as the altar was prepared, and all things were entirely ready, Abraham said to Isaac his son: 'O my son! I poured out a vast number of prayers that I might have thee for my son. And since it was God's will that I should become thy father, it is now His will that I shall relinquish thee. Let us bear this consecration to God with a ready mind. Accordingly, thou, my son, wilt now die, not in any common way of going out of the world, but sent to God, the Father of all men, beforehand, in the nature of a sacrifice. I suppose He thinks thee worthy to get clear of this world neither by disease, neither by war, nor by any other severe way, but so that He will receive thy soul with prayers and holy offices of religion, and will place thee near to Himself, and thou wilt there be to me a succourer and supporter in my old age; and thou wilt there procure me God for my Comforter instead of thyself.' Now, Isaac was of such a generous disposition that he at once answered that he was not worthy to be born at first, if he should now reject the determination of God and his father, and should not resign himself up readily to both their pleasures. So he went up immediately to the altar to be sacrificed. The rest we know from Moses. To which Josephus only adds that Abraham and Isaac, having sacrificed the ram, embraced one another and returned home to Sarah, and lived happily together, God affording them His assistance in everything.

'And Isaac dwelt by the well Lahai-roi.' That arrests us. That must have been intended to arrest us. And to make sure that it shall arrest us and shall not escape us, the sacred writer is not content with having told us that once; he tells us that again, and still more emphatically the second time. At the same time, having with such repeated point told us that, Moses leaves it to his readers to make of it what they are able to make, and what they like to make. Make anything of it, or not, there stands the fact—that, in broad Canaan, as soon as Isaac had a tent of his own to pitch, he pitched his tent toward Hagar's well. Hagar, you must remember, had been Isaac's mother's maid. Not only that, but Hagar had been Isaac's own first nurse. Isaac and Ishmael, the two innocent half-brothers, had learned their lessons together, and had played together, till the two mothers fell out, and till Hagar and her unlawful son had to flee to the wilderness. But, little children never forget their first nurse, especially when she has such stories to tell as Hagar had to tell little Isaac about the palaces, and the pyramids, and the temples, and the Nile, and the crocodiles of Egypt. And then, as her charge grew up, in seasons of trouble and sorrow and mutual confidence, Hagar would be led into telling the devout little lad her wonderful story of Beer-lahai-roi. And that heavenly story took such a hold of young Isaac that to the end of his life he never found himself within a day's journey of Hagar's well without turning aside to drink of its waters and to meditate and to pray and to praise beside its streams. Where, then, when he was choosing a site for his future tent, where should he choose that site after Moriah, but on a spot scarcely less solemn to Hagar's pious little nursling than Jehovah-jireh itself. Lahai-roi was one of the two most sacred spots on earth to Hagar's two boys; and, as sometimes happens, the boy of the two who was not her own, best remembered all she had told him, and shaped his course accordingly. It is no superstition to seek out the spots where God has come down to visit His people. It is not that God is any more there, or is any more likely to return there; but are better prepared to meet with Him there. And God comes to those who are ready to meet with Him wherever they are. There is no respect of places with God. And nothing draws God down to any place like a heart like His own. As often, therefore, as He saw Isaac's tears dropping into the water he was drinking, God again visited Isaac also. And Isaac could never walk round that well, or sit down beside it, or drink out of it, but his tears would come fast for poor ill-used Hagar, and for poor outcast Ishmael, till he wished again that he had never been born rather than that they should both be outcast from their proper home on his account. I, for one, thank Moses warmly for writing it, and then for underscoring it, that, as soon as Isaac had a tent of his own to pitch, he pitched that tent toward Hagar's holy well.

It is now the late afternoon before the day of Isaac's marriage. Abraham's servant has performed his errand to perfection, and he is now nearing his young master's tent with Isaac's bride under his charge. 'And Isaac went out to meditate in the field in the even-tide; and he lifted up his eyes, and saw, and behold, the camels were drawing near.' All that day Isaac had spent in prayer and in meditation. Isaac was greatly given to solitude and to solitary thoughts, and he had much that day to think upon. The day it was made him think. He thought of his father Abraham and his mother Sarah; and then he thought of his own wonderful birth as of one born out of due time. From that, he went on to think of Hagar his Egyptian nurse, and of Ishmael his half-brother, and of all the evil fate that had befallen both Hagar and Ishmael because of him. And then this well, whose sacred waters were now shining in the setting sun. And all that took place at this well; and that which Hagar exclaimed over this well, and which was never a day, scarcely ever an hour, out of Isaac's thoughts. And then Moriah, Mount Moriah, the mount of the Lord, had been so burned into Isaac's heart, that, for years and years, he felt its cords knotted round his arms, and saw its knife gleaming over his head. Till his heart gave a great bound as he suddenly looked up and saw the distant thread of Chaldean camels drawing slowly near with their precious burdens. And till they came near, and till Isaac met the rich procession, Isaac still prayed, and praised, and vowed to God, the God of Abraham, his godly father. It is a beautiful scene in the setting sun. 'And Isaac went out to meditate in the field at the even-tide; and he lifted up his eyes, and saw, and behold, the camels were coming. And Rebekah lifted up her eyes, and when she saw Isaac she lighted off her camel. For she had said to the servant, What man is this that walketh in the field to meet us? And the servant had said, It is my master. Therefore she took a veil and covered herself. And Isaac brought Rebekah into his mother Sarah's tent, and she became his wife; and he loved her; and Isaac was comforted after his mother's death.'

The prophetic travail of Rebekah in giving birth to the twin-brothers Esau and Jacob, and then Esau's sale of his birthright, fill one graphic chapter, and then after another chapter we are all at once introduced to Isaac's deathbed. And then, the space given to the deathbed scenes; the dramatic situations; the eloquence and the pathos; and at the same time the suppression and the severity of the composition,—all that of itself would kindle an intense interest in the story of Isaac's last hours. And then both the writer's pains, and the reader's strained interest and attention, are all amply rewarded as we stand by and look on, and lay to heart all that goes on around that distressing deathbed. 'And it came to pass that when Isaac was old, and his eyes were dim, so that he could not see, he called Esau his eldest son, and said unto him, My son; and he said to him, Behold, here I am. And he said, Behold, now, I am old. I know not the day of my death. Now, therefore, I pray thee, take thy weapons, thy quiver and thy bow, and go out to the field, and take me some venison. And make me savoury meat, such as I love, and bring it to me, that I may eat; that my soul may bless thee before I die.' The inspired writer had already been compelled to set it down, on the sad occasion of the barter of Esau's birthright, that Isaac loved Esau and despised Jacob, because he did eat of Esau's venison. And, altogether, the place that 'venison' holds on this page of the patriarchal history, and the part it plays in the tragedy now on the stage, compel us to consider and to think what it all means to us, and what it all warns us of.

When I read Isaac's whole history over again, with my eye upon the object, it becomes as clear as a sunbeam to me that what envy was to Cain, and what wine was to Noah, and what lewdness was to Ham, and what wealth was to Lot, and what pride and impatience were to Sarah—all that, venison and savoury meat were to Isaac. I cannot get past it. I have tried hard to get past it. Out of respect for the aged patriarch, and out of gratitude for the mount of the Lord and Hagar's well, I have tried to get past it; but I cannot. 'Take me some venison. Make me savoury meat such as I love, and bring it to me, that I may eat, and that my soul may bless thee before I die. And Esau went out to hunt for venison. And Rebekah said to Jacob, I will make savoury meat for thy father, such as he loveth. And she made savoury meat such as Isaac loved. And Jacob said, Sit up, and eat of my venison. And he said, Bring it near to me, and I will eat of my son's venison. And he brought it near to him and he did eat; and he brought him wine and he drank. And Esau he also made savoury meat, and said, Let my father arise and eat of his son's venison,' and so on till Isaac's deathbed reeks with venison. The steam of the savoury meat with which his two sons bid for his blessing chokes us till we cannot breathe beside Isaac's deathbed. But Isaac's ruling passion is still strong in death, so strong, that the very smell of Esau's venison-stained coat is sweet to the old patriarch's nostrils. My brethren, there is no respect of persons in the Bible. The Bible puts the simple, naked truth before everything else. Before the consistency, before the honour, and before the good name of the saints. Before propriety, before partiality, before what is seemly to be told, before what is consoling, before what is edifying even.

The inordinate and unseemly love of good eating has an undue hold of many otherwise blameless men, of many able men also, and even of many old men. Neither the grace of God, nor some true love of the things of the mind, nor the decays of nature, would seem to be able to root out or at all to weaken this degrading vice; so deeply is it seated in some men's habits of life and character. It would not be so much to be wondered at that out-of-door men like Esau should eat and drink with a passionate delight; but that a quiet, home-keeping, devout old saint like Isaac should let his table become such a snare to his soul,—that does startle and alarm us. And we see the same thing still. Sedentary men, bookish men, and men who are never out of their study, are sometimes as fond of savoury soup and venison as ever Isaac or Esau was. That they take too little exercise seems sometimes to make them seek their relaxation and refreshment in their table even more than other men. The greatest glutton I ever knew never crossed his doorstep. His only walk all the day was from his desk to his dinner-table, and then from his dinner-table back to his desk. Now, Isaac in his old age was the father of all such men. Isaac's very love for his sons depended on their skill and success in hunting. If a son of his could not hunt, could not run down and entrap venison, he might be a saint, but old Isaac had no blessing for him. Isaac was only happy, and full of good-humour and benediction, when he had just had another full meal. But he was sulky and peevish and fretful if his soup was short or out of season. If you would enjoy Isaac's benediction, you must get him after his dinner, and it must be of the best, and at the moment. Old Isaac, with his eyes so dim that he could not see, is the father of all those men who make their god their belly, who think too much and too often of what they shall eat and what they shall drink, who value their friends by the table they keep, and who are never so happy as when they are sitting over their venison and their wine. Isaac was the father of Ciacco in the *Inferno* and of Succus in the *Serious Call.* Of him also 'who makes every day a day of full and cheerful meals, and who by degrees comes to make the happiness of every day to depend upon that, and to consider everything with regard to that. He will go to church, or stay at home, as it suits with his dinner, and he will not scruple to tell you that he generally eats too heartily to go to the afternoon service.' And, lastly, Isaac in his infirm years, and in his increasing appetite, is the father of 'all those people, with whom the world abounds, who are weakly and tender merely by their indulgences. They have bad nerves, low spirits, and frequent indispositions, through irregularity, idleness, and indulgence.' Such to this day are some of Isaac's sons and daughters. Four rules for such.

1. Never accept a second helping at table.

2. Never rise from table without an appetite, and you will never sit down without one.

3. Never sit down at table till you have said this for a grace—What! Know ye not that your bodies are the members of Christ? Shall I, then, take the members of Christ and make them the members of a glutton? God forbid!

4. Only love God enough, and then eat anything you like, and eat as much as you like, said St. John of the Cross to his over-ascetical disciples.

XV

ESAU

OR PROFANE PERSON

ESAU lost his birthright with all its blessings largely through his lack of imagination. The things that are unseen and eternal had neither substance nor evidence to Esau compared with the things that are seen and temporal. Jacob, his brother, had many faults, but Jacob inherited the blessing because after all is said he had eyes and a heart for the unseen and the spiritual. But Esau had no such speculation in his eyes. The covenant promises made to his fathers had no interest, they had no existence even, to Esau.

They can take the promises who care for them; as for Esau, a bird in the hand is worth two in the bush. At the same time, Esau had many not wholly ignoble things about him. Esau was full of the manliest interests and occupations and pursuits. He was a very proverb of courage and endurance and success in the chase. He was the ruggedest, the brawniest, and the shaggiest of all the rugged, brawny, and shaggy creatures of the field and of the forest, among whom he lived and died. Esau had an eye like an eagle. His ear never slept. His foot took the firmest hold of the ground. And his hand was always full both of skill, and strength, and success. Esau's arrow never missed its mark. He was the pride of all the encampment as he came home at night with his traps, and his snares, and his bows, and his arrows, and laden to the earth with venison for his father's supper. Burned black with the sun; beaten hard and dry with the wind; a prince of men; a prime favourite both with men, and women, and children, and with a good word and a good gift from the field for them all. But, all the time, a heathen. All the time, an animal more than a man. All the time, all body and no soul. All the time, a profane person, who failed of the grace of God.

In that extraordinary solidity of style, in which Moses sometimes surpasses Dante himself, we have Isaac and Esau and Jacob set before us to the life in six or seven verses. 'And Jacob sod pottage; and Esau came from the field, and he was faint. And Esau said to Jacob, Feed me, I pray thee, with that same red pottage; for I am faint. And Jacob said, Sell me this day thy birthright. And Esau said, Behold, I am at the point to die; and what profit shall this birthright do to me? And Jacob said, Swear to me this day; and he sware unto him; and he sold his birthright unto Jacob. Then Jacob gave Esau bread and pottage of lentils, and he did eat and drink, and rose up, and went his way. Thus Esau despised his birthright.' This was not the first time that Esau and Jacob had exchanged words about that birthright. No man sells his birthright on the spot. He who sells his birthright, sells it many times in his heart before he takes it so openly as that to the market. He belittles it, and despises it, and cheapens it, at any rate to himself, long before he sells it so cheaply to another. No man, and no woman, falls in that fatal way without having prepared their fall for themselves in their hearts. Esau had showed his contempt for his birthright a thousand times, and in a thousand ways, before now. Everybody knew that Esau's birthright was for sale, if anybody cared to bid for it. Isaac knew, Rebekah knew, and Jacob knew; and Jacob had for long been eyeing his brother for a fit opportunity. It had for a long time back been marrow to Jacob's bones to hear Esau jesting so openly about his birthright over his venison and his wine; jesting and being jested about the covenant blessing. 'As much as you are able to eat, Esau! and anything else you like to name, to boot; only, say that you toss me to-day your worthless birthright,' said Jacob. 'Take it, and welcome!' said Esau. 'And much good may it do you! It has never been worth a haunch of good venison to me. You may have it, and my oath on it on the spot, for a good dish at once, and be quick, of your smoking pottage. Take it, and let me be done with it. Take it, and let me hear no more about it.' And Esau did eat and drink, and rose up, and went his way.

Esau's roving habits of life; his increasing distaste for the life and the religion of his father's house; and, now that he had cut himself so completely adrift by openly selling his birthright, with all its privileges, and obligations, and responsibilities—all that combined to throw Esau more and more into the company of the old Canaanite communities that lay all around the patriarchal settlements, Esau, alas! was all the time himself a true Canaanite at heart. Son of Isaac and Rebekah, and grandson of Abraham and Sarah, as he was, Esau had nothing of his forefathers or his foremothers in him, unless it was some of the dregs of their remaining vices; and, as the apostle has it, some of their springing up roots of bitterness. All that Abraham and Sarah, and Isaac and Rebekah, had passed through; all their trials, and all their triumphs, and all their attainments of faith and of obedience, had left no mark at all on Esau, their so profane descendant. And everything that Esau did, every step that he took in life, every choice that he made in life, and every bargain that he struck, only made that more and more manifest. A man's choice in his marriage, more than anything else in this life, makes it manifest what that man is, and where his heart is. Now, Esau's marriage, fatal step as it also was, was not the passionate impulse of a moment, any more than his sale of his birthright had been. Esau had hunted for years with the brothers of Judith and Bashemath. He had eaten and drunken and danced with the Hittite inhabitants of the land. He had sacrificed and sworn and vowed to their false gods of the fields, and of the streams, and of the unclean groves. Like every reprobate from a better life, Esau had far outdone the sons of Beeri and Elon in their impieties and debaucheries. Till, at last, and in open defiance of all decency and religion, he brought home two Canaanite wives to his father's covenanted camp. 'Now, all these things happened unto them for examples, and they are written for our admonition, upon whom the ends of the world are come.' And thus it is that we see the same things in the end of the world that has come upon ourselves. A child is born and baptized in a God-fearing house; and yet, by some fatality, or what shall we call it, he grows up as much outside the best life of his father's house as Esau all his days was outside the best life of Isaac's house. He is a little heathen among his brothers and sisters and school-fellows. His birthright is the Sabbath-day, and the Lords' table, and the society of the best people in the city, and, first a youthhood, and then a manhood, of purity and piety and the service of Christ in His church. But his first act of free and independent life is to sell all that, sometimes for a better salary; sometimes for the smile and the patronage of the open enemies of his father's faith; and sometimes for a coarser mess than even that. Years pass on till Esau sets up an openly heathen household in defiance of father and mother and all, which is ever after a grief of mind to Isaac and Rebekah. The tragedy is not so patent to us because we do not have Moses to write out our household histories, and Paul to comment on the writing, as in Esau's case; but to those who train themselves and accustom themselves to look on the world around them in this one single view as God's world, there is plenty of such profanity and self-reprobation going on among us every day.

What with the purpose of God according to election, and that purpose communicated to Rebekah when she went to inquire of the Lord; what with Isaac's love for Esau because he did eat of his venison; what with Rebekah's retaliatory love for Jacob; what with Esau's increasing levity and profanity, and Jacob's increasing subtlety; what with Esau's defiant Canaanite marriage; and now, to crown all, Isaac's old age, blindness, and fast-approaching end—what with all that, that was as unhappy a house as was at that moment on the face of this unhappy earth. So full is that house, covenant promises and all, of guilty secrets, guilty memories, guilty wrongs, guilty remorses, guilty intentions, and guilty hopes and fears. It has often been pointed out what a mercy it is that God keeps our own future, and the future of our families, to Himself; and does not burden, and entangle, and tempt us with a knowledge that we are not able to bear. Rebekah would have children; and then she would know the secret things that belonged to Him who was forming her children in her womb; and, then, not able to wade into, and to keep her feet in the deep places of God, she fell into a life-long snare and sea of trouble, and laboured all her days under a life-long cross. It would take a Shakespeare, as deep in grace as in nature, to put upon the stage that hell upon earth that opened its mouth day and night in Isaac's covenant tent. A more powerful and a more fruitful chapter for the sacred ends of tragedy was never written than the tragical chapter of Isaac's deathbed. The decayed life, and the still more decayed faith, of Abraham's only son Isaac; the cunning and treachery of Rebekah, the bride he had brought into his mother Sarah's tent in love; Jacob, the too willing tool of his cunning mother's chicanery and lies; the pitiful imposition perpetrated upon the blind old epicure; and, then, reprobate Esau's unavailing cry of remorse and revenge. Yes, verily. The ways of transgressors are hard! The wages of sin is death!

On the principle, then, that all these things about Esau are written for our admonition, how shall we be best admonished against Esau's profane and disastrous mind? To know the truth about him, and about ourselves, is the first thing for us all to set about to-night. Well, to begin with, we are all more or less like Esau in our birth, and in our birthright, and in our profane and brutish mind about our birthright. Like Esau, we have all been born inside the covenant. We have all been sealed with the seal of the covenant. We have all been baptized for a future far greater, and far more full of blessing, than that future which fell either to Esau or to Jacob. But we have all Esau's profane mind and hard heart in us also. And, if any one would but teach us; if any great writer or great preacher, if any wise father or loving mother could and would but take us early in hand, and tell us, and let us see, that all this life is not to make what is called money, or to attain what is called success, or to fill our belly with what is called pleasure, but that God Himself has set us here so to live, and so to choose, and so to act as to put off every day this profane mind, and to put on a sacred, a spiritual, a divine, a heavenly mind—if any one with authority and with influence would but tell and teach us that! For, like Esau, to begin with, we have no imagination. We have no eyes, neither or body nor of mind, for God, or for Jesus Christ, or for heaven, or for hell, or for holiness, or for eternal life. Before we are out of our boyhood we are become vain in our imaginations, and our foolish hearts are darkened, and we worship and serve the creature more than the Creator. And for this cause God gives us over to vile affections, and to a reprobate mind. That was Esau's early history; and that is the early and life-long history of multitudes among ourselves. There is an intellectual, and with it a spiritual stupidity—there is no other name for it—that has already taken possession of one out of every two children that are born in our most covenanted households. They soon declare and show themselves to be utterly insensible to everything intellectual, spiritual, moral, noble, and above the world that knows not God.

If they are rich and idle, they spend their days, like Esau, hunting down creatures of God that have more of God's image in them than their hunters have. They eat, and drink, and dress, and dance like Esau, with any Canaanite household which has sons and daughters like themselves. But they never read a good book. They never attend a good teacher. They have neither time nor taste for anything that pertains to the mind or the heart. Philo calls Esau a 'wooden' man; and the number of wooden men and women who sit at our dinner tables eating venison and drinking wine, and who are then driven all the noisy night after to our city assemblies, far outnumber those people who are made of finer or more spiritual material. Put off the wood and the earth, put off the insensibility and the profanity that are still in you all, my brethren. And put on mind, and heart, and understanding, and consideration, and imagination. Choose your reading. Choose your company. Choose your husband and your wife. Choose your birthright. Choose life, and not death; blessing, and not cursing; heaven, and not hell. You can, if you choose. You can, if you like. Only, lay this to heart with all holy fear, that there is insensibility, and stupidity, and profanity enough in you by nature, and up to this day, to make you, amid all your covenant surroundings, a reprobate of a far worse kind than ever Esau was, unless, with tears, you seek a place of repentance. And it will take all your tears, and all your time, and all the repentance, and all the remission of sins, that Christ can give you out of His place of exaltation, to enable you to escape his end at last who ate and drank, and despised his birthright.

Young men! come, come, and I will tell you! All of you who have not up to this night quite sold the whole of your birthright. Oh! never, never do it. Die, and we shall bury you with honour, and with assurance; but, oh! my son, my brother, never, never, till the day of your death, sell to man or woman or devil your divine birthright. Your birthright of truth, and honesty, and honour, and, especially, of chastity. Sell everything but that! There must be some men here to-night just at the crisis, and just in the temper, in which Esau came home so hungry from the hunt. There are men in this house who are saying this to themselves: 'I am alone. I have nobody to care for me. If I had, it would be different, and I would be a better man. But in all this big city, in all broad Scotland, there is no one for whose sake I need to keep my head above water. Though I go out of this house, and sell myself to hell to-night, no one will lament me. What profit shall it do to me to make any more stand against the gambling-table, or the dram-shop, or anything else!' My own son! ring my bell to-night, and I will talk with you and will tell you the rest. I have not lived to grey hairs in a city, and been a minister of city families, and city young men, without learning things about birthrights and their sale and their redemption too—things that cannot be told on the housetop. No minister in Edinburgh knows more or can speak better about these things than I can do. If you have no minister who can and will tell you about Esau, and about himself, and about yourself, and about Jesus Christ, ring my bell! It will be late that I do not open the door! I will be busy that we do not have another hour over Esau —you and I.

But what is to be said to those who are long past all that? What is to be said to those whose birthright has been sold past all redemption long ago? To those who have sold, not their birthright only, but their very selves, soul and body, so long ago, and so often since then? All this about Esau is agony to them. They are beside themselves with remorse and with misery. They are tired to death seeking for a place of repentance. They are beginning to seek for a field of blood, and some Sabbath night, unless God himself prevent them, they will go out like Judas. But God will prevent. He will come, and He will prevent all that from this time henceforth. 'Save from going down to the pit, I have found a ransom. O Esau, thou hast destroyed thyself; but in Me is thine help. Ye have sold yourselves for nought, but ye shall be redeemed without money. What fruit had ye then in those things of which ye are now ashamed? For the end of those things is death. For the wages of sin is death; but the gift of God is eternal life. Who is a God like unto Thee, that pardoneth iniquity, and passeth by the transgression of the remnant of His heritage? He retaineth not His anger for ever, because He delighteth in mercy. He will turn again, He will have compassion upon us, He will subdue our iniquities; and Thou wilt cast all our sins into the depths of the sea. Blessed be the God and Father of our Lord Jesus Christ, who, according to His abundant mercy, hath begotten us again to a lively hope by the resurrection of Jesus Christ from the dead; to an inheritance incorruptible, undefiled, and that fadeth not away, reserved in heaven for you, who are kept by the power of God through faith unto salvation, ready to be revealed in the last time.'

XVI

REBEKAH

AND THE WIFE SEE THAT SHE REVERENCE HER HUSBAND

A SWEETER chapter was never written than the twenty-fourth of Genesis, nor a sadder than the twenty-seventh, and all the bridge that spans the gulf between them is the twenty-eighth verse of the twenty-fifth chapter. The picture of aged Abraham swearing his most trusty servant about a bride for his son Isaac; that servant's journey to Padan-aram in the far east; Rebekah, first at the well, and then in her mother's house; and then her first sight of her future husband—that long chapter is a perfect gem of ancient authorship. But, the sweetness of the picture, and the perfection of the writing, only go to deepen and darken the terrible tragedy of Isaac's deathbed. That the ship was launched on such a golden morning only the more darkens the surrounding gloom when she goes to the bottom.

'And they said, We will call the damsel, and inquire at her own mouth. And they called Rebekah, and said unto her: Wilt thou go with this man? And she said, I will go.' Though no one knew it, and though she did not know it herself, Rebekah's heart had been Isaac's all the time. The story of Abraham her old kinsman's call; the aged Terah's enterprise and pilgrimage; Isaac's fair and princely youth, and then his offering on the altar—all that had been a household word in Rebekah's mother's house, and all that had for long fired Rebekah's so easily fired heart. And thus it was that, every day for long, as she went out to the well for water, she had looked away west over the vast sands of Mesopotamia, and had wished to heaven that she had been born a man-child, so that she, too, might have been called of God to go out to His land of promise, and there to have her part in the founding of a family of saints, and princes, and great men of God. And, now, what has God wrought for Rebekah! Is she beside herself? Is she awake, and is this broad daylight, and not a dream? Her heart bounds up to God and blesses Him, as she goes down to the well and waters camel after camel, the camels that are Abraham's and Sarah's and Isaac's camels. And never did woman's heart so go forth of her as Rebekah's heart did when Abraham's servant put an ear-ring of gold upon her face, and bracelets of gold upon her hands. Had Rebekah had to walk barefoot over all the burning sands that separated Padan-aram from the land of promise, nothing would have kept Rebekah back from an election and a call so divine, so sweet to her heart, and so welcome as was that warm argument of the aged Eliezer of Damascus. Hearken, O daughter, and consider, and incline thine ear; forget also thine own people, and thy father's house. Or ever I was aware, says the bride in the Song, my heart had made me like the chariots of Amminadib. And Rebekah said, Yes, I will go.

The single plank that spans the terrible gulf between Isaac's marriage-bed and his death-bed is laid for us in this single sentence: 'Isaac loved Esau because he did eat of his venison; but Rebekah loved Jacob.' And, standing on that plank, he that hath ears will hear that bottomless pit of married sorrow that Isaac and Rebekah had dug and filled for themselves and for their two sons, boiling up and roaring all around him. It sickens us to stand there and to think of such life-long sorrow after such a sweet start. There are years and years and years of secret alienation, and distaste, and dislike in that little verse. There are heart-burnings and heart-breaks; hidden hatreds and open quarrels; deceits and duplicities, and discoveries of deceits and duplicities, enough to make Isaac old and blind and dead before the time. When the two twin-brothers were brought up day after day and hour after hour in an atmosphere of favouritism, and partiality, and indulgence, and injustice, no father, no mother, can surely need to have it pointed out to them what present misery, and what future wages of such sin, is all to be seen and to be expected in that evil house. Eloquent with wickedness as the words are—Isaac loved Esau, but Rebekah loved Jacob—yet they make little impression on us till we have read on and on through chapter after chapter, full of the fruit of that wicked little verse. But, then, after we were glutted with the woes of that long and sorely chastised house, if we have any heart, and conscience, and imagination, we come back and stand on that reeling plank till the smoke of the torment of Isaac's and Rebekah's sin comes up like Sodom itself into our blinded eyes.

> Not in their brightness, but their earthly stains,
> Are the true seed vouchsafed to earthly eyes,
> And saints are lowered that the world may rise.

One of the very first fruits of that devil's garden that Isaac and Rebekah had sowed for themselves was the two heathen marriages that Esau went out and made and brought home, and which were such a grief to Isaac and to Rebekah. That great grief would seem to have been almost the only thing the two old people were at one about by that time. It was a bitter pill to Rebekah, those two marriages of Esau. And it was bitter only. She got no after-sweet out of it, as she might well have got. For the old disorder and disgrace still went on; only, henceforth to be increased and aggravated by the introduction of those two new sources of disorder and disgrace, Judith and Bashemath, into that already sufficiently disordered and disgraced household. Esau is greatly blamed by some preachers for his heathen marriages; but, surely, quite unfairly. We talk to Esau about the covenant, and what not. But Esau answers us that, for his part, he saw little covenant in his father's house beyond the name. And Esau might very well think that he could surely get a mother for his children from nearer home than Padan-aram, who would be as fair, and wise, and kind, and good to them as his covenant mother had been to him. Poor Esau could not say what Santa Teresa says about herself in her happy *Life of Herself*. 'It helped me, too,' she tells us, 'that I never saw my father and my mother respect anything but goodness.' And again: 'My mother was a woman of great goodness, and had great sense.' Poor, mishandled Esau could not say that to his children. The disrespect and utter lack of reverence that his mother showed to his father made Judith's respect and reverence to Beeri, and Bashemath's respect and reverence to Elon, an attraction and a refuge and a rest to Esau's restless heart. And I do not believe that the two Hittite women, whom Esau made his two wives, ever played him such a trick in his old age as Rebekah played his old father Isaac. My brethren, let our children not hear any less in our houses about calls, and covenants, and covenant promises, and covenant hopes; but let them see far more covenant fruit in family love, family fair-play, family reverence, and family oneness of mind.

As to Rebekah's treatment of her quiet, silent, retiring, fast-ageing husband, there is this to be said for her, that there is some reason to believe that she had not had a very good example set her in this respect in her old home. She had seen her old father Bethuel overlooked, slighted, often forgotten, and often pushed aside in his own house. Had Bethuel's daughter been made of the finest and most womanly-hearted stuff, that humiliating sight at home would have secured to her future husband all the more reverence and honour, deference and love. That Bethuel seldom spoke at his own table would have made a daughter of the finest kind to say to herself that, if ever she had a husband,—let her tongue be cut out before her husband was ever talked down in his own house. Only, Rebekah, with all her beauty, and with all her courage, and with all her ambition to be in the covenant line, lacked the best thing in a woman, covenant line or no—womanly sensibility, tenderness, quietness, humility, and self-submission. And, though that speck on her heart was so small as to be wholly invisible as long as she was still a maid, and a bride, and a young wife, yet it was there. And by the time that Rebekah became no longer a bride or a young wife, this speck had spread till both her heart and her character had wholly lost all wholesomeness, and sweetness, and strength. 'The one thing certain about a wife is that the result is different from the expectation—that is, if there were ever any particular and defined expectations at all. Age, illness, an increasing family, no family at all, household cares, want of means, isolation, incompatible prejudices, quarrels, social difficulties, all tell on the wife more than on the husband, and make her change more rapidly into that which she was not. Be she strong or weak, she is apt to revert to her own ways, if she has them, and if she has what is called a will of her own.' And, after a rest and some refreshment Isaac still went on: 'There will not be real union without much self-sacrifice; each chiefly bent on pleasing the other. To most men and women this is not easy; for, what with self-confidence, self-will, self-esteem, and selfishness pure and simple, they enter the marriage state with a foregone conclusion on all the points upon which difference is possible. And there are many. And they will remain stumbling-blocks and rocks of offence, unless one will give way to the other, or both are softened by higher influences.'

'And the wife see that she reverence her husband,' says Paul, with his eye on Rebekah. Yes; but what if she cannot? What if there is so little left that is to be reverenced about her husband? 'It is one of the best bonds in a wife,' says Bacon, 'if she think her husband wise.' No doubt. But what if he is not wise? What if he is a fool? What if a wife wakens up to see that she has yoked herself till death to a churl, or to a boor, or to an ignoramus, or to a coxcomb, or to a lazy, idle log, or to a shape of a man whose God is his belly, or his purse, or just his own small, miserable self? What is a woman, so ensnared, to do? Well, she will need to be both a true woman and a true saint, if she is to do right: if she is to do the best now possible in a life of such exquisite and incessant misery. But it can be done. It had been done. And it is being done all around her by thousands of her sisters in the strength of their womanhood, and by the help of God. Let her say: I would have him. I would not see what everybody else saw, and what some of my people were so bold and so cruel as to tell me they saw. I walked into it with my eyes shut. I thought that just to be married would be heaven upon earth. I was sure he would improve. I said that if ever woman helped a man to improve I would be that woman. And he said with such warmth that I was that woman to him, and that there was not another woman like me in the whole earth. I made this bitter bed with my own hands; and no one shall ever know, and last of all my poor husband, what a bitter bed it is to his weak and evil wife! That is the true line to take when a woman is told to reverence a husband for whom no one else has any reverence or affection. Let her determine to be a New Testament wife to him. Let her believe that Jesus Christ said, and still says, Take up thy cross daily! And let her rise up to believe and to see this, that a salvation for her immortal soul of a far deeper, a far more inward, a far more perfect, and a far more everlasting kind, lies for her in her unhappy marriage, than if she had been the proudest and most puffed-up wife in the city. These are they which came out of great tribulation, it is said in heaven over multitudes of such wives. Let her say to herself, then, every day, that this is her great tribulation. Let her put her finger on it and say, This is that through which I must go up, if I am to go up at all. And, at the worst, he is my husband. And if he is not all I would fain believe him to be, yet let me go on trying to believe it. And, perhaps, that will help him. I have not helped him as I promised and intended to do. I have dwelt on my own disappointment and shipwreck, and not enough on his. There are two sides to our married life. There is my husband's side as well as mine; and there is his mother's side as well as my mother's. Perhaps it will help him to overcome if I behave as if he had overcome. Perhaps, if I act as if I were happy, it may help to make him happy. Let me behave myself as if he were wise, and true, and noble, and every way good, and it will greatly help to make him all that. Is there not a Scripture somewhere which says that husbands are sometimes to be won by the conversation of their wives? And, that a wife's best ornament is a meek and quiet spirit? Let me be such a wife as I have never yet been. She who so bends her back to the burden will soon find that the load is not so heavy as she thought it was. What a pity it was that Rebekah did not go to Hagar's well for water every morning, and there talk to herself in that way till she went home to reverence her husband, saying all the way, Thou God seest me! What a pity it was that Rebekah did not do that!

XVII

JACOB

BE SURE YOUR SIN WILL FIND YOU OUT

THERE was no Old Testament saint of them all who, first and last, saw more of the favour and forgiveness of God than Jacob. And yet, with all that, the great sins of Jacob's youth and the great sinfulness of Jacob's heart both found him out every day he lived down to the day of his death. Of Jacob, and of Rebekah his mother, it may truly be said, Thou, O Lord, wast a God that forgavest them, though Thou tookest vengeance on their inventions. It is part of Moses' subtlety, as Philo calls it, to tell us how much more Rebekah loved Jacob than she loved Esau, whom Isaac loved; and then, to go on to give us two examples, and two examples only, of that love. The first example of Rebekah's motherly love is seen when she dresses up Jacob in Esau's clothes, and drills him into the very tones of Esau's voice, as also into all Esau's hearty huntsman's ways in the house, till she has rehearsed her favourite son Jacob into a finished and perfect supplanter. And then, her second love is seen in the terror and in the haste with which she ships off Jacob to Haran lest Esau in his revenge should send one of his shafts through the supplanter's heart. All that stands in Moses, and much more like that, both in and after Moses; and yet here are we, down in the days of the New Testament, still dressing up our daughters, and emigrating our sons, as if we had been the first fathers and mothers in all the world to whom God had said, I will give thee thy wages.

Esau had been all up and down the whole country round about a hundred times. That bold and cunning hunter would be days and weeks away from home when the season came round for the venison to be on the hills. But Jacob had never been out of sight of his mother's tent-pole till now. The fugitive spent his first night in a herdsman's hut, and his second night in the hut of a friendly native of the land; but after that all his nights were spent in the open air. And the first of Jacob's open-air nights is a night to be remembered, as we say. Poor Jacob! This is the beginning of the visitation of the iniquity of the fathers upon the children to the third and fourth generation. A Syrian ready to perish, were it not that man's extremity is God's opportunity.

And were it not that Jacob, and all his true seed, are known to themselves and to us by the hundred and sixteenth psalm: 'The sorrows of death compassed me, and the pains of hell gat hold upon me: I found trouble and sorrow. I was brought low, and He helped me.' And he took of the stones of that place and put them for his pillows, and lay down in that place to sleep. And he dreamed. God spake in divers manners in those early days. Jacob dreamed that night because Rebekah had neither a Bible nor a *Pilgrim's Progress,* nor a hymn-book, to put into his scrip beside his bread and his dates and his oil. No; nor, worst of all, a good example. Still, she may forget her sucking child that she should not have compassion on the son of her womb, yet will God not forget him. And thus it was that Jacob dreamed as he did dream his first night away from home. How dreadful is this place! Jacob had been taught to feel and to say how dreadful was that place where his father's altar was built; and those places where God had come down to talk with Adam, and Abel, and Noah, and Abraham, and Hagar. But Jacob had no idea that God was at Luz, or would ever come down to talk with him there. And, then, more than that, there was this. God's presence, God's holiness, but above all God's great grace, will always make the place dreadful to a great sinner. Dreadful, with a solemnising, awful, overwhelming dread that there is no other word for. How dreadful did all Jacob's life of sin look at Luz! He had had his own thoughts about himself, and about his mother, and about his father, and about his brother all these last three days across the wilderness. But it was not till that morning at Luz that Jacob learned to say: Against Thee, Thee only, have I sinned! How dreadful did his past life look now, as it lay naked and open under that gate of heaven and that shining ladder! The lasting lesson of that best of all mornings to Jacob is memorably preserved to us and to our children in our Second Paraphrase; and as often as we sing or say to God that noble piece we still reap into our own hearts the first sheaf out of the rich harvest of Jacob's life. We always read that chapter and sing that paraphrase on the Sabbath night before we emigrate another of the sons of Jacob; but, alas! too late; for by that time our family worship, like Isaac's that night, is but locking the stable door after the steed is stolen.

What a down-come it was from the covenant-heights of Bethel to the cattle troughs of Haran! What a cruel fall from the company of ascending and descending angels into the clutches of a finished rogue like Laban! Jacob had been all but carried up of angels from Bethel and taken into an inheritance incorruptible and undefiled; but, instead of that, he is taken down to Padan-aram, where he is cheated out of his wages, and cheated out of his wife, and cheated, and cheated, and cheated again, ten times cheated, and that too by his own mother's brother, till cheating came out of Jacob's nostrils, and stank in his eyes, and became hateful as hell to Jacob's heart. We say that Greek sometimes meets Greek. We say that diamond sometimes cut diamond. We calculate the length of handle his spoon would need to have who sups with the devil. We speak about the seller being sold. And we quote David to the effect that to the froward God will show Himself froward; and Paul to the same effect, that as a man soweth so shall he reap. Yes. Other people had been creating their fathers and their brothers all these years as well as Rebekah and Jacob. Other little boys had been taking prizes in the devil's sly school besides Rebekah's favourite son. Laban, Rebekah's brother, and bone of her bone, had been making as pious speeches at Bethuel's blind bedside as ever Jacob made at Isaac's. And now that the actors are all ready, and the stage is all built, and the scenery is all hung up, all the world is invited in to see the serio-comedy of the Syrian biter bit, or Rebekah's poor lost sheep shorn to the bone by the steely shears of Shylock her brother. 'What is this that thou hast done unto me? Wherefore hast thou so beguiled me?'—Jacob appealed and remonstrated in his sweet, injured, salad innocence. Jacob had never seen or heard the like of it in his country. It shocked terribly and irrecoverably Jacob's inborn sense of right and wrong; it almost shook down Jacob's whole faith in the God of Bethel. And so still. We never see what wickedness there is in lies, and treachery, and cheatery, and injury of all kinds till we are cheated and lied against and injured ourselves. We will sit all our days and speak against our brother till some one comes and reports to us what they say who sit and speak against us. And then the whole blackness and utter abominableness of detraction and calumny and slander breaks out upon us, till we cut out our tongue rather than ever again so employ it. It was Jacob's salvation that he fell into the hands of that cruel land-shark, his uncle Laban. Jacob's salvation is somewhat nearer now than when he believed at Bethel; but, all the same, what is bred in the bone is not got clean rid of in a day. It were laughable to a degree, if it were not so sad, to see Jacob, after all his smart, still peeling the stakes of poplar, and chestnut, and hazel where the cattle came to drink, till it came about that all the feebler births in the cattle-pens were Laban's and all the stronger were Jacob's. And till Laban had to give it up and to confess himself completely outwitted; and till he piously and affectionately proposed a covenant at Mizpah, saying, This pillar be witness that I will not pass over it to harm thee, nor thou to harm me.

Before we leave Laban and his enfeebled cattle, we take some excellent lessons away with us. And one of those excellent lessons is a lesson in the most perfect English style. The whole Laban episode is rich in gems of composition and expression. The Master of expression himself falls far below Moses more than once in these chapters. The prince in the *Tempest* is wine and water compared with Jacob. Even Burns has it better than Shakespeare:

> The man that lo'es his mistress weel
> Nae travel makes him weary.

But this is still better than either: 'Jacob served seven years for Rachel, and they seemed to him but a few days, for the love he had to her.' And there are other gems of the pen scattered lavishly about this same passage quite as good as that. Only, we are in quest to-night of better gems than gems of English, beautiful and rare and precious as they are.

We may emigrate our sons to the gold-fields of South Africa, or to the cattle-ranches of America or Australia, and they may make such a fortune there as to be able to come home after we are no more, and build in the West-end, and educate their children in this capital of learning. But as long as Esau lives, as long as that man or that woman lives whom our son supplanted so long ago, he will build his house over a volcano, and will travel home to it with a trembling heart. And Jacob's heart often trembled and often stood still all the way of the wilderness from Haran to the Jabbok. Your son will send home secret instructions to some old class-fellow who is now at the top of the law to effect a peace, if not forgiveness and reconciliation, at any price. And so did Jacob. Jacob took a great herd of Laban's whitest cattle: goats, and camels, and kine, and everything he could think of, and sent herd after herd on beforehand so as to quench the embers of his brother's wrath. We have a like instance in that Highlander who, on hearing Robert Bruce inveighing in the High Kirk against those sins of which he knew himself to have been guilty, came up to the great preacher and said, 'I'se gie thee twenty cows to gree God and Me.' But, to Jacob's consternation, Esau never looked at those lowing, snow-white herds, but put on his armour in silence, and came posting north at the head of four hundred men. When Jacob's scouts returned and told him all that, he was in absolute desperation.

Had he been alone it would have been easy. But, with all these women and children, and with all these cattle and other encumbrances, was there ever a man taken in such a cruel trap! But he had still one whole night to count on before Esau could be at the Jabbok. And here is his prayer that night, preserved word for word to us his sons; his instant prayer after the scouts came back: 'I am not worthy of the least of all the mercies, and of all the truth, which Thou hast showed to Thy servant: for with my staff I passed over this Jordan; and now I am become these two bands. Deliver me, I pray Thee, from my brother Esau, lest he smite me, and the women with the children.' That is a fine sentence about the staff. It is points like that in a prayer and in a psalm that touch and take captive both God and man. That staff at the first had been a birthday gift from his twin-brother Esau. The cunning hunter had cut it out of the wood one day, and had carried home his snares and his venison slung over it on his shoulder. When he saw that Jacob envied it, Esau smoothed the stout branch better, and straightened it out, and carved E. and J. into a true lover's knot under the handle of it, and laid it beside Jacob's lentil-dish on the morning of their double birthday. That staff felt like so much lead when Jacob took it into his hand to run from home; but he would need it, and, though it sometimes burned his hand to a red-hot cinder, somehow he never could throw it away. The staff stood sentinel over its dreaming master at Bethel, and with its help he waded the Jordan, and sprang the Jabbok, till he laid it down to water Rachel's sheep in Padan-aram. Jacob and his staff were a perfect proverb in Padan-aram. They were never found separated. Jacob never felt alone when he had his staff in his hand; and many a time he was overheard talking to it, and it to him. And now, at the return to Jabbok, with that staff he made his prayer and praise to God, as if it had been some sacred instrument of a priest which had power with God. And, no doubt, we all have a staff, or a pen, or a ring, or book, or a Bible, or something or other that has gone with us through all our banishments, migrations, ups and downs in life, and when our hearts are soft and our prayers come upon us we again take that old companion by the hand. You will have a blue old cloak, like Newman's, or a brown old plaid that you bought while yet you were in your mother's house,—I have one,—and you feel sure that you could pit that old plaid with a story hanging at every single thrum and tassel of it, against Jacob's so-travelled staff any day. You will give orders that that old wrap is to be your winding-sheet; and you will wear it, with all its memories of judgment and of mercy, under your wedding garment in heaven. 'With my staff I passed over this Jordan, and now I am become these two bands.'

And he took them and sent them over the brook, and sent over all that he had. And when the night fell upon him Jacob was left alone. But now, who can tell how near Esau may be by this time! That cunning, cruel, revengeful man! Till, as the darkness fell so obscure, every plunge of the Jabbok, and every roar of the storm, made Jacob feel the smell of Esau's coat and the blow of his hairy hand. Whether in the body, Jacob to the day of his death could never tell; or whether out of the body, Jacob could never tell; but such a night of terror and of battle no other man ever spent. It was Esau, and it was not Esau. It was God, and it was not God. It was both God and Esau; till Jacob to the day of his death could never tell Who the terrible Wrestler really was. Just before the morning broke, with one last wrench Jacob was left halt and lame for life. When, as if from the open heaven, he was baptized of the gracious Wrestler into a new name. For as He departed and the morning broke, the mysterious Man said to Jacob as he lay prostrate at His feet, Thou art henceforth no longer Jacob, but Israel, for as a prince thou hast power with God and with men, and hast prevailed.

Jacob's new name is a great surprise to us. We would never have called Jacob a prince. There are many other names and titles and epithets we would have given to this overtaken son of Isaac and Rebekah; this broken brother of Esau, whose sins have so found him out. But God proclaims Jacob ever after the Jabbok none of our names, but a prince. And for this reason. Prayer, such prayer as Jacob prayed that night, is the princeliest act any man can possibly perform. The noblest, the grandest, the boldest, the most magnificent act a human can perform on this earth is to pray; to pray, that is, as Jacob prayed at Peniel. No man is a prince with God all at once; no, nor after many years. Few men—one here and another there—ever come to any princeliness at all, either in their prayers or in anything else. Jacob had twenty years, and more, of sin and of sorrow, of remorse and of repentance, of gratitude for such a miraculous past, and of beaten-back effort after a better life, and then, to crown all, he had that unparalleled night of fear and prayer at the Jabbok; a night's work such that even the Bible has nothing else like it till our Lord's night in Gethsemane,—and it is only after that, and far more than Moses with all his honesty and all his subtlety has told us,—it is only then that Jacob is proclaimed of God a prince with God. You must understand that prayer, to be called prayer, is not what you hear people all about you calling prayer.

That is not prayer. Jacob's thigh was out of joint, and our Lord's sweat was as it were great drops of blood falling to the ground. Prayer is colossal work. There were giants in those days. Prayer takes all our heart, and all our soul, and all our strength, and all our mind, and all our life, sleeping and waking. Prayer is the princeliest, the noblest, the most unearthly act on this side heaven. Only pray, then; only pray aright, and enough, and it will change your whole nature as it changed Jacob's. Till, from the meanest, the falsest, the most treacherous, the most deceitful, the most found-out, and the most miserable of men, it will make you also a very prince with God and with men. Happy is he that hath the God of Jacob for his help!

XVIII

JOSEPH

THE LORD WAS WITH JOSEPH

JOSEPH, the future ruler of Egypt, was the late-born and the greatly-beloved son of Jacob and Rachel. Joseph inherited all his mother's proverbial gracefulness and sweetness and attractive beauty. And then Joseph's intellectual gifts were such that, taken along with the purity and the nobility of his character, they lifted him up out of a pit, and out of a prison, and set him in a seat of power and of honour scarcely second to the seat of Pharaoh himself. At the same time Joseph climbed up to that high seat through many great risks and out of many great sufferings; and he ran some of the greatest of those risks at the hand of his too-doting father. Were it not that our own hearts so continually condemn us, we would turn on Jacob with indignation for his mischievous treatment of Joseph. Can Jacob have forgotten the sea of trouble into which his father's favouritism, and his mother's indulgence, cast both themselves and their children? The woeful harvest of all that long past folly is still making both Jacob's life and many other lives as bitter as death to this day; and yet here is Jacob poisoning the whole of his family life also, and spoiling Joseph, just as Isaac and Rebekah had spoiled and poisoned their own and their children's lives when Jacob and Esau were still their children. We would denounce Jacob for his insane treatment of Joseph were it not that we are all ourselves repeating sins and follies every day from which we and our families have suffered for generations.

Joseph's coat of many colours was like to have been his winding-sheet, such was the envy and the hatred of his half-brothers at Rachel's well-favoured, richly-talented, and over-ornamented son. 'Our coats be of one colour; so should his,' grumbled Dan, and all Dan's brothers agreed with his spiteful and angry words. The patriarchs, moved with envy, says Stephen in the Acts, sold Joseph into Egypt. And Jacob, on his death-bed, when he was blessing Joseph, said of him that the archers had hated him, and had shot their arrows at him, and had sorely wounded him. It is usual for mankind, says Josephus on the text, to envy their nearest relatives and their best friends for their eminence and for their prosperity. And yet, if Dan would but wait a little, and would but command himself a little, the brightness will soon begin to fade out of his brother's many-coloured coat. Let a short season run and there will be nothing to pain Dan's eye and to wring and heat his heart. Some other fond father will soon begin to clothe his spoiled son in a coat full of more and more brilliant colours than Joseph's coat; till Joseph's coat will be so eclipsed that he also will join the archers' ranks, and will shoot at his rival with their envious arrows. Another author will soon rise and will take the public taste. His new books will soon be on every table, and his new name in every mouth, till that success which so galls you to-day will be completely forgotten by you and forgiven. His crowded pews will before long begin to thin out, and new orators will spring up and will attract and draw off that preacher's painful crowd. And if none of these considerations will quiet Dan's evil eye, and if he really feels his eye to be an evil and a wicked and a murderous eye, let him take his evil eye to God. To whom else can such an eye as that be taken? Let him lift his so sorely stung eye up to Joseph's God. Ask the God of love to consider you and to pity you. Ask Him not to spurn and spit on you. Ask Him to be merciful to your secret and incessant misery. Shut your door on God and yourself, and on your knees ask Him still to add to your brother's goodliness, and to his talents, and to his honour, and to his happiness, and to his usefulness; if only He will anoint your eyes with enough love, and if only He will take out of your eyes that same evil light that glanced so murderously in the patriachs' eyes as often as they again saw Joseph in his shining coat. Importune Him to enable you to love Joseph, till you enjoy, as if they were your own, those so many and so shining colours of his coat. If ever Almighty God has wrought that salvation in Dan, or in any of Dan's brothers on this side the new Jerusalem, ask Him, for Christ's sake, to do it a little to you.

Joseph was only seventeen years old when his two so intoxicating dreams came to him. You must always recall Joseph's unripe age, and his complete inexperience, before you blame him too much for the way he talked about his prerogatives and prospects of greatness. The time will come when all Joseph's splendid achievements, and all his matchless honour and glory, will not make Joseph open a lip about himself. But he was only seventeen as yet, and he had never been for an hour out of his father's flattering eyesight. And thus it was that Joseph's future modesty, and humility, and self-command, and knowledge of other men's hearts, and thoughtfulness for other men's feelings and temptations, had not yet begun to come to him. Had Joseph been but a little older, and had he been but once or twice at Dothan, he would have hidden his dreams in his heart like so many guilty secrets. But, innocent child that he was, he must up and out of his bed, and tell all his dreams to all the house. And so intent was he in what so much interested himself that he did not see the ugly looks on the faces of his brothers. And, like Joseph, till we are well past seventeen, and have been for some time away from home, we talk about nothing else but our own dreams also. Other men dreamed last night as well as we, but they never get their mouths open where we are. We talk the whole table down. We have just come home from the pulpit, or from the platform, or from the desk, or from the instrument, or from a visit, or from an entertainment, or from what not, and our vain hearts are full. We never think that all the other people at table are as full of themselves as we are. We never see that they also are bursting to get at the only topic that interests them, which is not at all the same topic that so interests us. We mistake that silence and that suspense. We think that all that silence and all that suspense means that all our audience are as full of our interests as we are ourselves, and are waiting to hear us. While all the time, they can scarcely command themselves with weariness and disgust. Be sure your company is as full of you as you are of yourself before you again give the reins to your galloping tongue. Be sure that they all worship you. Be sure that you are their god. Be sure that they are all your wife and children. Be sure that they have no interests, or occupations, or vanities of their own. Be sure of all their love and devotion and patience. In short, he sure that you are in heaven before you keep the whole house waiting to break their fast till you have told out to the end all your dreams of last night. And it came to pass that they stripped Joseph of his coat, his coat of many colours, that was upon him. And they took him and cast him into a pit, and then they sat down to eat bread. Is that another subtlety of Moses? Does Moses insinuate that Joseph's brothers had never till now sat down to eat bread in entire peace since the day that Joseph began to dream? With all their faults, Joseph would have been eating bread at that moment with the patriarchs but for his spotted coat and his irrepressible dreams. I overheard a conversation something like this not long ago: 'Shall we ask him to dinner, and invite So-and-so to meet him?' 'No, I think not.' 'Why?' 'Why? Because the last time he was with us he talked two mortal hours about himself, till everybody but himself must have seen contempt and disgust written as plain as day on every face. No. But if only he were not so full of himself, what a welcome guest he would be! And with such talents, and with such a position, what might he not do!'

There are some men, on the other hand, whom you can never waylay into once opening their lips about themselves. Two such men stand out enviably and honourably to me in my acquaintance. And they are just the two men in all my acquaintance I would most like to hear on themselves. But, no. Never they. Whether it is pride—I sometimes think it is; or whether it is scorn of their company—as it may well be; or whether it is absence of mind, or age, or experience, or knowledge of the hearts of men, till they will not commit themselves to men, I am sometimes divided; but, be it what it may, I never yet saw either of them take up a single moment of Joseph's time. There is such a thing as having too much of a good thing. And there is a golden mean in this matter also, if Joseph from the one side, and my two friends from the other side, could only strike it.

That dreadful pit in Dothan was the beginning of Joseph's salvation. The first night he spent in that pit recalled to Joseph's mind what his father told him of his first night from home, as also of that other night at the Jabbok. And as Joseph lay in that horrible pit, and dreamed and prayed, behold, the very same ladder of Bethel is let down into the bottom of the pit. 'I am the Lord God of Abraham, and of Isaac, and of Jacob thy father. And behold, I am with thee, and will keep thee in all places whither thou goest. For I will not leave thee till I have done all that which I have spoken to thee of.' And, all that night after, Joseph could think of nothing else but the sins of his youth; his vanity, his proud superiority and superciliousness to his brothers, his evil reports concerning his brothers, his talkativeness about himself, and all the temptations and provocations into which he had led his brothers. That deep pit was brimful of such remorseful thoughts and prayers, when Judah appeared at its mouth with cords and grappling irons to draw Joseph up to the daylight. But it was only to kill him with a far worse death; for that morning Joseph was sold to the Midianite slave-dealers of Egypt for twenty pieces of silver. Twenty pieces of silver was Joseph's whole price that day in Dothan. Those who know Joseph's after-history will flash forward their minds, and will contrast the Prime Minister of Pharaoh with that slave lad sold for that paltry price at the mouth of that pit that day. And, to-morrow, when you buy an apprentice, or a message boy, of his widowed mother for five shillings a week, think of Joseph for a moment, and say to yourself, Who knows what the future may have in store for my message boy and for me? Who knows how I may go down, while he goes up? Who knows the talents of God that may lie hidden in that friendless boy? Who knows what place he may be predestined to fill in the church and in the world? And even if he comes to nothing of all that; if he never becomes a great man, yet, even so, such thoughts, such imaginations, such forecasts will help you to treat him well, and will help to make you a good man and a good master, whatever your slave-boy may come, or may not come, to be.

The good work that the pit in Dothan began in Joseph, those still more terrible days and nights on the way down to Egypt carried on. Lashed to the loaded side of a huge cane-wagon, and himself loaded with the baggage of Gilead for the Egyptian market, Joseph toiled on under the mid-day sun, thankful to be left alone of his churlish masters in the red-hot air. Put yourself in Joseph's place. The fondling of his father; a child on whom no wind was ever let blow, and no sun was ever let strike; with servants to wait on his every wish, and to dress and anoint him for every meal; with loving looks and fond words falling continually upon him from the day he was born; and now, lashed to the side of a slave caravan, and with the whistling whip of his Ishmaelite owner laid on his shoulder till he sank in the sand. But you must add this to the picture, else you will not have the picture complete: 'The Lord was with Joseph, and Joseph found grace in the sight of the Lord.' Yes, the Lord was more with Joseph, more and better far, than ever He had been as long as Joseph was the spoiled child of his father, and the continual snare of his brothers. And there are young men in this city suffering hardships and persecutions in workshops and in offices as sore to bear as was Joseph's load of labour and ill-usage of the Ishmaelites. And the Lord is with them also as He never was so long as they were spoilt sons at home, getting all things their own way. And as they silently and prayerfully take up their cross daily, and wait out the will of God, they are thereby putting off a past that would have been their sure destruction—and had almost been—and are preparing themselves for a future as sure, and as full of the providence of God, as ever was Joseph's future. It is good for a man that he bear the yoke in his youth. He sitteth alone and keepeth silence, because he hath borne it upon him. He putteth his mouth in the dust, if so be there may be hope. He giveth his cheek to him that smiteth him; he is filled full with reproach. For the Lord will not cast off for ever; but, though He cause grief, yet will He have compassion according to the multitude of His mercies. 'How many saints,' William Law rejoices, 'has adversity sent to heaven! And how many poor sinners has prosperity plunged into everlasting misery! This man had never been debauched, but for his fortune and advancement; that had never been pious, but through his poverty and disgrace. She that is envied for her beauty may perchance owe all her misery to it; and another may be for ever happy for having no admirers of her person. One man succeeds in everything, and so loses all; another meets with nothing but crosses and disappointments, and thereby gains more than all the world is worth.'

Even if Potiphar paid thirty or even forty pieces of silver for his Hebrew slave, we know now what a good bargain he got that day. For that handful of silver the captain of Pharaoh's guard came into possession of all the splendid talents that lay hid in Joseph's greatly gifted mind, and all the magnificent moral character the first foundations of which had been laid in the pit in Dothan, and had been built up in God every step of the long wilderness journey. All Joseph's deep repentance also, and all his bitter remorse; all his self-discovery, and all his self-condemnation; with all his reticence and all his continence,—Potiphar took all that home from the slave-market that day in exchange for his handful of Egyptian silver. Joseph was now to be plunged into the most corrupt society that rotted in that age on the face of the earth. And had he not come into that pollution straight out of a sevenfold furnace of sanctifying sorrow, Joseph would no more have been heard of. The sensuality of Egypt would have soon swallowed him up. But his father's God was with Joseph. The Lord was with Joseph to protect him, to guide him, and to give him victory. The Lord was with him to more imprisonment, and then to more promotion; to more and more honour, and place, and power, till this world had no more to bestow upon Joseph. And, through it all, Joseph became a better and an ever better man all his days. A nobler and an ever nobler man. A more and more trustworthy, and a more and more trusted and consulted man. More and more loyal to truth and to duty. More and more chaste, temperate, patient, enduring, forgiving; full of mind and full of heart; and full, no man ever fuller, of a simple and a sincere piety and praise of God, till he became a very proverb both in the splendour of his services, and in the splendour of his rewards.

XIX

AARON

IS NOT AARON THE LEVITE THY BROTHER? I KNOW THAT HE CAN SPEAK WELL

WHAT a gifted house! What an honour to that man of the house of Levi who took to wife a daughter of Levi! What a rich slave-hut was that with Miriam and Aaron and Moses all born of God into it! What splendid wages to have three such children given to that son and daughter of Levi to nurse up for the Lord, and for Israel, and for all the world; three such goodly children as Miriam the prophetess, and Aaron the high priest, and Moses the deliverer and leader and lawgiver of Israel. Has there ever been another house gifted like that house in Goshen on the face of the earth? I have not heard or read of another house in all the world like the house of Amram of the house of Levi, and his wife God-my-glory. And, then, the sovereign distribution and allotment of their gifts and their graces and their offices, the dividing-out of the family genius, was no less wonderful than the immense amount of it. For, by that sovereign division and distribution Moses was made the first and the greatest of all the prophets of Israel. Aaron, again, must have been the most eloquent of all eloquent men, since the fame of his eloquence had reached up to heaven itself till it was acknowledged and talked of and boasted about there. What oratory must Aaron's oratory have been when God Himself both felt and confessed its power. I know, said the Divine Voice, that he can speak well. And, then, Miriam, in sacred drama, in sacred dance, in sacred song, and in sacred instruments of music, was quite worthy to stand out beside her two unapproachable brothers. While, all the time, each several one of the three was all the more dependent on the other two just because of the greatness of his own or her own special gift. The very magnitude of their own gifts made the others' gifts more necessary to them, till the whole house of Amram was a complete and a rounded and a perfect gift of God to all Israel. And till all that Israel could ever need as a nation and as a church, as fathers and as mothers, as masters and as servants, as slaves and as redeemed from slavery, as sinners and as the chosen people of God—all Israel was complete in Moses and Aaron and Miriam, even as they also were complete in God and in one another. Yes, indeed, what a highly honoured house was the house of that son and daughter of Levi, Amram and God-her-glory.

And Moses said unto the Lord, O my Lord, I am not eloquent. Neither heretofore nor since Thou hast spoken to Thy servant; but I am slow of speech and of a slow tongue. It was the depth and the weight and the fulness of Moses' mind that made him a man of such slow speech and of such a slow tongue. Moses had lived so long alone in Horeb that he had well-nigh forgotten the every-day language of every-day men. He had been so much alone with God that he felt like a man away from home when he met again with any man of many words. He had taken the shoes off his feet so often before God that he never could put them on again or walk in them with any ease or any freedom before men. I AM! was all that God had said to Moses, year after year, as Moses fed the flock of his father-in-law in the mount of God. And, who am I? was all that Moses answered God for forty years. Moses was a great philosopher, says Matthew Henry, and a great statesman, and a great divine, and yet he was no orator. And one great statesman of England speaking of another great statesman, says of him, He was without any power to be called oratory, and yet I never heard a man speak in the House of Commons who had so much power over the House. He had those great qualities that govern men, and that has far more influence in the House of Commons than the most brilliant flights of fancy, or the keenest wits. But, better than all his great philosophy and great statesmanship, Moses was a great divine, the greatest of Old Testament divines; the greatest because the first of all divines. And yet he was no preacher, as we say. In this Moses was somewhat like certain of our own great divines. They have such a depth and weight of matter that they also are slow of speech and of a slow style. Butler for one, and Foster for another. Whereas certain others of our great divines are like Aaron in this, that they can speak well. And yet we have sometimes heard of great divines and great preachers too who shrank back from the pulpit as much as Moses himself shrank. The call of Isaiah, and the call of Jeremiah, and the call of Calvin, and the call of Knox, and the call of Bruce all remind us of Moses' noble modesty, his fear of his office, his fear of himself, and of his fellow-men. And the Lord said to Moses 'Who hath made man's voice? Is not Aaron the Levite thy brother? And he shall be thy spokesman unto the people; he shall be to thee instead of a mouth, and thou shalt be to him instead of God.'

Cato the Censor defined a great orator to be nothing else than a good man well skilled in speaking. And Quintilian, in his *Institutes of Oratory,* has a noble passage on the great Roman's great text. Let all our young orators, and, especially, let all our sacred and Aaronic orators, study the delightful *Institutes,* that perfect treasure-house of ancient letters, ancient wisdom, and ancient truth and beauty. Now, Aaron was one of Cato's good men skilled in speaking. We are sure of that, because for Aaron's goodness as a man we have not only his long lifetime in the most sacred of all services, but also the psalmist's testimony that Aaron, with all his great trespass, was a great saint of God. And, besides, for his great skilfulness in speaking we have the great certificate of the Divine Voice itself. The sword had entered Aaron's soul also. The iron furnace of Egypt had been burning for long in Aaron's covenant heart also. But when Aaron looked at the tremendous and impossible task of delivering Israel out of Egypt, he felt that he was helpless and hopeless. At the same time, he felt sure that if there was a man on the face of the earth made of God on special purpose for such a service, it was just his own banished brother Moses. And thus it was that Aaron set out to Horeb to seek for Moses just at the moment when the bush began to burn on Horeb, and when the Lord began to speak to Moses out of the bush. 'Behold, Aaron thy brother cometh forth to meet thee, and when he seeth thee he will be glad in his heart. And thou shalt speak to him, and put words in his mouth; and I will be with his mouth and with thy mouth, and will teach you both what you shall both do. And he shall be, even he shall be to thee instead of a mouth, and thou shalt be to him instead of God.' And Aaron went and met Moses in the mount of God. And Aaron kissed Moses, and Moses told Aaron all that the Lord had said concerning him, till Aaron answered, and shrank back, and said: Surely it is not so. Surely the Lord did not so speak concerning me. I speak well! I speak for thee, my brother! I am not worthy to unloose thy shoe-latchet. I am not worthy to be of the same name with thee. I should always sit silent. I should never speak. My tongue will not tame. I need thee, my brother. I need thy wisdom. I need thy patience. I need thy counsel. I need thy command. Thou art the wisest and the best of men. Thou art a king in Israel. Moses, my dear brother! While all the time Moses felt more than ever before how all this must be of God. For even as Aaron so spake, Moses saw to his delight that Aaron had always the right word ready. No man could resist Aaron. No man could refuse Aaron. Pharaoh himself would not be able to resist and refuse Aaron. Moses felt beside Aaron that he would never open his mouth again. The right word always went away, somehow, when Moses opened his mouth to speak. Whereas Aaron had but to open his mouth and the right word always came out of his mouth. Till, with Aaron beside him, Moses felt that he could face without fear of failure both all Israel and Pharaoh with all his priests and all his magicians.

Now, as we have already seen, we have always had men among ourselves more or less like Moses, and other men more or less like Aaron. Men like Moses—that is, men of great originality, and of great depth and grasp and strength of mind. And yet men who have been of a stammering tongue. Carlyle has made Cromwell's 'mute veracity' noble and venerable to us to all time, and Lord Acton has told us that Dr. Döllinger knew too much to write much. On the other hand, what are those men to do, who, like Aaron, have no such depth, and grasp, and originality, and productivity of mind as Moses and the great thinkers and great scholars of our race have had? A common man and a man of no gifts may be set in a place, and may have a calling of God that he cannot escape—a place and a calling which demand constant speaking and constant teaching at his hands. A minister, for instance. He may not be a great scholar or a great thinker himself, but he is set over those who are still less scholars, and who think still less. Now, what is such a man to do? What, but just to take Moses instead of God. What, but just to find out those great divines and other great authors who have been so immediately and so richly gifted of God, and to live with them, and work with them, and make them his own, just as if God had given him all the great gifts He has given them. If I am a man of no learning and no originality, then I know men, both living and dead, who are; and they are all that, of God, and under God, for me. And, if I had to travel barefoot to Horeb for them; if I had to sell my bed for them, at any cost I would have them. I would take no rest till I found them, and then, as God said of Aaron, I would be glad when I saw them, and I would kiss them, and claim them as my own. We are not all the men of Moses-like genius and originality we might like to be. We are not all epoch-making, history-making, nation-making men. But we are what we are. We are what God has made us to be; and Moses himself is no more. And Moses may be as glad to meet me in my teachableness and in my love and in my reverence as I am to meet him in his magnificent supremacy and high solitariness of gift and of office. Yes; and who knows what our Master may graciously say to us after He has rewarded Moses for his magnificent talents and for his magnificent services? One thing is sure: we shall be satisfied with what He shall say to us, and we shall have no room left in our hearts wherewith any more to envy Moses for his god-like gifts and for his god-like services.

All went well with Aaron as long as he had Moses beside him to inspire him, and to support him, and to be to him instead of God. Aaron faced the elders of Israel, and scattered all their objections and all their fears as a rushing mighty wind scatters chaff; and the long struggle with Pharaoh and with his magicians has surely been preserved to us by Aaron's eloquent pen. The crossing of the Red Sea also, Mount Sinai, and the giving of the tabernacle and the law—it has certainly been by some one who could both speak well and write well also that all that wonderful piece has been put into our hands. And, whatever part Aaron and Aaron's great gifts may have had in all that, at and rate, all went well with Aaron through all that. Aaron did splendid service through all that, and both his great name and his great service would have gone on growing in love and in honour to the end if only he had never let Moses out of his sight. But always when Moses was for any length of time out of sight, Aaron was a reed shaken with the wind; he was as weak and as evil as any other man. Those forty days that Moses was away on the Mount brought out, among other things, both Moses' strength and greatness and Aaron's littleness and weakness in a way that nothing else could have done. 'Up, make us gods, which shall go before us; for, as for this Moses, we wot not what is become of him.' And Aaron went down like a broken reed before the idolatrous and licentious clamour of the revolted people. A man may be able to speak well when all men's ears are open to him, and when all men's hands are clapping to what he says, who is yet a very weak man, and a very helpless man, and a very mischievous man in a time of storm and strain and shipwreck. A man may be, if not one of Cato's orators, yet a great favourite with the multitude, who has no real root in himself. He may speak well under sufficient applause who has no nobility of character, and no strength of will, and no backbone or brow of courage, and no living and abiding faith in God and in the truth of God. It has often been seen, both in sacred, and in profane, and in contemporary history, how soon the man of a merely emotional, impulsive, oratorical temperament goes to the wall in the hour of real trial. It is popular clamour, and the dividing and receding wave of popular support, that tries a true statesman's strength. The loud demands and the angry threats of the excited people soon serve to discover whether the wonted leader is really able and really worthy to lead or no. And men of the oratorical order have so often flinched and failed in the hour of action and of suffering that our eloquent men are apt to be too lightly esteemed. The love of popularity, and the absolute necessity to have the multitude with him, is a terrible temptation to that leader of men and of movements in the church and in the state who has the gift of popular speech, and who loves to employ it. What would the people like me to say to them on that subject? Will they crowd to hear it? How will they take it? And what will be said about what I have said after I have said it and cannot unsay it? And, in my heart of hearts, can I let them go? Shall I not tune my pulpit just a touch or two, so as to attract this man, and so as to keep that other man from going away? Moses had his own temptations and snares that even he did not always escape and overcome; but it was the good speaker's temptations, it was the popular preacher's temptation, that led Aaron into the terrible trespass of the golden calf.

There is a fine sermon by the finest of English preachers under this fine title—"Saintliness not forfeited by the penitent." And though that unique preacher, after his provoking manner, gives with the one hand and takes away with the other all through that fine sermon, at the same time the sermon is full of subtle truth and exquisite beauty. No; by the true penitent neither saintliness nor service is ever forfeited. Blessed be God, both saintliness and service too are, in such a case, only the better secured and the more fruitfully employed. But then, in order to either saintliness or service being preserved and maintained in a penitent, his penitence must be of the very best kind. It must be penitence indeed. It must be a breaking, burning, consuming, and ever-deepening life of penitence, and that, too, both before God and man. And it was because Aaron's penitence was at once so saintly, and so laid out in service, that we hear so little, and in as many words, about it. We would be nearer the truth about Aaron if we put him at the very head of all Old Testament penitents, both for his own sins and for the sins of all other men. Luther speaks with Isaiah-like boldness when he says that Jesus Christ, by reason of the law of imputation, was the greatest sinner that ever was. Now, Aaron had to be Jesus Christ till Jesus Christ came. And while Aaron was Jesus Christ in type and by imputation, at the same time, and to give the uttermost reality and the uttermost intensity to that, he was himself Aaron all the time, Aaron of the golden calf and of many other untold transgressions besides. And you may be quite sure that Aaron never slew a sacrifice for sin that he did not lay the golden calf, and the nakedness, and the dancing, and the shame, and all the never-to-be-forgotten sin upon its bleeding head. You may be quite sure that Aaron never went into the holy place any day for the sin of others till he had gone first for his own sin. You may rely upon it that many an Israelite whose sin had found him out had a prayer offered for him and for his case at the altar such that the penitent never knew where all the compassion, and all the sympathy, and all the humility, and all the holiness, and all the harmlessness of his high priest came from. Little did the penitents in Israel think how much of his high priesthood Aaron had put on under Sinai and on the scene of that idolatrous and licentious revelry. Moses in his anger had ground the golden calf to ashes, and had sprinkled the ashes on the waters of the brook that ran down out of the Mount of God, till all the people drank of the sin-laden water. And to this day the children of Israel have a saying to this effect,—that when any terrible judgment of God, or any great remorse, or any great repentance comes upon them there is always an ounce of the ashes of the golden calf in it. And Aaron kept in the holy place, and beside the pot of manna and the rod that budded, a silver chest full of that same accursed ashes, and out of which chest he always sprinkled, and with many tears, all that he ate and all that he drank on every returning day of atonement. By these things priests pray, by these things prophets preach, by these things psalmists sing, and by things like these there comes to all sinful men the best life of their souls. John Foxe used to declare that both he and his people had got much more good out of his sins than ever either he or they had got out of his good works. And, though they did not know it, and would not have believed it, the penitents in Israel got far more good out of their high priest's trespass in the matter of the golden calf, than ever they got out of his broidered garments, and his silver bells, and his fair mitre upon his head.

XX

MIRIAM

AARON AND MOSES, AND MIRIAM THEIR SISTER

WATCH well, Miriam, and never let thine eyes off that ark of bulrushes. Watch that little ark with all thy wit, for no other maiden shall ever have such another watch till the fulness of time, when another Miriam shall watch over another child still more fair to God. Of those born of women only One shall ever be greater than thy little brother away down there among the flags by the river's brink. Watch well, Miriam, the brink of the river, and that ark among its waters, and thou shalt not want thy wages. For far greater riches are hidden in that little ark than all the treasures of Egypt. The civilisation and the sanctification of the whole earth is in thy keeping; the law and the prophets to come; the very Lion of the tribe of Judah Himself and all His kingdom, are all under thine eye to-day. O highly favoured Miriam, the sister of Moses. Only perform thy part well, and wherever this gospel shall be preached in the whole world, there shall this also that thou art doing be told for a memorial of thee!

What a witty little woman did Moses' sister prove herself to be that day! If it was all out of her own head, what a quick-witted little prophetess she was already! 'Shall I go and call to thee a nurse of the Hebrew women, that she may nurse the child for thee? And then, ye mothers among us, what amazing self-control that was in God-my-glory, the mother of Miriam and Moses. Just the proper proportion, and just the perfect mean, between a nurse's paid love for a fondling, and a mother's love for her own restored child. Could you have so hardened your heart till you got him home? And could you have always been on your guard to hold him at arm's length when an Egyptian neighbour came near as Moses' Hebrew nurse did? A mother worthy of prophets, and priests, and prophetesses; and, best of all, God-her-glory!

By the next time we see Miriam, Moses and Aaron and Miriam are at the head of the children of Israel. All Israel under their leadership have escaped out of the land of Egypt, and are standing on the shore of the Red Sea singing the praises of the

Lord like the sound of many waters. By this time Miriam herself in a prophetess, and is able to take the foremost place in the women's sacred songs and sacred dances. Some sharp-eyed scholars who are able to read between the lines assure us that they see tokens of Aaron and of his eloquence in the triumphant song that Miriam took down from Aaron's lips and taught to the devout and talented women, till Aaron and Miriam, with Moses so proudly looking on, made that day a day to be remembered for its songs and for its dances, as well as for its great deliverance, in the house of Israel. And we have the promise that if we flee from Egypt, and do not return to it, we ourselves also shall one day join Moses and Aaron and Miriam on the sea of glass, where, with the harps of God in our hands, we shall all sing together the song of Moses and the Lamb, saying, Great and marvellous are Thy works, Lord God Almighty; just and true are Thy ways, Thou King of saints. For Thou hast brought them in, Thou has planted them in the mountain of Thine inheritance, in the place, O Lord, which Thou hast made for Thee to dwell in; in the sanctuary, O Lord, which Thy hands have established.

But for her brother's marriage, Miriam would have been the sovereign woman in all Israel for all her days. But Moses' marriage was more than Miriam could bear. Miriam had been Moses' sister, and his mother, and his closest companion, and his most confidential friend now for forty years. Miriam had sat at the council-table with Moses and Aaron and the assembled elders of Israel. What Moses and Aaron were to the one half of the people, Miriam the sister of Moses was to the other half. Miriam was the first woman in Israel who had borne the honourable and universal name of a mother in Israel. And, but for the Moses' marriage Miriam would have shone beside Moses till her eye also was not dim, nor her natural strength abated. But Moses' marriage made Miriam as weak and as evil and as wicked as any weak and evil and wicked woman in all the camp. Set me as a seal upon thine heart! Miriam cried to Moses, in a storm of tears, when she saw the Ethiopian woman coming to take her place. Set me as a seal upon thine arm! For love is strong as death. Jealousy is cruel as the grave. The coals thereof are coals of fire, which hath a most vehement flame. What a life of torment did Miriam live in those days because of Moses' marriage! Her heart was full of hell-fire at Moses' innocent wife and innocent children, and even at her meek and innocent brother himself. Till her wild jeolousy kindled her wild pride, and her wild pride her wild, insane, and impious envy, and then her insane and impious envy soon led her into her fatal trespass against Moses and against God.

Aaron had great gifts of the intellectual kind, and he performed great services both of that and of the spiritual kind; but Aaron had little or no strength of character. Aaron could speak well when some stronger man inspired him and held him up, but that was all. Aaron never had much mind of his own. He was always weak in his will. He was easily caught up, easily tossed about, and easily swept away. His two great trespasses were at bottom not his own trespasses at all. In the one case it was the idolatrous and rebellious people, and in this case it was his envious and rebellious sister. We have not a thousandth part of what Miriam said to Aaron. There are days, and nights, and weeks, and years of insinuation, and suspicion, and wounded pride, and gnawing envy all gathered up into a few words, as the manner of Scripture is. 'Hath the Lord spoken only by Moses?' Miriam demanded of Aaron. 'Hath He not also spoken by us?' And Aaron had pride enough and ambition enough and envy enough smouldering in his own heart, that when Miriam blew long enough upon it, Aaron's heart also burned up into an answering flame. And all the time Moses was not blind. Moses was not deaf. And Moses' wife was not a stock nor a stone, though she was not a prophetess. And no little shame and pain—great distress and great and sore sorrow—was seen of the Lord in Moses' tent because of Miriam's abominable injustice and cruelty. But, all the time, Moses her brother was as if he were a deaf man who heard not, and a dumb man who openeth not his mouth. My lovers, said David, and my friends stand aloof from me, and my kinsmen stand afar off. They also that seek after my life lay snares for me; and they that seek my hurt speak mischievous things, and imagine deceits all the day long. Hear me, lest otherwise they should rejoice over me; when my foot slippeth they magnify themselves against me. For yet my prayer also shall be for them in their infirmities. And the Lord heard it. And the Lord spake suddenly unto Moses, and unto Aaron, and unto Miriam—Come out, ye three, unto the tabernacle of the congregation. And they three came out. Look at them. Pity them. Pray for them. Moses the leader and lawgiver of Israel, and Aaron the high priest, and Miriam the prophetess, and all Israel looking after them in terror, and the anger of the Lord kindling round about them. That is the wages of Miriam's sin begun. That is the fruit of all her envy, and insinuation, and detraction, and slander against her brother and her brother's wife. And that in Aaron is what comes of weakness and softness and easiness under temptation. Aaron feels now the full shame of letting Miriam come to his tent and sit and whisper and backbite, when he should have turned her to the door, prophetess and all. How they both wish now that he had! And the Lord called Aaron and Miriam, and they both came forth. What was it that ye two so sat and spake against your brother? In what had he hurt you? In what had he taken any word of Mine out of your mouth? In what had he failed in all his duty to Me? My servant Moses is not so, who is faithful in all Mine house. And the cloud departed from off the tabernacle; and, behold Miriam became leprous, white as snow. And Aaron looked upon Miriam, and behold, she was leprous. And for seven days and seven nights Miriam was shut out of the camp of Israel, and the people journeyed not till Miriam was brought in again.

Look well at Miriam, all you envious and evil-spoken women. Look back at Miriam's beginning. Look at her watching the ark of bulrushes. Look at her nursing her little brother in the house of her godly mother. Look at her in her rapture, like one out of the body with the joy of the Lord, at the Red Sea. And now see to what her wicked heart and her wicked tongue have brought her. Look at her with her hand upon her throat, and with a linen cloth upon her lip, and with her hoarse, sepulchral, noisome voice wandering far from the camp, and compelled to cry Unclean! Unclean! when any one came in sight. Look at all men fleeing from her. Look at her hiding her shame all day behind the sandhills of the wilderness, and coming out at night to look at the lights in Moses' tent and in Aaron's tabernacle. Look, O envy-filled men and women, look at your mother with her flesh half consumed upon her as if she had been seven days dead. Go out and walk all night with her. Go out and hide all day with her. Go out and cry her cry, all you who cannot endure to see or to hear the honours, and the successes, and the services, and the calling, and the gifts of God in your brother. Go out; your true place is not here. Your true place is outside the gates of all good and honest men. Your heart is hard and dry, and like a leper's dead body. Your very voice is hoarse as with the asthma of hell.

What a week that was in the camp of Israel! How many thoughts of how many hearts were that week revealed! Miriam's thoughts of her heart were that week revealed. For seven days and seven night she dwelt alone among the multitude of her own miserable, remorseful, despairing thoughts. What all her thoughts were that week let him tell us who is the chief of sinners, and whose sin has found him out to public exposure and public outcasting. What Aaron's thoughts were as he exercised his office on his sister, and pronounced it leprosy, and passed sentence upon her, and hurried her out of the camp, and shut the gate upon her—what Aaron's thoughts all that week were let him tell us who has had to bear witness against, and to sentence, and to execute judgment on some one in whose sin he himself had been a partaker. I tell you the lepers in Israel had extra-tender treatment at Aaron's hands ever after that awful week. I would like much to know what Moses' wife's thoughts were all that week. Her thoughts, I mean, about her banished sister-in-law. If I knew her thoughts that week on that subject, I would know then to a certainty whether Moses had married well or no. I would know then whether Miriam had any good reason and justification for resisting her brother's marriage. I would know then whether the Lord God had made that Ethiopian woman an help meet for Moses. I would know then whether she was black, but comely, and whether she was a good minister's wife or no. Was she glad in her heart when she heard of Miriam's leprosy? Did she laugh behind the door like Sarah? Did she say, Let her rot in the wilderness, for she deserves it? Was she sad all the eighth day and night after Miriam had been healed? Or, did she go up to the court of the Ethiopians, and there importune her brother Aaron to importune his God on behalf of his sister? Did she look out at the gate many times every day all that week, but could never see or hear Miriam for weeping? Did she buy the two birds for the cleansing of a leper with her own money, and did she have them all ready with her own hands for days before Aaron could as yet take Miriam back? I do not know. I do not read. Only, I know that the thoughts of no woman's heart in all Israel were more revealed all that week than the thoughts of that Ethiopian woman, Moses' much-injured wife. I can well believe that was the best week for the whole house of Israel till that week came when a Greater than Moses and Aaron and Miriam all put together suffered without the gate for their envy and for all their other trespasses. I can believe that that week's halt did more to secure and to hasten their subsequent march through the wilderness than a year of their best roads and their best weather. I can well believe that we have many psalms and the seeds of many psalms out of that fruitful week. I can easily believe that many future judges and prophets and priests in Israel were inquiring and thinking children for the first time that stand-still week. Why are we standing still? they would ask. Where is Miriam all this week? Why is Aaron always sad? Why is Moses always walking alone? Why is my mother always weeping so? And why, when the seventh day came to a close, was there such gladness again? Imagine for yourselves the questions and the answers in every tent in Israel that week. Imagine the wise answers, and the foolish answers, and the silences, and the embraced and the lost opportunities. Imagine the young minds that would open that week, and the young hearts that would break for the first time, and begin to bleed for sin for the first time, that week. It was that week!—they would often say after they were home in the promised land—it was that week in the wilderness!

Miriam did not live long after that week. It was not her age, and was not the dregs of the leprosy. Miriam died of a broken heart. All the sprinklings, and all the bathings, and all the thanksgivings, and all the benedictions of Aaron her brother; and all the love, and honour, and trust, and confidence of Moses her other brother; and all the sisterly tenderness of Moses' wife; and all the sports, and plays, and leaps, and laughters of Moses' children—all could not heal Miriam's broken heart. Miriam's name is never heard of again in Israel. From that week Miriam blotted herself out of all her brother's books. Miriam died to Israel and to all the world in the lazar-house of Hazeroth. Miriam's songs and dances were all past. Not even on the Sabbath-day would Miriam leave her weeping tent. Unclean! Unclean! If you would ever see or hear Miriam now you must venture and go out of the gate to where the lepers sit solitary, and where they follow the camp afar off. That is Miriam the prophetess, the sister of Moses and Aaron, who is taking out meat and medicine and linen for the lip of the lepers. She is sitting down with them. She is talking to them. She is telling them all about herself. She is pledging herself to speak to Aaron her brother for them. She will buy the two birds on her way home after dark. No. It was not years. And it was not sickness. But Miriam soon died. And Miriam sleeps at Kadesh in the wilderness of Zin till they shall awaken her with the song of Moses and the Lamb, saying, and she answering them with a timbrel, Just and true are Thy ways, Thou King of saints. Who shall not fear Thee, O Lord, and glorify Thy name? for Thou only art holy.

XXI

MOSES

NOW THE MAN MOSES WAS VERY MEEK, ABOVE ALL THE MEN THAT WERE UPON THE FACE OF THE EARTH

WERE I to let myself once expatiate on the whole of Moses' life I would not know where to begin or where to end. But my method and my endeavour in these expositions is the study of those Bible men and women in their moral character alone. My intention and my aim is to try to find out how the foundations of their moral character were laid in those Bible men and women; how their respective lives and characters were built up, what the instruments were, and what the occasions and opportunities by means of which those men and women made themselves what they were and are; as, also, to search out and ponder the wonderful ways in which God worked in and around those men and women to make them His workmanship also, created under His hand unto good works. And my present text is the very best text in all the Five Books of Moses for this purpose in the case of Moses himself. For the text is the copestone and the crown and the perfect finish of Moses' moral character and spiritual life. And our chief interest in all that Moses came through from the beginning to the end of his wonderful history is just to find out how it all contributed to and told upon his incomparable meekness and humility; that is to say, upon the perfection and the finish of his matchless moral character.

By all accounts Moses did not begin by being a meek man. The truth is, no truly meek man ever does so begin. It is not true meekness if it is found in any man at the beginning of his life. It may be sloth, it may be softness, it may be easiness, it may be indifference, it may be policy and calculation, it may be insensibility of heart, it may be sluggishness of blood, but true meekness is not. True meekness it is not till it has been planted, and watered, and pruned, and purified, and beaten upon by every wind of God, and cut to pieces by every knife of God, and all the time engrafted and seated deep in the meekness and in the gentleness and in the humility of the Spirit of God and the Son of God. It would be far nearer the truth to say that Moses, to begin with, was the hastiest and the hottest and the least meek and the least longsuffering of men. It was but a word and a blow with young Moses. And it was a word and a blow that laid you on the spot in your grave in the sand. No; the meekness of Moses was not a case of complexion, nor a matter of temperament, any more than it was the grace of a new beginner in godliness and virtue. Moses would by that time be well on the threescore and ten of our years, as we count our years, before it was written of him what stands written of him in our noble text.

I for one will all but exonerate and absolve that grave in the sand. The Egyptian slave-driver, as I take it, deserved all that he got. But if you still protest in your distance and security and indifference against the lynch-law of Moses, then you have Augustine on your side to support you. 'I affirm,' says that great father, 'that the man, though criminal, and really the offender, ought not to have been put to death by one who had no legal authority to do so. But minds that are capable of virtues often produce vices also.' Yes: and as I read this ancient narrative, and look human nature in the face, unless that young Hebrew had had this vice in his blood that day, he would never have had the virtue in after days that made him Moses. Unless he had had it in him, vice or virtue, to strike that bold blow at that insolent Egyptian, he would never have had it in him to strike off Israel's fetters. If he had hesitated and calculated and looked this way and that way that day, we would not have had his perfected meekness before us for our text to-night. I like to think of the son of Pharaoh's daughter out for a drive toward the land of Goshen that tempting sunset. I like to see the old nursling of God-her-glory still showing to all men what he had been suckled on. I rejoice to see that all the learning, and all the art, and all the luxury, and all the licentiousness, and all the dazzling prospects of Egypt have not emasculated Moses, nor made him ashamed of his oppressed kinsmen. You and I would have taken up discretional ground. We would have said that it would be eminently unwise to meddle between a master and his servant. We would have said that we had not time to go into the case. We would have told Pharaoh's second charioteer to drive on. We would have gained Augustine's approval. We would have been law abiding Britons that day. Unfortunately for Moses, it was not our calm Christian blood that was running in his veins that day; and thus it was that he had to pay with forty years' banishment for his sudden spring upon that Egyptian taskmaster, and for the life-long thanks of that delivered slave.

John Cairns refusing at forty to be called the Principal of Edinburgh University, and choosing rather to be the pastor of a despised dissenting congregation of his evangelical fellow-countrymen than to be a philosopher of European reputation, is the nearest thing I know to Moses at forty. Cairns and Keble. Having carried off as a mere boy the highest honours of the University, says Newman in his *Apologia,* Keble turned from the admiration which haunted his steps, and sought for a better and a holier satisfaction in pastoral work in the country. This, also, which is continually happening in Scotland, is not unlike the son of Pharaoh's daughter. The son of a shepherd, or of a stone-breaker, will take a bursary at school. He will thus get his foot on the lowest spar of the ladder. He has talents, and industry, and character, and religion. He takes his degree with classical or philosophical or mathematical honours at Glasgow or Aberdeen. His scholarship carries him up to Oxford or Cambridge. He becomes learned in all the wisdom of the Egyptians; as Philo has it, 'making himself master of all their disputes without encouraging any disputatious disposition in himself.' The news soon comes that he has taken the highest honours. The University takes him up and nourishes him for her own son. His way is open. There is nothing to which he may not aspire. The Scottish crofter's son may yet wear an English mitre. But, like Moses, it comes into his heart to visit his brethren in Argyll or Inverness, till he esteems a Gaelic congregation in his father's church and in his father's land a greater honour to him than all the honour and glory of England, as seeing Him who is invisible. Ouranius is a holy priest, full of the spirit of the Gospel, watching, labouring, and praying for a poor country village. When Ouranius was still a young man he had an ambition in his heart, a haughtiness in his temper, and a great contempt and disregard of all foolish and unreasonable people. But he has prayed away that spirit, and has now the greatest tenderness for the most obstinate sinners. The rudeness, ill-nature, or perverse behaviour of any of his flock used at first to betray him into impatience, but now it raises no other passion in him than a desire of being upon his knees in prayer to God for them. Thus have his prayers for others altered and amended the whole state of his own heart. This devotion softens his heart, enlightens his mind, sweetens his temper, and makes everything that comes to him instructive, amiable, and affecting. He now thinks the poorest creature in his parish good enough and great enough to deserve the humblest attendances, the kindest friendships, the tenderest offices he can possibly show them. He is so far from wanting great or learned or courtly people that he thinks there is no better conversation in the world than to be talking to mean and poor people about the Kingdom of Heaven. All this makes Ouranius more and more careful of every temper of his heart according to the strictest rules of temperance, meekness, and humility, that he may in some degree be like Abraham and Moses and Job in his parish ministry.

Some of you will know what forty years in the wilderness, and at the back of the Mount of God, have done for yourselves. You know how those years have reduced and subdued your too-high temper, and weaned you off from the shams and the sweetnesses of this world, and given you some eyes and some heart to suffer the loss of all things for the recompense of your reward in heaven,—in heaven, where the least and the lowest reward is greater riches than all the gain and all the glory of the present world. And if forty years have wrought such a change in such a slow-hearted scholar of God as you are, you will not wonder at the man Moses as he came back from the land of Midian. Any use you are, or are ever likely to be, or have now any hope or any ambition to be—it all has its roots in the great grace of God to you, and in any little humility and meekness that has come out of all that to you. And when you multiply all that, and yourself as the result of all that, by ten thousand, then you will have Moses in Midian, the herdman and the son-in-law of Jethro, the priest of Midian. Forgotten John Foster has a fine lecture on Jethro and Moses, in which that great preacher's philosophical and imaginative and spiritual power all come out. And all John Foster's power is needed to construct and to let us see Moses' life in Jethro's household, and out among his sheep, for those forty exiled years. Moses' magnificent powers of mind: his possession with him in his exile of all the learning and religion of Egypt; all Egypt's power and glory and cruelty and pollution, were before Moses as he wandered and pondered over Horeb; the past of his own people, and their future; his own wonderful youth and early manhood; that taskmaster's blood still upon his hands, and God coming nearer and nearer, and becoming clearer and clearer, more awful, but at the same time more good and more gracious every day,—forty years of that to such a man as Moses already was, that was God's way He took to make Moses the meekest man and the greatest prophet till Christ came. Nothing so occupies a man like Moses as solitude. Nothing so humbles a man like Moses as great gifts and great providences. And nothing so meekens a man like Moses as the sins of his youth; added to the corruption and the dregs of corruption that he still sees and feels in his own heart. And all that, and far more than we are told, or can ourselves divine—all that went from forty years and onwards to make Moses the meekest of men and the most prepared for his magnificent work.

There is another thing that God sometimes overrules and employs to break and humble and make more and more meek the hearts of His best servants, and that is family misunderstandings, family disputes, and family quarrels, and, especially, misunderstandings and disputes and explosions between husband and wife. And there are three most obscure and most mysterious verses in Moses' history that mean, if they mean anything at all to us, just such an explosion of ill-temper as must have left its mark till death on the heart of Moses and Zipporah. The best of wives; his help meet given him of God; the most self-effacing of women; the wife who holds her husband in her heart as the wisest and the best of men,—under sufficient trial and provocation and exasperation, even she will turn and will strike with just one word; just once in her whole married lifetime, as in that wayside inn on the way to Egypt, and as in Henrik Ibsen's latest and ripest tragedy. She does it only once; but when she does it, she does it as only the wife of a good man can do it. Till Moses lies done to death between his two best friends, who have both united to kill him that terrible day in that terrible inn. Zipporah may, or may not forget that day, and forgive it; but Moses never forgot it. And though he covers up that wayside scene as much as he may, no husband and no wife ever read that covert, and to all other readers enigmatical passage, without their hearts bleeding for Moses, and for Moses' wife, and for themselves. Moses' heart went to pieces that day between God and Zipporah, till he took his staff in his hand next morning, the solitariest, the meekest, and the most surrendered of men, and the most meet to be the best prophet of God and the best redeemer of Israel till the Man of all Sorrows came to leave Moses, and all his meekness and all his services to God and man, far behind.

It was on the occasion of the disgraceful attack of Miriam and Aaron on Moses at Hazeroth that this testimony was borne to Moses, that he was by that time the meekest man on the face of the earth. It was when Miriam and Aaron determined to pull down Moses from the supreme place that God had gifted him for and had put him into,—it was then that God set on Moses His open and His lasting seal to the greatness of Moses' office as a prophet, and the greatness of Moses' meekness as a man. 'That incident,' says Ewald, the great philosophical historian of Israel, 'furnishes a grand exemplification of the universal truth, that the best and the most capable man in a community is often the most misunderstood and the best persecuted.' And it was just this persecution that drew out the divine vindication and valuation that is here put of God upon Moses. Luther's translation of the Hebrew text is a fine stroke both of exegetical licence and of exegetical genius. Moses was very much plagued, Luther renders; he was plagued, indeed, above all the men which were upon the face of the earth. Yes; 'plagued' exactly describes the life that Moses had led ever since he was called of God to take Israel in hand: and all Moses' plagues came to a head in the matter of Miriam and Aaron and their envy and evil-speaking. But just then, or not long after then, the copestone and the full finish was put on Moses' meekness. God is fast putting His last touch to His servant's meekness and humility of heart when He shows him what a terrible temptation his great gifts and his great services are to his brother and his sister. For a man like Moses to see how his high place as God's prophet to Israel, and, especially, his sovereign superiority to all other prophets, was a constant source of sin and misery to Miriam and Aaron, his own sister and brother, plunging them into such envy and ill-will,—what a last blow to all Moses' remaining pride and ambition and self-exalting was that! And when we have eyes and a heart to take it to heart ourselves, how our very best things also are made a continual occasion to our brother of his worst things—our good his evil, our lifting up his casting down, our health his sickness, our life his death—when we lay that aright to heart, then there will be more men than Moses who will be meek above all the men that are on the face of the earth.

The perseverance of the saints, says an excellent old adage, is made up of ever new beginnings. So it is. And Moses' perseverance in meekness was exactly of that ever-beginning kind. For Holy Scripture exhibits and exposes Moses as back again at the very beginning of his meekness when he is on the very borders of the promised land. Moses, with humility and with fear let it be seen and said, was as hasty, and as hot, and as violent away on at the rock of Meribah as ever he was among the sands of Goshen. Moses struck the rock that late day with the very same stroke of angry passion with which he had killed the Egyptian in that early day. And all the rest of his days on earth, all the way from Meribah to Pisgah, Moses went mourning, praying, and importuning for his sin against meekness in his old age, as much and more than he had done from Goshen to Midian in the days of his youth. The perseverance of the saints is indeed made up of ever new beginnings. Put on therefore, as the elect of God, holy and beloved, bowels of mercies, kindness, humbleness of mind, meekness, long-suffering, forbearing one another and forgiving one another. If any man have a quarrel against any, even as Christ forgave you, so also do ye. And, again, a still meeker than Moses says to us every day, Take My yoke upon you, and learn of Me; for I am meek and lowly in heart; and ye shall find rest unto your souls.

Moses, the patriot fierce, became
 The meekest man on earth,
To show us how love's quick'ning flame
 Can give our souls new birth.

Moses, the man of meekest heart,
 Lost Canaan by self-will,
To show where grace has done its part,
 How sin defiles us still.

Thou, who hast taught me in Thy fear
 Yet seest me frail at best,
O grant me loss with Moses here,
 To gain his future rest.

XXII

MOSES THE TYPE OF CHRIST

A PROPHET OF THY BRETHREN, LIKE UNTO ME

I WISH that Moses had either told me less or had told me more about his mother. It is very tantalising to be told her remarkable name and to be told no more. Was "God-thy-glory" the remarkable name that Moses gave to his mother as often as he looked back at all that he owed to her, and as often as he rose up and called her blessed? Or was her very remarkable name her own invention? Was her striking name her own seal that she had set to her own vow which she made to her own God after some great grace and goodness of her own God? Or, again, did the angel of the Lord visit that daughter of the house of Levi on some Jabbok-like or Annunciation-night, and so name her as the sun rose upon her prayer? I call to remembrance the unfeigned faith that is in thee, wrote Paul to young Timothy, and which faith dwelt first in thy grandmother Lois, and in thy mother Eunice. And I call to remembrance also how God-her-glory dwelt in her husband's hut among the brick-fields of Egypt, and was nothing daunted, or dazzled, or seduced by all the state, and wealth, and power, and pollution of Egypt. She stayed her great heart on the God of Abraham, and Isaac, and Jacob, and Joseph, till she saw in her sleep a bush burning but not consumed, and till she, too, sang her own Magnificat. And then, one after another, she bore and suckled three such children as Miriam, and Aaron, and then the son of Pharaoh's daughter—bore and suckled all three on the same strong milk, till she weaned them from milk and put them on the marrow of lions. The oak has its roots round the rock, and men like Moses have their roots round their mother.

Neither do we know much about the mother of that Prophet like unto Moses. All that we know about the Virgin Mary might have been excellently gathered up of the angel into the remarkable name of Moses' mother. Mary said as much herself when she was with Elisabeth in the hill-country. My soul doth magnify the Lord, she said, and my spirit hath rejoiced in God my Saviour. How both those young mothers nursed their sons for God, and how they are now getting their wages from God, as they look upon their sons in their glory together, every mother among us must think continually. And no mother can think of Moses' mother, and of the mother of that Prophet like unto Moses, without asking of God, night and day, that their sons also may all in their measure be like Moses, and like that Prophet like unto Moses. And He went down, and came to Nazareth, and was subject unto them; but His mother kept all these things in her heart. And Jesus increased in wisdom and stature, and in favour with God and man. By faith Moses, when he was come to years, refused to be called the son of Pharaoh's daughter. By faith he forsook Egypt, not fearing the wrath of the king; for he endured as seeing Him who is invisible. In the old Hebrew, says Albert Bengel, the whole is ascribed to the mother.

Glancing at the Alexandrians among his accusers, Stephen, the witnessing deacon, said to them that Pharaoh's daughter took Moses up and nourished him for her son. And Moses, he added, was learned in all the wisdom of the Egyptians, and was mighty in words and in deeds. Now, the very opposite upbringing was appointed to our Lord. For his detractors never ceased to cast it up to Him that He had never learned letters like Moses: which was quite true. But the fact was, the letters of that day had nothing really to teach the child Jesus, else He would have diligently learned them. He did learn them as far as they were worthy to be called letters, and to be learned. You may be sure there were no children in all Israel at that day whose fathers and mothers taught them more diligently both when they sat in the house, and when they walked in the way, and when they lay down, and when they rose up, than Joseph and Mary taught both the letter and the spirit of Moses to Jesus and to His brothers and to His sisters. And then, as He grew up He had nature to observe and to study and to learn, and man, and, best of all, Himself. He had the carpenter's shop, and the carpenters,—an excellent school for a future preacher; and He had the sky and the sea and the mountains. The foxes in their holes, the birds in their nests, the lilies of the field outstripping Solomon in all his glory, the hen and her chickens, the mustard seed in Joseph's garden, the wheat seed in the fields around, and springtime, and summer, and harvest, and winter—that He was at school of His Father in all that, every sermon of His in after years is the abundant proof. But, best of all, He had HIMSELF. If 'Know thyself' was ever said with any fitness to any man, it was surely said with supreme fitness to the Man Christ Jesus. For He was the Mystery of Godliness Itself. He was God manifest to Himself first in the flesh. He was The Word of God. In Him were hid all the treasures of wisdom and of knowledge. Now, all our young preachers are to be as like Moses as they possibly can, and as like their Divine Master as they possibly can. They are all to be classical scholars, like Moses, if we can help it. But, above all, they are to be Christian men. Pascal went to hear a great preacher in Paris, and found a man in the pulpit. And that made all the difference to a man like Pascal. And we want to rear up true and genuine men for all our pulpits, men who shall set themselves resolutely to all learning, but who shall on that account be all the more men, and all the better men. It is not what the preacher has learned in the schools—it is not the preacher's literature—that impresses Pascal; it is the preacher himself. And what our examiners are bent upon is not conic sections, even Chaldee, in our candidates for the ministry; it is habits of work, and discipline of mind, and seriousness of purpose, and the ability, and the determination, and the perseverance to go on to old age, bringing out every Sabbath day to their people things new and old. Paracelsus denounced those doctors of medicine and those ministers of religion in his day who roasted pears all day.

Very much what the burning bush was to Moses—that His baptism at the Jordan must have been to our Lord. He that dwelt in the bush called Moses to the work of his life that eventful day on Horeb; and, so far as we can gather, our Lord received and accepted His full and final call also at the Jordan. So far as we can see, our Lord had the great seal of His Messiahship set upon His heart that day. And with that there came that unparalleled outpouring and indwelling of the Holy Ghost which made Him without measure equal to all His high call. Never did mortal man set out to such a task as that which was set to Moses at the bush. But what a far greater call was that which came to our Lord at Bethabara for our salvation! Look into your own heart and you will see there what Jesus Christ was called, and baptized, and anointed, and sworn in that day to do. You will never wonder and stand amazed and aghast at His awful task by studying it in any book—not even in the New Testament. But you will so stand, and so fall down, every day and all your days, if you only begin to study all the call and all the offices of Christ in yourself. As He so studied His call; as He saw more and more what was in the heart of man, and what came out of the heart of man, He sometimes seemed inclined to repent of and to resign His awful call, and to despair of His terrible office. And you will not wonder at that; you will expect that, when you look into yourself as He looks into you. But He went through with His call. He did not throw it up. He finished it. And He is finishing it still to-night in you and in me. And the Lord said, I have surely seen the affliction of my people which are in Egypt, and have heard their cry by reason of their taskmasters; for I know their sorrows. And the people believed; and when they heard that the Lord had visited the children of Israel, and that He had looked upon their affliction, then they bowed their heads and worshipped.

And Moses was in the mount with God forty days and forty nights; he did neither eat bread nor drink water. And it came to pass, when Moses came down from the mount, that Moses wist not that the skin of his face shone. And when Aaron and all the children of Israel saw Moses, behold the skin of his face shone, and they were afraid to come nigh him. On reading that we instinctively pass on and remember this. And He was transfigured before them. And His raiment became shining, exceeding white as snow; so as no fuller on earth can white them. There are some things there that go far down beyond our utmost depth.

At the same time, there are some things there that speak very plainly to us, and speak no parable. Did you ever happen to pass a looking-glass as you rose off your knees after an unusually long or unusually close season alone with God? Then you must have been startled and delighted to see that your plain, dull, old, haggard face was for the moment positively youthful and beautiful. Well, that was a ray or two of the identical same light that shone through Moses' skin of his face, and through our Lord's very raiment. Another thing. Moses neither ate bread nor drank water on the mount. And every meal you miss when you are in the Mount with God gives a new fineness, transparence, translucence, and fore-glow of glory to the skin of your face also. Then, again, you must often have seen two young lovers just parting, and as one of them passed you, you turned and looked after him for his face so shone out upon you. It was the light of heaven that filled his heart coming out at his face. All our lovers are so transfigured when they are still young. And it is only when they become old and cease to love that they become gross, and sodden, and stupid, and full of earth in their faces, and void of heaven. In paradise, Dante tells us, the more they love the more they shine. In heaven you will recognise and discover the great lovers of God and of man by the greater splendour and by the more exquisite beauty of their faces, and of their raiment, and even of the very street of gold they walk upon. What Moses said to Jesus on the New Testament mount about his ancient exodus from Egypt, and about the far greater exodus which should so soon be accomplished at Jerusalem—what would we not have given had Peter, James, and John but told us! But Peter was asleep as usual; and thus it is that we are left without a conversation we would have given—what would we not have given?—to have overheard.

Another thing in which Moses was a type of Christ was in the way he was envied and hated and detracted; and that, too, of his brother and sister, and of those he was serving with all his might, in season and out of season. For this is the diabolical distinction and supremacy of envy, that it boils up not in the hearts of enemies but of friends; in the secret hearts of brothers and sisters and bosom friends. The Athenians put it on Plato's tombstone—'Here lies a man much too great for envy.' Well, Moses was a much greater prophet that Plato, and yet he was not too great to Miriam and Aaron for envy. And Jesus Christ was a far greater prophet than Moses and Plato put together, and yet Pilate saw it in their evil faces, and heard it in their evil voices, that it was for envy His own had delivered Him.

Some of you will be thankful from the bottom of your heart that you read so much about such envy in the Bible. It makes you feel somewhat less lonely. But all that does not satisfy you. You sometimes wish that such envy had been far more in the Bible than it is. In your absolute agony, in your absolute madness, in your absolute despair, you will sometimes have the blasphemous wish that another Bible Character than either Aaron or Miriam or the elders of Israel—that He, with all His humiliation, and with all His agony, and with all His abandonment and darkness, had just had one of your days and nights of such envy. You feel as if you could then have had more hope in drawing near Him and of opening up your hell to His heart.

Another thing in which Moses and Christ are type and anti-type to one another is their consummate meekness under all envy and all detraction and all other ill-usage. It is a translation that is also an exposition and an illustration when Luther renders the Hebrew for meekness into the German for plagued; plagued and trampled on. For never were two servants of God so plagued, and so trampled on, and so ill-used in every way as Moses and Christ; and hence their never-equalled meekness. The divine use of envy, and detraction, and insolence, and ingratitude, like all that through which first Moses and then Christ were passed, was to give meekness her perfect work in them both. And as they were, so are we in this world. All that cruelty, and injustice, and impudence, and insolence, and unthankfulness that fill some men's and some ministers' lives so full—it is all because God has it in His plan for them to make them meek like Moses and meek like Christ. Learn of Me, our Saviour says to all such men, and ye shall have My peace of mind, and My inward rest and repose in yourselves also. Aaron and Miriam and all the people of Israel were to Moses what Jeremy Taylor calls "the instruments of his virtue." And so were all the bad men around our Lord. And so are all such men that are ordained and permitted to be round about us. May we all make as good a use of our instruments of virtue as Moses and Jesus made of theirs!

Those forty years of Moses in the land of Midian were great and fruitful years for Israel and for us. But those thirty-three years of Jesus Christ in Galilee and Jewry were far away and out of sight the greatest and the most fruitful years this world has ever seen, or ever again will see. All eternity itself—past, present, and to come—holds no such years for us as those thirty-three years of Jesus Christ. For during those thirty-three years God became man. God entered into man, and man entered into God, till God and man became for ever One. All through those supreme years the soul and the body of the Man Christ Jesus were being built up into an everlasting temple of God. All down those splendid years the soul and the body, the mind and the heart of Jesus Christ were being refined and transfigured, and made transparent and transpicuous, till he who saw and handled the Man Christ Jesus saw and handled The Very Word of Life. He in those happy days who saw and handled the Man Christ Jesus saw and handled Almighty God Himself. Hence at His baptism, His Father said: This is My Beloved Son, in whom I am well pleased. And, again, at His transfiguration—Hear ye Him. And thus it was that henceforth and as often as He opened His mouth and said, Verily, verily, I say unto you—all the ancient oracles fell dumb, Urim and Thummim themselves ceased to shine and seal, and Moses answered again and said, Send, O Lord, by the hand of Him whom Thou wilt send. As Peter, now for ever awakened out of sleep, had it in his great address—Moses said truly to the fathers, A prophet shall the Lord your God raise up unto you like unto me; Him shall ye hear in all things whatsoever He shall say unto you. For unto you first God, having raised up His Son Jesus, sent Him to bless you, in turning away every one of you from his iniquities.

And, to crown all, and to come to his nearest and his best to Christ, Moses in Israel's terrible extremity fell down before God and said, Blot me, I pray Thee, out of Thy book which Thou hast written, if Thou wilt not otherwise forgive Israel their sins. And, both for their sin and for his own sin, God took Moses at his word, and for a season and to some extent He did blot Moses out of the book which He had written. What a sad end was Moses' end, after such a great and such a noble life! And what a sad end was that of a far greater than Moses after a far greater and a far nobler life! And it was sin that did it to them both: actual sin to Moses, and imputed sin to Christ. But what is sin, do you ask? Well, sin passeth, like salvation, all understanding. Only look for yourselves at Moses shut out of Canaan, and look for yourselves at Christ shut up to Gethsemane and to Calvary, and you will see something of what sin deserves. And then stop and consider what you owe to Him who blotted Himself out of God's book for you and for all your sins. Let this cup pass from Me. But if not, then blot Me out of Thy book. Receive, O sinner, on the spot where thou sittest, receive and ever after keep fast hold of Him and of His salvation.

XXIII

PHARAOH

A NEW KING WHO KNEW NOT JOSEPH. . . .AND WHEN HE SAW THAT THERE WAS RESPITE HE HARDENED HIS HEART

WHEN King Ahasuerus could not sleep at night he used to have his chamberlains called in to read the books of the chronicles of the kingdom at his bedside. And as the reading went on King Ahasuerus would stop them and would ask them, What honour and what reward have been done to Mordecai for all this? And then when the king's ministers answered him that nothing had been done, the first orders that the king gave in the morning were that Mordecai and all his descendants should be set straightway among the men whom the king delighted to honour. Now it was just because Pharaoh the father did not have the history of Egypt read to him in that way that he and his son came to such a terrible end. Poor, misguided crown-prince, when he was still the crown-prince! His tutors and his governors had destroyed their royal charge for lack of knowledge. They had amused him, and flattered him, and let him run wild, and let him have his own way in everything, when they should have been bringing him up as David brought up Solomon, and as the wise men in the east brought up Cyrus. The only claim any man has to reign over other men is that he is wiser and better than they are. The divine right, as it used to be called, of every true king is grounded in his wisdom, and in his goodness, and in his truth, and in his justice; he is the best born, the best brought up, the best, read, the best experienced, the largest-minded and the noblest-hearted man in all the land. But the times are changed since Pharaoh's day. We are all kings, in a manner, in our day. We all have a crown on our head, and a sword and a sceptre in our hand. And, in our measure, we should all be instructed statesmen, like the royal patron of Mordecai and Esther; and it will go ill with us, and with those who come after us, if we are like Pharaoh, who had never heard of Joseph, and what Joseph had done for the land of Egypt. That will be the best election-time Scotland has ever seen, not when this or that party comes into power, but when every enfranchised man has already read about Wallace and Bruce, and about Cromwell and Milton, and about Hampden and Pym and about Knox and Melville and about Henderson and Rutherford and Chalmers. When all who have votes prepare themselves for the polling-booth in that way, then we shall see a House of Commons composed of the best and ablest men the land can produce; the most loyal, the most fair and just, the most God-fearing, and the least self-seeking of men. Then Ireland, and India, and China, and Africa, and Armenia, and Macedonia shall hold out their hands to England; and all lands shall both love and fear England and her Queen because of that knowledge and that righteousness which alone exalteth a nation, and which alone enthroneth and establisheth a sovereign.

Come on, let us deal wisely with them, said the ill-read and ignorant sovereign who sat on the throne of Egypt at the time when the children of Israel were fast becoming more and mightier than their masters. Come on, was his insane edict, let us deal wisely with them, lest they multiply and it come to pass that, when there falleth out any war, they join themselves to our enemies and fight against us. Therefore, they did set taskmasters over them to afflict them with their burdens. But the more they afflicted them the more they multiplied and grew. Till in a policy of despair this demented king charged all his people, saying, Every son of the Hebrews that is born ye shall cast into the river, and every daughter ye shall save alive. This is all that remains on the statute-book of Egypt to testify to the statesmanship of that king of Egypt who had never heard of Joseph the son of Jacob, the servant of Potiphar, and the counsellor and deliverer of the kingdom. That was the statute-book, and that was the sword and the sceptre, that this Pharaoh handed down to his son who succeeded him, and who was that new Pharaoh whom God raised up to show in him His power, and that through him His name might be declared throughout all the earth. A Pharaoh, says Philo, whose whole soul from his cradle had been filled full of the arrogance of his ancestors. And indeed, he was no sooner sat down on his throne, we no sooner begin to hear his royal voice, than he at once exhibits all the ignorance and all the arrogance of his ancestors in the answer he gives to Moses and Aaron: Who is the Lord that I should obey Him? I know not the Lord, neither will I let Israel go. Get you to your burdens. It is because you are idle that you say, Let us go and do sacrifice to the Lord. Go, therefore, for there shall no straw be given you, and yet you shall deliver your tale of bricks! The father had not known Joseph, and the son knew neither Joseph, nor Moses, nor Aaron, nor God. Moses! Moses is my slave, he shouted. Moses should be baking his tale of bricks all this time. What! Moses! of all men in the world, to come into my presence with a demand like that! Had Moses been some great ambassador who had come in a ship from some far country; had Moses and Aaron come with great gifts and in a great name to negotiate a royal league with Egypt, Pharaoh would have done them honour. A banquet would have been spread for Moses and Aaron, and the great council of the kingdom would have been called together to receive them, and to hear what they had to say. But Moses and Aaron! Why, they should have been at their tasks! Who are they, to come like ambassadors to me? No; to your bricks and to your burdens, you Moses and Aaron! And if only your minister were some great one, it would go so much better with him and with you. If he only came from some far-off city, and from some famous pulpit. If you only heard him preach once or twice in a lifetime, then you would attend to what he says; and you might, who knows, be prevailed on to do it. If your minister were only Dr. Chalmers, or Dr. Candlish, or Mr. Spurgeon. But he is nobody. And, besides, he has offended you, and has not always pleased you. And he is full of faults. And, besides, you know all about him. Moses had blood upon his hands in his youth, as Pharaoh's counsellors kept him well in mind. Yes, you stick to it like that royal spirit. It would be weak, it would be an impossible humiliation in you, to make any alteration in your heart or in your life for what your present minister says. Talk on after every sermon. Show your children after every sermon and every prayer of his how much better their father could preach and pray. Tell them about Disruption times. Laugh at their weak impressions and at their foolish praises, and tell them that they have never heard preaching to be called preaching. And if Pharaoh rises up in the day of judgment to condemn you, then stand up on the left hand and tell the Judge to His face that He never gave you and your children a chance. With such a minister, you never had fair play and a proper chance. Moses! Who, I would like to know, is Moses? Pharaoh was still shouting out that to his captains when the Red Sea rolled in and cut short his scorn.

What sign showest Thou, said the unbelieving Jews to our Lord, that we may see, and believe Thee? What doest Thou work? Let me see a miracle, said Pharaoh to Moses and Aaron, and then I will let Israel go. And to satisfy Pharaoh, and to soften his heart, Aaron cast down his rod before Pharaoh, and before his servants, and it became a serpent. But instead of saying, This is the Lord, and proclaiming an edict that the people should go free, Pharaoh called in his sorcerers and his magicians, and they did in like manner with their enchantments. And miracle succeeded miracle; miracles of judgment were wrought and miracles of mercy; but they all ended in the same way—Pharaoh's heart was only the more hardened. It looked a very innocent request. We would have said that it was a very promising and a very hopeful state of mind in Pharaoh to ask for some proof of the divine embassy of Moses and Aaron, and then he would obey. But, all the time, the evil seed of all Pharaoh's after life and death of sin lay at the heart of that innocent-looking, hopeful-sounding demand. For, innocent as it looked, and hopeful as it sounded, Pharaoh's demand put upon God, and upon Moses and Aaron, the first step of Pharaoh's repentance and obedience. If no miracle had followed his request, then Pharaoh would have felt fully justified in holding to his refusal. And, as it was, when his magicians did something sufficiently like Aaron's rod, then Pharaoh fell back and took his stand upon that, till the miracle upon which he had suspended his obedience was wrought in vain. No. Pharaoh's first step to his salvation, had he but taken it, was not to see a miracle, but to do what he knew to be right. Had Pharaoh said to his servants—Come, let us read in the book of the kingdom. Come, let us see what manner of life the people of Israel live in Goshen. What are their sorrows? What are their complaints? What are their requests? Then he would have soon after said, Yes, let them sacrifice to their God without molestation; and then let them come back again to their work. That was all that was asked of Pharaoh for the time; and, had he not been filled full from his cradle with the ignorance and arrogance of his ancestors, Moses and he would soon have come to terms, and Egypt and Israel would have been friends and allies to this day. But Pharaoh took a wrong turn and a false step when he still asked for evidence where he should have offered obedience; and that wrong turn and that false step laid him at last in the bottom of the Red Sea.

No. It is not more evidence you need. Or, if it is evidence, then it is the evidence of obedience and experience. It is not a course of Lectures on Apologetics you need. All the Bridgewater and Bampton treaties together would only mislead you and harden your heart. Neither is it a special providence, nor an extraordinary interposition on the part of Almighty God that you need. No. Be not self-deceived. For this cause, among others, God raised up Pharaoh that he might speak to you out of the Red Sea, saying Learn of me. Burn your books about miracles. If I had not bargained for miracles I would not have been here. Read books of obedience. Read books of prayer and repentance and obedience. Cease from debate and betake yourselves to be alone with God. Yes. A voice comes from the depth below, as well as from the height above, saying to us all, He among you that doeth the will of God, even he shall know of the doctrine, and shall not need to seek after a miracle. Do the will of God in the thing that lies nearest you, and in the thing that God has been so long asking of you; do it; resolve to do it; begin to do it to-night and before to-morrow; and then all past miracles in Egypt and in Israel, and all present providences and all coming experiences, will all work together to soften your heart and thus to strengthen and assure your faith. But turn away to-night from your first duty; make postponements; seek more convenient seasons; raise obstacles; make conditions; seek for signs, and put it off yourself, and put it upon God and upon His servants, to wait for you and to make terms with you, and from this night your heart will harden like Pharaoh's heart till your end is like his. Two young men are sitting in one seat, and, to look at them, you would say that they are not far from the kingdom of God. Their hearts are in the balance. They are almost persuaded. The intimation is made to them of the approaching celebration of the Lord's Supper. The time and the place are told them when their names may be entered for the Table. They both listen to the intimation. They both think about it; both in their own way. Yes, the one says, I have put it off too long. And I am no better. I think I will take what looks like God's word to me to-night. I will offer myself just as I am. And he does it. And his name is enrolled for the coming communion. He begins to-night and he goes on from to-night. The church is henceforth his church. The minister is henceforth his minister. He comes up to the church Sabbath after Sabbath now with a new interest in everything, and a stake of his own in everything. His heart softens and softens. And his faith clears up, and strengthens, and strikes root, and brings forth fruit; till, after years and years and years spent among us, he passes over into the promised land. His neighbour looks at the communion invitation also, and almost accepts it. No. I will wait, he says. I have some difficulties not yet resolved. I have not seen the unbelieving argument of that new book sufficiently answered. I must first read what is to be said on the other side. No, not to-night. No, not this communion yet. And he goes home. And, you could not detect it, it is so little, but his heart is just the smallest degree hardening to-night. He was at the sharp turning of the way, and he took, if anything, the wrong turn. He took Pharaoh's turn. May he turn again! Turn him, O Lord, before he goes on to Pharaoh's end.

The magicians led on Pharaoh so far, but a time came when their enchantments could carry them no farther. This is the finger of God, the outdone magicians had the insight and the honesty to say. This is the finger of God, and there is no use, and it would be death to us, to go on fighting with our enchantments against God's finger any further. Do, they advised Pharaoh —do what is asked of thee, and let the people go. But those magicians had done their evil work better than they knew. For, by that time, Pharaoh's heart was so hardened by their enchantments that he would not hearken to the too late advice of his old enchanters. Just so. We have seen it ourselves a thousand times. We have seen magicians who could begin a work of deception and delusion, but who could not stop the deception and undo the delusion when they fain would. We have seen philosophers putting nature in the place of God till their scholars went against both God and nature too. We have seen fathers and mothers indulging their sons, and letting them take their own way in religion and in life till they could not stop them. We have seen infidels, and scoffers, and gamblers, and drunkards, and all manner of profligates made by the score, as the magicians made Pharaoh; made, that is, little by little, till the work was finished, and till those who began it and carried it so far on were laughed at when they said, This, I fear, is the finger of God. The very sorcerers themselves at last believed, but Pharaoh still held out. They could set a bad work a-going; but, with all their advice, and with all their authority, they could not stop their evil work, nor in one iota undo it.

But stroke after stroke, plague after plague, fell upon Pharaoh till even he was brought at last to his knees. Then Pharaoh called for Moses and Aaron, and said, Entreat the Lord and I will let the people go. And Moses cried unto the Lord, and the Lord did according to the word of Moses. But when Pharaoh saw that there was to be respite, he hardened his heart and hearkened not unto them. Fatal Pharaoh! Everything that came to Pharaoh hardened his hard heart. God was fairly baffled with Pharaoh. God was completely defeated by Pharaoh. Good and evil, grace and judgment, plague and respite from plague—it was all one. Pharaoh's heart was hardened. Pharaoh was his name. What is your name? Well, when we substitute your name for Pharaoh's name in the terrible passage about the respite, we have in that passage the last chapter, the latest written-out chaper, of your evil life. Your present respite is fast running out, and up to this holy day you are still hardening your heart. You have gone on doing the things you swore to God and to man you would never do again. Because judgment against your evil work was not executed out, when it began to be executed, you have lifted up your heel to this very day in the face of God. There are men here to-night who were in that same seat on the New Year's day before last. And they have often remembered, sometimes with tears, but more often with a hard remorse as of hell, the text of that New Year's day address. The text that day was out of À Kempis, and it was this effect. That spiritual writer said to us that, if we would root out but one of our vices every new year, we should soon become perfect men. And, as I know, there were some men present here that New Year's day who were so touched and so taken with that striking counsel of À Kempis that they asked for a respite for that year. Now, that is a year and a half ago. They have had a whole half-year to the bargain, till their vice is all the deeper in their bodies and in their souls to this day. Stop to-night before you sleep. Stay up alone and set yourself to think what conceivable end God can have had in raising you up, and in filling your life so full of so many accumulated and aggravated sentences and respites of sentences? God tells us Himself for what purpose He raised up Pharaoh. And, read what God says about His purpose with Pharaoh in what light you like, and offer what explanations of it you like, still it remains a terrible story and a terrible sentence. What do you think, what do you suppose, God has raised you up for? Are you, do you think, would you believe, being sentenced and respited, sentenced and respited, and sentenced and respited again in order to show how far grace can go—your sin and God's grace? Who can tell, but that as Pharaoh stands to the end of time the proof of God's power, so you are to stand at the opposite pole as the proof of His long-suffering and super-abounding grace? Yes, that must be it in you. After so many respites, and so much sin after so many respites, if you die under respite, that must be it. Yes, this must be the key to your so often respited life—this: that, where sin abounded, grace did much more abound. And that, as sin hath reigned unto death in you, even so might grace reign through righteousness unto eternal life in you by Jesus Christ your Lord. May it be so!

XXIV

BALAAM

THE ERROR OF BALAAM

I SHALL take it for granted that you all have the Balaam chapters in the Book of Numbers by heart. You certainly ought to have those chapters by heart; for, taken together, they make up a narrative which Ewald pronounces to be unparalleled in effectiveness and unsurpassable in artistic finish. I shall assume, then, that you all have that artistic and effective narrative by heart, and I shall enter at once on some of the lessons I have been enabled to gather out of Balaam's awful history.

In the first place, then, that True Light which lighteth every man that cometh into the world kindled up in Balaam to an extraordinary brilliance and beauty. Balaam stands out in the selectest rank of those patriarchs and princes, those prophets and priests, who were raised up outside of the house of Israel in order that men might nowhere be left to live without a divine witness. To keep to the Old Testament—Melchizedek, and Jethro, and Balaam, and Job were all such divine witnesses to the profane lands in which they lived. Balaam, then, in his place, and to begin with, was a true and a greatly gifted prophet of Almighty God. Just listen to some passages out of Balaam's prayers and prophecies and exhortations, and judge for yourselves whether he was a man of divine gifts or no. 'And Balaam answered and said unto the servants of Balak, If Balak would give me his house full of silver and gold, I cannot go beyond the word of the Lord my God, to do less or more. And he took up his parable and said, Balak hath brought me out of Aram, saying, Come, curse me Jacob, and come defy Israel. But how shall I curse, who God hath not cursed? Or how shall I defy, who God hath not defied? Who can count the dust of Jacob, and the number of the fourth part of Israel? Let me die the death of the righteous, and let my last end be like his!' And, again, on the top of Pisgah, he takes up his parable in a way not unworthy of the place of Moses' grave: 'God is not a man, that He should lie; neither the son of man, that He should repent. Hath He said, and shall He not do it? Or, hath He spoken, and shall He not make it good? He hath not beheld iniquity in Jacob, neither hath He seen perverseness in Israel. Surely there is no enchantment against Jacob, neither is there any divination against Israel; according to this time it shall be said of Jacob and of Israel, What hath God wrought!' And on the top of Peor, that looketh toward Jeshimon, Balaam positively saw the day of Christ Himself afar off. 'I shall see Him, but not now; I shall behold Him, but not nigh. There shall come a star out of Jacob, and a Sceptre shall rise out of Israel, and out of Jacob shall come He that shall have the dominion.' And, to crown all. When Balak consulted Balaam, 'Wherewith shall I come unto the Lord, and bow down myself before the High God? Shall I come before Him with burnt offerings, with calves of a year old? Will the Lord be pleased,' inquired Balak, 'with thousands of rams, or with ten thousands of rivers of oil? Shall I give my first-born for my transgression, the fruit of my body for the sin of my soul?' 'He,' answered Balaam—'He hath showed thee, O man, what is good; and what doth the Lord require of thee, but to do justly, and to love mercy, and to walk humbly with thy God.' Could Moses, could Isaiah, could Paul himself have answered Balak better? No. The Great Prophet Himself never answered Balak better than that. Calvin is the prince of commentators, and Calvin has this on this passage: 'Certain it is that though Balaam was an impostor and full of deceits, yet he was endued with the gift of prophecy. This was the case, no doubt. God has often so distributed the gifts of His Spirit that He has honoured with the prophetic power even the ungodly and the unbelieving. The prophetic office was at that time a special gift, quite distinct from the grace of regeneration. Balaam, then, was a prophet.' A thing terrible to any man to think about; but terrible to a minister above all men to read, and to think, and to take home to his heart. For the gift of preaching, too, is a special and an official gift, altogether distinct from the gift of a new heart or a holy life. A man may be an impostor, as Calvin says; he may be full of deceit, and yet may be an eloquent preacher. Moses, as we have seen, could not preach at all, as our fault-finding people would have said. And even Aaron, who was Moses' mouth, never came within sight of the sacred eloquence of Balaam. In fact, I have a remorseful feeling within myself that Balaam's pulpit eloquence, and the dust that his pulpit eloquence cast in his own and other men's eyes, largely helped him to his ruin. Some eloquent preachers put all their religion into their eloquence. Some impressive preachers put all their tears into their pulpit voice, and all their repentance and reformation into those powerful appeals they periodically make to their own and to other flocks. That burning passage in the Book of Numbers should be appointed to all divinity students to make an exegesis and a homily upon it before they receive licence. They should have to bring out and exhibit from Balaam, and from other instances in church history, how fine natural gifts, and great learning, and great eloquence in the pulpit may all lie like so much far-shining whitening on the surface of a sepulchre. One of their points should be that official excellence often consists in a preacher with much secret corruption, and that a minister may have a great name, and may make a great income, who has no name at all, and no reward at all with God. Many will say to Me in that day, Lord, have we not prophesied in Thy name, and in Thy name have cast out devils, and in Thy name have done many wonderful works? And then will I profess unto them, I never knew you. What we ministers are in our closets, says John Owen, and not in our pulpits, just that we are in the scales of God: just that, and no more. Let us, then, who are ministers, or who are looking to be ministers, so live, lest, by any means, when we have preached to others, we ourselves should be cast away as reprobate Balaam was cast away.

Balaam's importunity in prayer: Balaam on his knees all night to know God's will, when he knew it all the time—a great deal of our own anxiety, and perplexity, and prayer, and importunity in prayer is made up out of the same self-deceit. 'I am afraid I cannot go; but tarry over the night till I see.' And Balaam actually went all night to God again about going to Balak. He was up a great while before day about going to Balak. Had God been a man, as Balaam in a fine sermon warned Balak He was not, then we would have said that Balaam was imposing upon God, and was laughing at Him behind His back. Had Balaam been a sincere and an honest man, he would have refused so much as to see Balak's second deputation of princes. He would have said to his servants that he was engaged and could not come down. He would have said to his servants to see that the princes of Moab and their companions and their camels had proper supper and lodging, as became a king's embassy; but that Balak had his last answer from him already. Had Balaam not been given over to making a great name for himself and a great fortune; had this prophet been working out his own salvation with fear and trembling, instead of making beautiful pictures of salvation, and astonishing people with his eloquence on salvation, then Balaam would have put on strength when he saw that long string of camels on their way to his house. Now is my time! Balaam would have said to himself—Now is my accepted time!

Now is the day of my salvation! A thorough honest man, as Butler says in his celebrated sermon on Balaam—a thorough honest man who would have known how set upon the praises of men and the wages of unrighteousness his own heart was, and had all along been; and he would have acted that day accordingly. But Balaam, with all his talents and with all his opportunities, was a thorough dishonest man.

With all his fine sermons Balaam has his price, said Balak to himself when his first princes came back without Balaam. And Balak sent again princes, more, and more honourable than they. And with a profanity and an impudence that might well have made Balaam blush and become a new man, Balak said to Balaam, Let nothing, I pray thee, hinder thee from coming to me. Neither thy God nor anything else. For I will promote thee to very great honour, and I will do for thee whatsoever thou askest of me. Come, therefore, I pray thee, curse me this people. The salmon is the king of fish; but, all the time, he is ridiculously taken. Ridiculously. Two or three inches of a sufficiently red rag drawn over a sufficiently sharp hook, and, with half an hour of a sufficiently strong and supple wrist, the fool is in your basket. In that self-same bare-faced, and rag-hooked way did Balak angle for Balaam, ay, and took him too. And in that self-same, bare-faced, and rag-hooked way are men and women being angled for and taken every day. A ribbon, a tassel, a shoulder-knot, a rosette, a garter, a feather, two or three empty letters before or after an equally empty name, and the fish is yours.

Yes, surely; go, if you would so much like to go, God said to Balaam as the day broke. At any rate, you may go so far. And you would have Me go against you, if you go all the way, take care what you say and do when you go. Beholding Balaam's insincerity, and being angry at it, says Philo, God said, By all means go. And Balaam's God is our God. And thus it is that as often as Balaam's insincerity, hesitation, sleepless anxiety about duty, prayer, and importunity in prayer are seen in us, He who gave way to Balaam gives way to us also, and says, Yes, surely. Our Maker does not place us under lock and key. He does not tie up our hands. He does not strike us lame or blind to make us obedient. He made us in His own image. He endowed us with free will. He did not intend us to be so many stocks and stones in His hands. Yes, certainly, He says; choose for yourself. What would you like best? Where is your treasure? Well, you are your own master. You are in this matter entirely in your own hands. There it stands in Holy Writ for all who are in hesitation,—If the men come to call thee, rise up, and go with them.

But the angel of the Lord stood in a path in the vineyard, a wall being on this side and a wall on that side. And when the ass saw the angel of the Lord she thrust herself into the wall, and crushed Balaam's foot against the wall. The dumb ass was doing her best to arrest and to save her eloquent master. And, had he not preached himself long past all hope of salvation, he would have divined the accident and interpreted the providence. Had he not been bereft of all sense and honesty, he would have turned his ass's head in that narrow lane, and would have carried his crushed foot home to rest it and to heal it, and to begin a new life after it. And ever after he would have caparisoned that ass with gold and silver, and would all but have made her his household god. And she would have deserved it all; for she did all she could do to save her devoted master, who had ridden her without a single swerve or stumble of hers to that day. But Balaam was too far gone for a bruised foot to bring him back. And, besides, the prevaricating angel practised upon the prophet, and perplexed the prophet's intellect and judgment, till he did not know what to do. We would never have taken that angel for an angel of the Lord had he not been so named of the sacred writer. For it is surely not usual with such angels at once to oppose a man and to push him on. I pity Balaam—what with his ass; what with that angel of the Lord; what with his crushed foot; and then with all his other bones out of joint, since his ass fell down under him. If it displease thee, said the so pious and so perplexed prophet to the two-faced angel—if it displease thee for me to go on, then I will turn and get me back again. By no means, said the angel. By no means. Having come so far, you are not to lose all your travel and go back. No; go with the men. They are waiting till you mount. Come, and I will help you to your seat. And Balaam mounted his ass with the help of the angel and came to Balak. Have any of you a crushed foot to-night? I have. I can scarcely stand before you to finish for pain and for loss of blood. And, as the Lord liveth, all His angels, with all their irony and all their evil help, shall not sophisticate me out of my soul to-night. I, for one, am to turn to-night in the path between the vineyards. I shall not ask any angel, from heaven or from hell, whether it displeases him or no. I am determined to turn to-night. I have gone far too far already. I bless God for my crushed foot. Indeed I do. I know what I am saying, if you do not know. But, if you do, then come with me. Come, let us return to the Lord our God; for He hath torn, but He will heal us; He hath smitten, but He will bind us up. Only, Balaam went with the princes of Balak.

And then, look and learn how Balak, once he had got a hold of Balaam, cadged the prophet about from one hill-top to another to get the proper place from which to curse Israel. The first point of view to which Balak took Balaam was to one of the high places of Baal. But, when Balaam saw Israel shining in her tents below, his curses all stuck in his throat. He could not do it. Come, then, said Balak, to a better place. I will take thee this time to a hill where thou shalt not see all their tents, and thou shalt curse them from thence. And Balak, not knowing what he was doing, brought Balaam to the top of Pisgah, till Moses' mantle fell on Balaam, and till Balaam was carried on in the Spirit to prophesy good things, and better things than ever, concerning Israel. Let us try the top of Peor this time, suggested Balak in his discomfiture. Build me then three three altars there, said Balaam, and I will see what I can do. But, no. The sight of Israel lying below made the spirit of blessing to come upon Balaam again, till Balak smote his hands together, and in his anger dismissed Balaam to his home without his wages, since he had not done his work. Yes, truly, this narrative is unparalleled in its effectiveness. For, with what sure effect it discovers Balaam's seed to this day. Do you know Balaam's seed when you see them, or when you are yourself one of them? That is one of Balaam's seed in the ministry, that preacher who does his best to tune his pulpit to please the king. He cannot do it; but, as Davison says of Balaam, the will is not wanting. Do you remember how James Stuart dragged Robert Bruce about, seeking a place and a point of view from which that great preacher and great patriot might be got to preach and to pray to the king's dictation? If our young ministers would have a life-long lesson and illustration in fearlessness, in fidelity, and in a good conscience to the end of a life of bribes on the one hand, and of persecution and banishment on the other, let them read themselves deeply into those two narratives so unsurpassable in effectiveness for a minister, the Life of Balaam in the history of Israel, and the Life of Bruce in the history of Scotland and of England. That church member also who changes his minister in the interests of his business, he is of the offspring of Balaam. And that other who changes his minister for the peace of his conscience, he also is Balak and Balaam seeking a spot where they can get at their sin without that restraint. You can live a life of uttermost selfishness, and worldliness, and wicked tempers, and idleness, and vanity, and vice, and total and absolute neglect of prayer in one church, and under one minister, that you could not long live under another. We cannot shut our eyes to men and women choosing their hill-tops and building and kindling their altars all around us every day, exactly as Balak and Balaam chose their hill-tops and built and kindled their altars in their day. And some of you may be strongly tempted sometimes to try a change of church or a change of minister for liberty of action and for peace of mind. But you cannot do it. Like Balaam, you know too much, and you have seen too many of the tents of Israel. You may try to shut your eyes, and you may let Balak lead you about promising you your wages, but you shall never see the place where you can give your whole heart to evil, or where you can sin on without an inward rebuke.

But, Balaam,—ass, and angel, and crushed foot, and Almighty God Himself notwithstanding, he would have the wages of unrighteousness. He would have Balak's gold. After his foot was whole again,—Balaam was a very clever man,—and he somehow got expectation and hope kindled again in Balak that Balaam might have changed his mind by this time. And, after some underground management, they met once again, Balak and Balaam, in the dark. You who know your Milton have there the identical advice that Balaam gave to Balak. It was the very same advice, to the letter, that Belial, the dissolutest spirit that fell, gave to the old serpent. Set women in their eye, counselled the old reprobate. And so for his so late but so successful counsel Balaam got his house filled with Balak's silver and gold when Israel sinned and fell in the wilderness.

Let me die the death of the righteous! That was Balaam's noble peroration on the high place of Baal. But as we pass on from the Book of Numbers, with its unparalleled effectiveness, to the end of the history in the Book of Joshua, we find in that book this: Balaam also, the son of Beor, the soothsayer, did the children of Israel slay with the sword among them that were slain by them. And then, the apostle Jude, in denouncing certain evil men who had crept into the ministry and into the membership of the church of his day, says, Woe unto them! For they have run greedily after the error of Balaam. They are spots in your feasts of charity, feeding themselves without fear; clouds they are without water; trees without fruit; wandering stars, to whom is reserved the blackness of darkness for ever. Such are some of the lessons of Balaam's lost life.

XXV

JOSHUA

JOSHUA, THE SON OF NUN, MOSES' SERVANT

WHERE were Gershom and Eliezer all this time? Were they both dead? Or, if living, had they no heart for their father's God till it had been better for them and for their father that they had had never been born? Can it be possible that even Moses had come so far short as this, in the supreme duty and fast-passing opportunity of bringing up his own sons? Had her husband been so cumbered with the exodus, and with the law, and with all the cares and labours of the leadership in Israel, that he had no leisure so much as to eat his meals beside Zipporah and her two sons? Had Moses been far too long in accepting a staff of elders to assist him in ruling and judging Israel? And were Gershom and Eliezer grown up and gone clean out of hand before their father had awakened up to that and was aware of it? But, when all is said, it is far less the father than the mother in this matter. Had Moses' house, then, been so divided against itself that it fell upon his two sons? And had Miriam and Aaron been right after all in their hot opposition to their brother's marriage with the Ethiopian woman? We ask these questions at the text, but we get no answer. We are left to look for the answers to all these questions in our own house, among our sons and daughters, and in our own heart and conscience. At the same time, though Moses had wholly lost hold of his own sons, there is this to be said for the father of Gershom and Eliezer: that he had an immense attraction for some other men's sons. There was nothing more remarkable about Moses than the openness of his heart and the freshness of his mind to double the age of ordinary men; as Isaac Walton says, God had blessed Moses with perfect intellectuals and a cheerful heart to old age; and the young men who were always about him had had a great deal to do with that. You will sometimes see stranger young men crowding around a minister in his classes and in his congregational work, and saving their own souls by so doing, while those young men that have been born in the family are never so much as seen or heard of. And that was always the case with Moses. There was quite a circle of young men continually around Moses, and

Joshua, the son of Nun, was the choicest and the most capable of them all. We know nothing as yet about Joshua—nothing but this, that he was not the son of Moses and Zipporah, but of a certain unknown man named Nun, of the tribe of Ephraim. Joshua had no such start in life as Gershom and Eliezer had, but by his high character and his great services he not only took their crowns from them, but at the same time he won a crown and a sceptre and a great name in Israel all his own.

It is stated again and again in the sacred history that Joshua stood before Moses and was his minister. Stood ready, that is, to run the great man's errands, and to set out with him on his hallowed expeditions, and, in short, to be more than a son to Moses in the absence of his own sons. 'He departed not out of the tabernacle' is another very remarkable testimony for that time concerning the son of Nun. Now, in that Joshua was exactly like his Great Namesake in the New Testament whose wont it was to go up to the synagogue of Nazareth every Sabbath day, and who said to His father and mother when they sought Him all through Jerusalem sorrowing: 'How is it that ye seek Me? Wist ye not that I must be about My Father's business?' Joseph and Mary had sought the child Jesus in all those places where other sorrowing fathers and mothers were seeking their lost sons also,—among the theatres, and the circuses, and the shows, and the races, and the wrestling arenas, and the inns, and shops, and streets of Jerusalem; but He departed not out of the temple. We, too, have boys sometimes among ourselves not unlike that. They love and choose and are always to be found among good things, in good places, and reading good books while yet they are still mere children. They take to the Sabbath-school, and to the church, and to the Bible-class, and to the missionary meeting as other boys take, and no blame to them, to cricket, and football, and fishing, and shooting. Wordsworth has two such boys:

> Never did worthier lads break English bread:
> The finest Sunday that the autumn saw,
> With all its mealy cluster of ripe nuts,
> Could never keep those boys away from church,
> Or tempt them to one hour of Sabbath breach,
> Leonard and James!

And as such boys rise to be young men they are already promising pillars in the house of their fathers' God. They are our Sabbath-school teachers, our elders and our deacons, our best preachers and pastors, and the heads of our seminaries and colleges. And Joshua, the son of Nun, was the first figure and far-off forerunner of all such young men as he stood before

Moses, and was his minister, and went up with him to the mount, and never departed out of the tabernacle.

There is no finer grace to be found in any young man's heart than his admiration and reverence for great and good men. We really are already what we love and admire and honour. And when a young man has eyes to see and a heart to love and honour those good and gifted men he reads and hears about; or, still better, those who live near him, nothing could be a sounder sign or a surer promise of his own future character than that.

> We live by admiration, hope, and love;
> And even as these are well and wisely fixed,
> In dignity of being we ascend.

The mother of Gershom and Eliezer, from the very little that we see of her, would seem to have been a froward, forward woman, and a rude and disrespectful wife; and a worse upbringing than that what child could ever have? But Joshua's nameless mother—judging her from her son, she must have been a true mother in Israel. And she had already her full wages paid her when she saw her son Joshua standing of his own accord before Moses and serving him as his minister. And if she lived to see him at the head of the tribes of Israel, and leading them on from victory to victory, she would feel herself to have been far more than overpaid for all the watchfulness, and all the care, and all the nights of prayer she had laid out on her noble boy. And thus it came about that through her, and through some other nameless mothers like her, what Moses missed so much at home he found so thankfully as often as he went abroad, when Joshua and his companions gathered round Moses to drink in his counsels and to execute his commands. But it was Joshua alone in all the camp who was all to Moses that John was to Jesus. Moses loved and trusted Joshua, and Joshua lay at Moses' feet. At the same time, the defect of Joshua's finest quality, as we are wont to call it, came out on an occasion, and was warmly and nobly rebuked by Moses, as we read in a very beautiful passage in the Book of Numbers. There was a day of Pentecost in Israel as Moses grew old, when the Spirit of the Lord fell on seventy of the elders of Israel in order to fit them to be Moses' assessors and assistants in ruling and in teaching the refractory people. And, as God would have it, over and above the selected seventy, there were two exceptional men on whom the Spirit fell also, till Joshua grudged and fretted at the way the people's eyes were drawn off his master and turned to Eldad and Medad as they prophesied in the camp. 'Forbid them, my lord!' said

Joshua, in his jealousy for Moses. To which speech of Joshua Moses made the golden answer: "Enviest thou for my sake? Would God that all the Lord's people were prophets, and that the Lord would put His Spirit upon them!" See John iii. 26, the margin steps in and says. And when we turn to John's gospel we find this fine parallel passage: 'A man can receive nothing,' said the Baptist, 'except it be given from heaven. Ye yourselves bear me witness that I said, I am not the Christ. The Christ must increase, but I must decrease.' It is beautiful to see Moses' best disciple so jealous of other gifted men, and all out of pure honour and love to his great master; and it is beautiful to see the same mistaken loyalty in John's disciples. But both Moses and John shine splendidly to all time in their rebukes to their disciples, and show themselves to be the true masters of such deserving disciples in their never-to-be-forgotten answers and lessons and reproofs. Moses, and John, and Paedaritus of Sparta, Moses' contemporary, who, when he was passed over and left out in the election of the Three Hundred, went home to his house beaming with happiness, it did him so much good to see that there were so many men in Sparta who were better men than himself.

For years and years, and all the time wholly unknown to anybody but himself, Moses had been schooling his own heart till the case of Eldad and Medad only called out into words what had for long been in his thoughts. Joshua had but put in rude and angry words the bitter jealousy that Moses had for years and years been battling with in secret. And Moses' magnificent answer to Joshua was but another proof of the incomparable meekness and sweetness of Moses' so subdued heart. And then, when long afterwards we find Moses suing for a successor who should take up his work and finish it, he does it in a way that proclaims Moses to have been a man after God's own heart long before David was born. 'Let the Lord, the God of the spirits of all flesh, set a man over the congregation, which may go out before them, and which may lead them out, and which may bring them in; that the congregation of the Lord be not as sheep which have no shepherd.' Noble soul! Great servant and great saint of God! Though his eye was not dim, nor his natural strength abated, yet because it was made clear to him that it was the will of God, and that the time had now come when he was to stand aside and give up his place to another man, he put off his harness and his honour without one murmur. The cross would, no doubt, have been somewhat less sharp had Gershom or Eliezer stood ready to take up the laid-down leadership, and it may well have been the last pang of that painful time to Moses that he had no son of his own to take his place, to finish his work and to transmit his name. Aaron, the high priest, under a like bereavement, held his peace. And so did his desolate brother, the great law-giver and leader of Israel. And the Lord said unto Moses, Take thee Joshua, the son of Nun, a man in whom is the Spirit, and lay thine hand upon him. And thou shalt put some of thine honour upon him, that all the congregation of Israel may be obedient. And Moses did as the Lord commanded him. 'A man in whom is the Spirit,' said the Lord, who gave to Joshua that great gift. The Spirit of the Lord had begun in Joshua from a child, from his mother's milk, indeed; and to him that hath shall be given, till by the time that Moses died we are reassured and rewarded as we read that Joshua, the son of Nun, was full of the spirit of wisdom, and the children of Israel hearkened unto him, and did as the Lord commanded Moses.

It is a great epoch to a nation and to a church, as well as a great testing time to all concerned, when an old leader has to put off his harness, and when a new and an untried man is summoned up to put on his harness for all the toils and crosses that await him. I was present once at such an impressive moment, and I often remember it. An old servant of God who had been a very Moses to multitudes in our land was about to die when he sent for the man who had been a very Joshua, a son and a servant to him, and from his death-bed addressed him in words of love and trust and prophetic assurance that must often come back to his heart, as they often come back to mine. And then the old leader put his arms round his successor's neck and kissed him, and lay down and died. Men like Moses and Joshua, and all who serve God and man, pass through extreme and painful experiences. The time had been when Caleb and Joshua stood absolutely alone with their life in their hand as all Israel bade stone them with stones. But never, all his days, was Joshua more or better the servant of God, and the best and the most far-seeing friend of the people of Israel, than he was just at that solitary, slanderous, murderous moment.

Just when Joshua was in the act of putting on his armour to attempt his first battle, he looked up, and, behold! a man stood over-against him with his sword drawn in his hand. 'Art thou for us?' demanded Joshua of the armed man; 'or art thou for our adversaries?' 'Nay,' answered the mysterious soldier, 'but as Captain of the Lords' host am I come.' And Joshua fell on his face, and said, 'What saith my Lord unto His servant?' And on the seventh day Jericho fell into Joshua's hands without sword or spear of Joshua.

Fell flat every stone wall of it before a blast of rams' horns only blown over Jericho in the name of the Lord. And Joshua from that day learned how to enter on the wars of the Lord in a way he never forgot. David, also, while yet a ruddy youth, had read the Book of Joshua in the intervals of feeding his father's flock. For we hear him as he puts off Saul's helmet of brass and coat of mail and takes five smooth stones out of the brook. Turning to Goliath, David said, 'Thou comest to me with a sword, and with a spear, and with a shield, but I come to thee in the name of the Lord of hosts. For to-day all this assembly shall know that the Lord saveth not with sword and spear, for the battle is the Lord's, and He will give you into our hands.' And all down sacred history, through Israel, and not less through England and Scotland, there have never failed prophets to preach how to war a good warfare, nor has the Lord's hosts lacked leaders like Joshua, who fell at that Divine Captain's feet and worshipped. Theodor Keim, in his volume of genius on our Lord's early life on earth, says that in His choice of a trade, which He was bound to choose, though He chose to be a carpenter, Jesus of Nazareth might have chosen anything else, anything but to be a soldier. But, surely, He was a soldier before Jericho, when He said to Joshua that He had come to him as Captain of the Lord's host. And we see Him in the thick and at the head of many a bloody battle all down the ages, till at last we are let see Him clothed with a vesture dipped in blood, and on His vesture and on His thigh a name written, King of kings, and Lord of lords. But we are not all soldiers, and we civilians have this same Divine Man as our forerunner and example as well as soldiers. For, in the manifold wisdom and abounding grace of God, the Son of God appears to each one of us as we enter life, and summons us to put the shoes off our feet as we stand on that holy ground. To the young soldier He appears in vision as a captain, to the young preacher He appears as a preacher, to the young pastor He is the chief shepherd, to the young merchant He is an example of successful buying and selling, to a master He appears as a master, and to a servant as a servant; sometimes He is a lover, sometimes He is a husband, sometimes a son, and sometimes a brother, and so on, till He never leaves any man at his entrance on life without a divine vision, and an ideal example, and a sacred summons to take his shoes off his feet. And all young men who, like Joshua, make their start on this holy ground,—they shall surely finish their course and keep the faith till the Captain of their salvation shall not be ashamed to call them His brethren. Loose thy shoes from off thy feet. And Joshua did so.

With all his clearness of head and with all his honesty of heart, Joshua made one great mistake in the opening of his military and diplomatic life. That great mistake arose out of his youth and inexperience, and he is not much to be blamed—by us, at any rate—for making that mistake. All the same, that mistake, once made, was disastrous and irretrievable. The Gibeonites were terrified to death at the approach of Joshua and his army. And they made as if they were come to him from a far country, a country that he would never have commission or interest to conquer, but with whose people it would be to his advantage in many ways to be good friends and in a league of peace. And their old shoes, and old bottles, and old bread, and their wily speeches, and other fine fetches completely circumvented Joshua, till he made a covenant of peace with a cruel, corrupt, and accursed people that he had been armed and ordained and commanded to sweep off the face of the earth. And for this, and for other like mistakes of ignorance, and simplicity, and overleniency, both Joshua and all Israel suffered long and bitterly. The mystical interpretation here tells us that pride was the sin of the Amorite, and envy the sin of the Hittite, and wrath of the Perizzite, and gluttony and lechery of the Girgashite and the Hivite, while covetousness and sloth were the corruptions of the Canaanite and the Jebusite. And then that same method of interpretation passes on to this, that many young men when they first enter on their inexperience of sanctification are cheated into sparing some of their pride under this disguise, and some of their envy under that. Gluttony and lust also come to them each under its own cloak of deceit, and covetousness and sloth also each under its own mask, till all their days many men are tempted and led into this and that besetting sin through early ignorance and simplicity and self-will. Still, just as Joshua put the Gibeonites to hew wood and draw water for the altar of the Lord when he could not root them out, so we may turn the remnants of our pride, and envy, and ill-will, and gluttony, and sloth to this same good use. These things will try us and will prove us, as the Scripture says, to see what is in our hearts, and whether we will serve God in spite of them or not. It was the thorn that was in the apostle's flesh that brought down this word to him: 'My grace is sufficient for thee, and My strength is made perfect in weakness.' And the children of the Gibeonites, while thorns in their eyes and scourges in their sides, and snares and traps to them, were at the same time hewers of wood and drawers of water for the congregation, and for the altar of the Lord to this day, in the place which the Lord shall choose.

Joshua never ceased all his life long to mourn over the great mistake he had made at Gilgal. He could not shut his eyes a single day to the disastrous results of that great mistake to himself and to all Israel. And when he was on his death-bed it all came back to him, till he summoned the heads of Israel around him to hear his dying apology and protest; 'Choose you out this day among all the gods of the Gibeonites and the other Canaanites the god that you and your children will serve; but know this, that as for me and my house we will serve THE LORD.' You all know, I suppose, what that meant on Joshua's dying lips that day. Joshua had never forgotten that day of days in the great days of his youth, when Moses took his young servant up with him to the top of the mount, ay, and even into the cleft rock itself.

From that awful day never a day, never a night, never an hour of a day or night, had passed over Joshua that he had not heard the Lord passing by and proclaiming, THE LORD, the LORD God, merciful and gracious, long-suffering, and abundant in goodness and truth, keeping mercy for thousands, forgiving iniquity, and transgression, and sin. Ever since that day on the mount and in the cleft rock the LORD, and no heathen god of them all, had been Joshua's God. Happy man who had such a revelation made to him in the days of his youth! Happy man, who could call all Israel to come and see that he was leaving a house behind him of the same experience, of the same fixed mind, and of the same assured and inherited happiness. Young men, still choosing a God for yourselves and for your household,—Joshua speaks to you out of his noble life, so nobly begun and now so nobly ended. Choose and say. Are you yourselves to be, and are you to bring up your children after you to be, Amorites, and Hittites, and Hivites, and Canaanites and Jebusites in the land? Are you to let ambition, and envy, and pride, and anger, and self-will rule in your hearts and be your household gods? No! Never, never! Not so long as you have still this day in your choice for yourselves and for your households the LORD, the LORD God, merciful and gracious, and abundant in goodness and truth. And Moses and Joshua made haste in the cleft rock, and they bowed their heads to the earth, and they said, If now we have found grace in Thy sight, pardon our iniquity and our sin, and take us for Thine inheritance. And from that day it was so.

XXVI

ACHAN

ACHAN OF THE TRIBE OF JUDAH WAS TAKEN

JERICHO was one of the largest and richest cities in all ancient Canaan. But for the terrible ban pronounced by Joshua, Jericho might have taken the place of Jerusalem itself as the chief city of ancient Israel. Jericho was an excellently situated and a strongly fenced city. Broad and lofty walls ran all round the city, and the only way in and out of the city was by great gates which were scrupulously shut every night at sundown. There were great foundries of brass and iron in Jericho, with workshops also in silver and in gold. The looms of Babylonia were already famous over all the eastern world, and their rich and beautiful textures went far and near, and were warmly welcomed wherever the commercial caravans of that day carried them. Balak's gold had long before now brought Balaam the soothsayer across the plains of Mesopotamia, and the gold and silver of Jericho had also drawn toward that city the travelling dealers in the woven work of the Babylonian looms. A goodly Babylonish garment plays a prominent part in the tragical history that now opens before us.

The rich and licentious city of Jericho was doomed of God to swift overthrow and absolute extermination, but no part of the spoil, neither thread nor shoe-latchet, was to be so much as touched by Joshua or any of his armed men. Nothing demoralises an army like sacking a fallen city. To spring like a tiger at a wall that reaches up to heaven, and then to extinguish all a tiger's thirst for blood and plunder, that is high ideal of a true soldier's duty. And it is a splendid certificate to Joshua's discipline, and to the morality of his army, that only one of his men gave way in the time of temptation. And the swift and heavy fall of Joshua's hand on that one man must have still more consolidated Joshua's authority, and transformed his wilderness hosts into true soldiers, where other soldiers would have been thieves and robbers. The army of Israel crossed the Jordan, entered the devoted land, besieged its cities, and marched from victory to victory under the banners of their respective tribes; very much as a modern army is made up of companies of men compacted together under the colours and the denominations of their respective clans and nationalities. Each of the twelve tribes of Israel had its own regiment, as we would say, marching and camping and entering battle under its own ensign; and thus it was that when the armies of Israel marched round Jericho on the way to their miraculous conquest of that city the standard of the tribe of Judah led the sacred host. Every single soldier in all Israel had heard Joshua's proclamation about Jericho; both what his men were to do till the walls fell, and how they were to demean themselves after the city had been given of God into their hands. But war is war; and the best of commanders cannot make war a silken work, nor can he hold down the devil in the hearts of all his men. In the hearts of many of them he may, if he first does that in his own heart; but scarcely in the hearts of them all. Night fell on the prostrate city, and the hour of temptation struck for Joshua and all his men. Blessed is the man that endureth temptation; for when he is tried he shall receive the crown of life. And Joshua and all his men received the crown of life that night,—all his men but one. Who is that stealing about among the smoking ruins? Is that some soldier of Jericho who has saved himself from the devouring sword? When the night wind wakens the embers again these are the accoutrements and the movements of one of Joshua's men. Has he lost his way? Has he been half dead, and has he not heard the rally of the trumpet? He hides, he listens, he looks through the darkness, he disappears into the darkness. No one has slept for joy in all the camp of Israel that night. And no one has slept for sorrow in one of Judah's tents that night. For, what is the fall of Jericho to them in that tent when it has cost them the life of their husband, their father, and their master? When the door of that tent is suddenly lifted, and the face of a corpse comes in, takes a spade, and buries a strange burden in the earth in the midst of the astounded tent. God giveth His beloved sleep. But—

> Methought I heard a voice cry, Sleep no more!
> Macbeth doth murder sleep, the innocent sleep!
> And still it cried, Macbeth doth murder sleep!

So the Lord was with Joshua; and his fame was noised throughout the whole country. But the men of Israel fled before the men of Ai, wherefore the hearts of the people melted and became as water. And the Lord said to Joshua, Get thee up; wherefore liest thou upon thy face? Up, sanctify the people, for there is an accursed thing in the midst of them. And Joshua rose up early in the morning, and brought Israel by their tribes, and the tribe of Judah was taken; and he brought the family of Judah, and he took the family of Zarhites; and he brought the family of the Zarhites, man by man, and Zabdi was taken; and he brought his household, man by man, and Achan of the tribe of Judah was taken. My son, said Joshua, give, I pray thee, glory to the Lord God of Israel, and make confession to Him; and tell me what thou hast done; hide it not from me. And Achan answered Joshua, and said, Indeed, I have sinned against the LORD God of Israel, and thus and thus have I done: When I saw among the spoil a goodly Babylonish garment, and two hundred shekels of silver, and a wedge of gold of fifty shekels weight, then I coveted them, and took them; and, behold, they are hid in the earth in the midst of my tent, and the silver under it. And all Israel raised over him a great heap of stones to this day. So the Lord turned from the fierceness of His anger. Wherefore the name of that place was called The Valley of Achor unto this day.

Everybody who reads the best books will have long had by heart Thomas à Kempis's famous description of the successive steps of a successful temptation. There is first the bare thought of the sin. Then, upon that, there is a picture of the sin formed and hung up on the secret screen of the imagination. A strange sweetness from that picture is then let down drop by drop into the heart; and then that secret sweetness soon secures the consent of the whole soul, and the thing is done. That is true, and it is powerful enough. But Achan's confession to Joshua is much simpler, and much closer to the truth. 'I saw the goodly Babylonish garment, I coveted it, I took it, and I hid it in my tent.' Had Joshua happened to post the ensign of Judah opposite the poor men's part of the city, this sad story would never have been told. But even as it was, had Achan only happened to stand a little to the one side, or a little to the other side of where he did stand, in that case he would not have seen that beautiful piece, and not seeing it he would not have coveted it, and would have gone home to his tent that night a good soldier and an honest man. But when once Achan's eyes lighted on that rich garment he never could get his eyes off it again. As Ã Kempis says, the seductive thing got into Achan's imagination, and the devil's work was done. Achan was in a fever now lest he should lose that goodly garment. He was terrified lest any of his companions should have seen that glittering piece. He was sure some of them had seen it and were making off with it. He stood in between it and the searchers. He turned their attention to something else. And then when their backs were about he wrapped it up in a hurry, and the gold and the silver inside of it, and thrust it down into a hiding-place. His eyes were Achan's fatal snare. It was his eyes that stoned Achan and burned him and his household to dust and ashes in the Valley of Achor. Had God seen it to be good to make men and women in some way without eyes, the fall itself would have been escaped. It was at Adam and Eve's eyes that the devil came into man's heart at first. In his despair to get the devil out of his heart Job swore a solemn oath and made a holy covenant with his eyes. But our Saviour, as He always does, goes far deeper than Job. He knows quite well that no oath that Job ever swore, and no covenant that Job ever sealed, will hold any man's eyes from sin; and therefore He demands of all His disciples that their eyes shall be plucked out. He pulls down His own best handiwork at its finest part so that He may get the devil's handiwork destroyed and rooted out of it; and then He will let us have all our eyes back again when and where we are fit to be trusted with eyes. It is better to go to heaven like a blind man led by a dog, says our Lord; ten times better than to dance all your days down to hell with Babylonian bangles on and all ornaments. Miss Rossetti is writing to young ladies, it is true; but what she says to them it will do us all good to hear. 'True,' says that fine writer, 'all our lives long we shall be bound to refrain our soul, and to keep it low; but what then? For the books we now forbear to read, we shall one day be endued with wisdom and knowledge. For the music we will not listen to we shall join in the song of the redeemed. For the pictures from which we turn we shall gaze unabashed on the Beatific Vision. For the companionships we shun, we shall be welcomed into angelic society and the communion of triumphant saints. For all the amusements we avoid, we shall keep the supreme jubilee.' Yes, it is as certain as God's truth and righteousness are certain, that the mortified man who goes about with his eyes out; the man who steals along the street seeing neither smiles nor frown; he who keeps his eyes down wherever men and women congregate,—in the church, in the market-place, at a railway-station, on a ship's deck, at an inn table,—where you will; that man escapes multitudes of temptations that more open and more full-eyed men and women continually fall before. You huff and toss your head at that. But these things are not spoken for you, but for those who have sold and cut off both eye and ear and hand and foot and life itself, if all that will only carry them one single step nearer to their salvation.

So Joshua rose early in the morning,—Joshua, like every good soldier, was an early riser,—and he brought all Israel by their tribes, and their families, and their households, that the Lord Himself might make inquisition, and might put His finger upon the marked man. Look at the camp of Israel that awful morning! It is the day of judgment, and the great white throne is set in the Valley of Achor before its proper time. Look how the hearts of those fathers and mothers who have sons in the army beat as if it were the last trump! Did you ever spend a night like that in Achan's tent? A friend of mine once slept in a room in a hotel in Glasgow through the wall from a man who made him think sometimes that a madman had got into the house. Sometimes he thought it must be a suicide, and sometimes a damned soul come back for a visit to the city of its sins. But he understood the mysterious noises of the night next morning when the officers came in and beckoned to a gentleman who sat surrounded by the luxuries of the breakfast table, and drove him off to a penal settlement. Groanings that cannot be uttered to you were heard by all Achan's neighbours all that night. Till one bold man rose and lifted a loop of Achan's tent in the darkness, and saw Achan still burying deeper and deeper his sin. O sons and daughters of discovered Achan! O guilty and dissembling sinners! It is all in vain. It is all utterly and absolutely in vain. Be sure as God is in heaven, that He has His eyes upon you, and that your sin will find you out. You think that the darkness will cover you. Wait till you see! Go on sowing as you have begun, and come and tell us when the harvest is reaped how it threshes out and how it tastes.

The eagle that stole a piece of sacred flesh from the altar brought home a smouldering coal with it that kindled up afterwards and burned up both her whole nest and all her young ones. It was very sore upon Achan's sons, and his daughters, and his oxen, and his asses, and his sheep, and his tent, and all that he had. But things are as they are. God gathers the solitary into families for good, and the family tie still continues to hold even when all the members of the family have done evil. Once a father, always a father: the relationship stands. Once a son, always a son, even when a prodigal son. Every son has his father's grey hairs and his mother's anxious heart in his hands, and no possible power can alter that. Drop that stolen flesh! There is a coal in it that shall never be quenched.

Achan, after all, as is sometimes the case, had all the time the root of the matter in him. Achan made a clean breast of it, and gave himself up to Joshua before all Israel, and walked out to the Valley of Achor without a murmur. But Joshua had no choice. Joshua could not help himself. Joshua was a man under authority. And Achan had to die. But the point and the proper end of the whole story to us is this: that a greater than Joshua is here. Joshua bore a Name greater than his own, but that only brings out all the better the blessed contrast between Achan and you. Make a clean breast of it, then. Go home to your tent to-night, take up the accursed thing out of its hiding-place, and lay it out before Joshua, if not before all Israel. Lay it out and say,—Indeed I have sinned against the Lord God of Israel, and thus and thus have I done. And if you do not know what more to say, if you are speechless beside that accursed thing, try this; say this. Ask and say, Is thy Name indeed Jesus? Dost thou indeed save found-out men from their sins? Art thou still set forth to be a propitiation? Art thou truly able to save to the uttermost? For I am the chief of sinners, say. Lie down on the floor of your room,—you need not think it too much for you to do that, or that it is an act unworthy of your manhood to do it; the Son of God did it for you on the floor of Gethsemane. Yes, lie down on the floor of your room, lay your head in the dust of it, and say this about yourself: Say that you, naming yourself, are the offscouring of all men. For thus and thus, naming it, have I done. And then say this,—

The dying thief rejoiced to see
That Fountain in his day—

and see what the true Joshua will stand over you and will say to you.

Therefore the name of that place is called The Valley of Achor to this day. Achor, that is, as it is interpreted on the margin, trouble; the Valley of Trouble. Why hast thou troubled us? demanded Joshua of Achan. The Lord shall trouble thee this day. The Lord troubled Achan in judgment that day, but He is troubling you in mercy in your day. Yes; be sure, in mercy. If I were suddenly to open your door to-night, and find you on your face, I would clap my hands with gladness. I would lie down on the spot beside you, and would share your trouble, and you would share mine, and I would lift you up and share your joy. It is not possible, you say. Look at your Bible again, and see. 'And Sharon shall be a fold of flocks, and the Valley of Achor a place for the herds to lie down in, for the people that have sought Me.' And, again,—'And I will give her her vineyards from thence, and the Valley of Achor for a door of hope; and she shall sing there, as in the day of her youth, and as in the day when she came up out of the land of Egypt.' Your soul, that is. Your soul shall sing there. There, in that Valley of Achor. There in that room. There where your sin found you out. There where I found you on your face. Yes; already your trouble is a door of hope. You will sing yet as you never sang in the days of your youth. You never sang songs like these in the days of your youth, or before your trouble came,—songs like these: The Lord will be a refuge for the overwhelmed: a refuge in the time of trouble. Thou art my hiding-place; Thou shalt preserve me from trouble; Thou shalt compass me about with songs of deliverance. He shall call upon Me, and I will answer him; I will be with him in trouble; I will deliver him and honour him. The sorrows of death compassed me, and the pains of hell gat hold upon me; I found trouble and sorrow. Though I walk in the midst of trouble Thou wilt revive me, and Thy right hand shall save me. O the Hope of Israel, the Saviour thereof in the time of trouble! You will sing that song in your Valley of Achor till this song shall be taken up over you by saints and angels,—These are they which came out of great tribulation, and have washed their robes, and made them white in the blood of the Lamb.

Second Series

GIDEON TO ABSALOM

XXVII

GIDEON

YE DID RUN WELL; WHO DID HINDER YOU?

WE are not told to whom we are indebted for the Book of The Judges, but whoever he was, he was a master of the pen, and the story of Gideon is his masterpiece. A powerfully built, middle-aged man of Manasseh is busy beating out a few blasted ears of corn in a secret winepress. He beats the sheaves softly lest the sound of his staff should tell the Midianites where the wheat is. He stops his work to dry his face and to wet his lips, but all the water in the well would not put out the fire that is in his eye, for the fire that is in his eye is his hot heart rising to heaven against the oppressors of his people. 'The Lord is with thee,' the angel of the Lord appeared at that moment and said to Gideon, 'for thou art a mighty man of valour.' Gideon thought that the angel of the Lord was mocking at him in so speaking. The Lord with me! and I have not meal enough to make my children's supper! I a mighty man of valour, when I am afraid to thrash out my few stalks of wheat on the thrashing-floor, but must hide myself in this hidden winepress! Call me not a mighty man of valour. Call me a God-forsaken coward! But the angel of the Lord only the more went on, 'Go in this thy might and thou shalt save Israel.'

No sooner had the angel of the Lord taken his departure than Gideon threw down his staff and went into the house where his mother sat mourning day and night for the loss of her sons slain at Tabor, each one resembling the son of a king. And Gideon said to his weeping mother, 'Awake, my mother, and sing to me the song of Deborah.' And while she only the more sat and wept, her son took out and whetted his sword and sharpened his axe. 'Sing to me,' he said, 'how Deborah and Barak arose and delivered Israel. Sing to me, ye daughters of Joash, of how the stars in their courses fought against Sisera.' Night fell; and at midnight, behold ten men, and each man with a pitcher and a lamp in it in his left hand, and with his axe in his right hand, stole out of his house and met Gideon. Their meeting was beside the altar of Baal and in the grove of Baal, which was built and planted in Joash's high place. For, how could Joash's son think to cast out a single Midianite as long as that unclean altar and those unclean trees stood beside his father's house? He could not. But at every blow of Gideon's swift axe new strength came into his arm. At every tree that fell before his axe his courage rose. And the light of God's countenance returned already to Israel in every star that shone down through the opening spaces in the grove of Baal. Why is *your* life is in such bondage and fear and famine to-night? Why have you not been fed to-day and every day with the finest of the wheat? Why are you not satisfied every day with honey out of the rock? Arise in this thy might, and the Lord will make of thee also a mighty man of valour. Be sure of this, that thy sure way to deliverance and peace and plenty lies for thee also through that levelled grove and over that prostrate altar.

> The dearest idol I have known,
> Whate'er that idol be,
> Help me to tear it from Thy throne,
> And worship only Thee.

The worshippers of Baal never neglected their morning devotions. 'Early will I seek thee,' they could say to their god with truth and a good conscience. And thus it was that before Joash was up that morning the men of the city were gathered already round his door, shouting and demanding, and saying,—'Bring out thy son Gideon that he may die: because he hath cast down the altar of Baal, and because he hath cut down the grove of Baal.' Many men who have not the courage to do a righteous deed themselves have the sense and the grace to be glad when other men do it. And sometimes you will see a father who is entangled in some evil or doubtful business, but has not the courage or the strength to cut himself and his house clear of it, a proud enough father when his son rises up and sets the whole household free. A vein of true humour ran in the Joash blood; for that morning the old man met the men of the city with a jest that scattered them all home, just as Gideon his son has enriched our literature to this day with more than one witty word and ready and racy answer. 'For shame!' said Joash, 'for shame, sirs! Stand back, and go home. Let Baal redress his own wrongs. Baal is a god: and you are only my everyday neighbours. Let Baal arise, but go you home.' And Joash brought out Gideon and baptized him Jerubbaal before them all, saying, 'Let Baal settle his own scores with my sacrilegious son.' 'Let her ladyship now save herself,' said John Knox, as he cast the wooden idol overboard. 'She is light enough; let her learn to swim.' After that, we read, was no Scottish man ever urged with that idolatry.

Gideon was a great favourite with Pascal. Gideon's fleece had taken a great hold of Pascal's imagination. You all know the fine story of Gideon's fleece. Gideon was a humble-minded man. Not Moses himself was a more humble-minded man than Gideon was, or more unwilling to come out and be a great man before Israel, 'Oh, my Lord, wherewith shall I save Israel? Behold, my family is poor in Manasseh, and I am the least in my father's house.' But, had Gideon not been poor in Manasseh, and the least in his father's house, God would have gone elsewhere for a leader to deliver Israel. And this is always the way of the Lord with men who are to do a great work for Him and for His people—'to that man will I look, saith the Lord, even to him that is poor and of a contrite spirit, and who trembleth at My word.' And God said to Gideon, What sign shall I show thee to assure and to confirm thee that thou art he who shall deliver Israel? And the quaint fancy of Gideon fell on a sheep's fleece now wet and now dry when all around it was now dry and now wet. A strange, indeed a fantastic, request to make of God. But, all the same, Gideon made it and got it. 'Is there humour in the divine mind?" asked one of his congenial students at Dr. Duncan, instancing, at the same time, what looked to him like some examples of something not unlike humour both in creation and in providence. 'It's true and it's no true,' was the old doctor's answer. And God did so that night; for it was dry upon the fleece only, and there was dew on all the ground. You have the whole story from 'a pen that ennobles and idealises all that it touches.' But you may not have read this addition from another pen, that Gideon's mother took that so versatile fleece of his, and cut it out, and sewed it up with her own hands into a soldier's mantle for her elect son: a mantle which he wore under his armour and next his heart in all his after-battles; and his men always witnessed that Gideon with his fleece on was full of hope when they were full of despair; and again, that he was full of a good captain's caution and forethought when they would have gone headlong to their own destruction. How often I wish with all the world that Pascal had been spared to develop his Thoughts and finish his Apology. What lessons I could then have read you out of Gideon's wonderful fleece! Pascal must have had something great in his mind about Gideon, for we see him taking down Gideon's name in his notebook again and again. But, as we know, Pascal did not live to digest his rich notebook into the great book of his life.

But it is time to come to Gideon's three hundred Ironsides, so to call them. Not a man of Colonel Cromwell's soldiers swears but he pays his twelvepence. No drinking, no disorders, no plundering, no impiety permitted. They were men that had the fear of God in them, and that made them put away all other fear. 'Truly they were never beaten at all,' boasted their colonel. 'My troops increase,' he wrote to his friend, Oliver St. John. 'I have a lovely company; you would respect them did you know them. They are no anabaptists. They are honest, sober, Christian men; and they expect to be used like men. The result was I raised such men as had the fear of God before them; such men as made conscience of what they did; and from that day forward they were never beaten, but wherever they were engaged against the enemy they beat continually. And truly this is matter of praise to God, and it hath some instruction in it.' You see, then, what an Ironside was. An Ironside was a soldier whose whole soul was ribbed and plated all round with sound morals and true religion. Colonel Cromwell's Ironsides were that, and so were Judge Gideon's. And Gideon's three hundred has still some instruction in it, as Cromwell says. And one of these instructions is this, that three hundred good and true men are far better for a great campaign of truth and righteousness than ten thousand men swept together by chance conscription, or picked up for a shilling a head in a public-house. The men are too many, said the Lord to Gideon. And the Lord took one of Gideon's own original and characteristic ways of weeding out that army of deliverance. The day was hot, and the ten thousand came to a river on their march. Their fathers in leaving Egypt had eaten their last supper without taking off their hats or their shoes. They ate that memorable supper standing, with a piece of the Passover lamb in one hand and with their staff in the other. And three hundred of Gideon's men out of the ten thousand remembered that supper that day, and they swore to themselves and to one another that they would not sit down to eat bread at a table, nor so much as lie down to drink water out of a river, so long as there was a single Midianite left alive in the land. And thus it was that without even taking off their helmets, the three hundred wet their lips out of the hollow of their hand, and were back again that moment in their unbroken ranks. As for Gideon, the dew glistening on his mother's mantle was water enough for him that day. 'Alexander, being parched with thirst in the desert, took the helmet full of water, but perceiving that the men of arms that were about him did thrust out their necks to look upon this water, he gave it back again unto them that had given it unto him, and thanked them, but drank none of it. For, said he, if I drink alone all these men here will faint. And what wonder if his men began to spur their horses, saying that they were not weary nor athirst, nor did think themselves mortal as long as they had such a king.' And all the best work and all the best warfare of the world is done still as it was done in Manasseh and in Macedonia; it is done by those men who are more intent on their work than on their wages: who think more about their armour than about their rations: who eat less that they may work more: and who lap up a mouthful and lose not a moment as they dash on to meet the enemy away past every running water.

But time would fail me to tell you all about Gideon: all about his battles, and all about his victories: about how he behaved himself in battle, and how he bore himself in victory. Like the Ironsides of England, the Ironsides of Israel said to their captain, 'Rule thou over us, for thou hast delivered us from the hand of Midian.' But Gideon said, 'I will not rule over you, neither shall my son rule over you: the Lord only shall rule over you.' And had Gideon only stopped there, what a noble name, and what a blameless name Gideon's name would have been to us to this day! But:

> The grey-hair'd saint may fail at last,
> The surest guide a wanderer prove;
> Death only binds us fast
> To the bright shore of love.
>
> I have seen
> The thorn frown rudely all the winter long,
> And after bear the rose upon its top;
> And bark, that all the way across the sea
> Ran straight and speedy, perish at the last,
> E'en in the haven's mouth.

And Gideon was that grey-haired saint; that sure guide; he was that straight and speedy bark.

'Rule thou over us,' said all the soldiers and all the people. And Gideon said unto them, 'I will not rule over you. But, he went on—and as he went on the devil entered into Gideon and he went on—'I would desire a request of you that you would give me every man the earrings of his prey.' And Gideon made an ephod of the earrings and put it in his city, even in Ophra; and all Israel went a-whoring after it, which thing became a snare to Gideon, and to all his house. It must have been the very devil himself. There is no other way of accounting for this terrible catastrophe. The devil has seldom since his first success had such another success over God and God's servants as he had in Gideon's awful fall. For Gideon, when he died, and long before he died, left Israel very much where he had found her when he cut down his father's unclean grove and overthrew his father's lewd altar. Gideon left Israel under the heel of her oppressors; or if not that just yet, then fast and sure on the way to that. Gideon's great sin, and Satan's great triumph over Gideon all arose out of this, that all through his magnificent life of service, in Paul's words, the law of Moses, the law of God, had never entered Gideon's heart. In Paul's words, again, Gideon did not know what sin was. He knew suffering in plenty; but, shallow old soldier as he was, he did not know the secret of all suffering. Gideon was as ignorant as the mass of you are what God's law really is, what sin really is, and what the only cure of sin really is. At bottom, and in New Testament words, that was Gideon's fall. And accordingly Gideon made a mock ephod at Ophra, while all the time God had made a true and sure ephod both for Himself and for Gideon and for all Israel at Shiloh. And God's ephod had an altar connected with it, and a sacrifice for sin, and the blood of sprinkling, and the pardon of sin, and a clean heart, and a new life; all of which Gideon, with all his high services, knew nothing about. Sin was the cause of all the evil that Gideon in his bravery had all his life been battling with; but, instead of going himself, and taking all his Ironsides and all his people up with him to God's house against sin, Gideon set up a sham house of God of his own, and a sham service of God of his own, with the result to himself and to Israel that the sacred writer puts in such plain words. Think of Gideon, of all men in Israel, leading all Israel a-whoring away from God! The pleasure-loving people came up to Gideon's pleasure-giving ephod, when both he and they should have gone to God's penitential ephod. They forgot all about the Midianites as they came up to Ophra to eat and to drink and to dance. Whereas, had they been well and wisely led, they would have gone to Shiloh with the Midianites 'ever before them,' till the God of Israel would have kept the Midianites and all their other enemies for ever away from them. Gideon was a splendid soldier, but he was a very short-sighted priest. He put on a costly ephod indeed, but it takes a great deal more than a costly ephod to make a prevailing priest. Gideon could hew down the enemies of Israel by the thousand; but, all the time, he was doing absolutely nothing to heal the real hurt of the daughter of his people. Gideon could not possibly heal that hurt as long as he did not know what it was nor where it lay.

Your time would not wait for me to make all the application. But, surely, there can be no need; if you have half an eye in your head you must long before now have made the application for yourself. I see, and you must see, men every day who are as brave and as bold as Gideon, and as full of anger and revenge against all the wrongs and all the miseries of their fellow-men; men and women who take their lives in their hands to do battle with ignorance and vice and all the other evils that the land lies under: and, all the time, they go on repeating Gideon's fatal mistake; till, at the end of their lives, they leave all these wrongs and miseries very much as they found them: nothing better, but rather worse. And all because they set up an ephod of their own devising in the place of the ephod and the altar and the sacrifice and the intercession that God has set up for these and all other evils. They say, and in their goodness of heart they do far more than merely say,—What shall the poor eat, and what shall they drink, and how shall they be housed? At great cost to themselves they put better houses for the working classes, and places of refreshment and amusement, and reading-rooms, and libraries, and baths, and open spaces, and secular schools and still more secular churches in the room of the cross and the church and the gospel of Jesus Christ; and they complain that the Midianites do not remove but come back faster than they can chase them out. But, as Joash or Gideon might have said in one of their humorous moments, all these things are so many apothecary's pills to protect a man from the earthquake. Only, there is much more fitness and sense and likelihood in the mountebank's prescription than there is in all your costly but unchristian ephods. Either the cross of Christ was an excess and a superfluity, or your expensive but maladroit nostrums for sin are an insult to Him and to His cross.... It only remains to say that from that day on which Gideon put on his ephod of earrings, his mantle which his mother made ceased to move on his bosom and to speak to his heart. From that day his mantle was no longer the miraculous fleece of his great days of victory; from that day and thenceforth it was only the dead skin of a dead sheep.

XXVIII

JEPHTHAH AND HIS DAUGHTER

IT IS GOOD FOR A MAN THAT HE BEAR THE YOKE IN HIS YOUTH

'PROSPERITY,' says Bacon, 'is the blessing of the old Testament, but adversity is the blessing of the New.' 'How many saints,' exclaims Law, 'has adversity sent to heaven! And how many poor sinners has prosperity plunged into everlasting misery! This man had never been debauched, but for his fortune and advancement; that had never been pious, but through his poverty and disgrace. She that is envied for her beauty may perchance owe all her misery to it, and another may be for ever happy for having no admirers of her person. One man succeeds in everything, and so loses all; another meets with nothing but crosses and disappointments, and thereby gains more than all the world is worth.' 'Adversity,' says Albert Bengel, 'transfers our affections to Christ.' 'Caius Martius,' says Plutarch, 'being left an orphan of his father, was brought up under his mother, a widow, and he has taught us by his experience that orphanage brings many disadvantages to a child, but does not hinder him from becoming an honest man, or from excelling in virtues above the common sort.'

Jephthah the Gileadite was the most ill-used man in all the Old Testament, and he continues to be the most completely misunderstood, misrepresented, and ill-used man down to this day. Jephthah's ill-usage began before he was born, and it has continued down to the last Old Testament Commentary and the last Bible Dictionary that treats of Jephthah's name. The iron had entered Jephthah's soul while yet he lay in his mother's womb; and both his father and his brothers and the elders of Israel helped forward Jephthah's affliction, till the Lord rose up for Jephthah and said, It is enough; took the iron out of His servant's soul, and poured oil and wine into the lifelong wound. Born, like his great Antitype, under a cloud, Jephthah, like his great Antitype also, was made perfect through suffering. Buffeted about from his birth by his brothers; trampled upon by all men, but most of all by the men of his father's house; called all manner of odious and exasperating names; his mother glad to get the servants' leavings for herself and her son; when a prophet came to dine, sent away to the fields to be out of sight; My son, his mother said, as she died on her bed of straw among Gilead's oxen—My son, shall not the Judge of all the earth do right? And from that day, if earth had been hell to Jephthah before, the one drop of water that had hitherto cooled his tormented heart was now spilt to him for ever, never to be gathered up again. For his mother was dead.

If at the death of his father Jephthah had got his proper portion of his father's goods, then Jephthah might have become as great a prodigal as his brothers became. But the loss of an earthly inheritance was to Jephthah, as it has been to so many men since his day, the gaining of an inheritance incorruptible and undefiled, eternal in the heavens.

And Gilead's wife bore him sons; and his wife's sons grew up, and they thrust out Jephthah, and said unto him, 'Thou shalt not inherit in our father's house, for thou art the son of a strange woman.' Then Jephthah fled from his brethren and dwelt in the land of Tob; and there were gathered vain men to Jephthah, who went out with him. 'Vain men'; yes, no doubt. But, then, we must remember that misery has always acquainted even the best of men with strange bedfellows. David's misery acquainted him with every one that was in debt, and with every one that was in distress, and with every one that was discontented, and he became a captain over them, as did Jephthah long before David's day. You must not sit in your soft chair and shake your head over Jephthah and David. They were not all highwaymen; they were not all unmitigated freebooters either in Adullam or in Tob. They were not unlike those Armenians or Greeks who have taken to the hills in our day against the Turks. Still, we must stand to the text; and it is to Jephthah's advantage that we do so stand. Yes; fill the mountain fastnesses of Tob as full as they can hold of vain men, and their captain's true character will only all that the better come out. Debtors, broken men, injured and outcast men, orphan and illegitimate sons, prodigal sons, and sons with whom their fathers were wearied out; with, no doubt, a sprinkling of salt here and there, as there always is among the most corrupt characters and the most abandoned men. But, bad as they were, Jephthah turned none of them away, but took them all the more into his own hand. I told you Whose type Jephthah was, and Who was his Antitype. And thus it was that he took that great rabble of refuse and of offscourings, and year after year gradually chastised them into an army of obedient and capable men. He took them to his own cave man by man, to sup with himself and to talk with himself. He listened to their story, and they listened to his. He told them what he would give them to do, and what he would give them for doing it. He made them captains over tens and over fifties and over hundreds. He trusted them, he praised them, he promoted them. And then he hurled them like a stone cut out of the mountain against the enemies of the King of Tob; till the elders of Israel in their absolute despair were compelled to approach and to beseech Jephthah to come down from his fastness and rid them of their enemies also.

It was a bitter pill to those elders of Israel. Some of the prouder stomachs among them would have died rather than swallow it. The stone which the builders had refused was become the head stone of the corner; and it broke every bone in their body to lift that stone up into its place. You know how you hate and fear and shrink back from meeting, not to speak of being beholden for your life to, the man or woman you once greatly injured. You will know, then, what it was to be an elder in Israel in that day and among the hills of Tob. Their hearts were as black as hell with remorse and with terror as they approached Jephthah's dreadful den and saw his naked savages glowering at them through their spears. Look at that poor elder of Israel of eighty. His old face is as white as his old hair. An old man like that should not be out on an errand like this. He drinks at every stream. He falls down with fear at every breath of wind. Who, you ask, is that so venerable figure they have placed at the head of the sacred deputation? Oh, that, you must know, is the ruling elder, to whose door Jephthah went in his despair when his mother was dying in Gilead's stable. That is the hand, so helpless to-day, that shut the door so sternly in Jephthah's face that day. That is the mouth, so dry to-day, that was so full of such evil names at Jephthah that day. And he would never have got through his mission to Tob that day unless Jephthah had made his daughter spread out some venison on a shelf of a rock and pour out some of the old wine of their mountains. That old elder's sin found him out that day, when the sweetest woman-child he had ever seen washed his feet, and anointed his head, and kissed his outstretched and deprecating hand. Jephthah's daughter shall never wash my feet! the old man had said; but she both washed his feet and kissed them too, in her beautiful honour to old age. Jephthah would have been more than a mere man, as, indeed, he sometimes was, if he had not reminded those elders of the old days. Only, if the deputation had had any sense; if they had not been so many idiots; if all their tongues had not been cleaving to the roofs of their mouths over Jephthah's hospitality and his daughter's devotion, they would surely have taken the upbraiding words out of his mouth. What a pity it is that Jephthah did not hold himself in to the end of the interview! What a lesson he would then have been to us in the New Testament art of taming an injured tongue! But let him who has always tamed his own tongue in Jephthah's opportunity cast the first stone at Gilead's disinherited and cast-out son. At the same time, Jephthah soon put a bridle on his mouth, and that lest his old wrongs should set sudden fire to what he knew was only waiting the match in the hearts of his men. And he was very glad when he got all those elders of Israel safely out of Tob and back again within the borders of their own land. He was angry with himself all down the long hill-road that he had ever told those wild men one word about the days of his youth. But by quick marchings and by strict orders Jephthah got his bodyguard held in till all danger was past.

THE LORD dwelt in those days at Mizpeh; THE LORD had a house and an altar at Mizpeh; and Jephthah opened all that was in his heart; past injury, present opportunity, and future surrender and service before THE LORD at Mizpeh. This is what we mean by masterly writing, sacred or profane. This: 'Jephthah uttered all his words before THE LORD in Mizpeh.' The truly masterly part was in Jephthah himself. But it is not every masterly part that gets such a masterly reporter. 'Before THE LORD,' I am much afraid, is only so much pen and ink to you even when it stands in these reader-arresting capitals. But, to Jephthah, Mizpeh was all that the Mount was to Moses when THE LORD descended there with His great Name. Tob, and Mizpeh, and all, were full of THE LORD and His Attributes to Jephthah. I expect to read in *The Athenæum* or *The Academy* some Saturday night soon that the land of Tob has been discovered and identified, and Jephthah's headquarters in it, with Exodus thirty-fourth and sixth and seventh still legible on its doorpost. Perhaps Dryasdust will then begin to open his eyes over his ordered article on Jephthah. Only, if they had been made to open they would surely have opened long ago at the last clause of the eleventh verse of the eleventh chapter of Jephthah's history. Time has failed me to make an exhaustive induction over the whole of the Old Testament, but I have a conviction that The Name of THE LORD occurs oftener in Jephthah's history than it does in the history of any other Old Testament saint, at any rate between the days of Moses and those of David. If the Name and Presence of THE LORD is the supreme distinction in any man's life and history, Old Testament or New, prosperity or adversity, then he that runs might surely have read in that Jephthah's character and Jephthah's standing in the true Israel. How I wish this fine narrator had taken time to tell us down to every jot and tittle all that Jephthah said and did when he uttered all his words before THE LORD at Mizpeh! Were this sacred writer on the earth in our day, and were he recasting his Judges in the light of the New Testament, I feel sure he would give us all Jephthah's words before THE LORD at Mizpeh, and that verbatim too, even if he had to leave out the Levite and his concubine. But this sacred writer knew his own business, and I can well believe it of him that he buried Jephthah's words before THE LORD at Mizpeh out of sight in order that we might have to dig for those words as for hid treasure—the hid treasure of the kingdom of heaven, as Jephthah had been taught by his mother about that kingdom, and had already taken, and will soon still more take, that kingdom by force.

Along with Jephthah we have Jephthah's father, and his mother, and his brothers, and the elders of Israel, and the King of Ammon, and Jephthah's daughter, and the daughters of Israel—but we have not one word about Jephthah's wife. Richard Owen, the great anatomist, from a few inches of fossil bone constructed a complete creature of a long past and forgotten world, and made it live and go about again before us. And from a few words of her daughter I can see and understand that nameless princess of the land of Tob better than I can see and understand some men and women who live next door to me. I conclude the long-dead mother from a single glimpse of her noble daughter. I see the mother of Jephthah's daughter the light of Jephthah's eyes in the dark cave of Tob. Those terrified elders owed their life that day to her. It was her love and her life and her death that so softened and so reconciled her husband. 'Yes,' she said to her father, after Jephthah had delivered her father's city,—'Yes, I will go with this man.' And when her daughter was born in Adullam that finished her work on her husband's savage soldiers. Always lions in war, they were now lambs in peace. 'My father,' said her daughter, long after her mother was dead and buried among her father's hills,—'My father, if thou hast opened thy mouth unto THE LORD, do to me according to that which hath proceeded out of thy mouth.' No, there can be no doubt at all about the mother of Jephthah's daughter. Moses had laid down a law that Jephthah was never to get a wife out of any family in Israel, nor was he ever to be let worship God in the same house with the virtuous elders of Israel. But men like Jephthah are above all such laws, and they break through them all as a lion breaks through a hedge. For Jephthah got of THE LORD in Tob a better wife and a better daughter too, than were to be seen in all Israel from Dan to Beersheba. And as for their tabernacle, he took it by storm, or, if not it, then that temple not made with hands, eternal in the heavens. Pericles' mother dreamed one night that she was brought to bed of a lion. And Jephthah's mother again and again had the same dream.

After all that, it does not at all upset me to read that Jephthah built an altar and offered up his daughter. That was their terrible way sometimes in those twilight, uncivilised, and unevangelical ages. What God bade Abraham and Isaac do on Moriah, that Jephthah and his daughter actually did at Mizpeh. No doubt, had God sent an angel and provided a ram, Jephthah and his daughter would have returned home together willingly enough. But God did better for Jephthah and his daughter than He did for Abraham and Isaac, and both Abraham and Isaac in their old age would have been the first to admit it. The finished work of this earthly life of fathers, and mothers, and sons, and daughters, is to hold them all as not ours but God's. It is really of little consequence in what age of the world, or in what dispensation of providence, patriarchal, Mosaic, pagan, or Christian, or just in what way, and just among what things, the mind and the heart and the will of Jephthah and Jesus Christ are worked out within us—If only they are worked out within us.

The one question is, Am I or am I not my own? Am I bought for a price or am I not? In all that do I not sin, nor charge God foolishly? In all that do I say, Lo, I come, in the volume of the book it is written of me? You take a right step. You take up a holy calling. You enter a holy covenant. You open your mouth to the Lord, and you put your hand to His holy plough. And, come what may, you never go back. You only all the more say, I will pay my vow. Thy will be done. My times are in Thy hand. The cup, shall I not drink it? All I have is Thine, said Jephthah. I had nothing. I had not even a name to be known by. No man would let me sit at his table. No mother would let me look at her daughter. No elder in Israel but spat in my face. It is all Thine. I am Thy servant, and the son of Thine handmaid; Thou hast loosed my bonds. Take it back again if Thou seest good; only let me redeem Thy people Israel. And God took Jephthah at his word, till wherever the Book of the Judges of Israel is read this that Jephthah and his daughter did shall be told for a memorial of them. And it was a custom in Israel that the daughters of Israel went to that altar once every year to lament the daughter of Jephthah the Gileadite four days in a year. And they came back from that altar to be far better daughters than they went out. They came back softened, and purified, and sobered at heart. They came back ready to die for their fathers, and for their brothers, and for their husbands, and for their God. Weep not for me, Jephthah's daughter said to them from off her altar and from out of heaven. Weep for yourselves and for your children.

And that the very fragments of such a history may be gathered up, and may not be lost, we are let read this on the margin—That though Jephthah had neither wife, nor son, nor daughter of his own any more, yet his palace at Mizpeh was only all that the more replenished and full of people. Old soldiers from the fastnesses of Tob were pensioned in that palace; prodigal sons worked in its fields: illegitimate sons sat at its table; foundling children played upon its doorsteps; nephews of its owner, the debauched sons of the rich brothers of his youth, became honest men—what between their uncle's house and the house of the Lord beside it. Long ago, when Jephthah first uttered his words before the Lord at Mizpeh, he read these words on the wall of that altar. These words: The Lord your God regardeth not persons, nor taketh rewards. He doth execute the judgment of the fatherless and the widow; He loveth the stranger, and giveth him food and raiment. Love ye, therefore, the stranger, for ye were strangers in the land of Egypt. And many of the sons of the elders of Israel ate the fat and drank the sweet at Jephthah's orphaned table, because of what Jephthah had read long ago on the Lord's wall at Mizpeh. For six years this life for others went on with Jephthah. He buried his grief as much as he might in warfare for Israel and in labours in her seat of judgment and among her outcasts, till he died in Mizpeh in midtime of his days. For he said, They shall not return to me, but I shall go to them, and so died.

XXIX

SAMSON

EVERY MAN THAT STRIVETH FOR THE MASTERY IS TEMPERATE IN ALL THINGS

SAMSON'S tragical story has been treated in three ways. Some commentators on the Book of Judges have treated the story of Samson as an excellent piece of Hebrew folklore. They have collected out of all the ancient books of the world wonderful tales of giants, and heroes, and demigods, with their astonishing feats of strength in war, and in love, and in jealousy, and in revenge; feats more or less like the feats of strength and of revenge we have in Samson. They have produced remarkable parallels to Samson's exploits out of Atlas and Cyclops, Hercules and Odin, and many suchlike mythological characters. And then their work on Samson has been done when they have illustrated his history with romances and legends of sufficient likeness and richness. Some evangelical preachers, again, have gone out to the opposite extreme, and have displayed Samson to us solely as a type and pattern of Jesus Christ. They have selected texts out of Samson's extraordinary history, and they have suspended excellent New Testament sermons on these adapted texts; hanging great weights on small wires. The former is the mythical way of dealing with Samson's history; the latter is the mystical way. But there is a third way. And the third way is the way that Paul takes, not only with Samson, but with all the patriarchs, and judges, and kings, and great men of Old Testament times. We have this apostle's way with all those Old Testament men and women set before us again and again in his own conclusive words: 'For whatsoever things were written aforetime were written for our learning, that we through patience and comfort of the Scriptures might have hope.' And again, 'All Scripture is given by inspiration of God, and is profitable for doctrine, for reproof, for correction, for instruction in righteousness.' And again, 'Now, all these things happened unto them for ensamples, and they are written for our admonition, upon whom the ends of the world are come. Wherefore let him that thinketh he standeth take heed lest he fall.' And yet again, 'Therefore, seeing we are compassed about with so great a cloud of witnesses let us lay aside every weight, and the sin which doth so easily beset us, and let us run with patience the race that is set before us.' Now, neither the mythical nor the mystical method shall be followed upon Sampson tonight. All my leanings and all my drawings, all my reading and all my experience—all combine to make me to sit at Paul's feet, and to pursue, so far as I am able, Paul's expository and homiletical methods. While listening attentively, then, to all that the mythologists and the mystics have to say on Samson; having done so, I feel all the more safe and sure in asking you to look at Samson as John Milton looked at Samson when he treated him with such 'verisimilitude and decorum.' For 'Tragedy, as it was anciently composed, hath been ever held the gravest, moralest, and most profitable of all other poems: therefore said by

Aristotle to be of power by raising pity and fear, or terror, to purge the mind of those and suchlike passions; that is, to temper and reduce the passions to their just measure.'

What more could God, or man, or angel of God have done for Samson that was not done? Every man must work out his own salvation with his own hands, or not at all; but, short of doing for Samson what neither God nor man could do, what more could God or man have done that was not done? From his birth, and for long before his birth, the gifts of God were simply showered on Samson. He had a father and a mother of the very best. Over and above what the Bible tells us about Samson's father and mother, Josephus, in supplement of the Bible, tells us that there was 'one Manoah, a person of such virtue that he had few men his equals, and without dispute he was the principal person in his country. And Manoah had a wife celebrated for her beauty, and excelling her contemporaries.' Now, Manoah and his wife had been prepared to be the father and mother of a great deliverer of Israel. And they had been prepared in the same way that God had often taken to prepare the parents of those children who were predestined to be great and famous men. Like Abraham and Sarah, like Isaac and Rebekah, like Jacob and Rachel, like Hannah, like Zacharias and Elizabeth, and like many more, it was as it were by a special and immediate act of creative power that Manoah and his wife got Samson their son at the hand of God.

And not only was Samson to be separated to God's service from his mother's womb; but, in order to make his separation and dedication both sure and easy and natural to him, his mother was separated and dedicated to God long before her child was born. 'Of all that I said to the woman let her beware. She may not eat of anything that cometh of the vine, neither let her drink wine nor strong drink, nor eat any unclean thing: all that I commanded her let her observe,' said the angel of the Lord a second time to Manoah. 'Not,' says Joseph Hall, 'that there is more uncleanness in the grape than in the fountain; but that wine finds more uncleanness in us than water finds; and that the high feed is not so fit for devotion as abstinence.'

> Desire of wine and all delicious drinks,
> Which many a famous warrior overturns,
> Thou couldst repress; nor did the dancing ruby,
> Sparkling, outpour'd, the flavour, or the smell
> Or taste that cheers the heart of gods and men,
> Allure thee from the clear crystalline stream:
> . . . . Nor envied them the grape,

Whose heads that turbulent liquor fills with fumes.
But what avail'd this temperance not complete
Against another object more enticing?
What boots it at one gate to make defence,
And at another to let in the foe,
Effeminately vanquished? . . . .

'I am weary of my life!' said Rebekah to Isaac over the marriage of Esau, and in terror of a like marriage of Jacob. And both Manoah and his wife said the same thing over Samson's marriage. How twice happy are those parents who get a child born in the Lord, and then live to see their child married in the Lord! What a crown of blessing it is to a godly mother to get a second daughter in her son's wife; and what a happy father he is who gets a second son in his daughter's husband! But, then, all the more, what a gnawing sorrow it is when a son or a daughter marries away outside of all sympathy with their father's house! Better, cries many a mother's broken heart—better they had never been born than to be mis-married. Samson's father and mother never saw another happy day after that day when their son—miraculous birth, Nazarite vow and all—went down to Timnath and saw a woman, a daughter of the Philistines, and said, Get her for me to wife. Then his father and his mother said to Samson, Is there never a woman of the daughters of thy brethren, that thou goest to take a wife of the uncircumcised Philistines? Was it for this day they had sanctified their unborn child? In his misery Manoah declared that he would never all his days pray for anything after this, lest it should turn to his bane, as his prayer for a son had so turned. For how is a child who brings such shame on his father and mother ever to fulfil the promise of his birth? How shall the son-in-law of an uncircumcised Philistine ever deliver Israel? Nor did all Samson's riddles, and jests, and sports, and revenges against the Philistines scatter or relieve the cloud that his first fatal step had brought on his father's and his mother's heart.

Though we look with fear for it, and almost expect it, and though Josephus actually says it, yet we are not told it in the Bible, and we simply cannot believe Josephus, that Samson broke his Nazarite vow. Could we believe Josephus in what he writes, what a treasure-house for Bible readers he would be. But wherever Josephus stands without corroboration and confirmation, we simply cannot believe a word he says. We shall, therefore, set it down to Samson's credit that, with all his licence and with all his riot, he never became a drunkard. But, then, as it always comes into my heart when I read of Samson's total abstinence—

What boots it at one gate to make defence,
And at another to let in the foe?

You are making a gallant defence at one gate, but what about all the other gates; and especially, what about the gates on the other side of the city? You keep, with all diligence, this and that gate of the body, but what about the more deadly gates of the soul? Plutarch tells us of a great Roman who was very brave; but, then, he was very envious of other brave men, and his envy did himself and them and the state more mischief than if he had been a coward. You work hard for God at your books and your visiting as a minister or as a Sabbath-school teacher, but you restrain prayer. You stand up for use and wont in public worship, and in pulpit and in published doctrine; but, then, you hate and hunt down the men who innovate upon you in these things. You go out, like Samson, against the enemies of God and His Church, but all the time you make your campaign an occasion for your own passions, piques, retaliations, and revenges. You do not touch wine, but how do you stand to all Samson's other sins? Death and hell will come still more surely into your hearts through the gates of envy, and ill-will, and hatred, and pride, and revenge, and malice, and unbelief, and neglect of God in prayer, than at those more yawning gates that all decently living men make a defence at. What avails this 'temperance not complete'?

Young men are not raised up among us nowadays with Samson's size and strength. The age of the Judges was a rude age, and God condescended to its rudeness, and raised up rude instruments to shape it. Samsons in body are not born among us in our day, but Samsons in mind are sometimes given us in room of them. And it is not seldom seen that our greatly gifted youths work as little deliverance for themselves and for us as Samson did for Israel. You hear of some young man's Samson-like feats of strength at the University or at the Divinity Hall. He rose from his shoulders upwards above all the men of his time. What was toil and defeat to them was but child's-play to him. Samson rent a lion that roared against him, as if it had been a kid. In the quickness and versatility of their minds our young Samsons set us riddles to which we Philistines cannot supply an answer. They make sport of our slow wits. They tie firebrands to foxes' tails, and turn the foxes in among our standing corn. But we endure it all, looking on it all as but the rough sport of young giants, and we wait with hope for the day when they shall be found working painfully among those very cornfields and vineyards over which they are now making their too destructive sport.

But it often happens with our promised deliverers also that they fall far short of far weaker men in the after-work they do for themselves and for us. A common man, over whose birth no angel did wondrously, will often at the end of the day far outstrip his brilliant neighbour who started with all heaven and earth looking on with applause and expectation. Genius is genius; but the oil-fed lamp of an honest mind and a humble heart will, not seldom, light its owner better home. Weak men must husband their strength. They have neither time nor strength to spare on those Samson-like feats that end in a day's amazement, but work no deliverance in the land. And, moreover, the very diligence and assiduity that their few talents compel them to, keep them from those idle and ruinous dalliances with the Delilahs of the flesh and of the mind that more affluent men are more easily led into.

But, still, in spite of it all, Samson actually judged Israel for full twenty years. At the same time, for some reason or other, a reason we can only guess at, the sacred writer tell us not one single word about what we would give a great deal to-night to know. Not one word are we told, neither about what kind of cases came up before Samson, nor how he managed his court, nor about the wisdom, or otherwise, of his judgments, nor about the manner of life that Israel lived for that whole generation under her gigantic judge. We sometimes hear it complained in our day that all the romance of the world is used up; that there is little or nothing left to the ambitious man of genius of these latter days but the most barren and most trampled spots of sacred and profane history. And, as a sad consequence to them and to us, that our dramatists and tragedians can never again give us such masterpieces as their forerunners have left behind them. Well, were I a sacred dramatist, I would ask for no better scope for my craft to-night than just the twenty years of Samson's judgeship. The whole magnificent drama of *Samson Agonistes* begins and ends, according to ancient rule and best example, within the space of twenty-four hours. Well, here are twenty untouched and absolutely silent years, during which the plot was laying deep and thickening fast toward the terrible catastrophe of Milton's masterpiece. Those twenty loaded years stand beckoning for a Milton or a Wells or a Browning to enter them, and to give us out of them a companion and a key to the *Agonistes* —a poem grave enough, moral enough, and profitable enough to satisfy the master of all these matters himself. Such an artist would let us see Samson repenting of having broken his mother's heart, and repenting with the passion of a hundred penitents poured into one. He would let us see the Lord turning again to give Samson another chance. He would let us hear evil men in Israel mocking at Samson and his seat of judgment because of Timnath and Gaza. He would raise pity and anger wherewith to purge our hearts as we saw Samson striving to do only what was right, with men of Belial all about him waiting for his halting, and dwelling on all his past wrong-doing. And his chorus would purge our breasts with fear and with terror as they lifted the veil and let us see the passions of lust, and jealousy, and hatred, and revenge that were all the time tearing at the great heart of Manoah's miserable son. Till one of those passions, even after he had judged Israel twenty years, again broke out, and laid Samson low, never to rise again in this world.

> Myself my sepulchre, a moving grave.
> Prison within prison,
> Inseparably dark!
> Nothing of all these evils hath befall'n me
> But justly; I myself have brought them on,
> Sole author I, sole cause. If aught seem vile,
> As vile hath been my folly.

But man's extremity is God's opportunity. And in such words as were possible to Samson's Old Testament biographer, that sacred writer tells us that in Samson also, where sin abounded, grace did much more abound, and that God's strength was made perfect in the day of Samson's weakness. That dark cell in Gaza—in Gaza, the scene of some of Samson's greatest sins—that shameful cell was a house of God, and a place of prayer and repentance to Manoah's overtaken and overwhelmed son. What a past Samson looked back upon as he sat at the mill! What he might have been! What he might have done! How he might have departed to his fathers and left Israel! Three thousand years dissolve, and *this* is Gaza. *This* is the mill with slaves. *This* man, and *that* man there, is Samson over again. Only, over again against light and truth that Samson never saw. 'What profit is there in my blood,' our Samson cries, 'when I go down to the pit? Shall the dust praise Thee? Shall it declare Thy truth? Hear, O Lord, and have mercy upon me. Lord, be Thou my helper. Turn my mourning into dancing, my dreaming into earnestness, my falls into clearings of myself, my guilt into indignation, my sin into fear, my transgression into vehement desire, and my pollution into revenge. Rejoice not against me, O mine enemy; when I fall, I shall arise; when I sit in darkness, the Lord shall be a light unto me. I will bear the indignation of the Lord, because I have sinned against Him, until He plead my cause, and execute judgment for me; He will bring me forth to the light, and I shall behold His righteousness. Who is a God like unto Thee, that pardoneth iniquity, and passeth by the transgression of the remnant of His heritage? He retaineth not His anger for ever, because He delighteth in mercy. He will turn again, He will have compassion on us; He will subdue our iniquities, and Thou shalt cast all their sins into the depths of the sea.'

XXX

RUTH

THE SAME IS MY MOTHER

Both the Bible, and all the books that take after the Bible, are full of fine stories of love. The love of the mother for her child. The love of the lover for her he loves. The love of the brother for his sister. The love of Jonathan for David, and of David for Jonathan. The love of Paul for his people Israel. The love of Christ for His own and for all men, and so on. But neither in the Bible, nor anywhere else that I know of, is there another such story of love told as the love of Ruth for Naomi; the love of this Moabite daughter-in-law for her Hebrew mother-in-law. Ruth's love for her dead husband's decayed mother is as pure as gold and as strong as death. Many waters cannot quench Ruth's love. And her confession of her love, when she is constrained to confess it, is the most beautiful confession of love in all the world. The world has nothing after Ruth's confession of her love like it. And Naomi said unto her two daughters-in-law, Go, return each to her mother's house; the Lord deal kindly with you, as ye have dealt with the dead, and with me. And Ruth said, Intreat me not to leave thee, or to return from following after thee; for whither thou goest, I will go, and where thou lodgest, I will lodge; thy people shall be my people, and thy God my God; where thou diest, will I die, and there will I be buried. The Lord do so to me, and more also, if aught but death part thee and me. No. There is nothing again like it. 'The same is my mother.'

'She clave to her mother-in-law,' says the Scriptures. Ruth's heart was so full of the cords of love to Naomi that those strong cords drew her out of the land of Moab and knit her deep into the lineage of Israel, and into the ancestry of Jesus Christ. And thus it is that our great seer discovers Ruth seated on her glorious seat in the rose of the seventh heaven, beside the glorious seats of the greatest dames of Scripture story—Mary, and Eve, and Rachel, and Beatrice, and Rebecca. Before Ruth had given Naomi the full proof of her love, that desolate woman had bestowed her highest praise on Ruth's past love, not only as a wife, but still more as a daughter-in-law. The Lord deal kindly with thee, as thou hast dealt with the dead, and with me. And the women of Bethlehem at once caught up this quite singular feature of Ruth's affection when they came to congratulate Naomi on the birth of Obed. 'Thy daughter-in-law,' they said to Naomi, 'which loveth thee, and which is better to thee than seven sons, hath borne him.' And in this salutation of theirs the women of Bethlehem are in entire harmony with the whole world about Ruth's so pure, and so noble, and so unparalleled love. Every language spoken among men has its own stock of cruel proverbs and satires and lampoons at the expense of their mothers-in-law. But Ruth and Naomi go far to redeem that relationship from all that obloquy. No only daughter of her own body could have been so devoted to Naomi as her son's young Moabite widow was. All the relationships of human life demand faith, and love, and patience, and forbearance, and good temper, and good sense, and good taste, and good feeling; but, perhaps, above all the other relationships of life that of a mother-in-law and a daughter-in-law demands all those gifts and graces. But, then, the relationship that offers scope and operation and reward for all those gifts of heart and graces of character is just that relationship that should be entered on by all men and women with much watchfulness, solicitousness, prayer, tenderness, sympathy, and loyalty; in short, with the mind and the heart of Ruth, that Moabitess maiden, and Naomi, that mother in Israel; that widow indeed.

Moses was as much opposed to Ruth's marriage as he had been to Jephthah's. A Moabite woman shall never be married by an Israelite man if I can help it, said that inexorable old law-giver; not to ten generations shall any of their offspring enter the congregation of the Lord. Yes, said Naomi, who had made up her mind to the interdicted marriage—Yes, she said to her more conservative and scrupulous husband, as she milked her kine under the top of Pisgah—Yes, she said, but marriage laws are made for men and women, and not men and women for marriage laws. And had Moses been here, she went on; had Moses been famished out of Bethlehem-Judah, as we have been; and had he been received and entertained of Ruth's and Orpah's fathers and mothers, as we have been, he would to a certainty have torn that revengeful leaf out of his law. Depend upon it, she said, as she saw her husband beginning to give way, depend upon it, Moses had altogether other Moabites in his mind's eye than Ruth and Orpah, and their so hospitable fathers, when he set down his retaliatory marriage laws. And Elimelech at last gave way. Nehemiah also, as well as Moses, visited the iniquity of the Moabite fathers upon the Moabite children to too many generations. For that merciless reformer and iconoclast contended with, and smote with his fists, and forcibly divorced the men of Jerusalem who had married Moabite women in his day. But, there again, this is to be said for Nehemiah, that the law-breakers of his day had not married such dear, sweet, generous-hearted women as Ruth and Orpah were. 'Because their fathers met not the children of Israel with bread and with water,' said Nehemiah. But, then, that was just what Ruth and Orpah and their fathers had done. They had met Elimelech, and Naomi, and Mahlon, and Chilion, not with bread and water only, but with wine, and milk, and honey, and spices, and all manner of Moabite fruits, till the land of Moab became to that famished-out family of Bethlehem-Judah a land of Moab indeed, a most delectable mountain, a place to dwell in, and to see their sons and their sons' sons settled in. And thus it came about that those two Israelite youths, Mahlon and Chilion, were married to those two Moabite maidens, Orpah and Ruth. And thus, through all that, it came in God's providence that a rich stream of Moabite blood ran first in King David's veins, and then through David's veins into the veins of a far greater King than David.

After the death of Elimelech, Naomi was a widow after Paul's own heart. Naomi was a widow indeed. She was desolate, but she trusted God, and continued in supplication and prayer night and day. She was in behaviour likewise as becometh holiness. She taught the Moabite young women about her to be sober, to love their husbands, to love their children, to be discreet, chaste, and keepers at home. In short, she taught them to be wives and mothers in Moab like the wives and mothers in Israel. I feel sure we shall not be far wrong to trace up a great part of Ruth's courage, devotion, extraordinary loyalty, and exquisite love, not so much to Naomi's schooling as to her example. She, no doubt, had something to get over, as well as her husband, when the two marriages first began to dawn upon her. At the beginning she, too, had her own struggle with her Hebrew pride when she saw that her two Hebrew-born sons were not to be married into some of the oldest and best of the families of

Bethlehem-Judah. But when she saw that was not to be, she bore no grudge against the two Moabite maidens, but went over to their side, and stood up for them against both Moses and Elimelech. And then; now among the joys of marriages, and now among the sorrows of death-beds, Naomi showed to those two Moabite women what a widowed wife and mother had to rest on in Israel; and one, at least, of her daughters-in-law laid the lesson and the example well to heart. Yes; behind all the nobleness, steadfastness, beauty, and tenderness of Ruth, I see inspiring and sustaining and maturing it all, the wise, chastened, weaned mind of one who was a mother in Israel and a widow indeed.

But you must not think of Naomi as a broken reed. You must not picture Naomi to yourself as a woman whose spirit was utterly and irrecoverably crushed. Widowhood with Naomi, and childlessness added to it, was not the dregs of life. It was not a few years of bitterness, and fretfulness, and listlessness, and ostentatious sorrow. No! Naomi is full of experience and full of resource. She knows the world. She knows the hearts of all the men and women about her. She knows the right way to act, and the right time to speak, widowhood, childlessness, and poverty, and all. With a rare and a delicate divination of how matters stood between Boaz and Ruth; knowing her kinsman and her kinswoman better than they knew themselves; Naomi struck the red-hot iron with the right stroke and at the right moment. Age and experience have their privileges, and Naomi possessed both age and experience, and employed them to purpose in the matter or Boaz and Ruth. 'Sit still, my daughter,' Naomi said to Ruth, while, all the time, her own heart was in a hidden flutter of love and of hope.

> Not obvious, not obtrusive, but retired,
> The more desirable.

What a blessing it is to a young man at Boaz's state of mind, and to a young woman at Ruth's stage of things, to have a mother in Israel, or a widow indeed, to whom to open their hearts! Or, still better, to have such a one to love them so that their hearts are divined and read before they are opened. One would think at first sight that a girl's own mother, or a young man's own father, was the natural adviser and bosom friend of their children. And that a parent should be the first to be confessed to, consulted, trusted in, and followed. And, again, that they should be the first to see and to take to heart all that is going on in their child's heart. But, as a matter of fact and experience, wherever the blame or the inability may lie, it is never, it is not once in a thousand, that a young man takes his father, or a young woman her mother, into their confidence and into their whole heart. And still less seldom does a father or a mother make it natural and easy and sweet for their child to do so. All the better, therefore, when our young people find a second father or a second mother in some friend older, wiser, more tried, and more skilled in the providences of God and in the passions of man than they are as yet themselves. Some one just to say, Sit still, my daughter. Some one just to say, with an anecdote to illustrate it, My times are in Thy hand. Some one just to say, I once knew a case exactly like yours. Or, better still, some one to tell them his own case, and to send them away with an *A Kempis* or an *Andrewes,* and this upon the fly-leaf, 'Your Father knoweth what things you have need of before you ask Him.' Then said Naomi to Ruth, 'Sit still, my daughter, until thou know how the matter will fall; for the man will not be at rest until he have finished the thing this day.'

The women are so delightful in this delightful little book that there is no room for the men. The men fall into the background of the Book of Ruth, and are clean forgotten. But this must not be. One, at any rate, of the men of the Book of Ruth deserves a better fate. One of them was certainly written for our learning. And more especially for the learning of all landlords and farmers and employers of labour. 'Then Naomi arose with Ruth, for she had heard in the country of Moab how that the Lord had visited His people in giving them bread, and they came to Bethlehem in the beginning of barley harvest. And Ruth the Moabitess said to Naomi, Let me now go to the field, and glean ears of corn after him in whose sight I shall find grace. And she said unto her, Go, my daughter. And she went, and came, and gleaned in his field after the reapers; and her hap was to light on a part of a field belonging to Boaz, who was of the kindred of Elimelech. And, behold, Boaz came from Bethlehem, and said unto the reapers, The Lord be with you. And they answered him, The Lord bless thee. Then said Boaz unto his servant that was set over the reapers, Whose damsel is this? And the servant that was set over the reapers answered and said, It is the Moabitish damsel that came back with Naomi out of the country of Moab.' Both Boaz's heart and his conscience were sorely struck within him at his servant's answer. For Naomi was a kinswoman of his own. He had known Naomi in better days. And he had heard of her widowhood, and of her return to Bethlehem; but he had not yet gone to see her, nor had he asked her to come to see him. He had made no inquiry of how she managed to live without husband or son. But here is a Gentile girl, a Moabite maiden, who has left her own proverbially abundant land to glean and to beg for the widow of his old friend Elimelech! And Boaz felt himself to be a beast on his own harvest field, while that gleaning Moabitess shone out like a princess in his eyes. 'Then said Boaz unto Ruth, Hearest thou not, my daughter? Go not to glean in another field, neither go from hence, but abide here fast by my maidens. The Lord recompense thy work, and a full reward be given thee of the Lord God of Israel, under whose wings thou art come to trust. So Ruth kept fast by the maidens of Boaz to glean unto the end of the barley harvest and of wheat harvest, and Ruth dwelt with her mother-in-law.' Time would fail me to tell all of the story of Boaz and Naomi and Ruth. Suffice it here to say that after two more chapters Boaz took Ruth, and she was his wife, and she bore a son. And the women her neighbours gave him a name, saying, There is a son born to Naomi, and they call his name Obed; he is the father of Jesse, the father of David.

Yes, Boaz is a splendid pattern to be set before all landowners, and farmers, and masters, and employers of labour. Courteous, solicitous, affectionate, devout, bountiful; Boaz greets his reapers in the harvest field as if they had been his sons and his daughters. He meets them in the morning with a benediction, as if he had been a priest, and they with a salutation answer him, The Lord bless our master. We hear him, indeed, in his jealousy for the reapers and the gleaners, issuing the strictest of orders to his young men; but Boaz's own character and example are his young men's best law. Just, honourable, and upright in the market and in the gate, he is kind, generous, and hospitable at home. He eats and drinks with a merry heart in the happy harvest season; but with it all he is at all times and in all places both temperate and chaste. A master to make his servants worship him. A mighty man of wealth, but forgetting and despising all that he possesses before beauty, and piety, and goodness, and truth. Altogether a husband worthy of Naomi's dear daughter Ruth, and after that what more can be said? From gleaning in his fields, and from falling at his feet, on till she sat at his table and lay in his bosom,—Ruth from first to last had nothing in her heart but pride, and respect, and love for Boaz. And he had neither act, nor word, nor look, nor wish to repent of, though Ruth had been found at his feet when his heart was merry. A happy pair, with a romantic history behind them, and with a future before them that it had not entered into their sweetest dreams to dream.

With all that, it is not at all to be wondered at that the Church of Christ, with such a dash of romance and mysticism in her heart, should have seen in Ruth's husband, Boaz, a far-off figure of her own Husband, Jesus Christ. For she, like Naomi and Ruth, was disinherited, disconsolate, despised, forgotten, and without kinsman-redeemer in her famine and all her deep distress, when His eye and His heart fell on her in the field. And how well He has performed a kinsman's part all the world has read in a Book that for truth and beauty far outstrips the Book of Ruth. How He has not only redeemed her, but has given her rest in His own house, in His Father's house, and in His own heart—what written book can ever fully tell? Boaz the Bethlehemite and Ruth the Moabitess made a noble marriage. Obed, and Jesse, and David, and Solomon, and Joseph, and Mary, and Jesus Christ—my Kinsman-Redeemer, and yours.

XXXI

HANNAH

A MOTHER IN ISRAEL

ABRAHAM and Sarah had no children. Isaac and Rebekah had no children. Jacob and Rachel had no children. Manoah had no children. Hannah had no children. The Shunamite had no children. Zacharias and Elizabeth had no children. Till it came to be nothing short of the mark of a special election, and a high calling, and a great coming service of God in Israel to have no children. Time after time, time after time, till it became nothing short of a special providence, those husbands and wives whose future children were predestined to be patriarchs, and prophets, and judges, and forerunners of Jesus Christ in the house of Israel, began their married life with having no children. Now, why was that? Well, we may make guesses, and we may propose reasons for that perplexing dispensation, but they are only guesses and proposed reasons. We do not know. We cannot guess; for it is only those who are intimately and eminently godly, and who are at the same time childless, who can have any experience and assurance of what God's motives are in that matter. And I do not know that any of that inner circle have anywhere come out and broken the divine silence. All the more—Why is it? Is it to spare and shield them from the preoccupation and the dispersion of affection, and from the coldness and the rudeness and the neglect of one another that so many of their neighbours suffer from? And is it to teach them a far finer tenderness, and a far rarer honour, and a far sweeter solicitude for one another? Or, on the other hand, is it out of pure jealousy on God's part? Is it that He may be able to say to them, Am I not better to thee than ten sons? Or, again, is it in order to make them meet, long before His other sons and daughters around them are made to meet, for that life in which they shall neither marry nor be given in marriage? Which of all these reasons, or what other reason, has their God for what He does with so many of His best saints? But all this time we have been intruding into those things of which he says to us—What is that to thee?

Elkanah of Mount Ephraim, Hannah's husband, was, as we say, a true gentleman. He would have been a perfect and a spotless gentleman but for one hard spot in his heart; a hard and a dark spot in his heart that came out in a hard and a dark spot on his life. It was because of that hard spot in Elkanah's heart that Moses had consented to let Elkanah take two wives. But Elkanah's shameful licence which he had taken in that matter had by this time sufficiently revenged itself on Elkanah and on his whole house: for by the time we are introduced to Elkanah and to his house, his transgression has been made so terribly his punishment, that his heart is as soft now, and as full of tears, as Hannah's heart is soft and a fountain of tears. And Elkanah's heart, far more than even Hannah's, was such a fountain. For to a man like Elkanah, to have done any one a great wrong, is, for all his after-days, to suffer far more than they can possibly suffer who only endure the wrong. I find a law, said Elkanah, as he went up out of his city yearly to worship and to sacrifice unto the Lord of hosts in Shiloh, that the greater the wrong done, and the greater the sorrow caused, the more all that comes back on him who did the wrong and caused the sorrow. But, Elkanah, sorrow upon sorrow at home, and yearly worship and sacrifice at Shiloh and all, never could undo the wrong he had done to Hannah and to all his house. He could only take every opportunity to sweeten a little, if possible, Hannah's great and bitter sorrow. But such was the cruel snare that Elkanah lay in, that every effort he made to lighten a little his own and Hannah's load, that effort only locked the teeth of the snare deeper than before into his soul. Elkanah could not move a finger to comfort Hannah's stricken heart without that instant provoking her adversary to fresh insults and fresh injuries. What Elkanah might have been driven to do had it not been for the worship and the sacrifices at Shiloh, we tremble to think of.

Of Peninnah, Elkanah's wife with children, we know nothing —nothing but what we hear from her own cruel and scurrilous tongue. Those of you who are living in the same house with a woman like Peninnah, you could best picture to us poor Hannah's life. The servants who most slighted and insulted Hannah, were Peninnah's prime favourites; and her children were sharp to find out how to please their mother and get their own way. The sacred writer does not keep us long in Peninnah's company: he hastens past Peninnah to tell us about Hannah, that sorely-fretted and sequestered woman, who waters her couch with her tears. But unless God was mocked on Mount Ephraim as He has never been mocked anywhere else, it does not need a prophet to tell us, if not Peninnah's past as a maiden and a young wife, then her future as an old mother and a widow. There were more sons and daughters of Belial being born and brought up in the house of Israel in these days, than Hophni and Phinehas. Take this child also, Belial had said to Peninnah over her successive child-beds, bring this one also up for me. And she did it. And you may take it for Holy Writ, though it is not written in as many words, that her children, when she was old, did not depart from the way in which she had brought them up.

I am filled with shame for myself and for my order as I see Eli sitting upon a seat by a post of the temple, and as I see Hannah's lips moving in prayer, and then hear Eli's rebuke of Hannah. 'Put away thy wine,' said Eli to Hannah. If he had said that to Hophni and Phinehas twenty years before, and had, at the same time, put away his own, Eli would have had another grandson than Ichabod to bear and to transmit his name. 'How long wilt thou be drunken?' said Eli to Hannah. I do not wonder that Hophni and Phinehas became prodigals. What else could they become with such a father? When the blind lead the blind, what can you look for? That temple post, and that doited old priest sitting idle in the sun, and Hannah drunk with sorrow, and the way that Eli looks at her, and the things he says to her—Rock of Ages, let me hide myself in Thee! Only to Thy cross I cling—as I see Eli, and myself in Eli, and my children in Hophni and in Phinehas and in Ichabod. I see in Eli my idleness, my blindness to my own vices, and to my children's vices, my blindness also to my people's trials and temptations—one provoking and another being provoked, one drunk with pride and insolence, and another drunk with ill-usage and sorrow. I see in Eli my brutish ignorance while all that is going on round about me; as also my headlong and unjust judgments, and the way I preach at my people when I should be away out of sight and deep in God's holy place in prayer for them and for myself and for my children. O my God, when Thou sayest that Thou wilt do a thing at which both the ears of every one that heareth it shall tingle, I understand what Thou sayest concerning whom Thou speakest. And I know, and I acknowledge, that had it not been for Thy long, long suffering, Thou wouldest have done all that to me and mine long before now. But, O my God, let Thy mercy endure for ever. Say to me that in Thy mercy I am to have this year also in which to rise off my seat and to acquaint myself with my people's sorrows, and to go out and in among them spending and being spent. Let me have the grace to preach to them out of Hannah's song, as I have never yet done. To preach to them, and to tell them that there is none holy as the Lord: neither is there any Rock like our God: that the Lord God is a God of knowledge, and that by Him actions are weighed: that He raiseth the poor out of the dust, and lifteth the beggar from the dunghill, and that He will keep the feet of His saints. But, all the time—

Could my zeal no respite know,
Could my tears for ever flow,
All for sin could not atone,
Thou must save, and Thou alone.

If Hannah was Elkanah's first wife, then there is nothing to be said but severe blame of Elkanah and deep sympathy with Hannah. But if Hannah was hoodwinked with her own wish to enter Elkanah's household as a second wife in those indecent days, then Hannah's bitter sorrow is just another harvest reaped according to the seed sown. How Hannah must often have envied, not the mothers of children so much, as those bright and merry maidens of Ephraim and Shiloh, whose souls were still their own. And how, as she went up to the temple and came home from it, she must have filled up the time with recalling the way the Lord had led her till she so let herself be misled by Elkanah. Had Elkanah been a bad man, Hannah would not have been misled by him. In that case, Hannah would not have been in this snare. But when it was too late, Hannah learned that evil in a good man is just as deadly as the same evil in a bad man; as deadly, and far more dangerous. Hannah would never have crossed the threshold of any but a good man. You would never, all her days, have seen Hannah the wife of a son of Belial. But when Hannah crossed good Elkanah's threshold, she had still to learn that a sin against purity, a sin against human nature and the human heart, will bring down just as heavy a punishment on a patriarch's tent as on a profligate's. Punishments of that kind are no respecters of persons. And even when some might think your person respected, it may be to this extent, to the great and gracious extent of forgiveness; while, all the time, a sharp vengeance is taken on your inventions. Elkanah and Hannah invented a sin against married life on Mount Ephraim, and, while they were forgiven for it, all the time the vengeance that was taken on it, and on them on account of it broke every bone in their body and every hard spot in their heart.

'Her adversary provoked Hannah sore to make her fret.' Little did her adversary think—only, people like Hannah's adversary never think—little, I was going to say, did Peninnah think what a life of sin she had plunged Hannah into. And little do we think—only one here and there has the power and the will, the mind and the heart so to think—how we plunge this man and that woman into a lifetime of deadly sin just by the way we provoke them to anger at us. Little do we think the sins that we are the true cause of, and of which we shall one day have to share the guilt. If you could see into this man's and that woman's heart, it would frighten you for once. We speak in a hyperbole about hell upon earth; but all the time there is one of the mouths of very hell in that heart that you have hurt till it so hates you. Exercise, I implore you, all your powers of imagination to put yourself in the place of that man or woman you so fret and provoke. Strive with all your might to put yourself inside his heart, so as to see and feel and sin and suffer as he does. Labour to see yourself as others see you. Be sure that Butler is right. Be sure that you differ from other people, as much as they differ from you; and that you are as offensive to other people, and that they are as full of wicked passions at you as you are at them. And, then, this is terrible. This, that the most obscure of us, the most innocent of us, nay, the very best of us, and the most blameless—we all have many hearts burning like hell underground against us. There are men we have never seen, and men who have never seen us, who are yet provoked and fretted out of all their composure and all their grace and truth at the bare hearing or reading of our names. We never saw them or they us; and if we had the opportunity we would forgive them and do them a service; yet such are the blind and furious passions of their hearts that our very names are a madness to them. Surely the thought of that should make us all walk softly and speak seldom and seek solitude and circumspection. Surely we should seek obscurity, and wish with all our heart that our so offensive name should never be spoken in this world again, or written or read. Nay, your very virtues are a provocation and a constant fury to men it would astonish you to be told about. Your very services, even to themselves; your very talents of which you are so innocent, and of which your Maker must bear the blame—what is there? —there is absolutely nothing in us, or about us, that does not provoke and exasperate somebody. Let God hide us all in the secret of His presence from the pride of men! Let Him keep us secretly in His pavilion from the strife of tongues!

Well, it was all that: it was Hannah's diabolical ill-usage at her adversary's hands, and it was still more, her own wicked and revengeful heart at her ill-usage: it was all that that made that saintly woman absolutely drunk sometimes with her sorrow. She staggered with her sorrow; she fell against the altar; she did not know what she was saying or where she was going; she actually forgot her own name, and did not answer when her name was spoken. Aaron himself would have been provoked to say to Hannah to put away her wine. Hannah was a saint; but she was a woman-saint; and hence her reeling heart. Hannah was able to command herself sometimes for weeks and months after she had been again at Shiloh. But something would happen in the household that would soon show that even Shiloh had made Hannah nothing better but rather worse; for her chastised and well-bridled tongue would all of a sudden break out again till, had it been in Greece or in Rome, she would have been called a fury rather than a woman and a saint. The milk of human kindness, not to say of womanhood, would suddenly turn to burning brimstone in Hannah's bosom. For days and weeks she would be able in the strength of the Shiloh meat to teach them their letters and to play with Peninnah's children better than if they had been Elkanah's and her own. She would toss them up in the air and make them light on their father's knee, till he clean forgot his sin and his shame and his pain. But the very next moment Hannah was within an inch of dashing them against the stones. Elkanah's happiness through any other wife but herself, and his rapture over her adversary's child's delightful ways, made Hannah sometimes go away to her bed like a she-tiger to her den. You will charge me with mocking you, and with an abuse of sacred words, when I call such a woman a saint. 'Among all the saints I have never found one,' said Santa Teresa, 'out of whose case I could take any comfort.' Well, speaking for myself, I can take comfort out of two saints. And one of them is Hannah of Mount Ephraim, and the other is Teresa of Mount Carmel. And out of another. 'Begone!' shouted the aged Philip, 'Begone! you do not know me. I am a devil if you know me!'

'Whom do men say that I, the Son of man, am? Some say that thou art Jeremias.' Our Lord makes no remark upon that. But I do not think that He was greatly offended to be so taken. Had He said anything about the men of Cæsarea Philippi who took Him to be Jeremias, I am mistaken if He would not have said that they were not far from the kingdom of heaven. For they had been drawn to Him just as we have been drawn to Hannah. They had seen Him in the Temple with His lips moving. No, they held, He is neither Moses nor Elias: He is the Man whose sorrow was like no other sorrow that has ever been seen. Pascal is continually preaching to us that the more spiritual light we have, the more spiritual sorrow we have. No wonder, then, that the Spiritual Light Himself was the Man of supreme spiritual sorrow. Who would not have been sad who had eyes to see what went on in Elkanah's house at Shiloh? No man but a blind and hopeless fool would have been other than sad over houses like the house of Elkanah and Peninnah, and Eli and Hophni and Phinehas. And the land was full of such houses in the days of our Lord, and thus it was that He was what the observing men of Cæsarea Philippi saw that He was. There are multitudes of men and women amongst us who are drunk and dazed with many kinds of sorrow. But it is only now and then that you will come—now in life and now in literature—on a man who is drunk and dazed with sorrow for sin. 'Pascal was greedy of happiness,' says Sainte-Beuve in a fine essay, 'but of a noble and an infinite happiness. He had that profound inquietude which attests a moral nature of a high order, and a mental nature stamped with the seal of the archangel! Pascal is of this leading and glorious race: he has more than one sign of it in his heart and on his brow: he is one of the noblest of mortal men, but he is sick, and he would be cured. Pascal sweats blood. Pascal clings to the Cross as to a mast in shipwreck.' His sister tells us that the noblest and most self-denying of brothers was sometimes so stupefied by reason of his own sinful nature that his very family affections were withered up in the terrific fires that burned his heart to ashes. And an intellectual and a moral nature like Pascal's; a spiritual sensibility like Pascal's; will always bring along with it Pascal's exquisite and awful sorrow. But let not your hearts be troubled, for it is a noble sorrow. It is a supernatural sorrow. It is the sorrow of the great saints; it is the sorrow of the Son of God. And as He was so are we in this world. Our present sorrow for sin is the exact measure and the sure seal of our future joy.

XXXII

ELI

HIS SONS MADE THEMSELVES VILE, AND HE RESTRAINED THEM NOT

'SEEST thou a man that is hasty in his words? There is more hope of a fool than of him.' Yes; but we have hope of Eli in spite of his hasty words. For Eli never forgave himself for his hasty words to Hannah. Eli had many bitter memories as he sat by the way-side watching for the ark of God. And one of the bitterest of those memories was the lasting memory of his insulting language to Hannah. No sooner was that hasty word gone out of Eli's mouth than he would have given all the world to have had that hasty word back again. 'Go in peace,' Eli said, 'and the God of Israel grant thee thy petition which thou hast asked of Him.' And all his days, in his sore remorse for what he had said to Samuel's mother before Samuel was born, Eli tried to make up for that insult to Samuel her son. Eli's extraordinary care over young Samuel; his extraordinary tenderness toward the child; and, as Samuel grew up, the old priest's secret fear at Samuel; and his growing reverence for him,—all that was all that Eli could do to undo the insult and the injury he had done to Samuel's mother.

Samuel was predestinated soon to succeeded to all Eli's forfeited offices. All Eli's high positions were soon to descend to Samuel. And Eli saw all that preparing to come about, and preparing to come about soon. But all that did not alter or abate by one iota Eli's notable goodness to Samuel. Eli could not have treated Hophni or Phinehas better than he treated Samuel, his immediate successor. Frederick Robertson, in his able apology for Eli, makes a great deal of the total absence of envy in Eli. But surely not with that great preacher's wonted insight. My tongue may be cleaving to the roof of my mouth with envy; I may be as blind with envy as Eli was blind with old age; the hair may have fallen off my head till I am bald with envy—and yet no man about me may so much as guess it. What Eli is to be praised for is this—not that he felt no envy of Samuel; but that, feeling envy every day, as he could not fail to feel it, he kept his envy down, and did not let it come out in his treatment of

Samuel. Of course Eli had envy of Samuel; all men have envy in their hearts who are placed by God in Eli's circumstances, and it is misleading and mischievous in the last degree in any preacher to say anything else. God alone could say whether Eli had envy or not. And He never says that about Eli or any other men. He says about Eli and all men the very opposite. The point with God is not whether I have envy or not; but it is this, how I deal with the envy that He knows I have. All that my fellow-men can see in me is not the envy of my heart, but that of my life. They can see and hear whether or no I backbite, and belittle, and detract, and depreciate; as also whether I consent and take part and pleasure with them who do. And while that is much to see and to judge, it is far from being all. If the Baptist had no envy and no jealousy of his fast-rising Cousin, then he has all that the less praise for his noble reply to his envious and jealous disciples. But if the Forerunner had to fast from his locusts to help him to subdue his pride; if it was only after many unwitnessed days and nights of sweat and prayer and blood that he was enabled to hand over John and Andrew to Jesus whom he had baptized but yesterday beyond Jordan; then John the Baptist is of some use to you and to me. But if John had no such envy and no such jealousy himself as his disciples had on his account, then he was not a man of like passions as we are. If John did not sometimes find himself hating Jesus in his heart till, in his agony, he threw himself over the bleeding rocks of the wilderness, then all I can say is, that Elizabeth's sanctified son was not made of the same rotten stuff with you and me.

Not only had Eli, with all his envy, a very real and a very deep love for little Samuel; but along with that, and kept alive by that, he had a real, a living, and deep faith in God, and in God's voices and visions and answers to men. Eli's fine benediction spoken over Hannah the next moment after he had mistaken her for a daughter of Belial; his open-hearted adoption of little Samuel to be his assistant and successor in the temple service; his rich and recompensing benediction pronounced on Samuel's mother because she had lent little Samuel to the Lord; his midnight lesson to his little elect companion; his solemn demand next morning to be told what the Lord had said to the prophetic child during the night; and his instant acceptance of the terrible message that little Samuel was compelled to deliver,—all that shows us that Eli, with all his shipwreck of life and opportunity and privilege, had the root of the matter all the time in him. There had been no 'open vision' for many a day in Israel. But Eli's mind had been open all the time. You will see men with great faults, and even with completely lost and wasted lives, who yet all through, and to the end, have a certain openness of mind to divine truth, and a certain sure and spontaneous sympathy with divine truth to whomsoever it comes, and through whomsoever it speaks. And poor old Eli was one of those open-minded and truth-loving men. If his own sins and his sons' sins had shut silent the divine vision, then Eli was all the more prepared to believe that the divine vision would hereafter speak to better men than he had been. And when the divine vision did begin to break its long silence, and to speak again,—for Eli to accept that vision, even when it came in the shape of a sentence of capital punishment on himself and on his house,—well, if ever faith had her perfect work in an open mind, it was surely in castaway Eli's open mind. What a lesson is here, and what a noble example to all old castaways among ourselves! The Spirit and the providences of God in His Church have stood still in our day. There has been nothing to call an open vision. We have sinned away the open vision. We have quenched the speaking Spirit. But, all the time, the Spirit of God is only waiting till we are out of His way, and then He will return and will not tarry. As soon as we are dead and gone, and obstruct the Spirit of God no more, Samuel will come, and the Lord will be with Samuel, and will let none of his words fall to the ground. But God's mercies always come mingled up with God's judgments, and if you have Eli's loving heart for the rising generation of God's ministers; and if with that you have a still living, if hitherto a too-barren faith in the ever-living God; in alleviation of your punishment, and in reward of your faith and your love, He will send the beginning of the returning vision before the end of your lost life. And even if that vision comes to condemn your whole life, and to pass sentence on you, and on your evil house; yet, even so, better that than to live and die in the long absence and the total silence of an angry God. Let us expect then, for our successors what we have sinned away from ourselves. Let us believe and be sure that the coming generation will see visions and hear voices that we have not been counted worthy to see or to hear, because of our great unfaithfulness and unfruitfulness, and because of our great blindness and disobedience.

And then, look at old Eli's splendid resignation and Gethsemane-like submission. 'It is the Lord: let Him do what seemeth Him good.' I shall never believe that Eli is lost. Broken neck; dead sons and daughters lying strewed all around him; the ark taken; the temple in ruins, and the glory departed, and all—

Eli is not lost. No man is wholly lost who lies lost before God like that. 'Though He slay me,' said Job. But He did not slay Job as He slew Eli. Job's patience, and meekness, and submission, and resignation were terribly enough tried; but they were not tried down to death as Eli was. And He who so rewarded Job, and who so supported and rewarded His own Son—no, I shall not believe it till I see it that Eli is among the reprobate. 'It is the Lord.' If anything will cover a multitude of sins; if anything will draw down the mercy of God, surely that cry of Eli's will do it.

Away back, at the beginning of his life, Eli had taken far too much in hand. Eli was not a great man like Moses or Aaron, but he took both the office of Moses and the office of Aaron upon his single self. Eli was both the chief judge and the high priest in himself for the whole house of Israel. The ablest, the most laborious, the most devoted, the most tireless and sleepless of men could not have done what Eli undertook to do. They called Origen 'Brazen-bowels,' he was such a sleepless student. But Eli would have needed both bowels of brass, and a head and a heart of gold, to have done the half of what he undertook to do.

And, taking up what was beyond mortal power to perform, the certain result was that he did nothing well, but did everything ill. Both his high priesthood at the altar, and his chief judgeship at the gate, and his sole fatherhood in his own house; both God's house and his own house, and the whole house of Israel, went to wreck and ruin under overladen Eli. It is startling and terrible to think that the unparalleled catastrophe of Eli's awful end had its first and far-back roots in what is as much a virtue, surely, as a vice: his determination to do two men's work with his own hands. But, whatever Eli's motives were for loading himself with all this plurality of offices and emoluments, the terrible catastrophe of his own end and his sons' end and the end of Shiloh—all this had its earliest roots in Eli's vaulting ambition and consequent incapacity and neglect. The mischief was widespread. But it was at home that the widespread mischief rose to a height that went beyond human remedy and beyond divine forgiveness. And may something of that same kind not be the explanation of some of those sad cases where the houses of able and good and devoted ministers come to such ruin? What with the pulpit of our land and our day—more than enough of itself; and what with the resulting and accompanying pastorate—more than enough of itself also for one man working at it in season and out of season; with so many public demands and claims, and with such incessant calls and encroachments at all hours of the day and night, there is neither time nor strength to do any part of a minister's work as it ought to be done. And one worried week follows another worried week till his children grow up and grow out of his knowledge. 'A bishop must be vigilant.' Yes; but a bishop in our day would need to have a hundred eyes and a hundred hands and a hundred feet. 'He must rule well the house of God.' Yes; but the apostle tells Timothy that he must know how to rule his own house first. It is a fine picture: 'One that ruleth well his own house, having his children in subjection with all gravity.' It would almost seem that Paul had had the ruins of Eli's house before his mind when he wrote that fine instruction. All other men have the grave sweet Sabbath-day to spend with their children, ruling and teaching them: all but ministers, and policemen, and some other slaves. But ministers have neither Saturday, nor Sabbath, nor Monday. And I never hear them complaining of that, unless it is when they think of their children. We call Eli old, and blind, and idle, and inefficient, and ignorant, and neglectful of his own children and of God's people; and so he was. But all that was not because he did nothing, but because he did too much to do anything well. Till, at last, broken in life and broken in heart, with his nation and his church and his household lying all in ruins round about him, we see Eli sitting by the wayside waiting for death. A terrible end to such a bold and ambitious beginning.

'Now the sons of Eli were sons of Belial; they knew not the Lord.' Impossible! you would protest, if it were not in the Bible. But just because it is in the Bible, we are compelled to ask ourselves how it could possibly come about that the sons of such a sacred man as Eli was could ever become sons of Belial. What! not know the Lord, and they born and brought up within the very precincts of the Lord's house! Were not the first sounds they heard the praises of God in His sanctuary? Were not the first sights they saw their father in his robes beside the altar with all the tables, and the bread, and the sacrifices, and the incense round about him? And yet, there it is in black and white; there it is in blood and tears—'The sons of Eli were sons of Belial; they knew not the Lord.' Let me think. Let me consider well how, conceivably, it could come about that Hophni and Phinehas could be born and brought up at Shiloh and not know the Lord? Well, for one thing, their father was never at home. What with judging all Israel, and what with sacrificing and interceding for all Israel, Eli never saw his children till they were in their beds. 'What mean ye by this ordinance?' all the other children in Israel asked at their fathers as they came up to the temple. And all the way up and all the way down again those fathers took their inquiring children by the hand and told them all about Abraham, and Isaac, and Jacob, and Joseph, and Moses, and Aaron, and the exodus, and the wilderness, and the conquest, and the yearly passover. Hophni and Phinehas were the only children in all Israel who saw the temple every day and paid no attention to it. And, then, every father and mother knows this, how the years run away, and how their children grow up, till all of a sudden they are as tall as themselves. And very much faster than our tallest children did Eli's children grow up. All things, indeed, were banded against Eli; the very early ripeness of his sons was against Eli. He thought he would one day have time but it was his lifelong regret that he had never had time. And, what with one thing, and what with another; what with their father's preoccupation and their own evil hearts; the two young men were already sons of Belial when they should still have been little children. 'Why do ye do such things? For I hear of all your evil dealings by all this people. Nay, my sons, this is no good report that I hear.' Like our own proverb, Eli is seen shutting the stable-door with many tears and sobs years and years after the steeds have been stolen. I have spoken of Job. Well, I always think that Job was the very best father in all the Old Testament, while Eli was surely the very worst. Job—let this passage be repeated to himself by every father every day from the first day he is a father, this golden passage—'Job was one that pleased God and eschewed evil. And it was so, when the days of their feasting were gone about, that Job sent and sanctified them, and rose up early in the morning and offered burnt-offerings according to the number of them all; for Job said, It may be that my sons have sinned and cursed God in their hearts. Thus did Job continually.' Our old ministers when they had a father at the pulpit-foot were used to make him swear that he would pray 'both with and for' his children. Now, it was just here that Eli went wrong. And it is just here that so many of ourselves go wrong, and our children. We scold and scowl at them, and we beat and bruise and lock them up, when we should pray both with them and for them. If, when they tell a lie, or steal, or speak bad language, or strike one another, or defiantly disobey us, we would neither lift a hand nor a tongue at them, but would take them to our place of prayer, and there pray both with and for them,—as sure as I stand here and you sit there,—there would be fewer sons and daughters of Belial in our houses. Let us do it. Let us, after Eli to-night, go home and do it. And if our children are grown up and gone away, let us all the more go after them, like Job, with that Sacrifice and that importunity which have the promise and the power to apprehend them and to bring them back. Thus did Job continually. You will all have it well in your mind how this all ended. How the ark of God was taken, and the two sons of Eli, Hophni and Phinehas, were slain. And how Eli, when he heard the evil tidings, fell from off his seat backward, and his neck brake, and he died. And how his daughter-in-law, her pains came upon her, and she answered not, neither regarded it; and how she named her son Ichabod, and so died.

'The Psalm of Ichabod, the son of Phinehas, the son of Eli, which he sang after that the Lord had repented Him of the evil, and had restored the priesthood to the house of Eli: I will confess my iniquity and the iniquity of my fathers. The fathers have eaten sour grapes, and the children's teeth are set on edge. But pardon the iniquity of Thy servant, according to Thy great mercy, and as Thou has been a father to the fatherless, so hast Thou been to Thy servant. I was a reproach among all mine enemies, but especially among my neighbours, and a fear to mine acquaintances. I was like a broken vessel. But I trusted in Thee, and Thou didst deliver me. I was cast upon thee from my mother's knees, and Thou didst hide me in the secret of Thy presence from the pride of men. Thou didst show me Thy loving-kindness in a fenced city. I am a wonder to many, but my boast is in God. Thou hast restored to me what the locust had eaten. Thou hast anointed my head with oil and made my cup to run over. Thou hast taken off my sackcloth and hast girded me with gladness. Come, all ye that fear God, and I will declare what He hath done for my soul. The sorrows of death compassed me, and the pains of hell gat hold on me; but Thou has brought up my life from the pit that I might show forth Thy praise. O Lord, I am Thy servant: I am Thy servant, and the son of Thine handmaid. I will pay Thee my vows which my mouth spake when I was in trouble. Bless the Lord, O my soul, and forget not all His benefits.' Thus sang Ichabod, the son of Phinehas, after the Lord had repented Him of the evil.

XXXIII

SAMUEL

BLESSED ARE THE PURE IN HEART
FOR THEY SHALL SEE GOD

Sir Joshua Reynolds has made all our children familiar with little Samuel. In the beautiful picture that sanctifies the walls of all our nurseries our children see and hear little Samuel kneeling and saying, Speak, Lord, for Thy servant heareth. And many a mother has taken the opportunity from that sweet picture to teach her child the same lesson that Eli taught the child Samuel. 'Sometimes when you are alone, my child, and both while you are yet a child, and after you are a big man, the same God of little children and of big men who spoke to little Samuel will come and speak to you. He will call you by name. If your name is Samuel, He will call and say, Samuel, Samuel, or whatever else your name is. And, be sure, my child, to answer at once. Be sure you say that moment, Speak, Lord, for Thy little servant heareth. And God will speak to you just as sure as He spoke to Samuel. Be sure He will. For He is about your path, and about your bed. Yea, the darkness hideth not from Him; but the night shineth as the day; the darkness and the light are both alike to God.' Good Sir Joshua has helped multitudes of good mothers to teach their children to pray.

Hannah lent little Samuel to the Lord according to her promise. That is to say, she lent Samuel to Eli the Lord's servant, to the temple at the Shiloh, which was the Lord's house. As soon as he was able to put on his own clothes and run about, his mother kept her promise. Hannah took Samuel up to Shiloh, and the child was young. And she said to Eli: O my lord, as thy soul liveth, I am the woman that stood by thee here, praying unto the Lord. For this child I prayed: therefore also I have lent him to the Lord: as long as he liveth he shall be lent to the Lord. And Samuel ministered before the Lord, being a child, and he was girded with a linen ephod. Little Samuel was the little doorkeeper of God's house in Shiloh. He ran messages also for Eli. He opened the doors of the tabernacle in the morning, and he shut them at night. He lighted the seven-branched candlestick at sunset, and he put it out at sunrise, and did everything his quick little hands and quick little feet could do to keep the house of God in order and beauty, serving the Lord. Once every year his mother came up to Shiloh to see her son, and to bring him a little coat that she made a little bigger and a little bigger every year till he grew to be a man. And after his mother was taken home to heaven and came no more to Shiloh, when Samuel the prophet needed another coat he had it always made of the same substance and of the same shape that his mother wove for him on her loom in Ephraim. It was her favourite substance and her favourite pattern, and the old prophet would never wear anything else. All his days the people knew Samuel by his 'mantle,' which was just his little coat made larger for a man. And he wears it to this day as he serves God beside his mother in heaven. When he came back from heaven to rebuke Saul for his sins, and to announce to that bad king his fast-approaching end, Samuel had still the very same mantle on. Only it was made now of finer linen, and it was cleaner and whiter than any weaver or fuller in Israel could weave it or whiten it. All the same, it was the very same mantle—the very same little coat his mother had made him when he was her little son, only of a substance now and a beauty fit for the heavenly Shiloh.

If Samuel's mother was still in this world when the ark was taken, and when Shiloh was laid waste, then the likelihood is that he went back to live with his mother till he should see what the Lord had for him to do. Wherever Samuel lived I am sure he lived a good life, and was never idle. Only, for the next twenty years, or thereabouts, Samuel is quite lost to us in that wild and lawless world. From about his twelfth to his thirtieth year, like Another, Samuel was ripening in secret for his future work as a great prophet. Ripening; because he had already been planted in the house of God in his early youth. In after-years Samuel's best-known name in Israel was 'The Seer.' 'Tell me,' said Saul on one occasion to a stranger he met, 'where the Seer's house is.' 'I am the Seer,' said Samuel; 'come with me, and to-morrow I will tell thee all that is in thine heart.' And if you will weigh that name of Samuel well, and will carry that name deep enough into the things of God and man, you could not have anything told about Samuel that would better help you to understand him. 'I am the Seer, and I will tell thee all that is in thine heart.' And, not only in Saul's heart, but in God's heart also. For God opened His mind and heart to Samuel, and when the people discovered that, all Israel from Dan to Beersheba knew that Samuel was established to be a prophet of the Lord. 'The Seer,' they said. 'Samuel, the Seer. The man amongst us who sees God, and who tells us what is in our hearts.'

When he was yet a child, Samuel was made a seer before he knew. He saw enough of God and man that terrible night to make him an old man and a seer before the morning. As he lay awake till the morning he saw what was the wages of all that wickedness that had so horrified him to see and to hear in Eli's sons. He saw, while yet a child, that the wages of such sin is death. And he saw what would be the end of all that to Eli also, his father in the Lord. Till it was no wonder that he hesitated to tell Eli all that he had seen and heard that terrible night. And all that must have worked powerfully together to make young Samuel the pure, prayerful, holy child before God and man that he early was and continued to be. His purity of heart and his love for holy things prepared Samuel early to be a seer; and the sights he saw both in heaven and in earth; both in God and in man, only perfected all his days what had been so early and so well begun.

And all happy children who have mothers like Hannah, and who all their days keep themselves pure in heart and pray like Samuel, they see God clearer and clearer all their days. They are still the seers in Israel. Every Scripture testifies to that, and every great saint and servant of God is a fresh proof of that. The impure in heart never see God. Hophni and Phinehas never saw God. The darkness shall cover us, they said, and it did. It did, till a Hand out of the darkness struck them down in their sin. They had no mother, and therefore they never saw God till they came to their awful end. Had Hannah been their mother; had Hannah adopted the two sacred orphans; and had she adopted them in time: then they, as well as Samuel, would have seen God; and all the awful overthrow of Eli's house, and God's house, and the whole of Israel would have been averted and escaped. Such blessedness is there in a good mother; in an early plantation in the house of God; and in a pure heart; for, then, with Hophni and Phinehas for Israel's high priests, and with Samuel for her prophet from Dan to Beersheba,—'I should soon have subdued their enemies, and turned My hand against their adversaries. He should have fed them also with the finest of the wheat; and with honey out of the rock should I have satisfied thee.' Mothers in Israel, would you have your sons to be seers and life-long servants of God? Now is your opportunity. Teach them early, as Eli taught Samuel. Teach them under the picture of Samuel hanging over their bed. And never lie down in your own bed without prayer for them till you are sure that they see God. And then you can take your well-earned rest. 'Lord, now lettest Thou Thy servant depart in peace, according to Thy word; for mine eyes have seen Thy salvation.' And, would any young man here see God? Would he see God in his own heart and mind and imagination, where God is best seen? Then let him keep God's temple clean. And then he will not only see God in his own mind and heart and imagination, but in Holy Scripture also, in Jesus Christ, in creation, in providence, in the means of grace, and eventually where Samuel now sees Him. The promise is plain, and the thing is true. 'Blessed are the pure in heart.' And again, 'If any man will do His will, he shall know of the doctrine.' And again, 'And holiness, without which no man shall see God.' The true doctrine of seeing God is written in Scripture with a thousand sunbeams, and every man's own life is to him the seal of it. Every pure man's life is to him the seal of it. And every impure man's life is no less to him the seal of the other side of it. Hophni and Phinehas's lives were the seals of it to them. And Samuel's life was the seal of it to him. And your life is the seal of it to you. And my life is the seal of it to me.

Blest are the pure in heart,
For they shall see their God:
The secret of the Lord is theirs;
Their soul is Christ's abode.

Without being prophets we could predict what kind of a judge Samuel would make when he sat down on the seat of justice. Seeing God; remembering what Abraham said to God on one occasion about the Judge of all the earth; able to tell men all that was in their hearts; Israel never had a judge like Hannah's son, Josephus says that Samuel had an 'inborn love of justice.' And so he had. Some men still, both in public and in private life, have that same love of justice born in them. And they are happy men, and all men are happy who have to do with them. Some other men, again, most men indeed, have an inborn love of injustice that they have to fight against all their days. The golden rule is written, as if with nature's own finger, on some men's hearts; while other men are never able all their days to learn that rule. Samuel was still 'The Seer' as he sat on the judgment-seat; but there was nothing enthusiastic, carried-away, or impracticable about Samuel. He was a clear-eyed, firm-handed, sure-footed, resolute-minded, righteous man, with an inborn sense of truth and righteousness: and all his opinions, and decisions, and sentences carried all men's consent and conscience with them. In ancient Rome they used to put on a white robe when they went out to ask for the votes of the voters, and it was for this that they were called 'candidates' in the language of Rome: spotless men, that is, in our language. But it was only one famous name here and another famous name there that came out of office as clean as they entered it. Look at Samuel laying down his office, and putting on his snow-white mantle. 'Behold, now, I am old and grey-haired: and I have walked before you from my childhood unto this day. Behold, here I am. Witness against me before the Lord. Whose ox have I taken? or whose ass have I taken? or whom have I defrauded? Whom have I oppressed? or of whose hand have I received any bribe to blind mine eyes therewith? And I will restore it to you. And they said, Thou has not defrauded us, nor oppressed us, neither has thou taken aught of any man's hand. And he said to them, The Lord is witness. And they answered, He is witness.'

Samuel was removed from his mother's side while still a child. No sooner was he at home in Shiloh than Shiloh fell, and he had again to change his home. In his office of judge he was continually on circuit dispensing justice and judgment up and down the land. And then when Saul became king, Samuel was compelled to retire into obscurity, and become of no reputation. Samuel was emptied from vessel to vessel till there was no lees left in the wine. The noblest thing, in some respects, in all Samuel's noble life was the way he took the providence of God in the establishment of the monarchy. The monarchy was a great innovation. It was a great revolution. And even more than that, it was a severe condemnation, if not of Samuel's own life, yet of his office and his order, which are sometimes dearer to a man than life itself. And, in addition to that, it was the deposition and dismissal of his two sons from the office and the rank to which he had raised them. Everything was against Samuel taking kindly to the thought of the new monarchy. All Samuel's past life had been spent in animating and purifying, and restoring the republic; but when he saw that a kingdom was coming in, instead of meeting it with resistance and obstinacy and lifelong hostility, the great man bowed to the will of God and the will of Israel, and cast in his lot with the new dispensation. Samuel had a great struggle with himself to do it; and he did not hide that struggle from Israel. But, that struggle over, Saul had no such loyal and faithful friend as Samuel the deposed judge. The State and Church of Israel shall have Samuel's service to the end. What there is out of the great past that is worth preserving he will do his best to preserve. What of the old order can safely be carried over into the new order he will do his best to carry that over. As far as Samuel is concerned Saul and his kingdom shall not only have fair play; but they shall have all Samuel's influence with God and with man. It is only a great man and a noble who can act in that way. And the more individuality of character, and the more independence of mind, and the more strength of will such men have, the nobler is the thing they do. It takes the very finest natures to pass over from one generation to another, and to work in the new generation as they worked in the old. It was splendidly done by Samuel. And it has been splendidly done, now and again, since Samuel's day. And, best of all, it has been splendidly done in our own day. And it is one of the finest sights to be seen among men when men have eyes and hearts to see it. It is only the old, and the ripe, and the much-experienced, and the men fullest of past service, who can do Samuel's service to our generation and the generation which is coming up after us. No amount of talent; no amount of loyalty; no amount of humility, even, can make up in the young—in young statesmen and in young churchmen—for the wisdom, and the experience, and the standing, and the influence of the aged. If the past time is to hand over its proper heritage to the present time, it is the old who can best do it. And I do not know that history, either sacred or profane, holds out a better example of this large-hearted, public-spirited wisdom than Samuel the deposed judge, and now the chief counsellor Saul.

But Samuel, deposed and superseded as he was, was full of new and still more fruitful ideas and intentions for Israel. And what did Samuel do to occupy his talents in his ripe age, and still to serve God and God's people? Never mortal man did a better, or a more fruitful thing than Samuel now did. Samuel planned and set up an institution, so to call it, that has made far more mark on the world than anything else that survives to us out of Israel or Greece or Rome. In his ripe and farseeing years Samuel devised and founded and presided over a great prophetical school in his old age. That school of the prophets to which we owe so much of Samuel himself; to which we owe David, and Gad, and Nathan, and all their still greater successors; that great school was the creation and the care of Samuel's leisure from office. How much of the Old Testament itself we owe to the prophets, and the preachers, and the psalmists, and the sacred writers, and other trained students of Samuel's great school, we have not yet fully found out. The day may come when all the Old Testament, as we now have it, will be traced back to that great institution that God honoured Samuel to plan and to set up as his reward for his pure heart, and his holy, studious, self-sacrificing life. And it is admitted—it is no fancy to say it—that our modern universities, divinity halls, and great public schools, have all their far-down roots in Mount Ephraim, and in Samuel's great college which he founded there. True, divine prophecy does not come by the will of man in prophetical schools, or anywhere else. School or no school, holy men of God will always speak as they are moved by the Holy Ghost. No man knew that better than Samuel; but at the same time, no man ever struck out a more fruitful line of action in the things of God than when Samuel laid the foundation of the sacred school of Ramah. Israel had already a divine deposit of religion and worship and morality and civilisation, all of which they had but to accept and assimilate in order to be the strongest, the safest, and the happiest nation on the face of the earth. But the divine law was too high and too good for Israel. Their hearts were hard, and they were not upright in God's covenant. And the new monarchy was already threatening to become a very stronghold of that hard, worldly, rebellious spirit. Saul, in spite of all that Samuel could do, was soon to become a complete shipwreck. But the throne was destined to stand long after Saul was cast out of it; and Samuel is determined to do his very best to secure it that Saul's successors shall have around them and over their people a class of men who, if not indeed prophets,—Samuel cannot secure that— the wind bloweth where it listeth,—yet Samuel can and will secure that there shall be an estate of learned and earnest-minded men, who shall watch over the religion and the morals of the people, in the prophetical spirit and in the prophetical name. And thus it came about that at Naioth in Ramah the first school of the prophets was set up. Ramah was Elkanah's old property; it had now come into Samuel's hands; and at Naioth, the quietest and sweetest spot of all his patrimonial estate, Samuel set up the first divinity hall; the first school for prophets and psalmists in Israel.

But, crowning all and sanctifying all was Samuel's life of prayer. Samuel was a proverb of prayer. The tradition of Hannah's psalm and prayer was well known to every young prophet in Samuel's school, and her best memories were perpetuated and transmitted in the devotional life and labours of her son. 'Moses and Aaron among His priests, and Samuel among them that call on His name.' As much as to say that Samuel stands at the head of all the men of prayer in Israel, just as

Moses and Aaron stand at the head of all the prophets and priests in Israel. The successors of Moses and Aaron were a glorious enough succession; but all that fades and vanishes away before the far greater glory of pure and unceasing prayer, and especially of unceasing intercessory and undeserved prayer. 'As for me,' said Samuel, 'God forbid that I should sin against the Lord in ceasing to pray for you.' Samuel said that as his answer to his sentence of deposition and banishment from being their head and their king in all but the name. Samuel, then, among them that pray for their enemies and for them that despitefully use them. Samuel among them that are cast off and forgotten after a lifetime of self-forgetful service. Samuel among them that cease not to pray for the prosperity of those who have taken their place in the world and in the Church, and in the hearts and the mouths of men. Samuel among them who have such a pure heart that nothing will ever turn their heart to gloom, or bitterness, or discontent, or retaliation, or to anything else, but to still more prayer.

Such, then, was some of the interest that the Lord paid to Hannah for the early loan of Samuel her son. And the Lord is the same yesterday, to-day, and for ever.

XXXIV

SAUL

AND SAMUEL SAID, I AM THE SEER, AND TO-MORROW I WILL TELL THEE ALL THAT IS IN THINE HEART

Dr. Newman, after attempting three times to preach on Saul, is compelled to confess that Saul's character continues to be obscure to him, and he warns us that we must be exceedingly cautious while considering Saul's so obscure character. Now, if Saul's character was still so obscure to the subtlest and the acutest of all our preachers, I cannot expect to be able to say much to purpose upon it. At the same time, with so much told us about Saul; and told us in such a plain, open, and straightforward style; and told us, as it must have been, for our instruction, we may surely hope to be able, amid all his acknowledged obscurity, to gather sufficient instruction out of Saul to justify us in taking him up for our subject this evening.

But, unhappily, the obscurity begins further back than Saul.

The obscurity begins with Saul's father and mother. We never hear of Saul's mother; but what kind of a father can Kish have been? We know all about Samuel. There is no obscurity about Samuel. All Israel, from Dan even to Beersheba, knew that Samuel was established to be a prophet of the Lord; all Israel but Kish and his son Saul. Hannah, and Samuel, and Eli, and Hophni and Phinehas, and Ichabod were all household words, as we say, in every household in Israel. Only, there was a man of Benjamin whose name was Kish, and he had a son whose name was Saul, a choice young man, and a goodly, but neither father nor son, neither Kish nor Saul, had ever heard of Samuel. Kish the father, and Saul the son, were so busy breeding asses that they made light of Samuel, and would not come. Samuel was an old man by this time. Samuel had grown grey in a service that made all Israel acknowledge and know God from the one end of the land to the other; but Saul, all the time, did not know Samuel when he saw him. 'Tell me, I pray thee,' said Saul to a stranger he met on his way when he was in despair about his father's lost asses, 'where is the Seer's house.' 'I am the Seer myself,' said Samuel. 'Come with me, and I will tell thee all that is in thine heart.' Yes, there is some quite inexplicable obscurity about Kish as well as about Saul; an obscurity that perplexes us, and throws us out at the very opening of his son's sad history. And yet, when we turn back and begin to read Saul's whole history over again with our eye on the object; when we stop and look round about us as we read, the ancient obscurity begins to pass off, but only to let alarm and apprehension for ourselves and for our own sons take its place. The prophet Samuel had been a public man, as we say, long before Saul was born. And, but for Saul, we would have said that there could not possibly be a child, or a youth or a grown-up man in all Israel who had not often sat at Samuel's feet and drunk in his divine words. But the most public men, after all, have only their own public. Saul staggers us and throws us out till we look at ourselves and at the men round about us, and then we soon see, what had before been obscure to us, that our inborn and indulged tastes, likings, dispositions, inclinations, and pursuits rule us also, shape us, occupy us, and decide for us the men we know and the life we lead. Josephus says that Samuel had an inborn love of justice. But Saul had inherited from Kish an inborn and an absorbing love of cattle and sheep; and, till they were lost, Saul had no errand to Samuel's city. Why hold up our hands at Saul's obscurity, and at Saul's ignorance of Samuel? We have it in ourselves. We also see what we bring eyes to see, and ears to hear, and hearts to love. To go no further; take just yesterday's journals. They were full of good books. They were full of public meetings, lectures, classes, sermons, speeches, till reading men, and thinking men, and men set on their own self-improvement and their own salvation from sin, do not know where to turn or what to do next, the doors of life are so many and so wide open. Let him who passed all that before him yesterday, and then laid out all this week, redeeming all the time, that he might read the best and hear the best—let that man, and let no other man, cast the first stone at stupid Saul and his stupid father. For Saul was not more stupid among the pastures of Benjamin than we are among the churches, and the classes, and the libraries, and the reading-rooms, and the booksellers' shops of Edinburgh. 'Behold now,' said Saul's servant when the asses were hopelessly lost, 'there is in this city a man of God, and he is an honourable man: all that he saith cometh surely to pass; now, let us go thither.' If you have no more sense of religion and life than Saul and his father had, at least, like them, see that you have a religious servant. Saul's servant knew Samuel. Saul's servant had sat at Samuel's feet as often as he had a holiday. He had bargained with Kish for a day now and then to see Samuel when he was on circuit, and to hear the prophet when he preached. And your servant who stipulates to get out to chuch, and takes less wages in order to do so, he will be able to tell you where the Seer lives when you have lost all, and yourself to the bargain. Insignificant people—the sacred writer does not even know that servant's name—have sometimes most important information. Saul was led up to the door of his earthly kingdom by the piety of his father's servant; and you may be led up some day to the door of the heavenly kingdom by one of your servants who has interests and acquaintances and experiences that up to to-night you know nothing about.

After Samuel had anointed Saul to the kingdom, we come upon this very obscure Scripture: 'And it was so that when Saul had turned his back to go from Samuel, God gave Saul another heart, and the Spirit of God came upon Saul, and he prophesied.' Saul, you exclaim, a prophet! Saul with 'another heart'! Saul with the Spirit of God upon him! You cannot understand. No. But words must be read in the light of facts; and Bible words in the light of Bible facts. Profession must be judged by practice, and faith shown by works. And 'another heart' judged what it is by what comes out of it. Nay, prophecy itself is only a sounding brass or a tinkling cymbal if the prophet has not charity. 'Another heart' has more meanings than one in Holy Scripture; and so has the Spirit of God; and so has prophecy. Isaiah prophesied of the atoning death of Christ, but so did Caiaphas. The Spirit of God came upon Jesus at the Jordan, but He came also upon Samson at the camp of Dan, and upon Balaam beside the altar of Baal. Matthew Henry in two or three words makes clear to us all the obscurity of Saul's 'other heart.' 'Saul,' says the most sensible of commentators, 'has no longer the heart of a husbandman, concerned only with corn and cattle; he has now the heart of a statesman, a general, a prince. When God calls to service He will make fit for it. If He advances to another station, He will give another heart; and will preserve that heart to those who sincerely desire to serve Him.' So He will. But that is just what Saul, another heart and all, did not sincerely desire to do. And here hangs the true key to the whole of Saul's sad history. He was elected and crowned king over Israel, but he was as ignorant all the time of the God of Israel as he was of Samuel, the great prophet of the God of Israel. The Spirit of God came upon Saul for outward and earthly acts, but never for an inward change of heart. Saul prophesied, whatever that may mean; what he said has not been thought worthy of preservation; but after he had so prophesied he relapsed and remained the same man he had been before. Saul was like ninety-nine out of a hundred of us preachers. The truth is, another heart, prophetical spirit and all, Saul all along was little better than a heathen at heart. And hence it is that what has often been called the profanity of Saul's character scarcely rises to the dignity of profanity. Saul's most presumptuous sins scarcely attain to profaneness. You must have some sense of what is sacred before you can be really profane. But Saul has no such sense. In his youth he had not one spark of insight or interest in the religious life and workshop of Israel. He had never heard of Samuel. What he could not but hear he immediately forgot. When his sin found him out, and when salvation was at his very door, the poor graceless castaway had no higher request to make of Samuel than this: 'Honour me, I pray thee, before the people.' All sure marks of a man who has not learned the very first principles of the divine life. No. Saul the anointed king of Israel had all the time neither part nor lot in the true kingdom of God. At the same time, in giving Saul another heart, the God of Israel gave Saul the greatest opportunity of his life to make himself a new heart. God suddenly made a break in the ungodly and heathenish life of the son of Kish. So much so that Saul for the moment was almost persuaded to become an Israelite indeed. Saul all his days was never so near the kingdom of heaven as when he said to Samuel, 'Am not I a Benjamite, of the smallest of the tribes of Israel, and my family the least of all the families of Benjamin? Wherefore, then, speakest thou so to me?' That is the language of a man whose heart is really touched for the time with divine grace. That is real humility; and humility is the root of all the graces, both natural and supernatural. And had Saul only dwelt on that thought; had he returned all his days to that thought; that thought dwelt upon and added to at every new occasion and fresh proof of God's goodness and his own ill deserts—that would soon have made Saul's heart a new heart; that would soon have made Saul another man. But it was not so to be with Saul. As time went on, and as trials and temptations beset Saul, a hard and stony heart, a spirit of rebellion, and pride, and envy, and jealousy, and despair took possession of Saul, and held possession of Saul to his terrible end.

No; there is no such obscurity about Saul getting another heart and yet that heart coming to nothing. We have all had the same thing in ourselves. We ourselves have gone out on an errand of duty or of pleasure, and have come back with another heart. We were for the time like new creatures. Very little more at that time would have made us new creatures altogether. Such surprises of providence, such opportunities of making ourselves a new heart, are occurring continually. Sometimes it has been at a time of sorrow, and sometimes at a time of joy and gladness. At the death of a father or a mother; at the time of leaving home to take our place in a lonely world; or, again, at that happy time when our loneliness was so graciously dealt with by God. God, I feel sure, lets no man become a married man, for instance, without giving him the great opportunity and the new start in religion He gave to Saul when He made him king of Israel. In the kingly heart that God gives to every bridegroom we are not far for the time from the kingdom of heaven. No man, the most heathen of men, ever became a bridegroom and a married man without having opportunities and intentions and commencements of a new heart and a better life. We have all had times when our hearts were too big for our bosoms. And at such times we were almost persuaded to become Christian men. Yes; at one time or other, and more than once, you have all had Saul's great opportunity. Did you or did you not embrace it? The bare remembrance of those times of another heart all but brings them back again. Bring them back. You can. You still can, if you choose. And though their first impression must be somewhat faded and spent, let your resolution in God be all the greater that even yet you are determined to make yourself a new heart out of them. Determine to do it, and God will see it done. Say it, and see if He will not.

Had Saul's change of heart only held, had his conversion only become complete, Saul would have been one of the greatest of all the Old Testament men. Saul was not a common man. He was a choice young man, and a goodly; there was not among the children of Israel a goodlier person than he; from his shoulders upward he was higher than any of the people. He had a splendid body and a stately gait, and the very sins of his soul had a certain lurid grandeur about them also. After God gave Saul another heart his life was full for a time of the finest promise. What could have promised better than his strict silence to his inquiring uncle about his anointing by Samuel? Where a weaker man would have had his head turned and his tongue loosed, Saul told his uncle that the stray asses were at last found; but of the matter of the kingdom he was strictly silent. We are bound to put a good construction on Saul's silence in that matter. It is but fair and just to set Saul's silence that day down to humility and modesty. As also when he hid himself among the stuff on the day of his election. As also when he held his peace at the men of Belial mocking at his election. As also after his first great victory. Bring the men who say, Shall Saul rule over us, said the people, and put them to death this day. But Saul said, There shall not a man be put to death this day, for to-day the Lord hath wrought salvation in Israel. If all that is not to be set down to Saul's humility, self-command, and magnanimity, not to say piety, then Saul's character is obscure indeed. We would have had no hesitation in setting all that down to the best motives had it not been that all his future so terribly belied all such modesty, humility, self-command, magnanimity, and piety. The great preacher did not say it till he had felt it to be quite impossible to draw out Saul's obscure life into a consistent and open piece. And the more we work on Saul under that great preacher and after him, the more we feel the obscurity and the mystery of Saul's dark character. It would take a Shakespeare to put himself into Saul's place and let us see the obscure working of Saul's heart under all his temptations. But he has gone away and left us to deal with such characters as Esau, and Balaam, and Saul, and Judas for ourselves. Only, there is one dark passage toward the end of Saul's insane life that we need neither Shakespeare nor Newman to open up to us. Saul's mad and murderous envy of David is as clear as day to every man who puts its proper name on what goes on every day in his own evil heart.

Who is your Saul, my brethren? Who is the man that stands in the way of your promotion? Who sits in the seat that should by this time have been yours? Who is the man that casts the javelin of slander and detraction at your good name? Who has cost you home and friends by his spite, and malice, and jealousy? Mark that man. Never let your eye off that man. God will bring that man to your feet one day· He will lie under your sword some day soon. But touch not a hair of his head. Touch not the skirt of his robe, neither the spear at his bolster, nor the cruse at his side. Remember who and what you are. Remember what Name you bear, and walk worthy that day of that Name. Love your enemies, bless them that curse you, do good to them that hate you, and pray for them that despitefully use you and persecute you. Therefore, if thine enemy hunger, feed him; if he thirst, give him drink. Be not overcome of evil, but overcome evil with good.

Oh! exclaims Thomas Shepard, the grievous shipwrecks of some great ships! We see some boards and planks lying in the mud at low water, but that is all!

XXXV

DAVID—IN HIS VIRTUES

ARISE, ANOINT HIM FOR THIS IS HE

JESSE the Bethlehemite, the father of David, and the far-off father of Jesus Christ, as the son of Obed, who, again, was the son of Boaz and Ruth. Jesse had an illustrious past to look back to. He was the tenth in direct descent from his father Jacob, and more than one shining name stood in his illustrious ancestry. But it is not his so illustrious past, it is the surpassing splendour of his future that makes us look with so much interest on David's father. We are not told as much about Jesse as we might like. He is already an old man when we first see him. And it is somewhat remarkable that we are told nothing at all about David's mother. The more so, that there would seem to have been nothing about Jesse to lead us on to think of him as either transmitting the extraordinary ability of his youngest son, or as discovering or fostering his youngest son's extraordinary gifts and character. Jessie's sole interest to us is in this, that he had David among his sons. We bow before the old Bethlehemite because of the branch that grew out of his roots.

Latest born of Jesse's race,
Wonder lights thy bashful face,
While the Prophet's gifted oil
Seals thee for a path of toil.

Twofold praise thou shalt attain,
In royal court and battle-plain,
Then comes heartache, care, distress,
Blighted hope, and loneliness;
Wounds from friend and gifts from foe,
Dizzied faith, and guilt, and woe;
Loftiest aims by earth defiled,
Gleams of wisdom sin-beguiled,
Sated power's tyrannic mood,
Counsels shared by men of blood,
Sad success, parental tears,
And a dreary gift of years.

For the Lord had said to Samuel, Fill thine horn with oil, and go, I will send thee to Jesse the Bethlehemite; for I have provided Me a king among his sons. God sees not as man sees, and God works not as man works. In providing Him a king, God worked in a way strange and unlikely to our eyes. We would not have committed our coming king to Jesse to bring up. It was a strange school for a future king—the lonely sheepfolds of Bethlehem. So we think who look at the outward appearance. David was forgotten and neglected by his father; he was scoffed at and trampled upon by his brothers; but you cannot sour, or starve, or poison, or pervert a nature like David's. There is a well-spring of piety and of poetry in David that makes David independent of adverse circumstances. Nay, he takes prosperity out of adversity. That ruddy stripling has his harp and his sling and his father's sheep, and what more does he need to make him happy? He has the glorious traditions of his far-off father Israel to dream about. Isaac, and Jacob, and Joseph, and Moses, and Joshua, and Jephthah, and Samuel: his poet's eye doth glance from the one to the other till they are all with him as he folds his flock under the stars of Bethlehem. 'Now, as they were going along and talking, they espied a boy feeding his father's sheep. The boy was in very mean clothes, but of very fresh and well-favoured countenance, and as he sat by himself he sang. Then said their guide, Do you know him? I will dare to say that this boy lives a merrier life, and wears more of that herb called heart's-ease in his bosom than he that is clad in silk and velvet. So they hearkened, and he sang:—

> The Lord's my Shepherd, I'll not want,
> He makes me down to lie
> In pastures green; He leadeth me
> The quiet waters by.'

And, again, 'When I consider the heavens, the work of Thy fingers, the moon, and the stars, which Thou has ordained; what is man, that Thou are mindful of him? and the son of man, that Thou visitest him?' And, again, this: 'Day unto day uttereth speech, and night unto night showeth knowledge. There is no speech nor language where their voice is not heard.' No; that was not an erroneous school for David. All his days the remembrance of those days was dear to him. A draught of the water of the well of Bethlehem, even to old age, would make King David pure, and free, and young, and himself again.

'And Saul's servants said to him, Behold now, an evil spirit from God troubleth thee. Let our lord seek out a man who is a cunning player on an harp: and it shall come to pass, when the evil spirit is upon thee, that he shall play with his hand, and thou shalt be well. Behold, answered one of Saul's servants, I have seen a son of Jesse the Bethlehemite that is cunning in playing, and a mighty valiant man, and a man of war, and prudent in matters, and a comely person, and the Lord is with him. Wherefore Saul sent messengers to Jesse, and said, Send me David thy son, which is with the sheep. And it came to pass, when the evil spirit was upon Saul, that David took an harp, and played with his hand. So Saul was refreshed and was well, and the evil spirit departed from him.' Browning's *Saul* is a wonderful piece of writing. The colour, the movement, the insight, the passion of that piece are astonishing. What a gift is poetic genius! And how well laid out by Robert Browning. Let all young men be readers of Robert Browning, and imitators of David in *Saul* in this, that what David put his hand to, you may depend upon it, he will carry that through. There is an inborn temper of masterfulness in David. David never does anything by halves. Energy, decision, resolution, devotion, finish, scorn of idleness, scorn of ease, love of labour, love of danger—you will always find virtues like these in young David. Saul's servants had all heard of David. David's harp had sounded farther than David ever dreamed. Plenty of shepherd-boys had a harp, but there was no man in all Israel who could make his harp play and work cures of the mind like David. David was a man of strong passion, good and bad: but no passion in David's heart was stronger than the noble passion to do with all his might whatsoever his hand found to do. Harp, or sling, or sword, or sceptre, or psalmist's pen—it was all the same. David was a cunning man, and the Lord was with David. It would soon change the face of the world if all our young men would but determine to put on David's masterful mind. How much power is wasted; how many talents are let rot; how many opportunities are lost for ever for want of David's eager, onward, hopeful, masterful mind. How few men come to anything eminent, or distinguished, or praiseworthy. Jesse's son was not the only son in Israel who had an ear for music. But he was the only owner of an ear for music who did his very best by his ear. All the men in Saul's camp had the best-made slings hung at their belts, but it was the homeliest piece of skin and cord in all Israel that delivered the smooth stone into Goliath's forehead. How much half-finished work is gathering dust in all our houses! How many books, bought or borrowed, and let fall out of sight unread! How many costly instruments of music that nobody can play! How many languages smattered over! What heaps of sluggard's litter lying all around us! How few of our children can translate a page to perfection, or polish a sentence, or play a tune, or patch a garment, or prepare or eat a meal so that you can say, The Lord is with them! In His name, what your hand finds to do, do it with all your might to Him who slumbers not nor sleeps. Whether it is learning a language, or preparing a speech, or singing a song, or composing a sermon or a prayer, or visiting a stair, or teaching and training up a class, or ploughing a furrow, or sweeping a house, lay it not down till you can say, It is finished.

The eighteenth chapter of First Samuel contains some of the most difficult and dangerous passages in David's whole life, and four times in that single chapter David's wisdom is remarked on. David, we read, went out whithersoever Saul sent him, and behaved himself wisely. And after the foolish women had aroused Saul's envy and endangered David's life with their thoughtless songs and silly dances, we read again that David behaved himself wisely in all his ways. Wherefore, when Saul saw that David behaved himself very wisely, Saul was afraid of David. And then, summing up David's residence at Saul's difficult and dangerous court, the sacred writer says that David behaved himself more wisely than all the servants of Saul; so that his name was much set by. I feel certain that the extravagant and ill-considered songs of the excited women pained David far more deeply than they pained Saul. Their coarse chants must have grated painfully on David's finely-strung heart. Their singing and dancing drove Saul mad. But all that—the women's folly and the king's jealousy—only made David a wiser and a wiser man every new day. If David could have shut the mouths of these mischief-making women, how willingly would he have done it. They could not understand what was the matter with the usually so open David, the victorious captain who rode past them in silence, and with a dark cloud on his countenance. It says much for David, and it says no little for the sound public opinion of Israel in that day, that David's name was celebrated for his wisdom. Men of a cold, cautious, reserved character far sooner gain and far easier keep the name of wise men than their fellows who are of warmer feelings and more general impulses. The fullness and the openness of some men's hearts obscure to the multitude the lucidity and the solidity of their minds. We are ready to think the man wise and able who is silent, and reserved, and proud, and whose temper and tongue are edged in all he says and does with slight scorn of other men. The warm-hearted man is a far wiser man than the cold-hearted man ever can be, but it takes a warm heart and a wise to see that. David must have had great strength of character and great solidity of judgment, and he must have had good and honest hearts round about him, fully appreciating him, and guiding public opinion concerning him, when, with so much openness, friendliness, geniality, and humility, he gained such a name for prudence and wisdom. The voice of the people is sometimes, after all, the voice of God.

David's fine humility is beautifully brought out in the matter of his marriage. Saul's diabolical design was to get David murdered in connection with his marriage. But, without having discovered that, David's humility of heart and delicacy of mind became, unknown to himself, a shield to save his life. A less humble, a less noble man, might very well, in David's place, have given loose reins to his imagination and his ambition, and let himself dream about the king's daughter. The more so, that, after the coarse custom of the time, Saul had promised his daughter to the man who should rid him of Goliath. And David had done that. But it had never entered David's fondest dreams that King Saul should fulfil his proclamation to an obscure man like him. Nay; even when Saul thought he saw a way of getting David killed in connection with his marriage, David scorned the proposal of the plotters. They might think as meanly of Saul and Saul's house as they chose; but let them not so speak to the king's armour-bearer. 'Seemeth it to you a light thing to be a king's son-in-law, seeing that I am but a poor man, and lightly esteemed!' David has not forgotten his father's house. David has more place and honour already than he knows how to bear. He would lay it all down and return to the sheepfolds of his youth if he only could. Whatever he may be to those foolish women, David is no hero to himself. To himself he is still the youngest son of Jesse the Bethlehemite. Well may Solomon say, looking back with a son's pride to his father's character and career, By humility and the fear of the Lord are riches, and honour, and life.

It is to David's lasting honour also that the land of Israel was not plunged into all the horrors of civil war. His men were increasing in numbers every day, and their extraordinary devotion to David, added to the rankling of their own wrongs, made them ready for anything. David's self-restraint was the one thing that stood between Saul and the loss of his throne and the loss of his life. It happened one day about that time that David and his outlawed men were hiding in a cave among the rocks of the wild goats, when, as Providence would have it, Saul, who was pursuing David, came up to that very cave to sleep. Now is David's opportunity. The Lord, said David's men, hath to-day delivered your enemy into your hand. David drew his sword and stepped down to where the sleeping king lay, and cut off the skirt of Saul's garment, and withdrew again into the darkness. His men wondered why he had not brought the king's head in his hand instead of the lappet of his robe. When Saul rose from his sleep and left the cave, David went to the mouth of the cave and called out, My lord, the king! Think of Saul's feelings when he looked up and saw David, whom he was hunting to death, standing on the spot where he had just risen from sleep, and standing with his sword in one hand and the skirt of Saul's robe in the other. When Saul looked up, David stooped with his face to the earth, and bowed himself. And David said to Saul, Wherefore hearest thou men's words against me? See the skirt of thy robe in my hand, and know that though some bade me kill thee, mine eye spared thee; for I said. I will not put forth mine hand against my lord, for he is the Lord's anointed. Is this thy voice, David? exclaimed Saul. My son David, thou art more righteous than I; for thou hast rewarded me good, whereas I have rewarded thee evil!

In the court, in the camp, in the caves of Engedi and Adullam, on the throne, in the sanctuary—all hearts, good and bad, fly open in David's presence. Like his New Testament Son, David's life, in its way, was the light of men. We see all the men and women of David's day in the light of David. All who come near David, ever after their hearts are naked and open to us. Saul, Jonathan, Merab, Michal, Nabal, Abigail, Abner, Joab, Uriah, Nathan, Shimei, Absalom, Solomon—we see them all in the light of David's blazing presence among them. There are some men who shut up every heart that comes near them. They chill, and cramp, and shut up every heart. But David warmed, and enlarged, and enriched, and lighted up, for good or for evil, every heart that came into his generation. Even Saul is no longer obscure after David enters Saul's court. It was David's heart. It was his talents; it was his character; it was his virtues; sometimes it was his vices; but it was always his heart. It was his heart; it was his love; it was his magnificent and unparalleled power of sympathy. It was the divine nature in David: it was Jesus Christ in David long before Jesus Christ came. Bring my soul out of prison, sang David in one of his most solitary and forsaken psalms. Bring my soul out of prison, that I may praise Thy name. The righteous shall compass me about; for Thou shalt deal bountifully with me. How well that prayer and hope was fulfilled in Israel: and how well it is fulfilled still among ourselves let David's psalms testify. Look how the righteous everywhere compass about David the sweet psalmist of Israel. Arise, anoint him: for this is he.

XXXVI

DAVID—IN HIS VICES

THE DECEITFULNESS OF SIN

BUTLER has a sermon on self-deceit which you should all read till you have it by heart. If you will listen to him, Butler will prove to you and will convince you that self-deceit, or internal hypocrisy, as he sometimes calls it, is the greatest of all your guilt, and is, in addition, the corruption of your whole moral character. He will show you also, in a way that will startle you, that David was guilty of this worst of all sins beyond any other saint or sinner in all the Bible. In Butler's sober, but most convincing and most solemnising words, David's is the most prodigious instance of the very wickedest and the very deadliest of all the vices of the vicious heart of man. All David's other vices were but skin wounds and surface sores that might soon have been bound up; at their worst, to borrow David's own words about them, they were but so many broken bones. But David's self-deceit was deep-seated, and it would have been deadly to David but for Nathan, or, rather, but for the Lord. As for David's fall, let it not be once named among you, as becometh saints. But, past speaking about as David's fall was, it was what followed his fall that so displeased the Lord. In the words of Butler's latest editor, 'it is safer to be wicked in the ordinary way than from this corruption lying at the root.' As Thomas Goodwin points out in his great treatise on the *Aggravation of Sin,* it was the 'matter of Uriah,' even more than the matter of Bathsheba, that awakened the anger of the Lord against David. That is to say, it was David's sin of deliberation and determination, rather than his sin of sudden and intoxicating passion. It was both matters; it was both sins; but it cannot be overlooked that it was after a twelvemonth of self-deceit, internal hypocrisy, and self-governing silence on David's part that Nathan was sent to David in such divine indignation. How a man like David could have lived all that time soaked to the eyes in adultery and murder and not go mad is simply inconceivable. That is to say, it would be inconceivable if we had not ourselves out of which to parallel and illustrate David, and thus to make David both possible and natural to us. Before you begin to read and think; as long as you confine your reading and thinking to the reading and thinking of children and fools, you will think it impossible that all the self-deceitfulness and internal hypocrisy that could possibly be in David and in the devil taken together, could have so blinded David to the blackness of his sin, and to the absolute certainty of God's dreadful judgments. But when you become a man in the books you read, and in the matters of your own heart; and especially in the superlative deceitfulness and desperate wickedness of your own heart, you will stop all your childish exclamations over David, and will say to yourself, I myself am David; I myself am that self-deceiving man. 'What the particular circumstances were with which David extenuated his crimes, and quieted and deceived himself, is not related.' No. They are not related; but we may guess at some of them to our own self-discovery and self-advantage. David would say to himself such things as these: 'I am the king, and Uriah and his wife are both my servants. All that he has in mine. She is not for such as he. She should be a queen, and she shall be. And I can make it up to him, and I will.' And then, after that, there was Uriah's disobedience and insolence to his king; his open disloyalty and his boasted indifference to his king's discovery and disgrace. 'Yes, the sword devoureth one as well as another,' David would say. 'And it might have devoured Uriah even if I had not written that letter.' And then, to repay, and repair, and cover it all up, David fetched the woman to his house, and she became his wife, and bare him a son. And, besides all that, it was all past: and why go back upon the past? David, you may be sure, had all these, and many more than all these, 'distinctions to fence with.' And then, what was wanting in all that, himself came in to complete and carry off the case; self, 'the most disingenuous and abominable principle that ever was.' Self, that utterly ungodly, diabolical, inhuman, inconceivably wicked, and detestable thing that was so strong in David and is so strong in you and in me. He who watches the workings of self in his own mind and heart he will not be forward to throw a stone at David: he will not be surprised at anything he reads about David or any other man. He will not wonder either at David's fall or at his subsequent self-deceit. I can fully, and down to the bottom, study the curse and shame and pain of self in no other heart but in my own; not even in David's heart. And I am warned of God that, with all my study and all my watchfulness and all my prayerfulness, the deceitfulness and the internal hypocrisy of my own heart will still deceive me. Well, all I shall say in answer to that is this, that if my heart is worse than I know it to be, then the God of all grace, with all the blood of His Son, and with all the patience and power of His Spirit, help me! Me, and all men like me; if there is another man like me in this matter on earth or in hell. My brethren, beware how you shield yourself from yourself, and use 'distinctions' when you are conversing with your conscience about yourself. To be pointed at, and told to his face that he was unclean, and cruel, and cowardly, and guilty of blood, was David's salvation. And to have some one injured enough and angry enough; or friendly and honest and kind enough, to call you to your face false, or cruel, or envious, or malicious, or hard-hearted, or ignorant and narrowminded and full of prejudice and party-spirit, or sycophantic to the great, and supercilious and harsh to the poor, or all that together, might be the beginning of your salvation. And would he then be your enemy who first told you that saving truth? Surely you will not think it. Let the righteous smite me, and it shall be a kindness. Let him reprove me, and it shall be an excellent oil that shall not break my head. But, far best of all, let my conscience smite me, and about my self-love and my self-deceit in me.

Butler points out at the same time that, portentous as David's internal hypocrisy and self-deceit was, it was all the time local and limited in David. That is to say, his self-deceit had not as yet spread over and corrupted his whole life and character. There was real honesty in David all this self-deceiving time. David gave scope, in Butler's words, to his affections of compassion and goodwill, as well as to his passions of another kind. And, while this is some comfort to us to hear, there is a great danger to us in this direction also. The whited sepulchres fasted twice in the week, and they gave tithes of all that they possessed. They made broad their phylacteries, and made long prayers, and were always to be seen in the synagogues, with their mint and anise and cumin. They made clean, no men made so clean, the outside of the cup and platter. Many of them had begun, like David, with only one thing wrong in their life; but it was a thing that they hushed up in their own consciences, till by that time the self-deceit was spreading and was well-nigh covering with death and damnation their whole life and character. David was rescued from that appalling end; but he was fast on the way to that end when the Lord arrested him. David all the time was administering justice and judgment as boldly, and with as much anger at evil-doers, as if there had never been a man of the name of Uriah on the face of the earth. And just because he was making men who had no pity restore the lamb fourfold; just because of that he was more and more confirmed in his own self-deceit. We would need Nathan and his parable at this point. Only, your self-deceit would make you miss his point, till he drove it home into your deceitful heart. You are the man. You are all the more severe with one class of sinners that you sin yourself so much with another and opposite class. You are terrible to see and hear on the sins of the flesh, because you are up to the eyes in the far more fatal sins of the mind. You despise and detest publicans and sinners, while you dine and sup and plot against Christ with Pharisees and internal hypocrites. We all turn away our eyes and our ears from parables like that. Yes, but Butler warns us that it is as easy to close the eyes of the mind as those of the body, as, also, that though a man has the best eyes in the world, he cannot see in any direction but in that to which he turns his eyes. Let the man, then, who would discover his own self-deceit, if there is one such here, let him turn his eyes in upon his own heart, and especially let him turn his eyes in the opposite direction in his own heart to that in which his easy and untempted virtue displays itself.

But so bold, and towering, and self-deceived is our self-deceit, that it invades and entrenches itself, not in the matters of morals only; it comes to its fullness and to a positive grandeur in our devotions; in our daily dealings with God Himself. Nothing can be more open and notorious than the self-deceit and utter hypocrisy of our psalms and our prayers. David says, and he says it, no doubt, from his own devotional experience, that if he regards iniquity in his heart, the Lord will not hear him. How much less would the Lord have heard him if he had carried out his iniquity openly, and had put all the deepest deceit of his heart into his psalms and his prayers, as we do. I do not read that David composed any penitential psalms during those self-deceiving twelve months. And yet there is no saying. There is no limit to the sacrilege and profanity of an internal hypocrisy. Be that as it may, if David did not, we do. What could be more self-deceitful than our public worship in this house? Stop and think over the next psalm that is given out, and say if you have forehead enough to sing it after you understand it. And, whether you do that or no, let any man venture to accept your psalm as sincere, and attempt to deal with you accordingly, and you will open his eyes. Let him venture with a counsel, or a correction, or a warning, or a reproof, and he will not take you at your word in the church or in the prayer-meeting again. Woe to the man who believes that you are in earnest as you prostrate yourself before God and man in your psalms and prayers. You will soon undeceive him if he thinks that you are broken and contrite in heart, or meek and lowly in heart, or that you lack wisdom, love the cross, wait for light, and are the little children of the kingdom of heaven. 'Julius goes to prayers, he confesses himself to be a miserable sinner, he accuses himself to God with all the aggravations that can be, as having no health in him; yet Julius cannot bear to be informed of any imperfection, or suspected to be wanting in any degree of virtue. Now, can there be stronger proof that Julius is wanting in the sincerity of his devotions? Is not this a plain sign that his confessions to God are only words of course, an humble civility of speech to his Maker, in which his heart has no share? If a man was to confess that his eyes were bad, his hands weak, his feet feeble, and his body helpless, he would not be angry with those that supposed he was not in perfect strength, or that he might stand in need of some assistance. Yet Julius confesses himself to be in great weakness, corruption, disorder, and infirmity, and yet is angry at any one that does but suppose his defection in any virtue. Is it not the same thing as if he had said, You must not imagine that I am in earnest in my devotion?'

He was a happy preacher whose pulpit awakened David and brought David back to God. Nathan took his life in his hand that day. But he had his reward. And what a reward it was!

Think of having David's soul set down to your account at the great day! What shall we ourselves owe to Nathan at that day for that sermon? We should never have had David's psalms but for Nathan's sermon. And what should we have done, I cannot conceive, without David's psalms. Preaching is magnificent work if only we could get preachers like Nathan. If our preachers had only something of Nathan's courage, skill, serpent-like wisdom, and evangelical instancy. But even Nathan himself would be helpless with some of you. You would have turned upon Nathan; you would have taken his good name and his life; you would have written a letter about him to Joab at Rabbah. Brutus never read a book but to make himself a better man. When will that be said about your coming to church? Happy the preacher who has so much as one Brutus a Sabbath day among his hearers! Happy the preacher who has a David among his hearers from time to time, so that he can pass on and say to him, The Lord also hath put away thy sin! We ministers must far more study Nathan's method; especially when we are sent to preach awakening sermons. Too much skill cannot be expended in laying down our approaches to the consciences of our people. Nathan's sword was within an inch of David's conscience before David knew that Nathan had a sword. One sudden thrust, and the king was at Nathan's feet. What a rebuke of our slovenly, unskilful, blundering work! When we go back to Nathan and David, we forget and forgive everything that had been evil in David. The only thing wanting to make that day in David's life perfect was that Nathan should have had to come to David. Now, what will make this the most perfect day in all your life will be this, if you will save the Lord and His prophet all that trouble so to speak, and be both the Lord and His prophet to yourself. Read Nathan's parable to yourself till you say, I am the man! And so ever after with every parable, and with every psalm, and with every prayer, and with everything of that kind. When we preach anything of that kind, all the time we are preaching, be you fast kindling your own anger against yourself. And as soon as we are done preaching, speak you out in yourself and at yourself, and say, As the Lord liveth, the man that hath done this thing shall surely die. And he shall restore the lamb fourfold, because he did this thing, and because he had no pity. And, always, when the thirty-second psalm is announced to be sung, and when innocent men and women and children are getting their instruments of music ready, be you getting yourself ready till you cannot wait for them. Blessed is the man!—lead the congregation, and sing. And, when, by a happy inspiration the fifty-first psalm is again given out, do you ejaculate up to David's God your daily thankfulness that there is such a psalm in existence. For it is new to you every morning and every night. Just hear a verse of it, and say if it is not. 'Behold, Thou desirest truth in the inward parts; and in the hidden part Thou shalt make me to know wisdom. Create in me a clean heart, O God, and renew a right spirit within me. Cast me not away from Thy presence, and take not Thy Holy Spirit from me.' 'I conceal nothing,' sobbed out Bishop Lancelot Andrewes every Lord's Day morning before he could face his congregation and his clergy. 'I make no excuses. I denounce against myself my sins. Indeed, I have sinned against the Lord, and thus and thus have I done. O Lord, I have destroyed myself. And Thou art just in all that has come upon me. I acknowledge my transgressions, and my sin is ever before me. I abhor and bruise myself that my penitence, Lord, O Lord, is not deeper. Help Thou mine impenitence, and more, and still more, piece Thou, rend, and crush my heart. Magnify Thy mercies toward the chief of sinners, and say to me, Thy sins are forgiven thee. Say, O God, unto my soul, I am thy salvation!'

And, then, David's 'way of lying.' Did any of you ever suppress and keep silent about your principles, say, at an election time? Did you ever hedge and double in your public life in order to get a post, or in order to stand well with those who have posts and pieces of bread to give away? Did you ever tune a speech or a sermon or a prayer to turn away the anger of a man whose anger you feared, or with an eye to a man you wished to stand well with? Or, did you ever 'tell a vain lie upon yourself,' ascribing something falsely or exaggeratingly to yourself through vanity or other self-interest? And, alongside of that, when and where did you last put forward, or allow another to put forward, a detracting word about your friend or about your rival, and hold back what you felt would be for his advantage? Then, the story of David and the priest of Nob is, in that case, written for your learning. You will see in that chapter how David obtained hallowed bread of Ahimelech, and what that bread cost Ahimelech and his house. 'Remove from me the way of lying, and grant me Thy law graciously. He points to the sort of his guileful heart,' says Goodwin, 'wherein his grief lay. David, among other corruptions, had a lying spirit sometimes.'

Or, again, were you ever driven to simulate sickness, or even madness, in order to get out of some dreadful crime or scrape you had fallen into? See, then, God's compassion for you at David's cost, in His having had that so humiliating chapter put into your Bible. What a state of mind must David have been in that day when the servants of King Achish led David like a madman or a wild beast to the borders of their land, and then let loose, as you would let loose and hound out a madman or a wild beast you were terrified at! O what a bottomless mystery and misery and agony of sin and shame the heart of man is, and most of all the heart of a man after God's own heart! From the same fountain will spring forth, on sufficient temptation and opportunity, the noblest deeds, and the most debasing and despicable. Had it not been in the Bible, we would have denounced that chapter as the cruelest, the most blasphemous, and the most utterly impossible slander. And, then, to have two splendid psalms as the immediate outcome of that sickening chapter! Truly they would need to be men in understanding, and not children, who read the Bible. For,

> Not in their brightness, but their earthly stains,
> Are the true seed vouchsafed to earthly eyes,
> And saints are lowered that the world may rise.

XXXVII

DAVID—IN HIS GRACES

A MAN AFTER MINE OWN HEART

DR. THOMAS GOODWIN says that David's youthful virtues differed from his old-age graces somewhat as wild marjoram differs from sweet. Now, the wild marjoram is little better to begin with than a useless wandering weed; whereas the sweet is a planted, a protected, and a most precious herb. Your meekness, and your humility, and your industry, and so on, proceeds the incomparable Puritan preacher, must spring up, not only out of your constitution and your temperament; it must spring up out of your heart, as your heart is more and more softened, and tamed, and humbled, and sweetened by the grace of God and by the indwelling Spirit of Christ. Many a man, the sometime President of Magdalene is continually warning us, may live and die a model and a praise of 'civil virtues,' who never all his days comes within sight of the first principles of gospel holiness. At the same time, marjoram is marjoram, whether it is found running wild on the sides of the hills, or is watched over, and weeded, and watered, and gathered till it makes our whole house full of sweetness and health with its odorous fragrance. And teachableness, and meekness, and gentleness, and submissiveness, and thankfulness, and suchlike, are what they are, even before they are engrafted on Him who is the true and original root both of our wild and fast-fading flowers, as well as of our most fragrant and most fruitful herbs.

I would fain begin David's shining graces by saying that faith in God is the true and real and living root of them all. I would fain begin with David's faith, were it not that there is no word in all our tongue that carries less meaning and less vision to most people's minds and hearts than just this so frequent sound—faith. As Pascal says, We all believe in that dead word God; but there is only one here and another there who really and truly believes in the living, ever-present, and all-present God. But this is David's shining distinction above all God's saints—unless there are two or three in the New Testament who equal and excel David. In his pure, courageous, noble youth; all through his hunted-down days; fallen and broken and full of the pains of hell; filling up his dreary gift of years,—David is always the same unconquered miracle of faith in God. Take and read and hear what David says to the Philistine giant about God, and you will see somewhat of his youthful faith in God. Then pass on to far on in his life, and open the hundred and thirty-ninth psalm; and I am safe to say that David, the author of that psalm, and Jesus of Nazareth, whom I may call the finisher of it, have been the only two saints and sons of God on the face of this earth who have ever taken up, understood, and imaginatively and unceasingly employed in their prayers that great believing psalm. And therefore it has been that they are the only two, father and son, to whom a voice came from heaven saying, Thou art a man after Mine own heart, and, This is My beloved Son, in whom I am well pleased. Jesus Christ was out of sight the greatest and the best believer this earth has ever seen. But the best of it is that He was beholden to David's psalms of faith, and trust, and resignation, and assurance to support and to give utterance to His faith in His father. The psalms of David, says Isaac Williams, were our Lord's constant prayer-book. When, therefore, you begin to ask after and to enter on the life of faith, open and read David's life and David's psalms, comparing them together; and then pass on to Jesus Christ, and then to the Apostle Paul. 'Faith is the modestest of all the graces,' says the princely preacher I began with, and at the same time, it is the most masterful. Wherever true faith is, it frameth the heart to the most childlike and friendlike dispositions towards God. Faith, my brethren, is a passion; it is a strong and a commanding instinct of our hearts after Christ, and after mystical union with Christ, so that we cannot be at peace and satisfied without Him.'

But, who is that roaring all the day long on the murderous wheel? Who is that stretched and stretched again on the rack all night till all his bones are out of joint—out of joint and broken in pieces with the hammer and the anger of God? The voice of whose roaring is that—According to the multitude of Thy tender mercies blot out my transgressions? And that—For I acknowledge my transgressions, and my sin is ever before me? Do you ask who that is? Do you not know? That is the prodigal son of the Old Testament. That is the same man who sometime went out against the giant, and against the bear, and against the lion in the name and in the strength of God. That is the anointed of the Lord. That is the King of Israel. That is the man after God's own heart. And he lies roaring on the rack—

Thus on us to impress
The portent of a blood-stained holiness.

For, holiness it still is; a true, a great, and an ever-growing holiness, though a holiness ever after to be stained with blood; but, also, to the end to be washed whiter than the snow in better blood. And a holiness, too, with a height, and depth, and a fire, and an inwardness, and a solemnity, and a far-sounding psalmody in it, of which would seem scarcely to be attainable in this life unless under the stain of blood, or of something that stains still worse than blood. Dreadful sin! that can only be propitiated by blood upon blood! Dreadful holiness! that can only be attained through tears and blood! But, blessed holiness that is still attainable by us all at that, or at any other price possible to be paid by God or man! As David's holiness was, and as all their holiness is, to whom David is set forth as a portent, and at the same time as an encouragement.

I was always exceedingly pleased with that saying of Chrysostom, says Calvin, 'The foundation of our philosophy is humility.' And yet more pleased with that of Augustine: 'As, says he, 'the rhetorician being asked what was the first thing in the rules of eloquence, he answered, Delivery. What was the second? Delivery. What was the third? still he answered, Delivery. So if you ask me concerning the graces of the Christian character, I would answer firstly, secondly, and thirdly, and for ever, Humility.' And thus it is that God sets open His school for teaching us humility every day. Humility is the grace of graces for us sinners to learn. There is nothing again like it, and we must have a continual training and exercise in it. You learn to pronounce by your patrons complaining that they cannot hear you, and that they must carry their cases to another advocate unless you learn to speak better. And, as you must either please your patrons or die of starvation, you put pebbles in your mouth and you go out to recite to yourself by the river-side till your rhetoric is fit for a Greek judge and jury to sit and hear. And so with humility, which is harder to learn than the best Greek accent. You must go to all the schools, and put yourself under all the disciplines that the great experts practise, if you would put on true humility. And the schools of God to which He puts His great saints are such as these. You will be set second to other men every day. Other men will be put over your head every day. Rude men will ride roughshod over your head every day. God will set his rudest men, of whom He has whole armies, upon you every day to judge you, and to find fault with you, and to correct you, and to blame you, and to take their business away from you to a better—to a better than you can ever be with the best pebbles that ever river rolled. Ay, He will take you in hand Himself, and He will set you and will keep you in a low place. He will set your sins in battle-array before your face. He will exact silence, and your mouth in the dust, and a rope on your head, and your heart a pool of tears, long after you had thought that you were to be set in a wealthy place. But let me say David at once. For it is David who rises before me as I speak of injuries, and insults, and detractions, and depreciations, and threats, and yet sorer, and yet severer and more immediate handlings by God Himself. David might have put Joab, and Shimei, and all the rest of his tutors and governors, in the front of the battle as he put Uriah; but he could not cast a piece of a millstone on his Maker from the walls of Rabbah, and he would not now if he could. And no more will he seek to silence a single one of his many reminders and accusers; no, not the most malignant, insolent, and unceasing of them all.

Once let David, or any other man, begin to taste the heavenly sweetness of true humility over against pride, and over against rebellion, and over against retaliation, and he will become positively enamoured and intoxicated with his humiliations. What once was death and hell to him will now be life and peace and salvation to him. What at one time he had almost committed murder to cover up, he will now hearken for from every house-top. When I was a child I used every Sabbath-day to read David's challenge to the giant, and I thought I was sanctifying the Sabbath over that Scripture. But for many years now, and more and more of late years, my Bible opens of itself to me at the place where Shimei casts stones and dirt at David, till David says, So let him curse, because the Lord hath said to him, Curse David. My children still read Goliath on Sabbath evenings, but I am on the watch to see how soon I can safely introduce them to Shimei. Shimei is the man for me and mine! Only, may I endure my schoolmaster to the bitter end better than even David did. Let me take insults, and injuries, and slights, and slings from men, and God's hand itself, as David that day took Shimei's curses. Nay, things that would seem to you to have nothing in the world to do either with my past sins or with my present sinfulness—let me have David's holy instinct, let me lay down David's holy rule, to look at everything of that kind that comes to me as so many divine calls and divinely opened doors to a deeper humility. Graces also grow by what they feed on; and humility grows by deliberately dieting itself on such humiliations as these, both human and divine. And evangelical humility grows by being fed, and by feeding itself on evangelical humiliations. If any one has the steadiness of eye and the strength of head, and the spiritual ambition and enterprise, to penetrate into this region of things, he will find a field rich in these and in many suchlike spiritual blessings in Jonathan Edwards's *Religious Affections.* I shall close up this grace of David by this specimen of mighty Edwards: 'Evangelical humiliation is the sense that a Christian man has of his own utter despicableness and odiousness, with an always answerable frame of heart. This humiliation is peculiar to true saints, for it is always accompanied with a sight of the transcendent beauty of divine things. And then, God's true saints all see, more or less, their own odiousness on account of sin, and the exceedingly hateful nature of all sin. Evangelical humiliation consists in a mean esteem of ourselves, as in ourselves nothing, and altogether contemptible and odious. This, indeed,' Edwards goes so far as to say, 'is the greatest and the most essential thing in all true religion.'

'The grey-haired saint may fail at last'; and the last sight we see of David is his deathbed shipwreck on that very same sunken rock he had steered past so often in the stormy passage of his life. On his death bed, David failed in that very grace which had been such a strength and such an ornament to his character on till now, and such a pride and such a boast to us. But the truth is, the only saint whose path has ever been as the shining light was not David, but David's far-off Son. And it was exactly where David so sadly struck and sank that his divine Son touched and attained to the top of His obedience, and gave to Himself the finishing touch of His full sanctification. Father, forgive them, He said, and gave up the ghost. I do not know that of all the bad blood of which all our hearts are full there is any that lasts longer than anger, and resentment, and ill-will at our enemies, at our detractors, and at those who despise and deride us. It is only the cold, firm fingers of death that will squeeze the last dregs of that worst of all bad blood out of our hearts. We would draw the curtains of David's deathbed if we dared. But we dare not, and we would not if we could. For, after all, David is not our surety. David is not our righteousness. David did not die the just for the unjust. Nor at his very youngest and best is David set forward as an example to the disciples of Jesus Christ. David at his best, as at his worst, is one of ourselves. David is a man of like passions with ourselves. David was cut out of the same web, and he was shaped out of the same substance as ourselves. He was a man of like passions with us, and, like our passions, his were sometimes at his heel, but more often at his throat. David held back his bad passions at Saul, and at Shimei, and at Joab, occasion after occasion, till we were almost worshipping David. But, all the time, and all unknown to us, they were there. Till, of all times and of all places in the world, David's banked-up passions burst out on his deathbed, that no flesh might glory in God's presence. But that, according as it is written, He that glorieth, let him glory in the Lord. And, like David, we sometimes master somewhat and smother down our passions of resentment and retaliation and ill-will. But with us as with David, at our best it is only a semblance and a surface of self-mastery. The bad blood is there still. And if it is not roaring in every vein as it used to do, the thick pestiferous dregs of it are all the more settled deep down in our hearts. Jeremiah is entirely right about us. He is divinely and entirely right about us. He is divinely and entirely right about the resentment, and the hatred, and the ill-will of our hearts at all who have ever hindered us, or injured us, or detracted from us, or rebuked us, or refused to flatter us. Yes, we will put our mouth in the dust, and a rope upon our head; and, as at the day of judgment, we will tell the truth, and will say it in words which the Holy Ghost teacheth: Yes, we will say, my injured and resentful heart is desperately and deceivingly wicked. Desperately, and deceivingly, and down to death wicked. But no longer than that. No longer after death. After death we shall be done both with death and hell; and after death we shall awake in His likeness who died, not cursing Judas, and Annas, and Caiaphas, and Herod, and the soldier with the spear, but saying over them all with His last breath, Father, forgive them, for they know not what they do. For even hereunto were we called.

There is one thing, so far as I remember, that David never failed or came short in. 'My honest scholar,' says Isaac Walton, when he is giving his companion a lesson in making a line and in colouring a rod, 'all this is told you to incline you to thankfulness; and, to incline you the more, let me tell you that though the prophet David was guilty of murder and adultery, and many of the most deadly sins, yet he was said to be a man after God's own heart, because he abounded more and more with thankfulness than any other that is mentioned in Holy Scripture. As may appear in his book of Psalms, where there is such a commixture of his confessing of his sins and unworthiness, and such thankfulness for God's pardon and mercies as did make him to be accounted, and that by God Himself, to be a man after His own heart. And let us, in that, labour to be as like David as we can. Let us not forget to praise Him for the innocent mirth and pleasure we have met with since we met together.' Would you know? asks William Law in his beautiful chapter on singing psalms—would you know who is the greatest saint in the world? Well, it is not he who prays most or fasts most; it is not he who gives most alms, or is most eminent for temperance, chastity, or justice; but it is he who is always thankful to God, who wills everything that God wills, and who receives everything as an instance of God's goodness, and has a heart always ready to praise God for His goodness. And then Law winds up with this, and I wish it would send you all to the golden works of that holiness-laden writer—Sometimes, he adds, imagine to yourselves that you saw holy David with his hands upon his harp, and his eyes fixed upon heaven, calling in transport upon all creation, sun and moon, light and darkness, day and night, men and angels, to join with his rapturous soul in praising the Lord of heaven. Dwell upon this imagination till you think you are singing with this divine musician; and let such a companion teach you to exalt your heart unto God every new morning in his thanksgiving psalms. Or make a morning psalm suitable to your own circumstance out of David's great thanksgiving psalms. You should take the finest and the selectest parts of David's finest and selectest psalms, and adding them together make them every morning more and more fit to express your own thankful hearts. And, till you have had time to compose a psalm exactly suitable to your own standing in grace, you might meantime sing this psalm of David every morning with a spiritual mind and a thankful heart:

Bless, O my soul, the Lord thy God.
And not forgetful be
Of all His gracious benefits
He hath bestow'd on thee.

For Thou art God that dost
To me salvation send,
And I upon Thee all the day
Expecting do attend.

XXXVIII

DAVID—IN HIS SERVICES

WELL DONE, GOOD AND FAITHFUL SERVANT

God is the only master with servants who accepts the intention for the action. God alone of all paymasters pays as good wages for the good intentions of His servants as He pays for their best performances. One of David's greatest and best services to God and men never went further than the good intention. But David was as much praised and as much paid for his good intention to build the temple as if he had lived to see the golden towers of God's house shining in the Sabbath sun. It will help on your salvation to lay it to heart that hell is paved with good intentions; and it will, at the same time, comfort every good and honest heart to be told that good intentions form some of the surest of stepping-stones to heaven. Think much about intentions. Give, and it shall be given you; good measure, pressed down, and shaken together, and running over, shall men give into your bosom. For with the same measure that you mete withal it shall be measured to you again. After which Bengel acutely annotates that it is by our hearts that we both mete out to others and have it meted out to ourselves. It would have gone hard with the poor widow if she had only had a farthing meted out to her in her Lord's judgment on her. But her Lord looked on her heart. And thus it is that she sits in heaven to-day among the queens who sit there on their thrones of gold, because she had such a queenly heart that day in the temple porch. Both from David's intended temple; from the poor widow's actual collection at the door of David's temple; and from Bengel's spiritual annotation let us learn this spiritual lesson, that our hearts are the measure both of our work and of our wages in the sight of God. You cannot build and repair all the churches and mission-houses and manses at home and abroad you would like to build and repair. You cannot endow all the chairs of sacred learning you would like. You cannot contribute to the sustentation and spread of the Christian ministry as you would like. You cannot visit and relieve all the fatherless and widows in their affliction as you would like. You cannot make the reading, or the religion, or the devotional life of your people what your heart is full of. You wish you could. So did David. David had magnificent dreams about the temple. He built the temple every night in his sleep. And had he been permitted he would not have slept with his fathers till he had dedicated a most magnifical house to the name of the Lord. But it stands in God's true and faithful word that it was all in David's heart. And He who looks not so much on the action as on the intention, He saw in this also a man after His own heart. May all David's good intentions, and generous preparations be found in all our rich people; and may all the widow's love and goodwill be found in all our poor people. For the heart is the measure. And as we measure out good words, and good wishes, and good purposes, and good preparations, and good performances in our heart, so will it be measured back to us by Him who sees and weighs and measures the heart and nothing but the heart.

'Thou hast shed blood abundantly, and hast made great wars; thou shalt not build an house to My name, because thou hast shed much blood upon the earth in My sight. But, behold, a son shall be born to thee, and his name shall be Solomon, and he shall build an house for My name.' When I first read that sentence of such terrible disappointment to David, I looked to see David all that night on his face on the earth. But I did not know David; I had not yet got into all the depths of David's deep heart. For, instead of refusing to rise up and eat bread with the elders of his house, David was never in a happier frame of mind than he was all that night. David not only said, 'It is the Lord,' but his heart broke forth in a psalm such that there is nothing nobler in his whole book of Psalms. David not only consented that it was both good, and right, and seemly, that hands like his should not touch a stone of the house of God; but, that his son should be chosen of God to build Him an house—that set David's heart on fire as never Old Testament heart was set on fire like David's heart. As we read the psalm that poured out of David's heart that chastised and disappointed day, David is a man after our own heart. A psalm of resignation, and self-sacrifice, and thanksgiving, and many other virtues and graces like that psalm, covers a multitude of David's sins. Then went David in, and sat before the Lord; and he said, Who am I, O Lord God, and what is my house, that Thou hast brought me hitherto? And this was yet a small thing in Thy sight, O Lord God; but Thou hast spoken also of Thy servant's house for a great while to come. And is this the manner of man, O Lord God? Would God we all had a heart like that! I have found David, my servant.

It makes it possible, and, more than possible, pleasant to a father to lie down and leave his work unfinished when he sees his son standing at his bedside ready to take up his father's unfinished work to finish it. Nay, I suppose a father who loved his son aright and enough would almost rather leave all his work and all his hope unfinished if he saw his son able and willing and chosen and called to take it up. This, no doubt, greatly helped David to resign his great hope of being spared to build the temple, that Solomon, his greatly-gifted, wise-hearted, pure, and noble-minded son was standing ready to take up and to carry out his father's long-intended task. Judging David that day by myself, David must have been a happy father and a thankful, as, indeed, the fine psalm he sang that day lets us see that he was. I myself would willingly lie down to-night and leave all my mismanaged and mangled life; all the mistakes and misfortunes and mishaps of my ministry; all the obstacles and offences I have been to so many of my people; all my wrong dividing of the word of truth; and all else that you know so well and sorrow so much over. I declare to you that I would lie down with a good will to-night and wrap my head out of sight in my winding sheet, if I saw my son standing ready to take up and repair and redeem my lost life. I would say, Lord, now lettest Thou Thy unfaithful and unfruitful and offensive and injurious servant depart in pardon, since mine eyes have seen Thy salvation begun in my son. And if I saw all my sons preparing for the ministry of Christ in the Church of Christ I would die in a far greater triumph than David's death-bed could possibly be. Well, why not?

> Come, my soul, thy suit prepare.—
> Thou art coming to a king;
> Large petitions with thee bring;
> For His grace and power are such,
> None can ever ask too much.

David did many other services, both intended and executed, both in the field, and on the throne, and in the house of God; but by far and away David's greatest service was his Psalms. The temple was built, and built again, and built again; but for two thousand years now not one stone of that so sacred and so stately structure has stood upon another. The very foundations of the temple have been razed out, sown with salt, and for ever lost. But the Psalms of David shine to this day with a greater splendour than on the day they were first sung. And long after the foundations of this whole earth shall have been ploughed up and removed out of their place, David's Psalms will be sounding out for ever beside the song of Moses and the Lamb. 'I have reared a monument of myself more lasting than brass.' And time, which has ground to powder so many temples of marble and of brass, has only set a more shining seal to the poet's proud boast. But how poor was his boast, and how short-lived will be his best work beside David's immortal Psalms! What a service has David done, not knowing that he was doing it; and not to his own nation only, but to the whole Israel of God. And not to Israel only, but to the God of Israel, and to the Redeemer of Israel. 'I have found David My servant, with My holy oil have I anointed him. I have exalted one chosen out of the people.'

I have said that David did a great service to the Redeemer of Israel, and I intended to say it. When I think of that service, all the other services that David has done by his Psalms shine out in a far diviner glory. I bless David's name for the blessing my own soul gets out of his Psalms every day I live. But when I trace that blessing up to its true source, I find that true and grace-gushing source in Jesus of Nazareth, whom I see growing in grace every day as He goes about in Galilee with David's Psalms never out of His hands. Think, people of God, of the honour to David, higher far than all the thrones on earth and in heaven,—the unparalleled and immortal honour of being able to teach Jesus Christ to sing and to pray. For, when the Holy Child said to Mary, Mother, teach Me to sing and to pray, what did Mary do, hiding all that in her heart, but put into her Child's hands David's golden Psalm beginning thus: The Lord is my Shepherd, I shall not want. And then, think of Him as He grew in wisdom, and in stature, and in strength of spirit beginning to discover Himself in this Psalm of David and in that. Think of the sweet start, the overpowering surprise, the solemnity, the rejoicing with trembling, the resignation, the triumph with which the growing Saviour was led of the Spirit from Psalm to Psalm till He had searched out all David's Psalms in which David had prophesied and sung concerning his Messiah Son. See Jesus of Nazareth on His knees in the Sabbath synagogue with this place open before Him for the first time,—Lo, I come; in the volume of the book it is written of Me, I delight to do Thy will,

O My God; yea, Thy law is within my heart. And, having once begun to read and to think in that way you will go on till you come to the cross, where you will see and hear your dying Redeemer with one of David's Psalms on His lips when He can no longer hold it in His hands. And He said unto them, These are the words which I spake unto you while I was yet with you, that all things must be fulfilled which were written in the law of Moses, and in the prophets, and in the Psalms, concerning Me. And they said one to another, Did not our heart burn within us while He talked with us by the way, and while He opened to us the Scriptures?

O two disciples, on your way that same day to Emmaus, how I envy you your travelling Companion that day! My heart burns to think of your Divine Companion opening up to you David's Messianic Psalms that memorable day. And when I think also of the multitudes that no man can number to whom David's Psalms have been their constant song in the house of their pilgrimage; in the tabernacle as they fell for the first time hot from David's heart and harp; in the temple of Solomon his son with all the companies of singers and all their instruments of music; in the synagogues of the captivity; in the wilderness as the captives returned to the New Jerusalem; in the New Jerusalem every Sabbath-day and every feast-day; in the upper room, both before and after supper; in Paul's prison at Philippi; in the catacombs; in Christian churches past number; in religious houses all over Christendom at all hours of the day and the night; in deserts, in mountains, in dens and caves of the earth; in our churches; in our Sabbath-schools; in our families morning and evening; in our sickrooms; on our death-beds; and in the night-watches when the disciples of Christ watch and pray lest they enter into temptation. A service like all that is surely too much honour for any mortal man! Then David went in and sat before the Lord; and he said, Who am I, O Lord God? and what is my house? And is this the manner of man, O Lord God? And what can David say more unto thee! for Thou, Lord God, knowest thy servant.

Then, take David's knowledge of God, and his communion with God. There is nothing like it in the whole world again. There are many mysteries of godliness not yet revealed to us; but, to me, the mystery of David's knowledge of God and his communion with God is one of the most mysterious. Had Paul sung David's Psalms, and sent, now the twenty-third Psalm to the Philippians, and now the thirty-second and the hundred and thirtieth to the Romans, and now the forty-fifth and the twenty-second to the Colossians, and so on, I would not have wondered. I would wonder at nothing after the coming of Christ, and after His death and His ascension. But it baffles me to silence to see such Psalms as David's before the day of Christ. And I have never, with all my search, seen an intelligent attempt made to face that mystery.

No; David is scarcely second to the Man Jesus Christ Himself in this mystery of mysteries, the mystical communion of the soul of man with the Living God. Such knowledge is too wonderful for us; it is so high that we cannot attain to it. 'O God, Thou art my God. Early will I seek Thee. My soul thirsteth for Thee; my flesh longeth for Thee in a dry and thirsty land where no water is; to see Thy power and Thy glory, so as I have seen Thee in the sanctuary. Because Thy loving-kindness is better than life, my lips shall praise Thee. My soul shall be satisfied as with marrow and fatness, and my mouth shall praise Thee with joyful lips when I remember Thee upon my bed, and meditate on Thee in the night watches. My soul followeth hard after Thee.' That would not have stumbled me had I come on it in the heart of the seventeenth of John itself. To David in the sixty-second, and in its sister Psalms, there is only I AM and David himself, in all heaven and earth. Against Thee, Thee only, have I sinned, David says in another Psalm. And, 'Thee, Thee only,' is the sum and the substance, the marrow and the fatness, the beauty and the sweetness of all David's communion Psalms. To know God, and to be in constant communion with God, this is life to David; this is better than life; this is love; this is blessedness. Then, again, it is told of Luther in his 'Table Talk,' that being asked one day which were his favourite Psalms—Why, to be sure, he answered, Paul's four Psalms,—'Blessed is the man whose transgressions are forgiven, whose sin is covered,' 'Have mercy upon me, O God,' 'Out of the depths,' and 'Enter not into judgment with Thy servant.' Do you not see, he demanded, that all these Psalms tell us that forgiveness comes without the law and without works? Forgiveness and peace come to him that believeth. 'That Thou mayest be feared.' That dusts away all merit; that teaches us to uncover our heads before God and to confess that forgiveness is of His grace and not of our desert at all. 'Even as David describeth the righteousness of the man unto whom God imputeth righteousness without works, saying, Blessed is that man.' David knew it experimentally. It was Paul's privilege to know it both historically and experimentally, as we say, and then to set it forth doctrinally, as we say also. And it is our privilege to have it in all these three ways, if we love and value such things above all other love and value. Even David without Paul was not made perfect. Nor will we be without them both. 'I have found David, My servant. And My mercy will I keep for him for evermore, and My covenant shall stand fast with him. My covenant will I not break, nor alter the thing that is gone out of My lips. Once have I sworn by My holiness that I will not lie unto David.'

But, with all that, the half, and the best half for you, has not yet been told you. After all that, listen to this. He that hath ears to hear, let him give ear to this. 'In that day he that is feeble in Jerusalem shall be as David, and the house of David shall be as God.' Does Feeble mind hear that? Then let him receive and rest on that. Let him wake up psaltery and harp at the hearing of that. And let all that is within him sing and play like David. Let him sing and play, and that with the mind and the heart and the spirit like David. Let him sing and play to God, and to God only, like David. Let him who is feeble in faith, and in repentance, and in holiness, and in communion with God, be much in the Psalms. Let the Psalms dwell richly in the feeblest among us, and the feeblest among us will yet be a man of more spiritual strength than David. Sing a heart-strengthening Psalm every morning, and a heart-cleansing and a heart-quieting Psalm every night. Seven times every remaining day of your earthly pilgrimage sing a Psalm. Let no place, and no conversation, and no occupation delude you out of your heart-refreshing Psalm. Fill the house of your pilgrimage with the sound of Psalms. Let the prisoners hear you. Let the angels hear you. Let God hear you. Let Him bow down his ear and hear you. And let Him say to His Son, and to His angels, and to His saints, over you and over your house, I have found a man after Mine own heart; with My holy oil have I anointed him.

XXXIX

JONATHAN

THY LOVE TO ME WAS WONDERFUL,
PASSING THE LOVE OF WOMEN

JONATHAN was the eldest son of Saul, and he was thus the heir-apparent to the throne of Israel. The crown prince was a young man of great mental gifts, and he was endowed also with many most impressive moral qualities. Handsome and high-mettled, full of nerve and full of heart, Jonathan was the pride of the army and the darling of the common people. His comrades, for his beauty of person and for his swiftness of foot, were wont to call him The Gazelle. In all that, the heir-presumptive was the son of his royal father's early and best days. But the piety, the humility, the generosity, the absolutely Christ-like loyalty, tenderness, self-forgetfulness, and self-sacrifice of Jonathan—all that the son had drawn from some far higher source than from his fast-falling father Saul. But for his father's great and disastrous transgressions, Jonathan would soon have been the second king of Israel; second in succession to Saul, but second to no king that ever sat on a throne in those great qualities of mind and heart and character that give stability to a throne and add lustre to a crown.

The first time that Jonathan and David ever saw one another was on the day when Goliath fell under David's sling. Jonathan had stood beside his father Saul, and had been a spectator of the never-to-be-forgotten scene. Brave and bold and practised in war as Jonathan by that time was, with all that he had not been bold enough to face the gigantic braggart. But, with all the army, with both armies, he had been astounded to see a Bethlehemite stripling, fresh from his father's sheep, step out into the open space to face the champion of the opposing host. And when the five thousand shekels of brass rang on the open plain no voice shouted over David so soon or so long as the voice of Jonathan, the king's son. And when Saul sent for David and talked with him, Jonathan's heart went out to David, and the soul of Jonathan was knit to the soul of David, and Jonathan loved David as his own soul. And from that day on till the day when David sang his splendid elegy over Saul and over Jonathan his son, the mutual love of Jonathan and David is described all along in words of such warmth and such beauty that there is nothing like them in literature again, if we leave out the love of Christ.

'And it came to pass that the soul of Jonathan was knit to the soul of David.' You knit things together that are of the same kind; things that are of the same substance, and fibre, and texture, and strength, and endurance. You knit a thread to a kindred thread. You knit a cord to a kindred cord. You knit a threefold cord to a threefold cord. You knit a chain of iron to a chain of iron; a chain of brass to a chain of brass; a chain of gold to a chain of gold; and a chain of gold of the same size, and strength, and purity, and beauty to a chain of gold of the same size, and strength, and purity, and beauty. Now Jonathan's soul was a chain of gold, of the same size, and strength, and purity, and beauty as David's soul. Jonathan, as being the elder man, had for long been looking and longing for a soul like David's soul to which his own soul might be knit; and before the sun set that day the son of Saul had found in the son of Jesse a soul after his own soul, and he was at rest. Jonathan's soul was that day knit to another soul, if possible, still more tender, and pure, and pious, and noble, and loyal than his own; till Jonathan was the happiest man in all Israel that day. And that pattern of friendship, knit that day between Jonathan and David, has been the ensample and the seal of all true friendships among men ever since. It was a sweet fancy of Plato that at the great aboriginal creation of human souls they all came from the hand of the God of power, and wisdom, and love, and holiness twain in one. All human souls came into existence already knit together like the souls of Adam and Eve, like the souls of David and Jonathan, like the souls of Jesus and John, like the souls of Christ and His church. But Sin, the great sunderer and separater and scatterer of souls, came in and cleft asunder soul-consort from soul-consort till all our souls since the fall start this lonely life alone. And all the longings, and cravings, and yearnings, and hungerings, and thirstings, and faintings, and failings that fill the souls of men and women—it is all in search of that brother-soul, that sister-soul, that spousal-soul that we have all loved long since and lost a while. And every true comradeship, every true courtship, every true espousalship, every true married life is the divine recovery and reunion of twin-soul to twin-soul, as all human souls were in the great beginning, and will for ever be in God and in God's house of love and rest and satisfaction. And had Plato read Hebrew, how he would have hailed Jonathan and David as another example of two long-lost and disconsolate souls, finding rest in their primogenial, spousal, re-knit, and never-again-to-be-separated soul.

'And Jonathan loved David as his own soul.' Had I read this for this once only, I would have passed over it as a permissible hyperbole in the sacred writer. But when I read again and again that Jonathan loved David as his own soul, till I come down to David's splendid hyperbolical elegy over the slaughter of Saul and Jonathan; and then, when I go back and read Jonathan's whole dealing with David in the light of that golden chain of hyperboles, I stop, and think, and say to myself that there must be much more here than stands on the surface. Till I find myself saying to this sacred writer, Lo, in all this speakest thou plainly, and speakest no hyperbole. Yes; happy, happy Jonathan! For it was not of thee that David spake in that bitter psalm. 'Yea, mine own familiar friend.' David said, but not of thee, 'in whom I trusted, which did eat of my bread, hath lifted up his heel against me.' Nor was it of thee in another still more bitter psalm, 'But it was thou, a man mine equal, my guide, mine acquaintance. We took sweet counsel together, and walked unto the house of God in company. The words of his mouth were sweeter than butter, but war was in his heart; his words were softer than oil, yet were they drawn swords.' No, happy Jonathan, it was not of thee. Nor was this of thee, 'Thou didst speak peace to thy neighbour, while mischief was in thy heart.' Nor this, 'Thou didst bless with thy mouth, whilst thou didst curse inwardly.' Thy tongue, saintly man, did not frame deceit. Thou didst not sit and speak against thy brother. Jeremiah never said of thee in the bitterness of his heart that he heard the defaming of many. Thou never saidest concerning the friendless prophet, Report, and I will report it. He excepted thee when he upbraided them all round, and said, All my familiars watch for my halting. Nor did David's Son after thou hadst kissed Him say to thee, Friend, wherefore art thou come? Nor did Hamlet ever say to thee, 'O villain, villain, smiling, damned villain! My tables—meet it is I set it down, that one may smile, and smile, and be a villain.' Thy sin never found thee out. Thou never knewest the plague of a villain's heart. Thou never criedst, Create in me a clean heart, O Lord! Isaiah said, but thou never needest to say, I am a man of unclean lips. Great Jonathan! Dear Jonathan! We kiss thy feet. Till thy great Antitype comes we shall see no man born of woman again like thee!

'Then Jonathan and David made a covenant because he loved him as his own soul.' Jonathan's love was like the love of women in this, that it led Jonathan to leave his father's house behind him and to give his hand and his heart in a covenant to David. A woman cannot find rest but in the house of her husband. Knit as her heart is, and will for ever be, to her father and to her mother, yet there is a soul somewhere in God's hand to whom she was knit before she was born, and when God opens His hand twin-soul leaps out to meet twin-soul and she is married in the Lord. Now, it was something like that. David, in the warmth of his heart and in the sharpness of his sorrow, said that the love of Jonathan to him was still more wonderful than that. No love can be more wonderful than the love of a woman when she loves in God; when the warmth, and the tenderness, and the faithfulness, and the endurance, and the self-sacrifice of nature is all deepened, and strengthened, and ennobled, and made everlasting in the transforming and transcending love of God. And it was because Jonathan's love had so much of a woman's love in it; and, added to that, so much of God's love, that David's rapture rose to such a sublime height over it. There was something in Jonathan's love that David had never met with in any of the women whose love he had ever been blessed with, Abigail's, or Michal's or Solomon's mother's love, or any love his fathers had told him of in their days. And the surpassing love of Jonathan stood so alone because it stood so in God. Jonathan's heart had for long been full of God, and God is love. Under Samuel's ministry, Jonathan's heart had early been knit to God, and thus it was that his heart so knit itself round David's heart, in whom he found a man after God's own heart. And thus it was that father, and mother, and crown of Israel, and all, were counted loss to Jonathan as soon as he found David who had been so found of God. You will see the same thing to some extent in your own house every day. True religion, the knowledge and the love of God in your child's heart, will compel him to seek friends outside of your door if you are without the knowledge and the love of your son's God. How happy is that son who can love and honour and open all his heart to his father and mother in the Lord! But how unhappy if not! Jonathan loved Saul his father with a noble, devoted, loyal, and truly filial love. He followed his father's falling fortunes till father and son and all fell at last in the field. But all the time Saul had a son at his side whose deep and pure and holy heart he could neither understand, nor value, nor satisfy. Saul had begotten a son in Jonathan who was as much greater and better than himself as heaven is greater and better than earth; I might almost say than hell. Jonathan made a covenant with David, and with the house of David; and in making that covenant, and in the very terms of it, Jonathan, as we see in the Scriptures of it, spake less to David than he spake to David's God, the Lord God of Israel.

'And Jonathan stripped himself of the robe that was upon him, and gave it to David, and his garments, even to his sword, and to his bow, and to his girdle.' A wife's marriage ring is the seal of her husband's covenant with her, and her covenant with him. The rainbow in heaven is the seal of God's covenant with Noah, and with the earth. The water is the seal of God's covenant in baptism; and the bread and the wine in the supper. And, in like manner, Jonathan's robe, and his garments, and his sword, and his bow, and his girdle, were the signs and the seals of Jonathan's covenant that he made that day with David. In the bread and in the wine, Christ and all the benefits of the new covenant are represented, sealed, and applied to believers. And in Jonathan's robe, and raiment, and sword, and bow, and girdle, the kingdom of Israel, and all its honour and power and glory, were represented and sealed to David by this extraordinary action of Jonathan. The son and heir of Saul stripped himself naked for the sake of his sworn friend. Jonathan was such a miraculous and sacramental friend to David, that he stripped himself bare in order to clothe, and adorn, and seal David to the throne of Israel. In his measure, and so far as was in his power, Jonathan did that day all that Jesus Christ did in the fullness of time. Jonathan was only the sinful son of a sinful father, whereas Jesus Christ was the Son of God. But nothing more is said even of the Son of God Himself in this respect, than that He stripped Himself bare for His enemies, and clothed them with His robe and with His diadem. Well, all that Jonathan does to David. Jonathan is a disciple of Jesus Christ, born out of due time. Jonathan is all but Jesus Christ Himself come already in the Old Testament. As Jonathan strips himself to the bone, you look at him doing it and you exclaim, How could he ever do it! My brethren, your amazed exclamation betrays you. It is natural to you, and it shows to all who hear you that you have not yet begun to strip yourself for friend or enemy. If you had, if you had once even begun so to strip yourself, you would not cry out in such astonishment how Jonathan could do it. If you knew it, how could he help doing it? How could he do anything else? How could he stop doing it, till it was all done? He could not. And neither can you when once you have begun to do it. For the first time you will taste what true life is when you strip yourself bare of your best robe to put it upon your rival: upon him who is coming up so fast to supplant you. And you will drink deeper and deeper of the fountain of life as you go on to strip off your sword, and your bow, and your girdle to put them upon him. Of such is the kingdom of heaven. To such, and to such only, will it be said, Come up hither. Such, and such only, are highly exalted at the last. Such, and such only as make themselves of no reputation now. If you do it as they did it, you will yet sit down beside Jesus Christ and Jonathan, but not otherwise. At no less price to you than to them. But at the same price to you as to them. And it is for this cause that you have a robe given you, and garments, and a sword, and a bow, and a girdle and a rival, and a supplanter.

And it was told Saul. And Saul sought David every day. And David saw that Saul was come out to seek his life. And David was in the wilderness of Ziph in a wood. 'And Jonathan, Saul's son, arose and went to David into the wood, and strengthened David's hand in God.' There is a two-edged sword in the French tongue to this effect, that there is something in the misfortunes of our best friends that is not wholly displeasing to our secret hearts. But not to Jonathan's secret heart. Let every man defend himself from that sword of God as he is best able. Here is Jonathan's defence and shield, this: 'And Saul's son arose and went to David in the wood, and strengthened his hand in God.' That is Jonathan's shield against that sharp sword, and the hand of God in His own word holds it up over Jonathan. Be sure you see the full truth and the full beauty of that visit of Jonathan to the wood of Ziph. David was in danger of losing his faith in God. Which, if he had lost, he would have been the coming king of Israel, and Jonathan's rival, no longer. And Jonathan seeing that, came to the wood of Ziph to strengthen David in God lest his faith should fail. Was there ever a nobler deed done on the face of the earth till the Son of God came to do such deeds, and to show us all the way? If I had been Jonathan, I would have looked to David to strengthen me. I would have insisted that I needed the sympathy and the strength. It would have been a long time before I would have left my palace in Gibeah to go down to the wood of Ziph to strengthen the hand of my best friend, if that strength was to carry him over my head and put me under his feet. And Jonathan said to David, 'Fear not, for thou shalt be king over Israel, and I shall be next unto thee."

Are any of you being sent at this moment to that school to which God sent Jonathan? Are humiliations, and disappointments, and losses, and defeats your tutors and governors? Then, take Jonathan's history home with you to-night to imitate it. Grudge not your neighbour his divinely ordained promotion or praise. But, rather, as you have opportunity, strengthen his hand in God. As many as I love, I rebuke and chasten, and humble and put down, and make second. But to him that overcometh will I grant to sit with Me in My throne, even as I also overcame.

He always wins who sides with God,
To him no chance is lost;
God's will is sweetest to him when
It triumphs at his cost.

The cross of Christ was made of a tree that had grown in the wood of Ziph, and yours will be made of the same shining timber.

XL

NABAL

THE MAN WAS CHURLISH

We see Nabal on two occasions only. On the occasion of the sheep-shearing ten days before his marriage, and then on the occasion of the sheep-shearing ten days before his death. Had David been in the wilderness of Paran at that sunny sheep-shearing immediately before Nabal's marriage and he had asked for the crumbs that fell from the bridegroom's table, David would have been set in the place of honour at the smiling sheep-master's right hand. All that happy time when their master went out to the sheep-folds, he said to the sheep-shearers, The Lord be with you. And they answered him, The Lord bless thee. The-Joy-of-her-father,—for that was the name of the sheep-master's beautiful bride,—was also the joy of her bridegroom, till he sent two hundred loaves of bread, and two bottles of wine, and five sheep ready dressed, and five measures of parched corn, and an hundred clusters of raisins, and two hundred cakes of figs to Adullam, so that every one that was in distress, and every one that was in debt, and every one that was discontented, ate and drank and said, Let the God of Abraham and Sarah, and Isaac and Rebekah, and Jacob and Rachel be the God of that great man in Maon and Abigail his bride. 'The Lord make the woman that is come into his house like Rachel, and like Leah, which two did build the house of Israel.' And because of the blessing of all the poor and needy round about, and because of the beauty and the good understanding of Abigail, her husband was the happiest and the most open-handed man that day among all the men in Maon. And the man was very great, and he had three thousand sheep and a thousand goats, and he was shearing his sheep in Carmel.

The Bible has a way of its own taking great leaps sometimes over long spaces of some men's lives. And thus it is that the next time we see Abigail's bridegroom we would not know him. And we are left of the sacred writer to compose the whole married life of Nabal and Abigail out of our own married lives. And the Bible, with great safety and great assurance, leaves us to do that. Because it knows that as face answers to face in water, so do betrothed, and married, and churlish lives in ancient Israel, answer to married and churlish lives among ourselves.

The second sheep-shearing scene is set before us in a chapter of great pictorial power. With quite extraordinary concentration and strength, Nabal and Abigail are made to stand out before us in their great pictorial chapter. Abigail is still a woman of a good understanding. But Matthew Henry says that her understanding was all little enough for her exercises in it, for the man was churlish and evil in his doings. Abigail to all appearances is the same woman she was at the first sheep-shearing, but her husband has sadly gone down. It was the season of the year when the most churlish of men were wont to melt for the moment into hospitality and self-enjoyment, and even Nabal held a feast in his house. David and his six hundred men were lying in exile in the adjoining wilderness. Persecuted and cast out as David and his men were, they never forgot that they were men of Israel; and up among the mountains, and out on the borders, they were a kind of volunteer protectors and patrolling police over the flocks and herds of men like Nabal. As a matter of fact, David had interposed again and again, and been a wall, as Nabal's shepherds themselves said, round them and their sheep against the sheep-stealing tribes. The starving exiles had looked for some reward for their work; but Nabal was Nabal. Till sheer famine made David send to Nabal's feast and ask a share of his hospitality to 'thy son David,' as he called himself in his courteous but bold message. But Nabal's softness of heart over his sheep-shearing was only skin-deep. 'Who is David,' Nabal snapped out, 'that I should share my feast with him and his vagabonds?' And no sooner did David hear Nabal's churlish and insulting answer than he said, and it was all he said, 'Gird ye on every man his sword.' But, as good providence would have it, Abigail had heard both of David's embassy and of her husband's churlish answer, and she lost not a moment. Sending on before her a present of meat and drink, she hastened after it, and met David and his four hundred men just in time. How Abigail behaved herself before the insulted and revengeful soldiers; with what tact and understanding she spake to David; and how she melted David and turned away his hot anger—all that we read in the matter and the manner of this sacred writer. And, then, in two verses of crowning strength of style we have Nabal's drunken debauch all night, and his sudden death of fear and hate and hardness of heart in the morning.

'Nabal was of the house of Caleb.' But there is a Latin proverb to this effect, that to be the son of a good father is the shame of a bad son. Now, Caleb was a good father. Caleb was a large-hearted, hopeful, God-serving man. And Caleb and his house held their large estates in the land of Israel on that tenure. The family property was a witness to their father's great services in a dark day in Israel. Caleb lived to a green old age, crowned with all the love and honour that Nabal had by this time wholly lost. By his birth Nabal had come into great possessions in Carmel; and, as if to make him a man like his father—as if to keep his heart soft and full of love to God and man,—God had added to all that a wife who shines high up among the household saints of the house of Israel. But, all the time, Caleb and Abigail, great inheritance and great dowry, happy home, and all, there was a 'stone of obstination' in Nabal's heart that nothing could melt or remove, till his whole heart was turned to stone and he died.

'Our master flew at David's messengers,' reported the young man to Abigail. 'He railed on them,' as we excellently read it in the text. He snarled and snapped at them, as Josephus so graphically has it. You see the man. You know the man. Your young men know the man. Your wife knows the man. Your children know the man. 'Who is David? And who is the son of Jesse? There be many servants nowadays that break away every man from his master.' It is a glass, this chapter, in which we all see our churlish selves to the life. Who is he? we demand, with all the contempt and scorn we can call up out of our contemptuous and scornful hearts. Who is he to speak to me and to treat me in that way? And we go on to put the worst construction upon him, and upon his family, and upon his friends. A parcel of vagabonds! snarled out Nabal. And how much of our own speaking and writing about people we do not like is exactly like that churlish outbreak of Nabal. And what mischief Nabal's tongue and pen work among us also! Nothing roots our wicked hearts deeper into our whole life and character than a snarling tongue or a railing pen let loose. And nothing puts David and his men into a more wicked and murderous temper than to be railed at as Nabal railed. Do not do it. Do not listen to it. Do not read it. It is the death of your heart to speak it and to hear it. When you speak it your conversation is in hell; and when you write or read it, it is the literature of hell. It kindles hell in him who is railed at, and it spreads, and it feeds hell in him who writes it, or reads it, or speaks it. Nabal's railing tongue kindled such an outburst of murderous hate in David and in his men that, another half hour and it would have been put out in Nabal's blood.

'The man was churlish,' says this shorthand writer, giving us Nabal's whole character in a single word. That is to say, Nabal had allowed and indulged himself in his snarling, snappish ways till he was known in his own house, among his shepherds, and all round about, as Nabal the churl. 'A devil at home' is one of the sure marks of Thomas Shepard's 'evangelical hypocrite. He shines like an angel in the church. Christ and mercy are never out of his mouth. He is much to be heard on closing with Christ. He is raised up to heaven with liberty and joy on Sabbath, and especially on communion days. But he is a devil at home.' Whereas we find that 'hyperbole of sin,' Lancelot Andrewes, on his knees night and day, 'to be kind to mine own.' And you will remember that other portrait of the same family in John Bunyan. Obstinate also gave a great sheep-shearing feast before his marriage. And his bride also led her bridegroom to church and market in a silken bridle—for a time. But time passes, and there passes away with time all the hospitality, humility, pliability, and sweetness of the churlish and obstinate man. It is not that he has ceased to love his wife and his children. It is not that. But there is this in all genuine and inbred churlishness and obstinacy, that, after a time, it comes out worst beside those we love best. A man will be affable, accessible, entertaining, the best of company, and the very soul of it abroad, and, then, the instant he turns the latch-key in his own door, Nabal himself was not worse, he sinks back into such an utter boorishness, and mulishness, and doggedness. He swallows his meal in silence, and then he sits all night with a cloud on his brow. He is silent to no children but his own; he is a bear to nobody but his own wife. Nothing pleases him; nothing in his own house is to his mind. And all the time it is not that he does not pray to love his own, like Andrewes; but there is a law of obstinacy in his heart that still makes him a devil at home. And then hear Christiana: 'That which troubleth me most is my churlish carriages to my husband when he was in his distress. I am that woman that was so hard-hearted. And so guilt took hold of my mind, and would have drawn me to the pond.' Yes, constant fault-finding; constant correction, and that before strangers; gloomy looks; rough words and manners; all blame and no praise —with these things we are all driving one another to the brink of the pond every day.

'And it came to pass in the morning, when the wine was gone out of Nabal, and his wife had told him all these things, that his heart died within him, and he became as a stone." Nabal died of a stone in his heart. Nabal died of pride and rage. Nabal died of a strange disease—indebtedness to his wife. Nabal would rather have died of David's sword than have been saved from

David's sword by the understanding and the interposition and the intercession of his wife. Nabal died rather than admit that he had played the fool through all that sheep-shearing time. Had Nabal kissed Abigail that morning; had he kissed her hand; had he kissed her feet; he would have been living to this day; and when he died like a shock of corn fully ripe, all Israel would have mourned that they had lost him, and David would have sung a psalm over him that we would have put upon the tombstones of all our magnanimous and much-lamented men. As it was, it became a proverb in Israel to ask when a madam, or a man possessed with a devil, or a man who took his own life, died, Died he as Nabal died? Take care, O churlish husband! Take care, O man with a heart of stone beginning in thy bosom. For Satan is fast entering into thee. Take care.

But, now, can such churlishness be cured? Can it really be cured? some of you who have that cruel stone for long spreading in your hearts will ask me. Yes, it can, if it is taken in time, and if it is treated in the right way. And the first thing in the cure is to admit and accept the disease. It is to say, I am Nabal. Had Nabal taken it to heart how it would end, as soon as he felt the tenderness, and the honourableness, and the nobleness, and the manliness of his betrothal and bridegroom days beginning to wear off his heart and his life; had he been man enough, and man of God enough, and husband enough to watch and know the stopping of his heart and the creeping-on coldness of his heart to God and man, and especially to Abigail; and had he confessed to himself his fears how all that would end, it would all have ended the entire opposite of how it did end. Had he been thankful also. Had he practised himself in going back upon Caleb and the inheritance he had got because of Caleb; had he taken his flocks and his herds, and all that he had, every sheep-shearing time, again from the hand of God! had he every night and every morning taken Abigail in all her understanding and all her beauty again from the hand of God; and had he prevented David's petition and sent him a share of the sheep-shearing feast before he asked for it—by all that, Nabal would have made himself a new heart, and he would have come down to us in as good a report as any of the elders of Israel. Kick, then, the dog out of your heart. Hammer the stone out of your heart, and you will get back the days of your first sheep-shearing; you will get back your bride, and your own tender, hopeful, noble, manful heart. But the one, the only real and sure cure for all our New Treatment Nabals is that supreme antidote and counter-poison to all churlishness, the cross of Christ. Whatever we start with, we always end with the cross of Christ. Try it, for it cures everything, and especially churlishness and all its bad effects. It cures churlishness in Nabal; and impatience, and weariness, and despair of life in Abigail; and anger and revenge in David. Come near to the cross, both Nabal, and David, and Abigail, and look and hear. Hear those churlish men as they pass by and wag their heads, and rail at David's Son cast out upon the cross from among men, while, all the time, He dies to save and bless them. Great Example! Great Refuge and Great Strength to us all! The Butt, the Jest, the Scoff, the Flout of all who pass by! We come to Thee. We need Thee. We have no cure for our hearts, and no pardon for our hearts but Thee. Churls, and churls' victims, we come to Thee. Railing and railed at, we come to Thee. Nabal, and David, and Abigail, and the shepherds, and the soldiers, we all come to Thee. We hang by our hands and our feet and our hearts beside Thee. We forgive all those who revile us, and buffet us, and despitefully use us beside Thee. We die, and are buried, and rise again, and sit beside Thee. Finally, be ye all of one mind, having compassion one of another, love as brethren, be pitiful, be courteous. Not rendering evil for evil, or railing for railing, but contrariwise blessing; knowing that ye are thereunto called, that ye should inherit a blessing.

XLI

MICHAL, SAUL'S DAUGHTER

SHE DESPISED HIM IN HER HEART

Never, surely, were man and wife more unequally yoked together than was David, the man after God's own heart, with Michal, Saul's daughter. What was David's meat was Michal's poison. What was sweeter than honey to David was gall and wormwood to Michal. The things that had become dearer and dearer to David's heart every day, those were the very things that drove Michal absolutely mad; furiously and ungovernably mad that day on which the ark of God was brought up to the city of David.

It was the greatest day of David's life. And, sad to say, it was the very greatness of the day to David that made it such a day of death to Michal, Saul's daughter. Michal, Saul's daughter, died that day of a strange disease—a deep distaste at the things that were her husband's greatest delight. A deep distaste that had grown to be a deep dislike at David, till that deep distaste and settled dislike burst out that day into downright hatred and deliberate insult. You must understand all that the ark of God was to David, and the home-bringing of the ark, before you can fully understand the whole catastrophe of that day. It would take me till midnight to tell you all that was in David's heart as he sacrificed oxen and fatlings at six paces, and leaped and danced before the ark of God all the way up to the city of David. And, even then, you would need to be a kind of David yourself before you would look with right reverence and love at David that day. For David was beside himself that day. David never did anything by halves, and least of all his worship of God. It was like that day long afterwards in that same city when we read that His disciples remembered that it was written, The zeal of Thine house hath eaten Me up. With all his might, then—and you know something of what all David's might in such matters was—with all his might David leaped and danced before the Lord till Michal despised him in her heart.

Those who are deaf always despise those who dance. The deaf do not hear the music. And, on the other hand, those who do hear the music, they cannot understand those who can sit still. David could not understand how Michal could sit still that day. But Michal's ear had never been opened to the music of the ark. She had not been brought up to it, and it was not her custom to go up to the house of the Lord to sing and play like David. Had Michal been married in the Lord; had Michal reverenced her husband; had she cared to please her husband; had she played on the psaltery and harp sometimes, if only for his sake—what a happy wife Michal would have been, and David what a happy husband! Had her heart been right with her husband's heart when he blessed his household every night; had she been wont with all her heart to unite with her husband when he blessed them every night and sang psalms with them; had she sung with him and said, We will not go up into our bed till we have found out a place for the Lord, an habitation for the mighty God of Jacob: how well it would have been. Lo! sang David alone with the handmaids of his servants, Lo! we heard of it at Ephratah; we found it in the fields of the wood. Arise, O Lord, into Thy rest; Thou and the ark of Thy strength. Had David not been so unequally yoked, Michal would have put on David's shoulder that day an ephod that she had worked for that day with her own hands; and as she put it on him she would have sung and said, I will clothe her priests with salvation, and her saints shall shout aloud for joy. And then all that day in Jerusalem it would have been as it was at the Red Sea when Miriam the prophetess took a timbrel in her hand, and all the women went after her with timbrels and with dances. But it was not so to be. For Michal sat at home that great day in Israel, and forsook her own mercy. Michal was not in the spirit of that day. And thus it was that she despised David in her heart when the very gates of brass and iron were lifting up their heads at David's psalm to let the King of Glory come in.

Not to speak of the past, had Michal done that day what any woman with any sense of decency left in her would have done—had she put on her royal garments and set out with David to the house of Obed-Edom, how differently for her and for David that day would have ended! For, once on the ground; once surrounded with the assembled people, the magnificent scene would have carried Michal away. The fast-dying ashes of her first love for David would have been blown up into all their former flame as she shared in the splendid salutation that David received from the assembled land. No ambitious woman, and least of all Saul's royal-hearted daughter, could have seen assembled Israel that day without being swept into sympathy with the scene. But Michal lost her last opportunity that morning. Michal did not overcome herself that morning. Her proud and unsympathetic temper got the better of her that morning, till David had to set out on the royal duties of that day alone. And as the day went on, Michal was left alone with a heart the most miserable in all Israel that day. And Michal's heart became harder and darker and fiercer as the day went on. Harder and darker and fiercer at David, and at all the ordinances and delights of that day. And then, when all Jerusalem rang with the ark just at her door, Michal stole to her shut window and saw nothing but David dancing before the Lord. At the despicable sight she spat at him, and sank back in her seat with all hell in her heart. You have had Michal's heart in yourselves, in your measure, on some Sabbath-day when you remained at home for some wrong reason, and when your husband came home with his face shining. And on other days, when you should have been at his side, but some distaste, some dislike, some pique, some catishness kept you at home to eat your heart all the time. And then the very high spirits of the party when they came home made your day end sufficiently like Michal's day. What a pity that David did not better prevail with Michal to accompany him to the fields of the wood that day!

The wife see that she reverence her husband, says the apostle. Yes; but even Paul himself would have allowed that it was impossible for Michal to reverence David all at once that day. Paul would have needed to have got Michal's ear early that morning when she tarried at home in the palace. Nay, he would have needed to have got her heart while she was yet Saul's daughter in Saul's palace. It is to tell a waterfall to flow uphill to tell Michal at this time of day to reverence David. Reverence does not come even at a divine command. Reverence does not spring up in a day. Reverence is the result of long teaching and long training. Reverence has it roots in the heart and in the character; and the heart and the character only come and bring forth reverence as life goes on. That may be all true, but the apostle does not say that. He does not say that any of the wives to whom he wrote were too late now to reverence their husbands. He speaks it to all wives, and he expects that all wives who hear it shall lay it to heart, and shall do it. And yet their husbands, their very best husbands, are in so many things so difficult, so impossible, to reverence. They fall so far short of their young wife's dreams and visions. They are so full of faults, and follies, and tempers, and habits to which no wife can possibly be blind. Most husbands are at so little trouble, after they have been for some time husbands, to make it easy, or indeed possible, for their wives to continue to love, and respect, and reverence them. All our wives have dreary, lonely, sorely disappointed days at home—partly our fault and partly theirs, but mostly ours—that we know nothing about. Now, what are they to do between Paul on the one hand demanding in the name of God that they shall love and reverence us, and us on the other hand with all our might making both love and reverence impossible? Well, with God all things are possible. Let our wives, then, take us, with all our faults and infirmities, and let them think that with all our faults and infirmities we are still their husbands.

And let them take this to heart also, that though we fall ever so far below ourselves, that is all the more reason why they should rise all the more above themselves. It does not divorce a wife from her affection and respect for her husband that he causes her much pain and shame: many a blush in public, and many a tear in private. His sins against good taste, his clownish or churlish habits, his tempers, his prejudices, his ignorance, his rude, insolent, overbearing ways, not to speak of still grosser vices —all that will not absolve a wife from a wife's solicitude and goodwill to her husband. All that will not discharge her from her command over herself. She must often see and feel all that like a wolf under her gown as she sits at the top of the table and her husband sits at the foot. But she must all the more learn to say her own grace to herself before she sits down to her temptation, till she is able to return thanks as she rises to go upstairs. All the time they are talking and eating and drinking at the other end of the table, she must set a watch on her ears and on her eyes and on the blood in her cheeks. She must be as full of guile as her husband is of meat and drink and himself. The keenest and cruelest eye must not find her out. Its deceived owner must be sent home saying, What a fool of a wife that brute, that bore, that goose has! I declare the blind thing is still in love with him! The wife see that she is hypocrite enough to throw dust into the eyes of her oldest, closest, and most familiar friend. Dante describes Michal as a woman who stood scornful and afflicted at her royal window. But let not even Dante's terrible eyes see either your scorn of your husband or your affliction on account of his exposure of himself. Throw dust even into Dante's blazing eyes. We are poor creatures, the best of us husbands; and, at our best, we are still full of appetites and egotisms and all the other dregs of our indwelling sin. But if Almighty God bears with us, and does not despise us and spurn us and refuse us His love, neither will you. And you will be well paid for it all, and well acknowledged. For when we praise God at last, and say, To Him who loved us! we will not forget you. The wife see, then, that she prays for and puts up with her husband. The wife see that she makes his self-improvement easy for her husband. And if, after all is done, there is an irreducible residuum of distaste, and almost dislike left, well, all the more let her see to it that she work out his and her own salvation under that secret, life-long, household cross. To your thorn, as to the apostle's Christ will come and will say, My grace is sufficient for it. My strength is made perfect even in such weakness as yours.

Being the woman she was, and having the husband she had, Michal could not but feel both scorn and affliction that day. But, when all is said for her, and all allowance made, she should not have spoken to David as it is recorded she did speak. She could not command her proud heart when she saw David dancing, but by the time he came home she should have had her tongue tamed and under a bridle. David was, no doubt, a great provocation and a constant cross to Michal. They were never made for one another. It was impossible they could ever be happy as man and wife, short of a miracle. David was all emotion, especially in divine things; whereas Michal was as proud and cold as if she had been a daughter of Lucifer, as indeed she was. David that day was like one of our own ministers coming home from the communion table. It takes a night and a day and more than that till the agitation and the emotion of a communion day subsides and settles in a minister's heart. And if he were met with a blow in the face about his sermon or his prayer or his table service as he opened his own door, that was exactly the reception that poor David met with at Michal's hands that day. The wife see, at any rate, that she holds her tongue. I do not now speak of communion time. There is no fear of any minister's wife speaking on that day as Michal spoke. But there are other times with ministers and with all men. Times when husband and wife do not see eye to eye. Times when their two hearts do not beat as one heart. Times of distaste, and disapproval, and difference of opinion, and positive dislike; when Michal, who is written for our learning, must be called to every wife's mind. Michal with her heart full of war, and her mouth full of wicked words, and her whole after-life full of remorse and misery for that evil day in her house in Jerusalem—Michal is a divine looking-glass for all angry and outspoken wives.

'It was before the Lord,' was David's noble answer to Michal's taunting and insulting words. That was the whole explanation of David's emotion and the sufficient justification of it. David's overflowing joy that day had its deep and full spring in that far-off but never-to-be-forgotten day when Samuel came to Bethlehem with his horn of oil. To understand David and to sing David's psalms, you must have come through David's experiences. You must have had David's birth and upbringing; David's election and anointing and call; David's sins and David's salvation; David's falls and David's restorations; David's offices and David's services in the church of God. No wonder, then, that so many of David's psalms are as much beyond your depth to-day as his dancing was beyond Michal's depth that day. Michal thought of her royal father Saul that day, and despised David. David thought of his poor father Jesse that day, and danced before the Lord. And, as he says, he would have danced all the same, and still more, had earth and hell both been all let loose to scoff and shout at him. 'Both less and more than king,' is Dante's whole remark on David's dance. As we shall be on that day when we look down at the hole of the pit from whence we were digged, and cast our crowns at His feet who took us from the dung-hill and set us beside David.

And then, the truly noble, the truly humble, and the terribly lonely man that he was, David took up the taunt of his godless and heartless wife, and wore it as a badge of honour before the Lord that day. Yes, he said, it will be as you say. I will seek and

I will find among the poorest and the most despised of God's people that which my own married wife denies me at home. And who can tell how many husbands here are in David's desolate case? Who can tell how many have to go out of their own homes to find the finest sympathy, and the fullest utterance, and the completest rest for their hearts? The wife see that her husband has not to go abroad to find his best friend, his most sympathetic and fellow-feeling friend, and, above all, in his religion. A minister once told me that he preached best and prayed best when his wife was at home. What a gulf there was between David and Michal; between Jesus and His brethren, not to say His mother; and between my desolate friend and his wife; My brethren, the Holy Ghost knew what He was doing, and for whom He was doing it, when He moved the sacred writer to put that day in David's life into our Bible. And this,—'Husbands, love your wives, even as Christ loved the church, and gave Himself for it.' And this,—'And the wife see that she reverence her husband.'

XLII

SOLOMON

LEST I MYSELF SHOULD BE A CASTAWAY

THE shipwreck of Solomon is surely the most terrible tragedy in all the world. For if ever there was a shining type of Christ in the Old Testament church, it was Solomon. If ever any one was once enlightened, and had tasted the heavenly gift, and was made a partaker of the Holy Ghost, and had tasted the good word of God, and the powers of the world to come, it was Solomon. If ever any young saint sought first the kingdom of God and His righteousness, and had all these things added unto him, it was Solomon. If the kingdom of heaven was ever like a lord's servant with five talents, who went and traded with the same and made them other five talents, it was Solomon. If ever there was any one of whom it could be said that he had attained, and was already perfect, it was Solomon. If ever ship set sail on a sunny morning, but all that was left of her was a board or two on the shore that night, that ship was Solomon. A board or two of rare and precious wood, indeed; and some of them richly worked and overlaid with silver and gold—it was Solomon with his sermons, and his prayers, and his proverbs, and his songs, and his temple. If ever a blazing lighthouse was set up in the sea of life to warn every man and to teach every man, it was Solomon.

Solomon was born of a father and a mother, the knowledge of which was enough to sanctify and dedicate both him and them from his mother's womb. If ever it was said over any child's birth, Where sin abounded, grace did much more abound, it was surely over the birth, and the birth-gifts and graces of Solomon. If ever a father's and a mother's son said when he was come to years, And is this the manner of man, O Lord God? that son come to years was surely Solomon. And, then, with a tutor and governor like Nathan—Judge, I pray you, betwixt me and my vineyard. What more could have been done to my vineyard that I have not done in it? And then his father's deathbed, and all those terrible tragedies on the back of that; all ending in Solomon sitting down on the throne of Israel amid such a blaze of glory. Solomon would have been made of stone not to have been moved to make those vows, and promises, and choices of wisdom and truth and righteousness, which we read so beautifully that he did make at the beginning of his reign in Jerusalem.

The Holy Child Himself never dreamed a better dream than that dream was which Solomon dreamed after that day of a thousand burnt-offerings on the altar of Gibeon. And a nobler choice was never made by any elect man in his most waking and most enlightened hours, than was the choice that Solomon made that night in his sleep. As soon as Lord Melbourne had announced to the young Princess Victoria that she was now Queen of England, he opened the Bible and read to the young sovereign the story of Solomon's dream at Gibeon. It was a stroke of genius. It was an inspiration. It was a prophetic Scripture in her case and in ours. Would God it had come half as true in his case who dreamed the dream! 'And the speech pleased the Lord that Solomon had asked this thing. And God said unto him, Because thou hast asked this thing, and hast not asked for thyself long life; neither hast asked riches for thyself, nor hast asked the life of thine enemies; but hast asked for thyself understanding to discern judgment. Behold, I have done according to thy words; lo, I have given thee a wise and an understanding heart; so that there was none like thee before thee, neither after thee shall anyone arise like unto thee. And I have also given thee that which thou hast not asked, both riches and honour; so that there shall not be any among the kings like unto thee all thy days.' And both the riches and the honour promised at Gibeon were all fulfilled in Jerusalem, till the half had not been told to Solomon.

Magnifical, a mountain of cedar and wrought gold, as Solomon's temple was, it is all gone to dust and ashes millenniums ago. As the Lord warned Solomon, the temple soon became an astonishment and a hissing. But the dedication prayer that Solomon offered on the opening day before the altar is a far better prayer to us to-day than it was that day on which it first fell from Solomon's lips. Stone and timber, gold and silver, crumble to dust and are forgotten. But once a piece like that is composed, and spoken, and taken down, and read, it lasts for ever. No doubt it may be said in suspicion and in depreciation of Solomon that kings are wont to get their speeches and their prayers written for them by their ministers, secular and sacred; and that what falls from a king's lips before his people need not have come from his heart. But in the case of a king of Solomon's birth and upbringing and great gifts, such a libel would never have been let light had it not been that it is a real relief to hear it. If Solomon actually, and all of himself, made and offered that wonderful prayer, then when we think of it, he is more a mystery of perdition to us than ever. That wonderful discovery and operation of our day which is called Biblical Criticism has let in a most piercing and searching and edifying light, not only upon Bible books, but also upon Bible men. And upon no man more than upon both Solomon and his books. 'The prayer of Solomon,' says a scholar of no less grace and genius than of scholarship, 'so fully reproduced, and so evidently precomposed, may well have been written under Nathan's guidance.' He does not say positively that it was so precomposed and written. But he evidently believes, for his part, that it was; and he says what he does say in this matter for the sake of those who will let him say it, and not for those who will not. Had Solomon lived up to that prayer; no, I must not say that, for no man could do that, not Nathan himself; but if Solomon in all his unspeakable sensualities and idolatries had ever given the least sign or symptom that he felt shame for his life, or remorse when he remembered his prayer: had it not been for that, I, for one, could never have let it light on my mind that any one but Solomon himself composed what is here called Solomon's prayer. But I must say it is both a relief and an edification to my mind that the greatest castaway in the Bible may not have been the original and real and only author of one of the greatest and best prayers in the Bible. I can hold up my head better when I am opening a church and am reading and expounding this prayer, when I think of Nathan's pure and noble soul rather than of Solomon, who is so soon to be such a scandal and reprobation. I do not know how you feel about a matter like that. But I shall always return to that splendid prayer with the author of the parable of the one little ewe lamb before my mind, rather than the reprobate lover of no end of strange women, and the fatal father of Rehoboam. I can imagine many open-minded young men here, and many open-minded old men like Jonathan Edwards, who will go back to the prophetic precomposition and the prophetic reproduction of this great prayer with thankfulness to God for the splendid service that Christian scholarship is doing to Holy Scriptures, and not least to Solomon's psalms and songs and prayers and proverbs in our open-eyed, believing, and truly reverential day.

Our own Lord Bacon always comes to my mind when I think about Solomon. For Bacon also took all wisdom and all knowledge, past, present, and yet to be discovered, for his province. Bacon also spake of trees, from the cedar tree that is in Lebanon, even to the hyssop that springeth out of the wall. He spake also of beasts, and fowls, and of creeping things, and of fishes. Bacon, like Solomon, put tongues into trees and made them speak proverbs. The streams round Verulam and Gorhambury ran excellent books to Bacon, till he extracted wisdom absolutely out of everything. Solomon's House in *The New Atlantis* is the best commentary that will ever be written on the wisdom of Solomon. Bacon's Essays are our English Book of Proverbs, and an English Ecclesiastes could easily be collected out of Bacon's Letters and Speeches. For he, too—

> he felt from time to time
> The littleness that clings to what is human,
> And suffered from the shame of having felt it.

And then, with it all, Bacon's superb genius followed by his awful fall, makes us almost believe that Solomon has come back to this earth again in the lord chancellor of England. Only, how happy it would have made us had Nathan found among Solomon's parchments, and in Solomon's own handwriting, a psalm or prayer like that which Bacon's executors found in his dead desk. Will you join me in the following petition out of Bacon's prostrate prayer: 'Most gracious Lord God, my merciful Father from my youth up, my Creator, my Redeemer, my Comforter. Thou, O Lord, soundest and searchest the depths and secrets of all hearts. Thou acknowledgest the upright in heart,

Thou judgest the hypocrite, Thou ponderest men's thoughts and doings as in a balance, Thou measurest their intentions as with a line, vanity and crooked ways cannot be hidden from Thee. Lord, I have loved Thy assemblies. I have mourned for the divisions of Thy Church. I have delighted in the brightness of Thy sanctuary. Thy creatures have been my books, but Thy Scriptures much more. I have sought Thee in the courts, in the fields, and in the gardens, but I have found Thee in Thy temples. Thousands have been my sins, and ten thousand my transgressions; but Thy sanctifications have remained with me, and my heart, through Thy grace, hath been an unquenched coal upon Thy altar. As Thy favours have increased upon me, so have Thy corrections; so as Thou hast been always near me, O Lord, and ever as my worldly blessings were exalted, so secret darts from Thee have pierced me; and when I have ascended before men, I have descended in humiliation before Thee. Besides my innumerable sins, I confess before Thee that I am debtor to Thee for the gracious talent of Thy gifts and graces, which I have neither put into a napkin nor put it as I ought to exchangers, but have misspent it in things for which I was least fit, so as I may truly say my soul hath been a stranger in the house of my pilgrimage. Be merciful unto me, O Lord, and guide me in Thy ways, and afterwards receive me to glory.' No. That is not Solomon come back again. Would God it were! Solomon has nothing like that to come back with. That is Solomon's father come back to fallen Bacon. That is the man after God's own heart.

What malice there must be in our hearts when God's very best gifts to us, and our very best blessings, are turned by us to be our temptation and our snare! David's terrible fall took place not among the cruel rocks of his exile, but on the roof of the king's palace in Jerusalem. And it was Solomon's very wisdom and wide understanding; it was his great riches; it was his wide dominion; it was his largeness of heart and his long and peaceful life that all worked together to make his path so slippery and so deadly. It is not to be wiser than what is written to say that it was not a vulgar and an everyday sensuality that made Solomon in the end such a castaway. There was that in it. But there were more things, and more seductive and dangerous things in it than that. There was this: There was what the inspired text calls largeness of heart—very much what we would call in our day openness and breadth of mind, hospitality and catholicity of mind, even to sympathy and symbolism with beliefs, with ways of worship, and with ways of no worship, against which it had been the divine call and whole ministry of Moses, and Aaron, and Joshua, and David to warn and to protect the children of Israel. That Solomon should go down to Egypt, of all places on the face of the earth, for his queen; that Pharaoh's daughter should sit on the throne of David, that must have given a shock to the more conservative, and sober, and thoughtful, and religious, and far-seeing minds in Israel—a shock that we wonder we do not hear more about it while Solomon is yet young and yet alive. We shall hear plenty about it when he is dead, and when Rehoboam's teeth are set on edge. No doubt, largeness of heart, even as the sand that is on the seashore, and breadth and openness of mind, and a catholic and a hospitable temper, and the charity that believeth all things and hopeth all things, is all of God, and is all to be seen in Jesus Christ and in His church. At the same time, such is the malignity of our hearts, that even charity itself has its temptations and its snares when it becomes our charity. Even grace itself, says Shepard, is flesh in respect of God. And Solomon's largeness of heart soon ended in sheer flesh itself. His wisdom as his life went on descended not from above. The wisdom that is from above is first pure, then peaceable. We see it every day. We see men absolutely revolting against all smallness of heart. They loath all your bigotry, and narrowness, and hardness, and suspicion, and superstition. They see a soul of good especially in things evil. They fraternise with men and with movements that their fathers abominated. They pare down and prune away the decalogue, and the creed, and the catechism, and the books of discipline of their godly upbringing. They rehabilitate and reinvest names and reputations that were a shame and a reproach in their father's house. They go down to Egypt for a wife, and they bring up her false gods with her. 'And it came to pass that, when Solomon was old, his wives turned away his heart after other gods; and his heart was not perfect with the Lord his God, as was the heart of David his father.' And, if not in them, then in their children, all that Moses, and Aaron, and Joshua, and David had won for them and for their children at a great price is surrendered up and sold for naught, till the old great price has to be paid for it again in their children's sin, and suffering, and defeat, and captivity. Every generation has its own sword sent to it: its own peculiar trial of faith and holiness and severe obedience. And there is no shipwreck of faith and holiness and severe obedience in all the world that is written more for the men of our generation than just the terrible shipwreck of Solomon amid his wealth, and his wisdom, and his largeness of horizon and hospitality of heart, even to strange women and to their strange gods, till that end came which always comes.

The books of Solomon so-called—the Proverbs, the Ecclesiastes, and the Song—had a great struggle to get a footing inside the Old Testament. Each one of Solomon's books had its own difficulty to those who sifted out and sealed up the Hebrew Bible. There was something in all the books that were in any way associated with Solomon's name that made the Hebrew Fathers doubt their fitness for a place in Holy Scripture. There is one fatal want in them all. There is no repentance anywhere in Solomon. There is no paschal lamb, or young pigeon, or bitter herb among all the beasts, and birds, and hyssop-plants of which Solomon spoke and sang so much. There is no day of atonement, or so much as one of the many ordained sacrifices for sin, in any of Solomon's real or imputed writings. Both the sense of truth and the instinct of verisimilitude kept back all those who ever assumed Solomon's name from ever putting a penitential psalm, or a proverb of true repentance, in Solomon's mouth. The historical sense, as we call it, was already too strong for that even in the deathbed moralisings and soliloquisings that have come down to us under Solomon's name. There is no thirty-second, or fifty-first, or hundred and thirtieth Psalm of David in all the volume of 'Psalms of Solomon' that were composed in the century before Christ. No; there is no real repentance, real or assumed, anywhere in Solomon. There is remorse in plenty, and weariness of life, and discontent, and disgust, and self-contempt, bitterer to drink than blood. There is plenty of the sorrow that worketh death; but there is not one syllable of the repentance to salvation not to be repented of. 'All taste for pleasure is extinguished in the king's heart,' wrote Madame de Maintenon from the deathbed of Louis the Fourteenth. 'Old age and disappointment have taught him to make serious reflections on the vanity of everything he was formerly fond of.' Bathsheba might have written that letter from her dying son's bedside. Vanity of vanities, groaned out Solomon, with his heart full of the ashes of a lost life. All is vanity and vexation of spirit. Dreams at Gibeon, building of temples and kings' houses, largeness of heart, gifts of prophecy, a tongue of men and angels, proverbs and songs and Songs of songs—all is vanity if there is not along with it all constant repentance, daily self-denial, and a heart more and more perfect with God. The wise men of the east, wiser than Solomon, have a proverb upon the secret worm that was gnawing all the time in the royal staff upon which Solomon leaned. What, to end with, is the secret worm that is gnawing in your staff on which you lean?

XLIII

SOLOMON, AND A GREATER THAN SOLOMON

BEHOLD, A GREATER THAN SOLOMON IS HERE

WE have, as I believe, a suddenly passing, but a true and a deep glimpse into the working of our Lord's mind when He says, 'Behold, a greater than Solomon is here.' And there is nothing in heaven or in earth, in God or in man, so interesting to us as the working of our Lord's mind; especially when His mind is working upon Himself. Well, as it appears to me, we have here an example of how our Lord read, and thought, and saw, and felt about Himself, till He had fully discovered Himself, and had fully and for ever taken possession of Himself. The apostle says that it is not wise in us too much to measure ourselves by ourselves, or to compare ourselves with ourselves. But He who is the Wisdom of God itself here measures and compares Himself with Solomon, and that, to us, in a most intensely interesting and instructive way. As the Holy Child read the story of Solomon, as that beautiful and so tragical story is still told in the First Book of the Kings—as He read and saw how Solomon was born of David and Bathsheba; how he was named first the Divine Darling, and then the Son of Peace: how the young king chose wisdom and understanding as his royal portion; how wise he already was, and how wise he became, above all the wise men of the East; what a great kingdom he had, and what untold wealth, and what far and near renown he had; what a service he did in building and furnishing the House of the Lord; how the Queen of Sheba came to Jerusalem to hear his wisdom; and then, after all that, Solomon's songs and sermons and proverbs—as the Child Jesus read all that, and asked questions about all that; and then, when He became a man, and saw Himself as in a glass in all that,—ere ever He was aware, the Holy Ghost had witnessed it and had sealed it on His mind and on His heart, that, in all that He, the Son of Mary, was made of God a far greater than Solomon. The same thing must have come to Him as He read, and prayed, and pondered about David, and Moses, and Abraham, and Adam, till our Lord stood alone among all men, and above all men, and till of the people there was none with Him. And this went on, and increased in all clearness and in all assurance, till He was enabled and constrained to say, I and My Father are One. In some such way as that, as I believe, our Lord was led up of the Spirit from strength to strength, till He stood before God and Man the Messiah of Israel, the Son of God, and the Saviour of all them that believe.

Let us, then, if so be it may be given to us, follow out some of the steps that our Lord took in His own mind till He was able to say to the Scribes and Pharisees who would see a sign from Him, 'Behold, a greater than Solomon is here.' They were all at one as to Solomon's extraordinary greatness in the matter of his birth. Now, though our Lord was not born at once in David's house, He was born none the less in David's line; so much so, that there was no name by which He was oftener named, and no name He was more ready to answer to, than just the name, Son of David. The Syrophœnician woman came out of the same coasts, and cried unto Him, saying, Have mercy on me, O Lord, thou Son of David. And her daughter was made whole from that very hour. Have mercy on us, O Lord, thou Son of David, the two blind men sitting by the wayside cried, and immediately their eyes received sight, and they followed him. Blind Bartimæus also: Jesus, thou Son of David, have mercy upon me. And after a short conversation he also received his sight and followed Jesus in the way. Hosanna to the Son of David, Hosanna in the highest, the multitude cried, singing at His last entry into Jerusalem. Now, Solomon in all his glory never went beyond that. Israel had no nobler salutation for any of her kings than to call him the Son of David. But our Lord was both Son of David and Son of God. It is on those two strong foundation-stones that Paul builds his Epistle to the Romans. 'Jesus Christ our Lord, which was made of the seed of David according to the flesh, and declared to be the Son of God with power.' No wonder that Isaiah, who foresaw His glory, said that His name would be called Wonderful! To be at one time begotten of God from everlasting, and to be born of Mary in the fullness of time; and to be, and to continue to be, God and man in two distinct natures, and one person, for ever, how wonderful is that! Yes; truly, it is far less than the truth to say that a far greater than Solomon is born here.

The exquisitely-told story of Solomon's choice leads us to think of the many untold dreams and visions that must have come to the Holy Child Jesus, and of the many sleeping and waking choices He must have made both before and after His first visit to Solomon's temple. It was after Solomon had offered sacrifices on the altar at Gibeon that the Lord appeared to him and said, Ask what I shall give thee. And we may well believe, that after

Jesus at twelve years old saw Jerusalem and the temple and the passover for the first time, a dream would come to Him that night through the multitude of that day's business; a dream, and a voice, and a choice, and a benediction that would all send Him home to Joseph and Mary saying, Wist ye not that I must be about My Father's business? And then, what with dreams, and visions, and temptations, and trials, and right choices, and victories day and night untold, our Lord came forth to begin His Messianic life in Israel, as much greater than Solomon as heaven is greater than earth, and as the Son of God is greater than the Son of David. What we know not now about the Mystery of godliness during those eighteen, during those thirty-three years—the most wonderful years this wonderful world has ever seen—it will be our discovery and delight to know when Wisdom shall have builded her house, and hewn out her seven pillars, and mingled her wine, and furnished her table. 'I have yet many things to say unto you, but ye cannot bear them now.'

The second Psalm, the forty-fifth Psalm, the seventy-second Psalm, and the hundred and twenty-sixth Psalm, all have Solomon's name associated with them in one way or other. But no New Testament man can read those Psalms without this coming up on his mind, that a far greater than Solomon is here also. How completely Solomon has passed out of the second Psalm, and how entirely Jesus Christ has taken possession of it till His enemies be made His footstool. "Yet have I set my king upon my holy hill of Zion. I will declare the decree: the Lord hath said to me, Thou art My Son; this day have I begotten thee. Ask of Me, and I shall give thee the heathen for thine inheritance, and the uttermost parts of the earth for thy possession.' And the forty-fifth Psalm has been made into action-sermons, into table-services, and into prayers and praises at communion-seasons, till, not once in a thousand, do we ever think for a moment of Solomon and Pharaoh's daughter. It is blasphemy to speak to us about 'Solomon in all his glory' when we see and sing Jesus Christ. 'Thou art fairer than the children of men; grace is poured into thy lips; therefore God hath blessed thee for ever. Thou lovest righteousness, and hatest wickedness: therefore God, thy God, hath anointed thee with the oil of gladness above thy fellows. Hearken, O daughter, and consider, and incline thine ear; forget also thine own people, and thy father's house; for He is thy Lord, and worship thou Him.' And then The Song. Whatever may be the last word to be said about The Song, the Church of Christ has taken such possession of The Song of Songs for her Husband and for herself that it will be His and hers for ever. The Song of Solomon will be sung like the voice of many waters at the marriage-supper of the Lamb. 'I sat down under His shadow with great delight, and His fruit was sweet to my taste. He brought me to the banqueting-house, and His banner over me was love.'

The Proverbs, also, of Solomon, the son of David, king of Israel. 'A wise man will hear, and will increase learning; . . . to understand a proverb, and the interpretation; the words of the wise, and their dark sayings. . . . Go to the ant, thou sluggard; consider her ways and be wise; which, having no guide, overseer, or ruler, provideth her meat in the summer, and gathereth her food in the harvest. . . . I went by the field of the slothful, and by the vineyard of the man void of understanding. And, lo, it was all grown over with thorns, and nettles had covered the face thereof, and the stone wall thereof was broken down. . . . So shall thy poverty come as one that travelleth; and thy want as an armed man. . . . If the tree fall toward the south, or toward the north, in the place where the tree falleth, there shall it be.' . . . And again, When the almond tree shall flourish, and the grasshopper shall be a burden; or ever the silver cord be loosed, or the golden bowl be broken, or the pitcher be broken at the fountain, or the wheel broken at the cistern. . . . All well worth coming from Sheba to Jerusalem to hear such parables as these, and much more as good as these. But those who went out among the vineyards, and the sheepfolds, and in the sowing time, and in the reaping time, and suchlike, in Galilee, and Samaria, and Judea with our Lord, they would be the first to exclaim to themselves, Behold, a greater than Solomon is here also. Solomon, at his best, was of the earth, earthy. Jesus Christ is always the Lord from heaven; and, carrying the kingdom of heaven always in His heart, He saw that kingdom everywhere and in everything—in land and sea and sky. What if earth, said the angel to Adam—

> Be but the shadow of heaven, and things therein
> Each to other like, more than on earth is thought?

But that is just how it is when the Lord of angels takes His disciples out among the things of earth, and points out to them how the kingdom of heaven is like this beast, and that bird; this herb, and that tree; this sower with his seed-basket, and that reaper with his reaping-hook; this enemy sowing tares, and that husbandman sifting with his sieve and winnowing with his winnowing-fan; this woman leavening her meal, and that woman sweeping the house; this lost sheep, and that lost son; this marriage with its five wise and its five foolish virgins, and that great supper where they were compelled to come in. No; never man spake like this man. And all men felt it. 'And it was at Jerusalem the feast of the dedication, and it was winter. And Jesus walked in the temple in Solomon's porch. Then came the Jews round about Him, and said unto Him, How long dost Thou make us to doubt? If Thou be the Christ, tell us plainly. Jesus answered them, My sheep hear my voice, and I know them, and they follow Me: and I give unto them eternal life; and they shall never perish, neither shall any man pluck them out of My hand. And many believed on Him there.' Yes. An infinitely greater than Solomon stood and spake in parables in Solomon's porch that day.

But it was the wisdom of Solomon that brought the Queen of Sheba to Jerusalem, and it was her visit to Jerusalem to see Solomon, that gave us our present text. The Queen of the South, to her immortal honour, came from the uttermost parts of the earth, as our Lord so picturesquely has it, to see the wisdom of Solomon. Never king nor queen set out on a nobler errand than did she of the South; and, according to the beautiful history, she was not only wholly satisfied with what she saw and heard, but she testified to Solomon and said that the half of what she had seen and heard in Jerusalem had not been told her in Sheba. Now, there is no richer, finer, more beautiful, and more winning word in the whole of the Old Testament than just this same word 'wisdom.' And then, when we pass over into the New Testament, we find Wisdom exalted, and honoured, and glorified, and made one of the many names of Him, than whom, and than whose name, there is none other name given among men whereby we must be saved. The Solomonic books have some incomparably splendid passages on wisdom; and if Solomon had fallen, and repented, and risen again, and begun again, till he ended in living up to his own sermons on wisdom, what a glory, both in sacred letters and in a holy life, Solomon's name would have been! 'Wisdom,' says Sir Henry Taylor, one of the wisest writers in the English language, 'is not the same with understanding, talents, capacity, ability, sagacity, sense, or prudence,—not the same with any one of these; neither will all these taken together make it up. Wisdom is that exercise of the reason into which the heart enters—a structure of the understanding rising out of the moral and spiritual nature. It is for this cause that a high order of wisdom, that is a highly intellectual wisdom, is still more rare than a high order of genius. When they reach the very highest order they are one; for each includes the other, and intellectual greatness is matched with moral strength.' And then this fine essayist goes on to point out how Solomon's great intellectual gifts, coupled as they were in him with such an appetite for enjoyment, together became his shipwreck. And Bishop Butler, as I think, the very wisest of all our English writers, though he does not, like Sir Henry Taylor, name Solomon, he surely had him in his eye when he penned that memorable and alarming passage about those men who go over the theory of wisdom and virtue in their thoughts, talk well, and paint fine pictures of it, till their minds are hardened in a contrary course, and till they become more and more insensible to all moral considerations. I wish the great preacher had gone on in the Rolls Chapel to a sixteenth sermon on Solomon and his fine pictures of wisdom. But in lieu of Butler let Sir Henry Taylor's *Notes from Life* be read by all men who lack wisdom. Our Lord also made fine pictures of wisdom, and virtue, and the kingdom of heaven; but He was constantly correcting His pictures and counselling His hearers that the true wisdom, and the true kingdom of heaven, stands not in the head, but in the heart; not in light, however immediately it comes from heaven, but in both light and love; not in theories, however brilliant and beautiful, but in practices; and in practices, the humbler, the more obscure and despised, and the more full of crosses and crooks they are, the better they are for the purpose.

Our Lord did not absolutely shut great and gifted men like Solomon in all his glory out of the kingdom of heaven, but He did the next thing to it. For, while admitting that all things are possible with God, at the same time, both His own life and all His preaching went to proclaim that great intellect, with great station, and with great appetite for enjoyment, divine possibility and all, were, and would be, all but absolutely fatal to Solomon, and to all Solomon-like men. A far greater intellect than Solomon's was in our Lord; He was ordained and anointed to a far greater station and seat; and He had the capacity, if not the appetite, for far greater enjoyment. But all that was all balanced in our Lord, and built up into moral character, by great humility, great submissiveness, great labours, and great love. As I do the will of my Father; as I in everything submit Myself to the will of My Father; and as I thus learn more and more of the will of My Father, both to submit Myself to it and to do it; so do ye, He was constantly teaching. And ye also, like Me, shall both know the doctrine that it is of God, and shall come at last with Me to His heavenly kingdom. Here, then, is wisdom, as John says in the Revelation. And here is the mind which hath wisdom. A greater than Solomon in all his wisdom is indeed here.

And when the Queen of Sheba, so we read, had seen all Solomon's wisdom, and the house that he had built, and the meat of his table, and the sitting of his servants, and the attendance of his ministers, and their apparel, and his cupbearers, and his ascent by which he went up into the house of the Lord, there was no more spirit in her. Solomon had built two houses—one a house for the Lord and another a house for himself. And what the Queen of Sheba saw we also see to this day in the sixth and seventh chapters; and, at this distance of time and space, as we read them we feel like her about them. But, proud of his house of God as Solomon was, he had grace enough to say that the heaven of heavens could not contain the God of Israel, much less this house that he had built. And as time went on in Israel, it became more and more clear that Solomon's temple, from heaven as it was at that time, became more and more a hindrance, rather than a help, to God dwelling on the earth; till Christ came in the temple of His body, and till Paul built up beside that temple, and leaning upon it, the similar temple of the believer's body. And then John Howe comes to us in our own day, and in our own tongue, with his *Living Temple,* a piece that Paul would have given orders to read to all churches. And I promise the student of these things, who will begin with Solomon and go on to John Howe, that he will write to me after he has read it all, and will say, that there is no spirit left in him as he lays down the Plato of the Puritans on *That Notion that a Good Man is a Temple of God.*

But my time has failed me. And all I shall attempt to say more at this time is this, that if the Queen of Sheba was so overpowered as she saw the meat of Solomon's table, and the sitting of his servants, and the attendance of his ministers, and their apparel, and his cupbearers, what would she have said had she ever sat down at the Lord's Table? I wonder what she would have said when she went south about the Lord's Table, and the meat upon it, and the sitting of His servants, and the attendance of His ministers, and their apparel, and His cupbearers. No, she would have said, the tenth of that had not been told me. Thy wisdom, O Thou Greater than Solomon, she would have broken forth, and Thy prosperity, far exceedeth all the fame that I had heard. Happy are Thy men, happy are those Thy servants, which stand continually before Thee, and hear Thy wisdom. And blessed be the Lord Thy God which delighted in Thee, to set Thee on the throne of Isreal.

XLIV

THE QUEEN OF SHEBA

THE QUEEN OF THE SOUTH SHALL RISE UP IN THE JUDGMENT WITH THE MEN OF THIS GENERATION, AND CONDEMN THEM

I SHALL take up somewhat high ground with you concerning the Queen of Sheba. For, so far as I have seen, that wonderful woman has never had adequate justice done to her. As I see her, the Queen of Sheba came to Jerusalem on the very highest of errands. She was moved to undertake her journey by the very strongest and the very loftiest of motives. And she saw and heard and took home in her heart far more than her very highest expectations. And while the sacred writer has told us her story in his very best manner, at the same time, it is our Lord's acknowledgment and confession of her in the judgment—it is this that lifts her up in my eyes till I see her among the foremost of those who shall come from the east, and the west, and the north, and the south, and who shall hear the wisdom, and taste the grace, and share the glory of a greater than Solomon in the Jerusalem which is above, and which is the mother of us all.

The first thing that is told us concerning the Queen of Sheba is this, that she had heard in Sheba concerning the Name of the Lord. It may very well be that this has bribed my eyes and perverted my judgment in the matter of the Queen of Sheba. The Name of the Lord so construes and so glorifies the whole of the Old Testament to me that the more I read the Old Testament tne more I find nothing else in it worth its ink but the Name of the Lord. If I once find the Name of the Lord in the life of any Old Testament man or woman, I can never again forget that man or that woman. And, on the other hand, however great, and good, and wise, and famous any man is, if the Name of the Lord is not his strong tower, I fear I do not do that man full justice. If this sacred writer means nothing more by it but a sonorous and a stately turn of expression when he mentions the Name of the Lord as the motive of the Queen of Sheba's mission to Jerusalem; if he means as little by it as the run of the commentators say that he means, then, all I can say is that he has set a trap for my feet in the text. You all know the Name of the Lord, and I hope you all feel about that Name with me. You remember it, and never an hour of any day can you forget it. The Name of the Lord is written all over Moses and David and Isaiah in letters of gold, a finger deep. For the Name of the Lord is 'The LORD God, merciful and gracious, long-suffering. and abundant in goodness and truth, keeping mercy for thousands, forgiving iniquity and transgression and sin.'

Well, it had all come about under the good hand of God somewhat in this way. It simply must have all come about somewhat in this way. Some of those merchantmen who went down to the Red Sea in ships, and did business for Solomon all along its shores in gold, and silver, and ivory, and apes, and peacocks, and almug-trees, and what not, one of their ships on one occasion was Queen of Sheba. And as the seamen of Israel filled their water-driven in for want of fresh water near the summer palace of the pots, it was an ordinance that they should sing, saying, Spring up, O well; in the Name of the Lord, spring up! When, who should pass by but the Queen of Sheba herself with her maidens with her? Sing still another of the songs of Zion, she said to Solomon's sailors. At which they sang a psalm that a prophet who was in their ship had taught them to sing on the occasion of a great tempest they had just passed through. 'These see,' they sang, 'the works of the Lord, and His wonders in the deep. For He commandeth, and raiseth the stormy winds, which lifteth up the waves thereof. They mount up to the heaven, they go down again to the depths; their soul is melted because of trouble. Then they cry unto the Lord in their trouble, and He bringeth them out of their distresses. Oh that men would praise the Lord for His goodness, and for His wonderful works to the children of men!' And, then, at the Name of the Lord, and without being told to do it, all the seamen standing on the shore lifted up their hands to heaven and proclaimed the Name of the Lord, and worshipped, saying, 'The LORD, the LORD God, merciful and gracious.' And ever after that day the Queen of Sheba watched at her window for the ships of Solomon, till, above all else, the Name of the Lord took entire hold of her heart. The Queen of Sheba had lords many and gods many of her own. She and her people had their gods of the sea and their gods of the land; their gods of war and their gods of wine; their gods of the night and their gods of the day, and many more. But there was no name of any god given in Sheba that took such hold of the Queen of Sheba's heart as did the Name of the God of Israel. Till she took a very great train, with camels that bare spices, and very much gold, and precious stones, there came no such abundance of spices as these which the Queen of Sheba brought to Jerusalem, because of the Name of the Lord.

Even Homer himself was sometimes seen to nod. And that is the explanation of Matthew Henry's unaccountable slander that some of the Queen of Sheba's questions that she put to Solomon, some were frivolous, some were captious, and some were over-curious. I do not see what business the best of commentators has to say that, unless it be to teach us always to read our Bible with our own eyes and with our own hearts for ourselves. And when I read with my own eyes all I can find about the Queen of Sheba, I see neither caption, nor frivolity, nor idle curiosity about her. And I cannot think there could have been, since our Lord sets His seal upon her, and takes her and her questions as His accusation and condemnation of the Pharisees of His day. The sacred writer knew far more about the Queen of Sheba than the minister of Chester did; and what he says about her questions is this, that they were hard to Solomon to answer; especially when she went deep down into her heart for her questions. 'All that was in her heart.' I suppose the sacred writer means all matters, or, at least, very many matters connected with the throne and the state of Sheba. Affairs of state, as we would say: her anxieties about her treaties of war and peace; her seat of judgment and justice over her own people; royal-family matters also, no doubt; and matters, maybe, still nearer her heart. The Queen of Sheba had heard in the south country all about Solomon's dream at Gibeon. She had it all read to her when her royal cares would not let her sleep. And, ever since, she had kept all these things in her heart against her long-intended visit to Jerusalem. But from the day when she first heard the Name of the Lord, from that day her heart had grown every day and every night deeper and fuller of hard questions; questions so hard that I doubt if she broke them all even to Solomon. At the same time, her heart in Sheba at its fullest of hard questions was not a New Testament heart, and could not in Sheba be. Of no New Testament heart does the New Testament ever say that its owner ever told to any man all that was in her heart; unless it was to our New Testament Solomon. And, then, He is such a Solomon that He does not need that communication to be made to Him. For He is wiser in men's hearts than all men; than Ethan the Ezrahite, and Heman and Chalcol and Darda, the sons of Mahol; and His fame is now in all the nations round about. Only, in His wisdom He will have it that we come, if it is from the uttermost part of the earth, and tell Him as if He did not already know all the hard questions of our hearts; and then there will not be anything hid from the King that He will not tell us. Oh, no, sacred writer! you do not really mean us to understand that the Queen of Sheba told to any man all that was in her heart. We quite well understand what you mean. She told Solomon so much about herself and about her people, and got so much help and advice from Solomon, that 'all that was in her heart' is just your hyperbolical and impressive way of putting her before us in your great regard for her, and in your great admiration of him.

Matthew Henry is more like himself when he goes on to say that we may be sure that Solomon gave the inquiring Queen a *rationale* of the temple and all its offices and all its services. That is a handsome retraction and apology for what he had said so rashly and so censoriously about the frivolity and the captiousness of the Queen's questions. You could not possibly give a *rationale* of the communion service of this house on a communion Sabbath-day to a frivolous and captious-minded man. Now, the temple was just the Lord's Supper already in type and prophecy. And when you try it, there is no subject in heaven or earth more impossible to rationalise to a frivolous or a captious mind than just what lies behind the Lord's Supper: the substitution and the propitiation made for sinners by the blood of Christ. The Queen of Sheba was like one of those children in Israel who asked their fathers at every passover supper, What mean ye by this service? Only, she was not a child, but a woman of a strong understanding and a deep heart, and both Solomon and the high priest and the prophet, all three together, were at their wits' end; it took them all their might to open up all the parts of the temple and its sacrifices to her satisfaction: the reason of this, and the reason of that; the use of this and the use of that; the antitype of this, and the antitype of that—she both hearing them and asking them questions. Till, when they had taken her through it all, there was no more spirit left in her to ask any more. I can believe it. For to this day nothing more completely subdues the spirit than the hard questions of the heart when they are honestly put and fully met and answered in the house of the Lord, and at His table. Nothing satisfies and silences the heart like the *rationale,* that is to say, the revelation of the truth and the grace of God to the heart that is hungry both for His truth as it is in Jesus, and for His grace as it is in Jesus also, and in Jesus alone.

No; there was neither captiousness nor frivolity in the Queen of Sheba when she came out of her own country, and neither was there detraction, nor depreciation, nor envy when she returned home. What say you? Had I been in her place, I do not feel guilty that I would have been either captious or frivolous in the house of God or in Solomon's own house. But I would have had things in my heart worse than captiousness or frivolousness; things that I would never have told to Solomon, or to Nathan, or even to the high priest over the scapegoat. Had I been a king, and had I been shown through Solomon's temple, and through his palace, and through all that the Queen of Sheba saw in Jerusalem, I know only too well what would have been in my heart. Ay, even when I was being taken over the Lord's house and was being instructed in its sacrifices. Bishop Lancelot Andrewes has no more private devotion than that is where we come upon him praying to God to be delivered from his envy of another man's grace. Oh, where will that sin of sins, that so besetting sin, not intrude itself! If all this good queen's appreciation, and admiration, and congratulation was absolutely sincere and without offence in the sight of God who seeth the heart, well does she deserve all the honour that both the Old Testament and our Lord bestow upon her. Only, Blessed be His name, even if you are sick till you have no spirit left in you at the sight of other men's great houses, and great riches, and wise words, and fame, and great happiness—even so, Blessed be his name, He will not despise you nor spit upon you. He will only take you all that the more and all that the deeper into His temple, and will show you all that the more riches of His grace, till He has given to you all you desire. And, Lord Jesus, all our desire in this matter is before Thee and is not hidden from Thee. It was a true report, she said, that I heard in mine own land, of thy acts and thy wisdom. Happy are thy men, happy are these thy servants, which stand continually before thee, and that hear thy wisdom. Only, had she known it, and seen the end of it, she was far more happy herself; as much more happy as it is to be faithful over a few things, and to admire rather than to be admired, and to bless than to be blessed, and to give than to receive.

Returning toward the same south a thousand years after the Queen of Sheba, the Ethiopian eunuch sat in his chariot and read Esaias the prophet. Esaias had not yet risen in the day of the Queen of Sheba; but she had the best reading of her day in her hand as she rode south. She had Solomon's prayer at the dedication of the temple in her hand. And the place in the prayer which she reads and prays all the way from Jerusalem to the south is this—'Moreover, concerning a stranger, that is not of Thy people Israel, but cometh out of a far country for Thy Name's sake. For they shall hear of Thy great Name, and of Thy strong hand, and of Thy stretched-out hand. When the stranger shall come and pray toward this house, hear Thou in heaven Thy dwelling-place, and do according to all that the stranger calleth to Thee for, that all people of the earth may know Thy Name, to fear Thee, as do Thy people Israel. All Ethiopia and all the south has not yet been explored. And who can tell but that the foundations of a long-lost temple may yet be laid bare in that ancient and honourable land; a temple, too, with no middle wall of partition with its excluding inscription engraven upon it; but in room of that an open door with this evangelical writing in gold of Ophir over it: 'Doubtless Thou art our Father, though Abraham be ignorant of us, and though Israel acknowledge us not. Thou art our Father. Thou, O Lord, art our Redeemer. THY NAME is from everlasting.' And then this beside it in the same gold from a Psalm for Solomon: 'The kings of Tarshish and of the isles shall bring presents; the kings of Sheba and Seba shall offer gifts. And He shall live, and to Him shall be given of the gold of Sheba: and blessed be His glorious Name for ever; and let the whole earth be filled with His glory.'

XLV

SHIMEI

AND DAVID SAID, LET HIM ALONE, LET HIM CURSE

SHIMEI was a reptile of the royal house of Saul. When Shimei saw David escaping for his life out of Jerusalem, Satan entered into Shimei, and he came forth and cursed at David as he passed by. And he cast stones at David, and cried, Thou bloody man, thou man of Belial, he cried. The Lord hath returned upon thee all the blood of the house of Saul. Behold, thou art taken in thy wickedness, because thou art a bloody man. Why should that dead dog curse the king in that way? said Abishai to David. Let me go over and take off his head. But the king answered to Abishai, So let him curse, because the Lord hath said unto him, Curse David. Let him alone, and let him curse, for the Lord hath bidden him. And still as David went on his way, Shimei also went along on the hillside over against David, and he cursed as he went, and he threw stones at David and cast dust. But David held his peace; for David had said to Abishai, It is the Lord.

Political and ecclesiastical party spirit turn us all, on occasion, into reptiles like Shimei. Shimei knew as well as you do that David had never shed a single drop of Saul's blood. So far from that, David's men were astonished and offended at David that he had let Saul go scot-free again and again when he had him in his power. And Shimei knew that quite well. But Shimei hated the truth that he knew. It was not Shimei's interest to admit the truth that he knew. He would not let the truth light on his mind for one moment, especially about David. Nothing was right that David did. Everything was wrong that David had any hand in. If you had a word to say for David, Shimei would follow you about also with curses and stones and dust. Shimei had everything to expect from Saul, and he knew that he had nothing to expect from David; and, therefore, David was a bloody man and a son of Belial. You know Shimei. At any rate, all who know you intimately know Shimei. Charity seeketh not her own, is not easily provoked, thinketh no evil; rejoiceth not in iniquity, but rejoiceth in the truth. But you never yet knew a fierce political or ecclesiastical partisan who had charity. When our political and ecclesiastical partisans begin to have charity we shall no longer need to offer the Lord's prayer every day, and say, Thy kingdom come.

Abishai looked up and saw a dead dog barking and biting out of his own kennel-door in Bahurim that day. But it was the Lord to David. David had nothing to do with the fall of Saul on Mount Gilboa; but the fall of Uriah in the front of the battle before Rabbah was ever before David, and never more so than it was that day as he crossed the Kedron, and passed through Gethsemane, and descended upon Bahurim. So let him curse, for the Lord hath said to him, Curse David. To such a divine use was Shimei put of God that greatest day of David's life. For Shimei that day perfected the good work on David that Absalom and Ahithophel had so well begun. Shimei was David's crowning means of grace that day. That day adorns and seals all David's psalms, and it was Shimei that did it. David had only to point with his finger to the hillside, and Shimei's insult and injury would have ceased for ever. But what profit would Shimei's blood have been to David? David had more sense. David had more grace. David knew himself better than that. And he know God better than that. There is a Shimei that you wish he were dead. He is such a trial and torment to you. He so hampers and hinders you. He is such a rival to you. He is such a thorn in your pillow, and such a crook in your lot, and such a cross on which you are crucified, and are to be crucified, every day you live. You count up how old he is, and you promise yourself to have so many years of relief and enjoyment after he is in his grave. Oh no! Oh no! Let him live. Let his doctor lengthen his days. Let his bow long abide in its strength. Let him see all the days of his fathers. Let him close your eyes. Let him stand over your grave. Let him inherit your substance. Let him live long after you and rejoice in your portion. For it is the Lord. It is your salvation. And who, then, shall say to the Lord, Why hast Thou done this? Shall the thing formed say to Him that formed it, Why hast Thou made me thus? O the depth both of the wisdom and knowledge of God! How unsearchable are His judgments, and His ways past finding out! For who hath known the mind of the Lord? Or who hath been His counsellor?

Now, what is true of bad men is equally true of all our other bad surroundings, and all our other adverse circumstances, as we call them. For they also are all set of God, and kept of God, and made of God to operate on us for a good use. God sets to each one of us all the special surroundings, good and evil, of our several lives. It is too high for us to attain to and to understand. How He can do that to you, and to me, and to all other men, as much as to you and me, that surpasses us. But over-work and difficulty and impossibility are only true of men; they are not true of God. The Divine Nature is not like human nature; at least, not in things like that. God is everywhere, and He is wholly everywhere; and all His power, and all His wisdom, and all His grace, and all His truth, are with, and for, and around, and within every man. And thus it is that He sets every man's circumstances to him, good and bad, as much and as well as if He had no other man on His hand in earth or in heaven. When Almighty God creates another soul; when He elects to eternal life another new sinner; when He regenerates and begins to sanctify another new saint, He, from that moment, besets him behind and before, and lays His hand upon him. And when we awake to all that, we fall in with it all with unceasing wonder and with unceasing thanksgiving. O Lord, Thou hast searched me, and known me. Thou compassest my path and my lying down, and art acquainted with all my ways. Whither shall I flee from Thy Spirit? How precious, also, are Thy thoughts unto me, O God! How great is the sum of them! He believes nothing who does not believe that. He knows nothing who does not know that. He has not begun to live who lives not always under that. And he will soon come to see God in everything that befalls him; and not God only, but God his Sanctifier and his Saviour. And then he will not let one atom of his most adverse circumstances be altered, lest he should thereby lose something of his full salvation. And when any of his friends, for his protection, or for his peace, or for his comfort would fain remove out of his life aught that tempts and tries him; aught that tramples on him and humbles him; aught that plagues him and vexes him and leads him into sin, like David to Abishai at Bahurim he says to him, Let it alone, for it is the Lord. You say to me rare things about design, and adaptation, and environment, and means to ends, and final causes, and what not; and you both astonish and edify me. But if you fear God, and come, I will tell you how He environs my soul, and how He adapts you and all you say and do, to the good of my soul. If you could see and study my soul, even as I see it and study it, you would see something to make a science out of it. You would see a design and an end and a final cause, the greatest and the best—your soul under sanctification and mine—a final cause and an end next to God Himself. You would see all things in my world and in my generation, all working together upon me for my good. And all so secretly, so exquisitely, so intricately, so surely, and so infallibly working together of God. No. If you love my soul and its salvation, you must not alter by a single hair's breadth any single thing of all my circumstances; not, at least, till you are sure that I have got its divine end and design out of it. Especially not my trying, and tempting, and searching, and sifting, and sanctifying circumstances. And least of all Absalom and Ahithophel and Shimei. Every hour of every day; every man I meet; every word that enters my ear; every sight that enters my eye; all my thoughts within me that like a case of knives wounds my heart—it is all the Lord! If this life were all, then, I admit, it might be different. If you denied the resurrection of the body and the immortality of the soul, then I could understand you. But I cannot understand a man who believes in the sanctification and the eternal life of his own soul escaping the only and sure path of life like that. It is the Lord, and He is set upon my salvation. He is set upon my humility, my submissiveness, my meekness, my gentleness, my resignation, my contentment, my detachment, my self-denial, my cross, my death to sin, my death to myself, my unearthliness, my heavenly-mindedness, my conformity to Christ, and my acceptance of Him—and what a splendid use is all that to which to put all the things that otherwise would be so much against me! And David said to Abishai, and to all his servants, Let this Benjamite alone, and let him curse; for the Lord hath bidden him. It may be that the Lord will look upon mine affliction. And as David and his men went by the way,

Shimei went on the hill's side over against David, and cursed David, and threw stones at him, and cast dust.

The magnificent use to which God puts the greatest of all His people's evils must not be attempted before a common congregation. Had we an elect-enough and a sympathetic-enough audience, this would make a splendid subject for the evening of the Lord's day. But we would need to have before us only the heavenly-minded, and the much-exercised, and the teachable, and the child-like; while all the frivolous and the captious, and all those given to disputes and debates about divine things should stay at home. There are plenty of materials for this great head of our subject lying scattered over the whole face of Holy Scripture. And the great masters have sometimes taken up this subject, after Holy Scripture. Samuel Rutherford, for example, comes often upon it in his Letters and in all his books. But after he has said all that it is possible to say upon it, he exclaims, Oh! what a deep is here, that created wit cannot take up! Jonathan Edwards takes it up with all his matchless wit in his fine letter to Thomas Gillespie of Carnock, and elsewhere in his golden works. And what do you say to Shakespeare himself?

> O benefit of ill! now I find true
> That better is by evil still made better!
> And ruined love, when it is built anew,
> Grows fairer than at first, more strong, far greater.
> So I return rebuked to my content,
> And gain by ill thrice more than I have spent.

And then, of death, the wages of sin. Can any good be said of death? Yes; by the proper man. 'Death,' says Thomas Shepard, 'is the very best of all our gospel ordinances. For in all His other ordinances Christ comes, on occasion, to us; but in a believer's death Christ take us to be for ever with Him.' A fair specimen of Shepard. And, to bind up this bold anthology with George Herbert:

> Death, thou wert once an uncouth, hideous thing,
> Nothing but bones.
> But since our Saviour's death did put some blood
> Into thy face;
> Thou art grown fair and full of grace,
> Much in request, much sought for as a good.

This brings us to David's deathbed; and David's deathbed has never been without its own difficulties to thoughtful and reverential readers. For Shimei with all his good and all his bad uses comes back again to David's deathbed to tempt and to try David, and to discover what is in David's dying heart. The deathbed sayings of God's saints have a special interest and a delightful edification to us; but David's last words to Solomon about Shimei —we would pass them by if we could. Three or four several explanations of those terrible words of David have been offered to the distressed reader by able men and men of authority in such matters. I shall only mention some of those offered explanations, and leave you to judge for yourselves. Well, some students of the Old Testament are bold to take David's dreadful words about Shimei out of David's mouth altogether, and to put them into the mouth of the prophet who has preserved to us David's life and death. Those awful words, they say, are that righteous prophet's explanation and vindication of the too late execution of Shimei by Solomon after his reprieve had come to an end with the death of David. Others, again, and they, too, some of our most conservative and orthodox scholars, say to us that the text should run in English in this way: 'Hold him not guiltless; at the same time bring *not* his hoar head down to the grave with blood.' You will blame me for my too open ear to such bold scholarship; and you will think it very wrong in me to listen to such bad men. But the heart has its reasons, as Pascal says, and my heart would stretch a considerable point in textual criticism to get Shimei's blood wiped off David's deathbed. Another interpretation is to take the text as it stands, and to hear David judicially charging Solomon about a case of too long delayed justice against a blasphemer of God and the king. And then the last explanation is the most painful one of all, and it is this, that David had never really and truly, and at the bottom of his heart, forgiven Shimei for his brutality and malignity at Bahurim. And that all David's long-suppressed revenge rushed out of his heart against his old enemy when he lay on his bed and went back on the day on which he had fled from Jerusalem. You can choose your own way of looking at David's deathbed. But, in any case, it is Bahurim that we shall all carry home, and carry for ever henceforth, in our hearts. We shall have, God helping us, David's Bahurim-mind always in us henceforth amid all those who insult and injure us, and say all manner of evil against us falsely; and amid all manner of adverse and sore circumstances, so as to see the Lord in it all, and so as to work out our salvation amid it all. And the Lord will look upon our affliction also, and will requite us good for all this evil, if only we wisely and silently and adoringly submit ourselves to it.

XLVI

JOAB

AND DAVID SAID, I AM WEAK THIS DAY THOUGH ANOINTED KING

JOAB, the son of David's sister, was a man of the very foremost ability. Had it not been for David, Joab would have climbed up into the throne of Israel. As it was, he stood on the steps of the throne and faced the king all his days. Notwithstanding their family relationship, David and Joab were much of an age, and that, no doubt, helps to account for a good deal that went on between the uncle and the nephew. Joab was a stern, haughty, imperious, revengeful man. His only virtue was a certain proud, patronising loyalty to his king. Joab's ambition might surely have been satisfied, for he was in more respects than one the most privileged man in the land. Even the king himself was afraid of his commander-in-chief. The sovereign took his orders meekly from his subject. After his own contemptuous way, Joab was always true to David. That is to say, he made short work with any one else who was false to David. And he performed some splendid services both as a soldier and a statesman in the extension and consolidation of David's kingdom. In his own well-read and picturesque way, Dean Stanley describes Joab very aptly as the Marlborough of the empire of Israel.

Over-ambition, to put it all in one word, was Joab's besetting sin; over-vaulting ambition. But what more would Joab have had? you may well ask. Only, do not ask that any more about Joab, or about any other ambitious and self-seeking man. Look into your own heart and answer. If you look well into your own heart, you will see there that as long as any one else has anything at all of his own, it does not matter how much you have. Joab was king in all but the crown. King, and more. But as long as his weaker uncle wore the crown, Joab's heart raged like hell. Jonathan gave over to David all that he possessed, and all that he ever expected to possess, and died a king. Joab envied David and every one else all that they had, and died an outcast. Pride, jealousy, malignity, revenge, assassination, with now and then a gleam of satanic loyalty lighting up his terrible heart—such is the son of Zeruiah. The land trembles as Joab rises on the stepping-stones of murdered men to the shining top of power and honour, only to fall under the sword of a too-slow justice an outlaw from the love and the pity of all men.

David was all heart, and passion, and sensibility; while Joab was all self-will, and pride, and as hard as a stone. David's sudden and unparalleled exaltation was never forgiven him at home. His brothers and his sisters were sufficiently proud of David toward all their neighbours; at the same time they could never enough let him see how much they thought themselves as good as he was when they were alone together. But it was Joab who carried all that to a head. David and Joab were by far the ablest members of a very able household; but David was hampered with his heart, till Joab, having no heart, got the mastery. And thus it is that, already, and before David has well sat down on the throne, we hear him saying such things as these: 'The sons of Zeruiah,' David burst out, 'be too hard for me. I am this day weak, though anointed king.' And you may be sure that when that so unkingly speech was reported to the sons of Zeruiah, it did not make them any the less hard for David. Joab's temper was not any sweeter, nor his hand any lighter, after that and many suchlike deplorably foolish speeches of David. Already David lay and writhed in a net of ten thousand invisible threads and stings; and a chain of iron is soon to be forged for David by his own besotted hands. Men of much heart are always men of much mischief to themselves and to other men. To keep much of a heart with all diligence every moment—what a superhuman task is that! To keep much of a heart, to keep it in, to keep it down, to keep it open, but not too open—who is sufficient for these things? David yielded to Joab out of simple good-nature yesterday, and again to-day, and he will yield something far more important to-morrow, and so on. Each time he yields it is an act of rare courtesy, fine consideration, and most beautiful good-feeling and good-will—all touched, at the same time, with a certain tincture of fear. In any other world but this, and to any other man but Joab, David's heart would be an open heaven. But as it is, David wakens up too late to find out that he is king in nothing but in name. Neither his royal word, nor his personal liberty, nor his children, nor his tears over his dead children, are his own. Such is the mischief of too much heart and too little will in one member of a family, and too little heart and too much will in another. Let both look at David and Joab, and learn, and lay to heart. For we are all in this world, and in families, for this end, to learn how to rule our hearts; now to reduce and now to enlarge; now to harden and now to soften our hearts. The heart is the man. In this world, and in the world to come, the heart alone is the man. And we are in this world and in its families to make ourselves an everlasting heart.

'It is worse than a crime,' says an astute politician, 'it is a blunder.' And though it was a clear enough crime in David to pass by Joab's murder of Abner, it came out afterwards to be a most terrible blunder. All David's after-life might well have been different but for that blunder. There might have been no 'matter of Uriah,' and no rebellion of Absalom, and none of the many other miseries that so desolated David's house, had he not committed this fatal blunder of letting Joab live. David knew his duty quite well. 'The Lord shall reward the doer of evil according to his wickedness,' David proclaimed over Abner's mangled body. Yes; but David held the sword for no other purpose than to be the Lord's right hand in rewarding all the evil that was done in Israel in his day. But, then, Joab was the most powerful and the most necessary man in Israel, and Abner had no friends, and David contented himself with pronouncing an eloquent requiem over Abner, and leaving his murderer to go free in all his offices and all his honours. Joab was deep enough to understand quite well why his life was spared. He knew quite well that it was fear and not love that had moved David to let him live. It was a diplomatic act of David to spare Joab, but David was playing with a far deeper diplomatist than himself. Very soon we shall see this respited assassin ordering David about and dictating to him, till we shall pity David as well as blame him. Joab's impunity speedily shot up into an increased contempt for David, till secret contempt became open insolence, and open insolence open and unavenged rebellion. Was it not a blunder?

In the corrupted currents of this world,
Offence's gilded hand may shove by justice,
And oft 'tis seen, the wicked prize itself
Buys out the law: but 'tis not so above;
There is no shuffling, there the action lies
In his true nature; and we ourselves compell'd,
Even to the teeth and forehead of our faults,
To give in evidence.

'And it came to pass in the morning that David wrote a letter to Joab, and sent it by the hand of Uriah. And he wrote in the letter saying: Thou shalt set Uriah in the forefront of the hottest battle, and retire from him, that he may be smitten and die.' That dreadful letter shows us David's desperation, indeed; but it shows us also David's estimate of Joab. Had Jonathan been spared to be second to David this would never have happened. David would never have dared to send such a letter as that to Jonathan. But Jonathan was taken and Joab was left, and David had Joab for his tool to impress on our hearts the terrible portent of a bloodstained holiness. But how could Joab have the utter depravity and the cold blood to do it? you ask. How could he plan an attack, and sham a retreat, and risk a defeat, and all to murder a noble, spotless, unsuspecting comrade? It was not soldierly obedience. Joab did not care one straw for the king's letter. When it suited him, Joab could tear up the king's letters and throw them in his face. Unless you can tell us, we shall never in this world know why Joab murdered Uriah after that letter. Unless you are astute enough, and wicked enough, and then honest enough to tell us, we shall not know till the day of judgment what all passed through Joab's heart when he read that letter, and read it again with his glancing eyes. Joab had some sufficient motive for following out David's detestable orders. But unless you find out Joab's motive among your own motives, we shall have to leave him alone. It was like Pilate and the chief priests with our Lord between them. They also had their motives. Only, their motives are as plain as day, while Joab was a deep man—deeper, quite possibly, than any man here. And it came to pass that, when Joab observed the city, he assigned Uriah unto a place where he knew that valiant men were on the wall. And Uriah fell. And David said to Joab's messenger, Let not this thing displease thee. But the thing that David had done displeased the Lord. And the Lord had Joab in His hand henceforth as the rod of his displeasure, and Joab had David's letter in his hand till, if there is a man on the face of the earth to be pitied from that time forward, it is David.

Better a living dog than a dead lion. David was the first lion of the tribe of Judah, and it is sad to see how his teeth and his claws were broken, and his sinews cut, by his tormentors. You are but a dog beside David. Only, you have this, that you are still alive, and young, and free, and unsold as yet, whereas David is dead. You are too young to have written any letters yet worth any one keeping. 'Destroy this letter as soon as you have read it,' David wrote at the top of it. 'Under the strictest seal of secrecy, and on the king's own business,' Uriah read on the envelope, and handed it with all speed and respect to his chief. 'Read and burn instantly,' wrote David in state cipher. But Joab was not the man to throw an autograph letter of the king ino the fire. Joab recollected what prices such letters bring in the auction rooms, and, instead of burning David's letter, he folded it carefully, and buttoned it up in his breast-pocket. That letter was still deep down in Joab's breast-pocket when Benaiah at David's demand fell upon him and slew him in spite of the horns of the altar. You are still in your innocence, and have written no letters. And were you my only son, may I bury you first before you write your first letter to Joab.

Tool turned tyrant—that shortly sums up Joab and David for the next thirty years. Only an insult here and a humiliation there has been preserved to us out of the daily insults and humiliations that Joab heaped upon David. Joab had no more pity than a tiger, and the tiger's claws were never out of David's flesh from the matter of Uriah down to David's death. David had said unto Nathan, I have sinned against the Lord. And Nathan had said unto David, The Lord also hath put away thy sin, thou shalt not die. But David had far better have died and been buried beside his sin. Thou answeredst them, O Lord our God; Thou wast a God that forgavest them, but Thou tookest vengeance of their inventions. And Joab was just the instrument to glut himself in the divine vengeance. 'Joab insolently falls foul of David.' is one of Matthew Henry's plain-spoken remarks. And again, 'He calls David a fool to his face.' We have only one in a thousand of Joab's insolent speeches to David's face. But the sacred writer surely selects and preserves his very best instance of tool turned tyrant and his insolent speech, in the case of Absalom. Joab ran Absalom three times through the heart right in the teeth of David's command to spare and save Absalom alive. And then, when David broke out in that terrible sorrow which sounds in our hearts to this day, Joab would not have it. There has been enough weeping now for Absalom, said Joab to David. Let there be no more. And David dried his eyes on the spot like a cowed child, and turned to the business of the kingdom, cursing Joab all the time in his heart. It was David's sad case that made our Lord say in David's city a thousand years after, Verily, verily, I say unto you, whosoever committeth sin is the servant of sin. And all Scripture is full of the same warning. Know ye not that to whom ye yield yourselves servants to obey, his servants ye are whom ye obey? For of whom a man is overcome, of the same he is brought in bondage. All this of David and Joab is only the life of some of ourselves sold for nought, and written out with all plainness of speech, and put of God into our hands.

I have been sorely tempted to take up the mystical interpretation of Shimei and Joab. Those two Scripture characters so lend themselves to the mystical method. Those two thorns in David's flesh—and there are more like them—so suit into the secretest depths of our own spiritual experience. Those two bad men were, each in his own wicked way, of such rich and indispensable use to David, if David was to be searched out, hunted down, laid low, and saved at last. They so struck in, made of God and kept of God for the very purpose, to tempt, and to vex, and to humiliate, and to weaken, and to keep broken David's broken heart. They, Joab especially, were ever with David. Joab with his insolence, and his cruelty, and his family familiarity, and his equality in years, and all that eating in and growing, on to David's deathbed—I declare it is another parable of that cunning Nathan, and not a true and honest history at all! It is a subtle allegory all the time; and that, too, of our own life. Yes, that is it. It is my life and yours; if your life is at all like mine, or is going to be, you who are yet young. It is our own life under sin, as Paul says, and under grace. Under forgiveness, and then under vengeance, as David says, and had such a good right to say. Only, come, all ye who would learn beforehand the ways of God, and we will tell you as good as anything that ever was told even of David. As good. As sad. As painful. As awful. And still more amazing in its grace. Shimei cursing and throwing stones. Joab, first tool and then ever after tyrant. We will show you such a letter. A sackful of such letters. And the writer of them walking softly, and never ceasing from prayer and tears on account of them all his days. O sacred chronicler, look well to your laurels! If once we take pen in hand, where would you be—Shimei, and Joab, and Absalom, and Ahithophel and all! O Lord, open Thou my lips, and I will show forth Thy praise. Then will I teach transgressors Thy ways, and sinners shall be converted unto Thee. Thou are my hiding-place; Thou shalt compass me about with songs of deliverance. Thou shalt hide them in the secret of Thy presence from the pride of men. Thou shalt keep them secretly in a pavilion from the strife of tongues. Be of good courage, and He shall strengthen your heart, all ye that hope in the Lord.

XLVII

ABSALOM

I WILL RAISE UP EVIL AGAINST THEE OUT OF THINE OWN HOUSE

POLYGAMY is just Greek for a dunghill. David trampled down the first and the best law of nature in his palace in Jerusalem, and for his trouble he spent all his after-days in a hell upon earth. David's palace was a perfect pandemonium of suspicion, and intrigue, and jealousy, and hatred—all breaking out, now into incest and now into murder. And it was in such a household, if such a cesspool could be called a household, that Absalom, David's third son by his third living wife, was born and brought up. But be not deceived; God is not mocked: for whatsoever a patriarch, or a prophet, or a psalmist soweth, that shall he also reap. For he, saint or sinner, that soweth to his flesh shall of the flesh reap corruption.

Maachah, Absalom's mother, was the daughter of a king. And this, taken together with his distinguished appearance and his princely manners, gave Absalom the pre-eminence over all his brethren. Absalom inherited all the handsomeness, manly bearing, and beauty of his father's handsome and manly house. The sacred writer expatiates with evident relish upon Absalom's extraordinary beauty. In all Israel there was none to be so much praised as Absalom for his beauty. From the sole of his foot even to the crown of his head there was no blemish in him. And the hair of his head is a proverb to this day.

A little ring of jealous and scheming parasites, all hateful and hating one another, collected round each one of David's wives. And it was in one of the worst of those wicked little rings that Absalom grew up and got his education. Absalom had a sister, named Tamar, who was as beautiful as a woman as Absalom was as a man. And how her beauty became the occasion of her ruin in that horrible household the sacred historian tells us with sufficient plainness of speech. Suffice it here to say that Absalom determined, sooner or later, to wash off his sister's terrible wrongs in the blood of the wrongdoer. And, then, as the divine vengeance would have it to be, that wrongdoer to one of David's fairest daughters was one of David's favourite sons. The Septuagint frankly tells us that David loved the wrongdoer so much that he could not so much as rebuke him for his brutality. But, after giving his father two full years to avenge his sister's ruin, Absalom took the law into his own hand till Amnon fell, when his heart was merry with wine, under Absalom's revengeful sword. And, then, all the plots and counter-plots connected with Absalom's revenge, and flight, and restoration, and too-late reconciliation to his father; his deep-laid schemes to wrench the kingdom out of his father's hands; and then his defeat and murder by Joab—all that, if we have the courage to look at it, will give us a picture of the men and the times, humiliating beyond all words, and never to be forgotten. David and his wives and concubines and mixed-up children, Tamar and her half-brother Amnon, Absalom and Jonadab, Joab and the wise woman of Tekoa, Ittai and Shimei, Ahithophel and Hushai, and the righteousness and the grace of God reigning over them all. Truly, all Scripture is given by inspiration of God, and is profitable for doctrine, for reproof, for correction, for instruction in righteousness; that the man of God may be perfect, thoroughly furnished unto all good works.

It is this so terrible plain-spokenness of the Bible that makes it so precious to all who are in earnest about themselves and their children. Had this sacred writer not been in earnest in his work, we should have had an altogether different David. And we make an altogether different David to ourselves in spite of the sacred writer, and in spite of all that David himself can say and do. The David that we set up for ourselves has always a halo round his head and a harp in his hand, and his eyes fixed on the heavens. We are willingly ignorant that David had ever any other wife but Solomon's mother, as also that she had ever any other son but Solomon. And, then, our Solomon is always dreaming his dream at Gibeon, and when he is not choosing wisdom for himself he is always writing inspired proverbs about wisdom for his son. While all the time David prevents the night-watches with psalms like this: I will behave myself wisely in a perfect way. O when wilt thou come unto me? I will walk within my house with a perfect heart. I will set no thing of Belial before mine eyes: I hate the work of them that turn aside; it shall not cleave to me, and so on. A David like that in our Bible would have delighted us, and would not have offended and shocked us. No. But then neither would he have been of any real use to us when we went to our Bible for real use. It is when we go to our Bible for real use, for the experiences of men of like passions with ourselves, it is then that we discover and see the pen of God in the Bible life of David. And it is from that pen that I gather these closing lessons out of the life of David and out of the death of Absalom.

'The inconceivable evil of sensuality' was surely never more awfully burned in upon any sinful house than it was upon David's house. David himself is a towering warning to all men, and especially to all godly men against this master abomination. And, all the more that he sinned so terribly against such singular grace. David, to use his own words, was as white as snow as long as he was young, and poor, and struggling up, and oppressed, and persecuted, and with Samuel's horn of oil still sanctifying all the thoughts and all the imaginations of his heart. But no sooner had David sat down on the throne of Israel than his life of sin and shame began. And all the woe upon woe of his after-life, almost every single deadly drop of it, came down out of that day when he first introduced open and unblushing sensuality into his palace in Jerusalem. There was military success, and extended empire, and great wealth, and great and far-sounding glory in David's day in Israel; but beneath it all the whole ground was mined and filled to the lip with gunpowder, and the divine tinder all the time was surely burning its way to the divine vengeance on David's house. Our doctors, our lawyers, our ministers, and many of ourselves, will all subscribe to Newman's strong words in one of his sermons—'The inconceivable evil of sensuality.'

You sometimes hear speak about the historical imagination, and the right and the fruitful uses of the historical imagination. Well, here is the history of young Absalom, and you must bring your imagination to bear upon it. You must read all the chapters about David's manner of life in Jerusalem, and all the chapters in which Absalom's name comes up, and then you must imagine yourself to be Absalom, and to be in his place. I dare not put in words what you will see when you read Second Samuel with your eye upon the object. For one thing, Absalom did not see his father David at all as we see him. He saw him as his enemies then saw him, and as infidels and scoffers see him now. It was impossible that Absalom could look on his father with our admiring eyes. 'It helped me, too,' says Santa Teresa in her happy 'Life of Herself'; 'It helped me much that I never saw my father and my mother respect anything but goodness.' 'It poisoned me at my father,' said Absalom to Ahithophel; 'the life we all led in our several stews.' Yes, polygamy is indeed a dunghill. Only, it is a dunghill with hell at the heart of it. We have nothing like the city of David on this side the Dardanelles. And no real lesson for our day and our household can be got out of Absalom's early life. Unless it is that far-fetched lesson to that fatal house where there is a father who is no father. And to that house where the father and the mother are full of divided lives, divided interests, divided counsels, divided tastes, and divided desires for themselves and their children. The sons and the daughters of such divided fathers and mothers will need neither history nor imagination to see and to feel with poor Absalom. Only, this lesson to such fathers and mothers is all but too late and irrecoverable.

The Hebrew Bible for some unaccountable reason is silent where the Greek Bible speaks out boldly about David, and delivers a great lesson to all of us who are fathers. The law of Moses was plain. It is to be read in the Book of Leviticus to this day. 'It is a wicked thing. And he that does it shall be cut off in the sight of all the people. He shall bear his iniquity.' Well, Amnon did it. Amnon was worse than if he had been the actual murderer of his own sister. But what do we read on this matter in the Septuagint? We literally read this: 'Notwithstanding Amnon's sin David did not trouble the spirit of Amnon his son, because he loved him, and because he was his first-born.' But, not to trouble the spirit of your son for his sin is to trouble other people's spirit all his days, ay, and your own spirit and his too, to the bargain. The Greek Bible has recovered for us one of the lost links in David's downward career, and in the downward career of Absalom his son. For it was David's unwillingness to trouble Amnon that made Absalom in the cause of his sister first a murderer, and then a conspirator, and then, after a life of terrible trouble, himself a mangled corpse under the revengeful and murderous hands of Joab, that other arch-troubler of Israel. 'Praise them openly, reprehend them secretly,' is the second of Lord Burleigh's ten precepts to his son concerning his children. But David did the very opposite of that with Absalom. All Jerusalem heard David for two years reprehending his half-pardoned son Absalom openly, till Absalom was exasperated out of all endurance, and till the last link of sonship was broken for ever between David and Absalom.

But, with all that, it is the terrible cry that comes out of the chamber over the gate of Mahanaim that makes the name of Absalom so well known and so full of the most terrible lessons to us. 'O my son Absalom, my son, my son Absalom! Would God I had died for thee, O Absalom, my son, my son!' Yes, that is love, no doubt. That is the love of a heart-broken father, no doubt. But the pang of the cry, the innermost agony of the cry, the poisoned point of the dagger in that cry is remorse. I have slain my son! I have murdered my son with my own hands! I neglected my son Absalom from a child! With my own lusts I laid his very worst temptation right in his way. It had been better Absalom had never been born! If he rebelled, who shall blame him? I, David, drove Absalom to rebellion. It was his father's hand that stabbed Absalom through the heart. O Absalom, my murdered son! Would God thy murderer had been in thy place this day. And the king covered his face, and the king cried with a loud voice, O my son Absalom, my son, my son!

Come all you who are fathers and mothers, come to the chamber over the gate of Mahanaim, and let us take counsel together as to how we are to bring up our children to virtue and godliness and everlasting life. Let us read all Holy Writ on this subject together; and after Holy Writ, all other good and true books that in any way bear upon this supreme subject. Let us set ourselves to gather together all our experience and all our observation, and let us counsel and correct and comfort one another concerning this one thing that we do, our children. Let us take time to it, and pains, and pursue it until we succeed in it. Let us search the Scriptures up to the top and down to the bottom for this pearl of great price. Let us set on one side all the fathers and mothers in Israel to whom God hath ever said, I know him that he will command his children and his household after him, and they shall keep the way of the Lord, to do justice and judgment, that the Lord may bring upon Abraham that which He hath spoken of him. And then let us set on the other side David and all those fathers and mothers on whom God took vengeance, and said, Now, therefore, the sword shall never depart from thine house. I will raise up evil against thee out of thine own house. Let us collect into a secret and solemn book all such instances; and let us, husband and wife, minister and people, and one anxious parent with another, let us meet together, and confer together, and pray together, saying, This one thing will we do. Why do men and women combine and consult together about everything else but the thing in which so many are ignorant, so stupid, and so full of fatal mistakes? If we asked our happy neighbours, they would surely tell us the secret of their success in their children. How did they come so well and so soon to understand their children? How early did they discover what manner of heart was already in their children? And at what age did they begin to deal with the hearts of their children? What amount of time did they set aside and keep sacred for reflection and for prayer to God for their child; naming their child and describing him; and how did God's answer begin to show itself first in the parents and then in the child? When did your child first begin to show some sure signs of saving grace? And how did that grace show itself to your satisfaction and thanksgiving; first in one child and then in another? Tell us about the Sabbath—how it was observed, occupied, and sanctified as your children grew up? About the church also and the Sabbath-school? About the books that were read on Sabbath-days and week days; both by your children alone and of their own accord, as also with you all reading together; one reading and all the rest listening? Things like that. All that you can tell us about such children as yours will be eagerly listened to and attended to. What priceless stores of experience, and observation, and success and defeat are lost all around us just because we do not speak more to one another about our ways with our children; our hopes and our fears; our neglects and our recoveries of neglects; the things that one household is so happy in, and the same things that cause such unavailing remorse in another household. Yes, this whole matter must surely be collected together and made into a science soon, and taught in every true church to every young father and young mother as their very life.

Third Series

AHITHOPHEL TO NEHEMIAH

XLVIII

AHITHOPHEL

I AM not going to whitewash and rehabilitate Ahithophel. I am neither to extenuate nor am I to denounce Ahithophel. I shall put myself back into Ahithophel's place, and I shall speak of Ahithophel as I see and feel Ahithophel to have been. I shall do my best to put myself first into Ahithophel's place, and then into David's place, and then I shall tell you exactly and honestly what I see and what I feel, first as to Ahithophel, and then as to David. But, to begin with, who was Ahithophel, and what were the facts?

Well, Ahithophel was far and away the ablest and the most famous politician, as we would say, in that day. The counsel of Ahithophel was a proverb in Israel in David's day. There was no one fit to hold the candle to Ahithophel in that day, unless it was Hushai the Archite, another of David's astutest counsellors. 'For the counsel of Ahithophel,' says the sacred writer, 'which he counselled in those days, was as if a man had inquired at the oracle of God: so was all the counsel of Ahithophel both with David and with Absalom.'

> Of those the false Ahithophel was first:
> For close designs and crooked counsels fit,
> Sagacious, bold, and turbulent of wit,
> Restless, unfixed in principles and place,
> In power unpleased, impatient of disgrace;
> A fiery soul, which, working out its way,
> Fretted the pigmy body to decay,
> And o'er-informed the tenement of clay.

So Dryden describes Lord Chancellor Shaftesbury in his *Absalom and Ahithophel,* that very able but still more truculent and time-serving piece. Matthew Henry is always worth consulting. 'Ahithophel was a politic, thinking man, and one that had a clear head, and a great compass of thought,' and so on. If the traditional interpretation of the fifty-fifth and some other Ahithophel psalms is true and is to be taken, David and Ahithophel had been bosom friends from their boyhood up. Ahithophel may not have been exactly a Jonathan, and yet he may have been a very dear and well-deserving friend for all that.

David and Ahithophel were such close companions, indeed, that had it not been for Jonathan, the proverb might have run thus—David and Ahithophel: so was the soul of David knit to the soul of Ahithophel. Jonathan strengthened David's hand in God, it is true; but this out of David and about Ahithophel is almost as good. 'A man, mine equal, my guide, and mine acquaintance. We took sweet counsel together, and walked unto the house of God in company.' Till, when David's time came to be lifted up of God into the throne of Israel, Ahithophel was proud to lay all his magnificent gifts of sound advice and incomparable counsel at David's feet. And Ahithophel continued to do that for all the best and most shining years of David's kingdom. David never made a law, nor gave a judgment, nor proclaimed a war, nor negotiated a truce, nor signed a peace, till Ahithophel had been heard, and till his advice had been taken. But the sacred writer has already given you all that, and far more than all that in one of his incomparably strong and satisfying sentences; it was, he says, as if a man had inquired at the oracle of God.

All that Ahithophel was to David in the council-chamber, all that Eliam, Ahithophel's only son, was in the army. The father's splendid talents for counsel came out in the shape of soldierly service in the son; and the son was as devoted to David in the field as his father was in the chamber. Now, Eliam had a daughter at home, a beautiful woman-child, who was the one ewe-lamb of her father Eliam and her grandfather Ahithophel. And it so happened that Eliam had a very trusty under-officer among the captains of the mighty men, whose famous name was Uriah. This Uriah was not an Israelite—he was a Hittite; but he was as brave and as loyal to David as if he had been an Hebrew of the Hebrews. And his high talents and his great services had carried him to the very top of the six hundred, where he stood clothed with worth and with honour beside Eliam the son of Ahithophel. With his whole soul Uriah loved Eliam's daughter, and both Eliam and Ahithophel gave to young Uriah the desire of his heart. David's devoted bodyguard had their quarters built for them in the city of David, and just under the walls of David's palace; and when Uriah came home on furlough, he was the happiest man in all Jerusalem with such a wife, and with Eliam and with Ahithophel. As time went on, and as Ahithophel counselled for David, and as Eliam and Uriah fought for David, David's power increased till the King of Israel denied himself nothing on which he had once set his heart. And in an evil hour he set his heart on Uriah's wife, who was also Ahithophel's one grandchild. And it does not need an oracle of God to tell us how Ahithophel took the ruin of his grandchild and the murder of her husband. Ahithophel would have been Jesus Christ Himself to have continued after all that to take sweet counsel with David, and to walk with David unto the house of God in company. I do not like to listen to all the names you would have called Ahithophel and Eliam had they still remained in David's service, and had they still eaten David's bread, with Bathsheba in David's bed and with her husband in his grave. I do not know what all you would have called Eliam and Ahithophel had they winked in that way at David's adultery and blood-guiltiness.

It was all that Ahithophel could do: he shook the dust off his feet, and Ahithophel returned home out of the city of David to his own city of Giloh. And no sooner had Ahithophel left David than the Lord sent Nathan to David. And Nathan said to David, Thus saith the Lord God of Israel, I anointed thee king over Israel, and I delivered thee out of the hand of Saul. And I gave thee thy master's house, and gave thee the house of Israel and of Judah; and if that had been too little, I would moreover have given unto thee such and such things. Wherefore hast thou despised the commandment of the Lord, to do evil in His sight? Thou hast killed Uriah the Hittite with the edge of the sword, and hast taken his wife, Ahithophel's granddaughter, to be thy wife, and hast slain Uriah with the sword of the children of Amnon. Now, therefore, the sword shall never depart from thy house. For thus saith the Lord, I will raise up evil against thee out of thine own house. For thou didst it secretly, but I will do this thing before all Israel and before the sun. And, after that, our hearts stand still as we watch how the vengeance of God came down on David's head, and how the vengeance of God travelled, as it always does, on stepping-stones which David laid for it with his own hands. As thus: And Amnon loved Absalom's sister.... But David did not trouble the spirit of Amnon, because he was his first-born. . . . And Absalom's servants did to Amnon as Absalom had commanded. And Absalom fled and went to Geshur, and was there three years. . . . And David said, Let him return to Jerusalem, but let him not see my face. . . . And Absalom stole the hearts of the men of Israel. . . . And Absalom sent for Ahithophel the Gilonite, David's counsellor, from his city, even from Giloh. And the conspiracy was strong, and the people increased continually with Absalom. For the counsel of Ahithophel, which he counselled in those days, was as if a man inquired at the oracle of God; so was all the counsel of

Ahithophel with Absalom as it had been wont to be with David.

Absalom had no head of his own. But he had what was better than ten heads of his own, for he had a head to know those who had heads and to send to their cities for them. And with Ahithophel's head like the oracle of God, and with his heart rankling against David like hell, the conspiracy was strong, and the people increased continually with Absalom. Ahithophel was worth ten thousand men to Absalom, and no one knew that better than David. And one told David, saying, Ahithophel is among the conspirators with Absalom. And David said, O Lord, I pray thee, turn the counsel of Ahithophel into foolishness. And then David took Hushai, his next astutest counsellor, to Ahithophel, and filled him with guile and sent him back to deceive Absalom and to counteract all the counsels of Ahithophel. Which he did. For at the end of all their cross-counsels we read this report and this reflection of the sacred writer on it all: And Absalom said, The counsel of Hushai the Archite is better than the counsel of Ahithophel. For the Lord had appointed to defeat the good counsel of Ahithophel, to the intent that He might bring evil upon Absalom. Ahithophel gave two of his deepest counsels to Absalom. Ahithophel has been called Judas, and all manner of evil names, for his first counsel that he gave to Absalom. And, no doubt, Ahithophel's first counsel sounds in our ears at this time of day abominable enough. But you will believe all things, and will hope all things even about Ahithophel. You will judge neither Ahithophel nor any other man, 'without necessity, nor without knowledge, nor without love.' For Absalom had said to Ahithophel, Give counsel among you what we shall do. And Ahithophel gave Absalom a counsel that you know already, or if you do not know it you will read it at home. Nothing, certainly, could sound worse. But, when I put myself in Ahithophel's place, for anything I know, the so subtle and so sorely injured Ahithophel may honestly enough have said something like this to himself. Something, possibly, like this: 'Has not David cast himself completely out of the throne? Has he not destroyed himself? Has he not thrown down the sceptre? Has not the Lord turned against him? And did not the Lord's righteous servant say that the Lord would do this same thing to David that David had done before all Israel and before the sun? I am only counselling Absalom to fulfil as the hand of the Lord what the Lord swore that He would do Himself to David.' Ahithophel's extraordinary and superhuman subtlety may honestly enough have led him to think that he saw in his counsel both prophecy, and policy, and payment back again into

David's own bosom of all that David had done to other men, and to no man more than to Ahithophel himself. But whatever may be said about Ahithophel's first counsel, his second counsel to Absalom is pronounced to be good by the sacred writer; but, then, what of that, when the Lord had appointed to defeat it that the Lord might bring evil upon Absalom? When we are working upon Ahithophel in this way, and when our minds and our hearts are full of Ahithophel, we cannot but wish that we had been told some more about him, and especially about his latter end. But the sacred writer has to hasten on. He has David and Absalom so much on his mind and on his heart that he draws a black border round Ahithophel's deathbed in these terrible words, and then leaves him: And when Ahithophel saw that his counsel was not followed, he saddled his ass, and arose, and gat him home to his own house, to his city, and put his household in order, and hanged himself, and died, and was buried in the sepulchre of his father.

Now, as you know, Ahithophel, from that day to this, has been stoned in his grave at Giloh, and all manner of names called at him as he lies there: Deserter, traitor, apostate, Judas Iscariot, suicide, and all manner of evil names, because he left David and joined Absalom. And, no doubt, had Ahithophel seen to the end, as he should have seen; had Ahithophel known all that we knew,—and if he had been a better man he would have known more than even he was let know,—had he known the half of what we knew, Ahithophel would have held fast to David, let David do what he liked. But Ahithophel lived in the day of David and not yet in the day of Christ; and he suffered at the hand of David what neither you nor I have ever suffered at any man's hand. And if he did not live and die in David's service, and if you will never forgive him for that; then, if it will do you any good, you can go home casting stones all the way at Bathsheba's broken-hearted grandfather. My business to-night is neither to whitewash Ahithophel nor blacken David, even were that possible, but to let you see yourselves in them both as in a glass. How, then, have you always acted toward those of your former friends who have injured you and yours? Did you shut your door this morning and pray in secret, saying, Forgive me my trespasses against God and man, as I forgive him—naming him—who has so trespassed against me? When you stood here praying to-night, did you forgive some enemy? Ahithophel should have conquered himself. Ahithophel was not a Hittite. Ahithophel was well read in all the law of Moses, if not yet in the law of Christ. Ahithophel should have gone on with his work in the city of David. He should have said—what, indeed, had he got his great head and his deep heart for but to say it with them?—Vengeance is not mine. I have eaten David's bread when he had plenty, Ahithophel should have said, and he shall come to Giloh now and eat my bread. Yes, Ahithophel, like the oracle of God he was, should have called to mind this psalm of David, and said: It shall be an excellent oil, which shall not break my head; for yet my prayer shall be for David in all his calamities.

And, then, on the other hand, though it is not written out, I for one shall continue to believe it, that David in his best moments took it all home to himself that Ahithophel was gone over to Absalom. David knew quite well all the time whose grandchild Uriah's wife was. As soon as David came to himself he must have foreseen all this. David was not so quick in the uptake as Ahithophel, but he was not a fool,—when he came to himself. David knew as well as all Jerusalem did what it was that had thrown Ahithophel over to Absalom's side. We see it every day in our own parties in the church, in our parties in the city, in our parties in our families. We have the gall and wormwood in ourselves that it was we ourselves that did it. It was our bad temper, our bad tongue, our want of thought, our want of love, our want of patience, our want of humility that threw this old ally and that old adviser, this able man and that rich man, into the opposite camp. We all know men who have, to all appearance, gone over for ever from truth and goodness, and from the winning to the losing side, because of us. Every time we meet them on the street, every time we hear their name spoken, every time we call them in any way to mind, something says within us—You did it. We ministers especially have our own very heavy hearts on this account. Our neglect of duty, our laziness and procrastination at a moment that went in a moment, and that we shall look back to with remorse all our days; our hot-headedness, our domineeringness, our indiscretions of speech, and our follies in conduct. Where is that family? Where is that former friend? Where is he who was once to us as the oracle of God? Where is that man, mine equal, my guide, and mine acquaintance? We took sweet counsel together, and walked unto the house of God in company. Why is he no longer here? Why is he where he now is?

And, then, what did David think when Ahithophel's terrible end was told him? And what did Bathsheba think? Did she curse David to his face when it was told her what her grandfather had done to himself? Did Uriah's wife fling David's psalms in his face in her agony of horror and self-disgust? Did she scream in her sleep till all Jerusalem heard her as she saw in her sleep her grandfather's gallows at Giloh? Or was this prophecy fulfilled before it was spoken: In that day there shall be a great mourning in Jerusalem, the house of David apart, and their wives apart, till there shall be a fountain opened to the house of David for sin and for uncleanness? And then did David go out to Giloh, and over the sepulchre of the suicide did David fall down and cry, past all consolation, O Ahithophel, the friend of my youth and my best counsellor, Ahithophel! Would God I had died for thee! O Ahithophel, mine equal, my guide, and mine acquaintance! If he did—then this would come in, The sacrifices of God are a broken heart. What did David think, and what did Bathsheba think? True. But what would you think if the first thing you saw to-morrow morning was the suicide of some one who has been the victim of your lust or your lies? Pray, man, pray. In God's name, pray. And though the poison may be bought, and the rope put up, God can do it. God can deliver you. With God all things are possible. Pray, you great sinner; pray, you great fool, pray. Pray, lest the newspaper run blood on your hands some morning, as the letters from Giloh ran Ahithophel's blood on David's hands. Pray for your Ahithophel without ceasing, and for all your Ahithophel's house. Give God no rest till He has remitted to you Ahithophel and all his injuries, and till He has repented of the evil He has reserved out of Ahithophel and out of his house against you. Every day you live, and till the day of your death, beseech the living God to make it all up to your Ahithophel and to set it all down to your account.

XLIX

MEPHIBOSHETH

MEPHIBOSHETH has been an enigma of motive and a study in self-interest from David's day down to our own day. Wherever the heart of man comes in you have always an enigma of motive and a study in self-interest. Wherever the heart of man plays a part you are soon out of your depth. There are many devices in a man's heart, and counsel in a man's heart is like deep water. The sacred writer sets us the enigma of Mephibosheth and his servant Ziba; but he gives us no hint at all as to how we are to decipher that enigma. He tells us Mephibosheth's story from the outside and on the surface, and so leaves us to make of the inside of it what we can. By that time both Mephibosheth and Ziba and David had long passed away; and already their motives and their mainsprings may well have become a sacred riddle in Israel. Given the story of Mephibosheth, and the story of Ziba, first at the flight of David and then at his victorious return, and then—was Mephibosheth a heartless, selfish, contemptible time-server, while Ziba, his servant, was a prince beside him? Or, was Ziba a lying scoundrel, and Mephibosheth a poor, innocent, ill-used, lameter saint? Let us see the surface of the story.

Mephibosheth was the son and heir of Jonathan, David's oldest and best friend. Mephibosheth, the future king of Israel, was only five years old when Jonathan his father, and Saul his grandfather, both fell in the same battle on Mount Gilboa, and with their fall their family fell from the throne. In the terror that took possession of Jonathan's household that terrible day, Mephibosheth's nurse caught up the child and fled with him in her arms. But in her haste she let the little prince fall, and from that fall Mephibosheth was lame in his feet all his days. Years pass on. David sits in the throne of Saul and Jonathan and Mephibosheth, and his enemies are all subdued round about David. In his remembrance of God's great mercies, and in the magnanimity of his heart, David often called Saul and Jonathan to mind. And David said, Is there yet any that is left of the house of Saul, that I may show him kindness for Jonathan's sake? And there was of the house of Saul a servant whose name was Ziba. And when they had called him unto David, the king said unto him, Art thou Ziba? And he said, Thy servant is he. And the king said, Is there not yet any of the house of Saul, that I may show the kindness of God to him? And Ziba said unto the king, Jonathan hath yet a son, which is lame on his feet. And the king said unto him, Where is he? And Ziba said unto the king, Behold, he is in the house of Machir, the son of Ammiel, from Lo-debar. Then King David sent and fetched Mephibosheth out of the house of Machir, the son of Ammiel, from Lo-debar. And David said unto him, Fear not, for I will surely show thee kindness for Jonathan, thy father's sake, and will restore thee all the lands of Saul thy father, and thou shalt eat bread at my table continually. So Mephibosheth dwelt in Jerusalem, for he did eat continually at the king's table, and was lame on both his feet.

Years passed on again, till Absalom by fair speeches and skilful courtesies had stolen the hearts of all Israel, of all of which Mephibosheth was a silent student, eating at David's table continually. And Absalom sent for Ahithophel the

Gilonite, David's old counsellor, from his city, even from Giloh. And the conspiracy was strong, for the people increased continually with Absalom, but Mephibosheth still ate at the king's table. And there came a messenger to David, saying, The hearts of the men of Israel are gone after Absalom. And David said unto his servants, and to them that sat at his table, Arise, let us flee. And the king went forth, and all his household after him. But Mephibosheth was lame on both his feet. And when David was a little past the top of the hill, behold, Ziba, the servant of Mephibosheth, met David with a couple of asses saddled, and upon them two hundred loaves of bread, and an hundred bunches of raisins, and an hundred of summer fruits, and a bottle of wine. And the king said to Ziba, What meanest thou by these? And Ziba said, The asses be for the king's household to ride on, and the bread and the summer fruits for the young men to eat, and the wine that such as be faint in the wilderness may drink. And the king said, Where is thy master's son? And Ziba said to the king, Behold, he abideth in Jerusalem; for he said To-day shall the house of Israel restore to me the kingdom of my father. Then the king said to Ziba, Behold thine are all that pertained to Mephibosheth. A few days after that the great battle was set in the wood of Ephraim, and of Absalom's side there was a great slaughter of twenty thousand men. And it was on that day that David went up to the chamber over the gate of Mahanaim, and wept; and as he went there he said, O my son Absalom; my son, my son Absalom! would God I had died for thee, O Absalom, my son, my son!

So the king returned and came to Jordan. And Shimei, who had cursed and stoned David on the day of his flight from Jerusalem, hasted first and came down to meet King David. And Shimei fell down before the king and said, Let not my lord impute iniquity unto me, neither do thou remember that which thy servant did perversely the day that my lord the king went out of Jerusalem, that the king should take it to his heart. For, behold, I am come the first this day to go down to meet my lord the king. And the king said to Shimei, Thou shalt not die. And the king sware unto him. And Mephibosheth also, the son of Saul, came down to meet the king. Our too otiose English is unjust to Mephibosheth; or else it has taken Mephibosheth's infirmity in his feet much too seriously. Mephibosheth was not so crippled in his intellects, at any rate, as to stay in Jerusalem till the king came home. He was too eager for that to congratulate the king on his victory. We all know how the mind overmasters the body, and makes us forget all about its lameness, on occasions. And Mephibosheth was at the Jordan all the way from Jerusalem almost as soon as Shimei himself. Four hundred years before, just at the same place, when the inhabitants of Gibeon heard what Joshua had done to Jericho and to Ai, they did work wilily, and went and made as if they had been ambassadors, and took old sacks upon their asses, and wine bottles old and rent and bound up, and old shoes and clouted upon their feet, and old garments upon them, and all the bread of their provisions was dry and mouldy. And Joshua said, Who are ye, and whence come ye? And they said, From a very far country thy servants are come, because of the name of the Lord thy God. And Joshua made a league with them, to let them live; and the princes of the congregation sware unto them. And all that about Joshua and the Gibeonites came back to David's mind when he saw Mephibosheth lifted down from off his ass. For Mephibosheth had not dressed his wooden feet, nor trimmed his beard, nor washed his clothes for grief, so he said, from the day that the king departed. Nor had he taken time to-day to make himself decent for such a journey, such was his joy that the king was coming back again to Jerusalem. Yes, but what came of thee that morning, Mephibosheth? asked David. I looked for thee. I was afraid that in the overthrow some evil had befallen thee. Thou art not able to bear arms for me; but thy father so strengthened my hands in God, that to have seen the face of his son that morning, and to have heard the voice of Jonathan's son would have done for me and for my cause what thy father did. My lord, said Mephibosheth—but 'the tale was as lame as the tale-bearer.' Ziba had stolen his ass just as he was mounting him to come with the king—and so on. David did not stoop to ask whose ass this was that Mephibosheth had got saddled so soon this morning. Say no more, Mephibosheth, said David, as he saw Jonathan's son crawling so abjectly before him. Dr. Kitto complains of David's tart answer to Mephibosheth. But if David was too tart, then with what extraordinary and saintly sweetness Mephibosheth received the over-tartness of the king. 'Let Ziba take all my estates to-day, forasmuch as my lord the king is come again in peace to his own house.' No, there was nothing cripple in Mephibosheth's intellects. 'Mephibosheth was a philosopher, says Dr. Parker. 'I find no defect of his wits in Mephibosheth,' says honest Joseph Hall. And the king spared Mephibosheth, the son of Jonathan, the son of Saul, because of the Lord's oath that was between them, between David and Jonathan the son of Saul.

Now, the first thing that goes to our hearts out of this miserable story is this, that Mephibosheth was the son of Jonathan. But Solomon, as he moralises in one place on fathers and sons with Jonathan and Mephibosheth before him, tells us to rejoice with trembling when our sons are born to us, for who knoweth whether they shall be wise men or fools?

> Rarely into the branches of the tree
> Doth human worth mount up: and so ordains
> He who bestows it, that as His free gift
> It may be called.

The poor child's accident while he was yet a child may well have been at the bottom of it all. Diminutive and dwarfed persons, deformed persons, and greatly crippled persons are sometimes so thrown in upon themselves as to make them melancholy, morbid, and misanthropic. If their hearts are bad, their bodily disabilities will sometimes work in their hearts to a deep and a malignant wickedness. Both true history and truthful fiction have taken firm hold of this frequent fact in human life. I do not know that the other side has been so often brought out—that great bodily infirmity and disability, alongside of a renewed and a humble heart, will sometimes result in a sweetness and a saintliness of a most uncommon kind. In poor Mephibosheth's case, it would seem as if his early and life-long infirmity, taken along with the hopeless loss of his brilliant prospects, had all eaten into his heart till he became the false, selfish, scheming creature that David found him out to be.

Hephæstion loved Alexander, while Craterus loved the king. And Jonathan was like Hephæstion in this, that he loved David at all times, whereas his son Mephibosheth resembled Craterus in this, that he preferred David on the throne to David off the throne. Jonathan strengthened David's hand in God in the wood of Ziph; but Mephibosheth, like another classical character, fled the empty cask. How Mephibosheth's heart had overflowed with gratitude to David when the royal command came that he was to leave Machir's house in Lo-debar, and was henceforth to take up his quarters in the king's house in Jerusalem! All Mephibosheth's morosity and misanthropy melted off his heart that day. But such was Mephibosheth at the bottom of his heart that, as he continued to eat at David's table, Satan entered ino Mephibosheth and said to him in his heart that all this was his own by original and divine right. All this wealth, and power, and honour, and glory. But for the bad fortune of his father's royal house on Mount Gilboa, all this would to-day have been his own.

'Ingratitude,' says Mozley, 'is not only a species of injustice, it is the highest species of injustice.' And the ingratitude of Mephibosheth grew at David's table to this high injustice, that he waited for both David and Absalom to be chased out of Jerusalem, that he might take their place. There is no baser heart than an ungrateful heart. And it was Mephibosheth's ungrateful heart that prepared him for the baseness that he was found out in both at the flight of David and at his victorious return.

The virtues were invited once
  To banquet with the Lord of All;
They came,—the great ones rather grim,
  And not so pleasant as the small.
They talked and chatted o'er the meal,
  They even laughed with temp'rate glee;
And each one knew the other well,
  And all were good as good could be.
Benevolence and Gratitude
  Alone of all seemed strangers yet;
They stared when they were introduced,—
  On earth they never once had met.

Dean Milman says that the writings both of Tacitus and Dante are full of remorse. And it is, as I believe, in our own remorse that we shall find the true key to Mephibosheth's heart and character. When a government goes out of power, when a church is under a cloud, when religion has lost her silver slippers, and when she walks in the shadow of the street, and when any friend of ours has lost his silver slippers—then we discover Mephibosheth in ourselves, and hate both him and ourselves like hell. And commentators have taken sides over the case of Mephibosheth very much as they have found that contemptible creature skulking in themselves, and have had bitter remorse on account of him. 'I am full of self-love, fear to confess Thee, or to hazard myself, or my estate, or my peace. . . . My perplexity continues as to whether I shall move now or not, stay or return, hold by Lauderdale, or make use of the Bishop. I went to Sir George Mushet's funeral, where I was looked at, as I thought, like a speckled bird. . . . I find great averseness in myself to suffering. I am afraid to lose life or estate. Shall I forbear to hear that honest minister, James Urquhart, for a time, seeing the stone is like to fall on me if I do so?' And then our modern Mephibosheth has the grace to add in his diary, 'A grain of sound faith would easily answer all these questions. I have before me Mr. Rutherford's letter desiring me to deny myself.' And though you will not easily believe it, the author of that letter himself has enough of Jonathan's crippled and disinherited son still in himself to give a tang of remorse to some of his very best letters. 'Oh,' agonises Samuel Rutherford, 'if I were only free of myself! Myself is another devil, and as evil as the prince of devils. Myself! Myself! Every man blames the devil for his sins, but the house and heart devil of every man is himself. I think I shall die still but minting and aiming to be a Christian man!'

This, then, is the prize for finding out that enigma of motive, Mephibosheth's hidden heart. This is the first prize, to receive of God the inward eye to discover Mephibosheth ever deeper down in ourselves. And the eye never to let Mephibosheth for a moment out of our sight as he sits at David's table feeding his ingratitude, and his duplicity, and his calculation of his chances. To see him also as he waits on providence in Jerusalem to hear how the battle is to go. And then to see him in his hurry to get to Jordan, where he arrives by a sport of providence just at the same moment with Shimei. If all that is the riddle of the sacred writer, and if all that is the right answer, then the reward of our skill is that we shall be made both able and willing to see Mephibosheth in everything in ourselves. For are we not told that all these Old Testament men are there as our examples? And that the wheel of providence is still turning in our day as it turned in their day? One man goes up on that wheel of God and another man goes down. One cause prospers and another cause decays. And in the manifold wisdom of God it is all ordered and overruled, as if both the wheel, and He whose wheel it is, and all the men, and movements, and governments, and churches, and everything else that is tied to that wheel were all tied to it and lifted, now up and now down, in order to discover us to ourselves, and to send us to His feet, who will not cast away even Mephibosheth himself if he comes to His feet in time. Our own good name and fame also, all our possessions, and all our expectations are all tied on to that wheel, for our hearts to be discovered and denounced, and for deliverance to be wrought in us from the dominion of such a heart. Every day, by the sovereign and electing grace of God, we are surely making some way in this knowledge of the wickedness past finding out of our own hearts, and some progress in the clearing out and conquest of that wickedness. Every day we are surely putting ourselves more and more in the place of our neighbour, and are doing more and more to him as we would he did to us. Till at last—O blessed hope!—every tang and taint of Mephibosheth's heart shall be taken out of us, and till truth, and righteousness, and fidelity, and gratitude, and courage, and love shall for ever reign in us and around us and over us. Even so, come quickly, Lord Jesus!

L

BARZILLAI

BARZILLAI, to put it all into one word, was an aged, venerable, hospitable Highland chief. Barzillai, by this time, was eighty years of age, and he was as full of truth, and courage, and good-will, and generosity as he was full of years. From within the walls of his lofty keep in far-off Gilead, Barzillai had watched the ways of God with His people Israel in the south country all through the days of Eli, and Samuel, and Saul, and David, and Joab, and Jonathan, and Mephibosheth, and Absalom, and his humble heart and his hospitable house had always been open to the oppressed, and to the persecuted, and to the poor. And thus it was that when David fled from Jerusalem to escape from Absalom, and when David made his final stand at Mahanaim, Barzillai lost no time in coming down to David's assistance. The sacred writer is at particular pains to tell us the whole of that truly Highland hospitality with which Barzillai replenished the king's camp at Mahanaim. Beds, we read, and basons, and earthen vessels, and wheat, and barley, and flour, and parched corn, and beans, and lentils, and parched pulse, and honey, and butter, and sheep, and cheese of kine for David, and for his people that were with him. For Barzillai said, The people are hungry, and weary, and thirsty in the wilderness. Then come the two chapters about the successful battle; after which, when David sets out to return to Jerusalem the sacred writer takes up the noble name of Barzillai again in this fine passage: 'And Barzillai the Gileadite came down from Rogelim, and went over Jordan with the king to conduct him over Jordan. And the king said to Barzillai, Come thou over with me, and I will feed thee with me in Jerusalem. And Barzillai said unto the king, How long have I to live that I should go up with the king to Jerusalem? I am this day fourscore years old, and can I discern between good and evil? Can thy servant taste what I eat or what I drink? Can I hear any more the voice of singing men and singing women? Wherefore, then, should thy servant be yet a burden to my lord the king? Thy servant will go a little way over the Jordan with the king;

and why should the king recompense it me with such a reward? Let thy servant, I pray thee, turn back again, that I may die in mine own city, and be buried by the grave of my father and my mother. And when the king was come over the king kissed Barzillai and blessed him; and Barzillai returned to his own place.' A beautiful old man, and a beautiful incident in a far from beautiful time.

Now, to begin with, Barzillai was a true Highlander in his splendid loyalty to David in his distress. Many men who had sat at David's royal table, and who had held their hands at David's royal liberality; many such men hedged and held back till they should see whether David's sun was to set, never to rise again, or not. Where is thy master? said David to Ziba, the servant of Mephibosheth. But Barzillai was not Mephibosheth. There was no lameness in Barzillai's allegiance to David. Barzillai did not wait to see how the wind would blow. The old hero took his ancient tower, and his great estate, and his own future, and the future of his family all in his hand that day. And, had Absalom succeeded, Barzillai would have been an outlawed and a sequestered man; and all the omens, to those who went by omens, looked that way that day. But Barzillai had steered all his eighty years by the fixed stars of truth, and righteousness, and duty, and loyalty, and he would steer by the same sure stars to the end. Even had David's cause been as bad as it was good, Barzillai's loyalty would have been noble to contemplate. Wrong-headed and short-sighted as was our own Highland loyalty to the Stuart House, there was not a little that was noble and brave and beautiful in it. It was a mad project to think to solder the crown of Charles Stuart to the crown of Jesus Christ; at the same time, there was a pathos and a poetry in it that still touch our hearts to this day. But Barzillai's loyalty to David was as sane-headed as it was warm-hearted. It was far-seeing and as sure-footed as it was warm-hearted and open-handed. David, on the throne or off the throne; David, in Jerusalem or in Mahanaim, is our divine king, said Barzillai to his household. The God of battles will do as seemeth Him good in this business, but our duty is clear, and it is pressing. Make haste and make up a present for David, and let it be the best. And say to the king that Barzillai, his servant, follows after the present as fast as his fourscore years will let him. Had Barzillai been tempted to hedge at dangers, and to calculate chances, and to weigh likelihoods, and to find excuses, he would not have wanted materials. No doubt David had done not a little to bring this terrible overthrow upon himself. And a cautious man would have considered all that. There are always sufficient reasons why a deliberating and a considering man should stand aloof for a time from a fallen man. But Barzillai had no head for such reserves and calculations. David was David to Barzillai, and as long as Barzillai has a roof over his head and a morsel of meat on his table, David shall not want. David's adversity was only all the more Barzillai's duty and opportunity.

And, every day, we all have Barzillai's duty and opportunity too, if only we have Barzillai's mind and heart. Not that kings and princes lie in want in our neighbourhood every day; but good causes do, and needy and deserving men, and old and distressed friends. There is not a day passes but our boldness, and our courage, and our loyalty, and our fidelity are put to the test. There is not a day that we do not hear some censuring, fault-finding, detracting, and injuring word spoken against an absent friend. And what do we do? Do we let it pass? Do we in our heart of hearts like to hear it? Do we silently, or with a half-uttered consent fall in with it? How seldom do we stand up as we would be stood up for! How seldom do we pluck out the false and spiteful tongue! Let us be men the next time. Let us be Barzillai the next time, if Absalom, and Ahithophel, and Mephibosheth, and all the miserable house of Israel are all arrayed against David. Let them know from Jerusalem to Mahanaim that there is one man in Israel who is a man and is not a dog.

Barzillai's truly Highland courtesy, also, is abundantly conspicuous in the too-short glimpse we get of the lord of Rogelim. For, how he anticipated all David's possible wants! How he put himself into all David's distressed place! How he did to David as David would have done to him! How he came down from his high seat, with all his years on his head, in order with his own hand to conduct the king over Jordan! And, then, with what sweetness of manner and music of speech he excused himself out of all the royal rewards and honours and promotions David had designed and decreed to put upon him!

> The service and the loyalty I owe,
> In doing, pays itself. Your Highness' part
> Is to receive our duties; and our duties
> Are to your throne and state children and servants,
> Which do but what they should, by doing everything
> Safe towards your love and honour.
> The rest is labour which is not used for you.

The humility, also, of that Old Testament hero is already our

New Testament humility in its depth and sweetness and beauty. A perfect and a finished courtesy has always its roots struck deep down into humility; which humility, again, has its roots struck deep down into the grace of God. In lowliness of mind let each esteem others better than themselves. Be kindly affectioned one to another with brotherly love; in honour preferring one another; submitting yourselves one to another in the fear of God. Yea, all of you be clothed with humility, for God resisteth the proud and giveth grace to the humble. Humility and courtesy are the court manners of the kingdom of heaven. A true, a finished, and an unconscious courtesy is the perfected etiquette of the palace and the presence of the great King.

And, then, there can be no doubt about Barzillai's Highland hospitality. Highland hospitality is a proverb of honour among us; and Barzillai's hospitality was the same proverb in the whole after history of Israel. As hospitable as Barzillai of Rogelim, they used to say. A bishop must be like Barzillai of Rogelim, wrote Paul to both Timothy and Titus. One would think that the two asses that stood as laden and waiting for David on the top of the hill had marched straight out of Barzillai's butler's pantry. As indeed, so they had. For Ziba, who had saddled and so loaded them, had first learned how to saddle and how to load an ass when he lived at Lodebar. He had found out how much charity a strong ass could carry when he and his master lived on charity at Rogelim and Lodebar. A couple of asses saddled as they used to saddle them at Rogelim and Lodebar could carry two hundred loaves of bread, and a hundred bunches of raisins, and a hundred of summer fruits and a bottle of wine. But it is not great lords only like Barzillai of Rogelim and Machir of Lodebar and Shobi of Rabbah who are summoned to show hospitality. No class of men could be poorer than were the bishops of Paul's day, and yet the apostle enjoins Titus and Timothy to ordain no man who is not given to hospitality. And the same apostle reminds the poor Hebrew laity that some men in old times have entertained angels unawares. But the truth is, true Highland hospitality is in the mind and in the heart of the host and hostess. A poor widow's hut will show you Highland hospitality in the way she comes out and offers you a drink of milk or even of water. You cannot tie up the hands of a hospitable heart. Does not Aristotle himself tell us that munificently-minded man is seen as well in his present of a ball or a top or a picture to a little child as in a temple or a sacrifice or a banquet to a God? And has not a Greater than Aristotle told us that the widow's mite will be extolled for its splendid munificence wherever His munificent gospel is preached? Hospitality and munificence and magnanimity are in the mind and in the heart, and it is the mind and the heart that are accepted and acknowledged of God. 'With what measure you mete, it shall be measured to you'; so our Lord lays down His last-day law. And then Bengal annotates our Lord's law thus: *Mensura est cor*. The measure is the heart, with its capabilities, desires, anxiety to impart blessings to others, and loving obedience. And thus it is that hospitality, with its present blessedness and its everlasting rewards, is not a matter of wealth or poverty, any more than it is of race or region.

Barzillai's passionate love of his Highland hills and valleys is another fine feature in this ripe old saint. As also his brooding, emotional, melting, Gaelic-like eloquence when he opens his whole heaven-minded heart to David. Like Moses also in his old age, Barzillai has numbered his days, and has applied his heart to wisdom. Like Paul also, if his outward man must perish, then Barzillai will see to it that his inward man shall not be squandered abroad and lost. No! 'Let the king pardon and discharge his servant,' Barzillai said. 'The king, I fear, forgets how old I am. This is my birthday, and I am fourscore years old to-day. No; it is not for an old man like me to go up to Jerusalem. My time is past to be eating and drinking as they will eat and drink in Jerusalem when God sends back their king to his people. I would be a burden to myself and to the king's servants. But take my son, if it please thee, and let him see Jerusalem. But as for me, the king will let me return home to die and to be buried beside my father and my mother. I shall need all my time; for I am fourscore years old this day, and how shall I go up with the king to Jerusalem?' Who can help loving octogenarian Barzillai, with his 'courtesy in conversation,' and when, like Pompey in Plutarch, he 'gave without disdain, and took with great honour'? And the king kissed Barzillai and blessed him, and Barzillai returned to his place at Rogelim.

And in this also the wise and good Barzillai is surely a beautiful lesson to all old men. Barzillai shows us how to take our advancing years. He shows us how to apply our hearts to wisdom as we number our days. He shows us also how, with all willingness, and sweetness, and courtesy, and divine wisdom to leave cities, and feasts, and crowds, and trumpets, and honours, and promotions to younger men, and to apply our whole remaining strength, and our whole remaining time, to end our days as our days should be ended. Barzillai having showed us how to live, shows us also how to die. Barzillai dies the same devout and noble and magnanimous man he has all his days lived. We have not as yet learned to live; and how then, can we know how to die? We die like a man run down in a race. We. die like a man who has not lived half his days. We die while yet this word is in our mouth, To-day or to-morrow I will go to such a city, and will buy and sell, and get gain. We die like a fox taken in a trap. We die like a rat poisoned in a hole. But Barzillai died like the heavenly-minded man he had always lived. Barzillai died like our own Highland laird, Fraser of Brea. For Fraser of Brea died still 'laying his pipe' ever closer and closer up and up to the fountain, till the Lamb which is in the midst of the throne led him to the living Fountain itself, and till God wiped all tears from his eyes.

LI

HEMAN

HEMAN was 'David's seer in the matters of God.' Now a seer is just a man who sees. He is just a man who has eyes in his head. Other men also have eyes indeed, but then, they do not see with their eyes as a seer sees. A seer stands out among all other men in this, that he sees with all his eyes. Heman, then, was a seer. And he was a seer in this. Heman saw constantly a sight that to most men even in Israel was absolutely invisible. Heman saw, and saw nothing else, but his own soul. From his youth up Heman had as good as seen nothing in the whole world but his own soul. And, after he was well on in life, Heman was moved of God to set down the sight of his own soul in the eighty-eighth Psalm. David, on occasion, was a wonderful seer himself. But David had not given himself up from his youth up to the things of his own soul as Heman had done. David was a man of affairs, and he had many other matters to see to besides the matters of God and of his own soul; but Heman saw nothing else. Separate me Heman and Heman's soul, the Holy Ghost had said. And it was so. And David, discovering that, made Heman the king's seer. Saul also in his day had sought out a seer. Only, the seer that Saul sought out was a seer who could see stolen sheep on the mountains a hundred miles away. Whereas David sought in Heman a seer who could see both David's soul and his own; and who could see sin in David's soul and in his own when no other eye in all Israel could see it. My sin is ever before me, said

David, when his eyes were once opened. And it was to Heman, under God, even more than to Nathan or Gad, that David owed that ever-present sight. 'In the matters of God Heman was the King's seer,' says the sacred writer. God had many matters, first and last, with David; but God's first matter with David, as with all men, was David's sin and David's soul. And Heman from his youth up had been kept so close at God's school for seers in the matters of sin and the soul, that David sought out Heman and established him in Mount Zion as the King's most private, most trusted, and most highly-honoured seer. This, then, was Heman, the seer of David in the matters of God.

'My soul is full of troubles,' says this great seer, speaking about himself in the eighty-eighth Psalm. What led Heman to speak about himself in that way to a people who could not understand what he said, we do not know. What led Heman to speak and to publish abroad this most melancholy of all the Psalms we are not told. He speaks in this Psalm as he was moved to speak by the Holy Ghost: but more than that we do not know. It may have been to console David in some of his many inconsolable seasons. It may have been to rebuke David by letting him see that a saint of God who had never sinned as David had sinned, had, nevertheless, been cast of God into depths that even David had never known. Or it may have been that there might be a Psalm grievous enough for our Lord to recall it and to repeat it during His three hours' darkness on the cross. Or it may have been because God, in His far foreknowledge, saw some one in this house this night that no other Psalm would suit but this saddest of all the Psalms. Who can tell? Now, Heman's soul so full of troubles, you must understand, was not on account of Heman's outward estate. It was not Heman's actual sin like David's. Neither was there any terrible trouble, like David's, among his large family of sons and daughters. Heman had brought up his sons and daughters far more successfully than David had done. For all Heman's sons and daughters assisted their father in sacred song in the house of the Lord. Some of the worst troubles we see and hear men's souls to be full of all around us come to them through their children. But that was not Heman's case. At the same time Heman cannot take a happy father's full joy out of his talented and dutiful children because of the overwhelming trouble of his own soul. He cannot sing and play with his gifted and gracious children with all his heart as other happy fathers sing and play. And that is another trouble to Heman's soul already so full of troubles. It is a terrible price to pay for his post as David's seer to have a soul like that.

It is a terrible baptism into the matters of God to have a soul from his youth up so full of inconsolable troubles.

'My soul is full of troubles,' says Heman, 'till I am driven distracted.' Every day we hear of men and women being driven distracted through love, and through fear, and through poverty, and through pain, and sometimes through over-joy, and sometimes, it is said, through religion. It was thought by some that the Apostle Paul was quite distracted in his day through his too much thought and occupation about divine things. And our Lord Himself was again and again said to be beside Himself. And no wonder. For if love, and fear, and pain of mind and heart, and sometimes over-joy have ever driven men distracted: who ever had all these things, and more, on his mind and on his heart like our Lord? To see what was in man, and what comes out of the heart of man: and to see all that with such holy eyes and with such a holy heart as His, and then to see and understand how all that so concerned Himself—had the very Godhead not held Him up, no mortal mind and heart could have endured under the sight. No wonder that Jesus of Nazareth was often, even to His mother and His brethren, like a man that should be kept close watch over at home. The Second Evangelist was a remarkable seer in all the matters of our Lord. He saw things in our Lord that no other Evangelist had the eyes to see: and he writes about our Lord in words that no other Evangelist can command. And one word he writes in goes so near describing absolute distraction that we shrink back from truly and fully translating it. We water it down till we say that our Lord was sore amazed and very heavy. To be made sin sore amazed our Lord. It almost drove Him beside Himself. A terror at sin, and a horror: a terror and a horror at Himself, took possession of our Lord's soul in the garden till He was full of trouble beyond all experience and imagination of mortal men. It was not death. Death is nothing. Death is nothing to sin. Death and all its terrors did not much move our Lord. He went up to meet death with a serenity and with a stateliness of soul that confounded and almost converted those who saw it. No; it was not death. It was sin. It was that in which our mothers conceived us. It was that which we drink up like water. It was that which we are all full of from the sole of the foot even unto the head. It was sin. It was hell-fire in His soul. It was the coals, and the rosin, and the juniper, and the turpentine of the fire that is not quenched. The pains of hell gat hold upon Him, He found trouble and sorrow till He was well-nigh distracted. Now there was no Old Testament saint so like our Lord in all that was as Heman. And in the measure that we have our Lord's eyes and Heman's eyes wherewith to see sin, in that exact measure will we each one of us fill up what is behind of these tremendous distractions. As it is, our brain sometimes reels in its distracted globe. We know that we sometimes talk distractedly. We know that we terrify and torment other men. We terrify and are a torment to ourselves when no one knows it. We tremble sometimes at the thought of what this may yet grow to if it goes on, as it will go on, all our days. But be not too much cast down. Comfort my people. Say to them that for all their present shame they shall yet have double. Say to them that this is wisdom. Say to them that this is the only mind that hath the true wisdom. Say to them, and assure them, that this is the beginning in them of the wisdom, and the truth, and the love, and the salvation of their God and Saviour Jesus Christ.

Now, with all that, this is not to be wondered at that Heman says next. Anything else but this is not to be expected from Heman. Heman makes it an additional complaint, but it is a simple and a necessary consequence of his own troubled and distracted soul. 'Thou hast put mine acquaintance far from me. Lover and friend hast thou put far from me, and mine acquaintance into darkness.' Job, Heman's spiritual equal almost, has the very same complaint again and again. 'He hath put my brethren far from me, and mine acquaintance are verily estranged from me. My kinsfolk have failed me, and my familiar friends have forgotten me. All my inward friends have abhorred me; and they whom I loved are all turned against me.' And no wonder. Who that could help it would live in the same house with Heman? With such a morose and melancholy man? Friends and lovers, the oldest, and the warmest, and the best—they all have their several limits. Most men are made with little heart themselves, and they are not at home where there is much heart, and much exercise of heart. They flee in a fright from the heights and the depths of the high and deep heart. It needs a friend that sticketh closer than a brother to keep true to a man who has much heart, and who sees and feels with all his heart. Heman had wife and child: he had David, and Asaph, and Jeduthun also; and a whole choir-seat full of smiling acquaintances; but all that only made him feel the more alone. Asaph, also, in the same seat, felt the same loneliness. 'Whom have I in heaven but Thee? And there is none upon earth that I desire beside Thee.' Much as Heman and Asaph had in common, they were all the time such strangers to one another when their distractions were upon them that they felt, as we say, as far as the poles asunder. When thou prayest, said our Lord, enter thy closet. That is to say, enter thine own distracted heart, And there is One, and only One, with thee in thy lockfast heart. David and Asaph and all,—there is nothing that sifts out lover and friend like prayer; the prayer that is, that takes up the troubles and the distractions of the soul. When our Lord took His distracted soul to His Father, the most that His lovers and friends could do for Him was to fall asleep three times outside the door. Heman, besides being the king's seer, was also an eminent type of Christ, both in the distracting troubles of his soul, and in the fewness and in the infidelity of his friends.

Down to Gehenna, and up to the Throne,
He travels the fastest who travels alone.

Now all that, bad as it was, would have been easily borne had it been a sudden stroke and then for ever over. Had it been a great temptation, a great fall, a great repentance, a great forgiveness, and then the light of God's countenance brighter than ever all Heman's after-days. Had it been with Heman as it was with David: 'For His anger endureth but a moment; in His favour is life; weeping may endure for a night, but joy cometh in the morning.' Or had it been with Heman as it was with Isaiah: 'For a small moment have I forsaken thee; but with great mercies will I gather thee. In a little wrath I hid my face from thee for a moment; but with everlasting kindness will I have mercy upon thee, saith the Lord thy Redeemer.' Josiah and Jeremiah bore their yoke also all their youth; but Heman bore his yoke all his days. Heman is now an old man; but like the woman in the gospel he is nothing better but rather worse. There are troubles and distractions in a man's youth sometimes that turn his hair grey before its proper time. But in most cases, by God's goodness, a life like that either comes to an early end altogether, or some great relief and great recovery comes in His grace from God. For the Lord will not cast off for ever. He doth not afflict willingly, nor grieve the children of men. But Heman's yoke from his youth up has been of that terrible kind that it has eaten into his soul deeper and deeper with every advancing year. Had Heman lived after Paul's day he would have described himself in Paul's way. He would have said that the two-edged sword had become every year more and more spiritual, till it entered more and more deep every year into his soul. And since souls like Heman's are absolutely bottomless and shoreless; and since the law of God is infinitely and increasingly holy and just and good; how could a man like

Heman escape being every day of his life more and more sold under sin? He could not. All that Heman had hitherto come through was like child's-play at trouble and distraction compared with this. For his troubles have now taken on an inwardness and an incessancy such as an old saint of God once said would surely some day drive her into the pond.

God forbid, when God is a little displeased with any of His saints, that I should by a single hair-breadth help forward their affliction. God forbid that I should in anything make the heart of any righteous man more sad and should take away from him any of his true refuges. Before I do that may my tongue cleave to the roof of my mouth. At the same time, I will risk it lest they be refuges of lies. I will risk it so that some one here present may perchance be discovered to himself and so saved. Heman's sad case has sometimes been set down to God's sovereignty. And so may all your sadness, possibly. But I would not have you believe that too easily. The chances with you lie all the other way. Are you quite sure that this deep darkness of yours is quite unaccountable to you short of God's sovereignty—short of His deep, hidden, divine will? I doubt it, and I would have you doubt it. I would have you make sure that there is no other possible explanation of this darkness of His face. All the chances are that it is not God's ways that are so distractingly dark, but your own. Look yet closer and yet deeper into yourself for the bottom of this dark mystery. If I were you I would let no man, not even an angel of light, cheat me out of my soul with any of his antinomianisms about the divine sovereignty. Is it not rather a divine controversy? Lean to that explanation. Look as you have never yet looked, and see if there is not some sinful way in you that is the cause of all this darkness on God's part, and all this distraction on your part. The only thing you can think of is such a little thing, that, if it is a sin, it is not worth God's pains to take so much notice of it, and to punish you so persistently for it. It is not a thing for God to stand upon; it is such a small affair. Well, if it is so small, all the more put it away. Put it away for a time at any rate, and, if light does not come, then return to it, of you cannot live without it. Only, there is a sermon of authority which says, Be ye therefore perfect; and it is through terrible distractions, and darknesses, and severities, and sanctifications that this perfect salvation comes to some men: and it looks to me as if you were one of them.

And to close with, there is a singular use in Heman for ministers. When God is to make a very sinful man into a very able, and skilful, and experimental minister, He sends that man to the same school to which He sent Heman. This was God's way, on the side of His sovereignty, with the Servant of the Lord also in the 50th of Isaiah. 'Who comforteth us in all our tribulations,' says Paul also, 'that we may be able to comfort them which are in any trouble. His own troubles and distractions give a minister 'a lady's hand,' as an old writer has it, in dealing with troubled and distracted souls. Now, who can tell what God has laid up for you to do for Him and for men's souls when you are out of your probationership of trouble and distraction, and are promoted to be a comforter of God's troubled and distracted saints? He may have a second David, and far more, to comfort and to sanctify in the generation to come; and you may be ordained to be the King's seer in the matters of God. Who can tell? Only, be you ready, for the stone that is fit for the wall is not left to lie in the ditch.

LII

JEROBOAM

God may have that in his heart for you, which you must not once let enter your heart for yourself. Your name may be written in the divine decree for something, the bare thought of which you must cast out of your heart like poison. And all Jeroboam's great talents, and all his great services, and all his great prospects, and all his great temptations, and all his great sins—all happened to him for ensamples; and they are all written for our admonition, upon whom the ends of the world are come.

But we must go back to the first beginning of Jeroboam's great temptations and great transgressions. It was King Solomon's many and terrible falls from godliness and from virtue that first set such a fatal snare before Jeroboam's feet. Solomon by this time was rushing insenate to his own ruin, and to the ruin of his royal house. If it were not written all over the Bible we would not believe it. Solomon's beautiful dream at Gibeon, his splendid prayer at the dedication of the temple, his wisdom, and his understanding, and his largeness of heart—it is all clean forgotten now. It is all become now like the morning cloud and the early dew. Can this be the same Solomon? Can this be that Solomon to whom the Lord appeared twice? For Solomon went after Ashtoreth, the goddess of the Zidonians, and after Molech, the abomination of the Ammonites. Then did Solomon build an high place for Chemosh, the abomination of Moab, in the hill of God that is before Jerusalem, and for Molech, the abomination of Ammon. In his old age, and when he should have been by this time a rare and a ripe saint of God, Solomon added this also to his other transgressions, an insane passion for building palaces both for himself and for his heathen queens, and temples and altars for their cruel and unclean gods, and great fortifications, and all manner of proud and costly and reckless public works. And, with it all, there was this also: Every stone of all Solomon's temples and palaces and heathen altars was laid wet with the blood of an oppressed and exasperated people. The prophet Samuel had foretold all this to the elders of Israel, and had got little thanks from them for so foretelling it. But every jot and tittle of God's great prophet had by this time been long proved true; and every warning word of his was now like a fire in the bones of Solomon's miserable subjects. As they bled to death under the whip of the tax-gatherer and the task-master, the people gnashed their teeth at their fathers and at themselves. For had not Samuel told it thus to their face? 'He will take your sons and appoint them for himself, for his chariots, and for his horsemen; and he will set them to ear his ground, and to reap his harvest, and to make his instruments of war. And he will take your fields, and your vineyards, and your oliveyards, even the best of them, and will give them to his servants. And he will take your menservants and your maidservants, and your goodliest young men, and will put them to his work, and ye shall be his servants. And ye shall cry out in that day, and the Lord will not hear you in that day.' Well, that day was now fully come. And it was amid all the terrible oppression and suffering of that day that Jeroboam rose so fast and so high in Solomon's service. Jeroboam's outstanding talents in public affairs, his skilful management of men, his great industry, and his great loyalty, as was thought, all combined to bring the son of Nebat under Solomon's royal eye, till there was no trust too important, and no promotion too high for young Jeroboam. And then, to crown it all, as time went on Satan more and more entered into Jeroboam's heart. And Jeroboam allowed Satan in his heart, and listened to Satan speaking in his heart. 'You are a greatly talented man. There is no other man in all the land fit to be your equal. Solomon is old, and his son is a fool. And who is to be king after Solomon dies? Thinkest thou ever who is fit to be king? Saul was but the son of Kish. David himself was but the son of Jesse. There has never been, and there never will be, respect of persons with the God of Israel. Jeroboam, you love your widowed mother. Play the man, then, but a little longer, and your mother will live to hear the cry of the people before she dies, this so sweet cry to her ears, Long live King Jeroboam!' And Jeroboam kept all these things and pondered them in his heart.

All this time, Ahijah the prophet, with those terrible eyes of his, was sleeplessly watching both the fast-coming fall of Solomon, as well as the immense industry and steady rise of Jeroboam. Ahijah's eyes, like a flame of fire, saw, naked and open, all that was hidden so deep in Jeroboam's heart; and he heard, as with God's own ears, all that Satan said to Jeroboam in his heart. Ahijah watched Jeroboam at his work, and he saw, till he could not be silent, that Jeroboam was fast undermining the walls of Jerusalem in his heart, all the time that he was receiving praise and promotion for building those walls up with his hands. 'Lay down thy plummet,' said Ahijah in hot anger to Jeroboam one day—'lay down thy measuring line, and come out to the potter's field with me.' And Jeroboam laid down his building and came out after Ahijah. Then Ahijah suddenly turned and stripped off his new garment that was upon Jeroboam, and tore it up into twelve pieces, and said, 'Thus and thus hast thou torn up the kingdom of Solomon in thine heart. And it shall be so. Take thee ten of these torn-up pieces and hide them with thee till all that is in thine heart shall come true.' And then the prophet, softening somewhat, went on to tell the trembling builder that if he would but cast Satan and all his counsels and all his hopes out of his heart from that day, then the God of Israel would make him a sure house, so that he and his seed should sit on the throne of Israel for ever. And Ahijah thrust the ten torn pieces upon Jeroboam and departed. And Jeroboam returned to his work on the wall of Jerusalem with his heart all in a flame. And it came to pass that when Solomon heard of all that, Solomon turned to be against Jeroboam. And Solomon eyed Jeroboam as Saul had eyed David, and as we all eye those gifted men who are fast rising to push us out of our seat. And just as David fled to Ramah from the javelin of Saul, so Jeroboam fled to Egypt from the same weapon of Solomon. And not Joseph, and not Moses himself, rose so fast and so high in Egypt as Jeroboam rose. In a short space of time the fugitive overseer of Solomon's works had actually become the son-in-law of Pharaoh himself. Jeroboam was born king and statesman; and both Israel and Egypt, both heaven and earth, confessed it to be so. And if only Jeroboam had tarried the Lord's leisure, and had kept his heart clean and humble, Jeroboam would soon have been king over all Israel, he and his sons, till the Messiah came Himself to sit down on David's undivided throne.

All this time, matters went on from bad to worse in Jerusalem, till Solomon died and Rehoboam his son reigned in his stead. But with all that God's prophets and God's providences could do, neither Solomon nor his son altered their insane and suicidal ways one iota. In their utter exasperation and despair the oppressed people at last took the strong and desperate step of sending a secret embassy to Egypt to beseech Jeroboam to return and deliver them from their miseries. And Jeroboam left Egypt at once, and came back with the Hebrew ambassadors. And, whatever may have been in Jeroboam's heart, no fault at all can be found with the words of his ultimatum to Rehoboam. 'Thy father made our yoke grievous; now, therefore, make thou the grievous service of thy father and his heavy yoke lighter, and we will serve thee.' But Rehoboam was demented enough to answer Jeroboam and the people with this insolence: 'My father chastised you with whips, but I will chastise you with scorpions.' At that, 'To your tents, O Israel,' rose the cry of rebellion till it rent the air. 'Now see to thine own house, O David.' So Israel rebelled against the house of David that day. And Jeroboam was made king over the ten tribes that day. There was none that followed the house of David but the tribe of Judah only.

Now, here is our first admonition. Had Jeroboam on the day of his coronation, and henceforth, but taken Ahijah home to be his counsellor, Jeroboam had ability enough, and divine right enough, to have built up Israel into a great kingdom for God and for himself. But Jeroboam never loved Ahijah. He both feared and hated Ahijah. He was never at home, as we say, with Ahijah. He was never happy when he was alone with Ahijah. His heart, neither on the wall nor on the throne, was ever single enough for Ahijah's all-searching eyes. And thus it was that Satan still kept his place in Jeroboam's heart, and was still Jeroboam's counsellor in all the affairs of the state, and in all the affairs of the family, till Jeroboam's great fall, from which he and his people never recovered, came about in this way. The ten tribes continued to go up to Jerusalem to Solomon's temple to worship God. And as they did so Jeroboam began to fear lest, in their worship together, Judah and Israel should both so return to the Lord together, that the breach in the kingdom would be healed, and he and his son cast out of his rebellious throne. The fact is, we have here before us in black and white, to this day, the very identical words that Jeroboam at that time spake in his heart. He said this in his heart: 'If my people go up to do service in this way in the house of the lord at Jerusalem, then shall the hearts of this people turn back to Rehoboam, and they will kill me and my son with me.' Whereupon Jeroboam took counsel, and made two unclean idols of gold, and said, It is too much for you to go up to Jerusalem; behold thy gods, O Israel, which brought thee up out of the land of Egypt. You are not to suppose that Jeroboam was so stupid as to believe what he said and did that day. No. But he knew how stupid, and, indeed, how brutish at bottom his people were, as well as how superstitious. He knew well, also, how party spirit and ill-will had all along prevailed between Samaria and Jerusalem; and, the bad man that he was, Jeroboam deliberately set himself to traffic, and to establish his throne, in the sensuality, in the stupidity, and in the ill-will of his hood-winked subjects.

But, happily for us all, there is nothing in God's name to usward that is more sure and more true than is His long suffering, and His immense patience, and the many calls to repentance that He sends us before He finally casts us off. And, lest Jeroboam should lose himself through his fear and hate at Ahijah, God actually condescended to set the old and faithful prophet aside and to send a new prophet to Jeroboam: a prophet whose eyes had not yet read Jeroboam's heart, and against whom Jeroboam could have taken up no umbrage. Unless we both know ourselves and hate ourselves, we shall be certain both to hate and put away from us the preacher who tells us to our faces what is in our heart, as Jeroboam hated and put away Ahijah; which hatred of Jeroboam at him was all the time one of Ahijah's surest seals, both to himself and to Jeroboam, that he was a true prophet of the heart-searching God.

With all that, Jeroboam was not a common man. And Jeroboam's sins were not the sins of a common man. It is only kings, and kings' counsellors, and popes, and bishops, and ministers, and elders, and such like, who can sin and make nations and churches and congregations to sin. But they can do it. And they are doing it every day. All who divide, and keep divided, nations, and churches, and families, and friends in order to make a name, or a living, or a party, or just a despite for themselves out of such divisions, they are the true seed of Jeroboam. All who inflame and perpetuate such divisions lest they should lose their stake of money, or of influence, or of occupation, or of pure ill-will; all able men who prostitute their talents to write or speak about men on the other side, as they would not like themselves to be spoken or written about—let them lay it to heart in whose lot they shall surely stand when every man shall give an account of himself to God. But common and mean men are not incapacitated and shut out by their commonness and meanness from sharing in Jeroboam's royal sin. The commonest and meanest man among us has more than enough of this terrible power of both sinning himself and making other men to sin. Every man among us has, in countless ways and on countless occasions, first sinned himself and then made other men to sin. Go back honestly into your past life and see. Take time; take a true light back with you, and look around, and see. Come up, as you shall one day be compelled to come up through your past life whether you will or no, and see. Some of them are dead and gone to judgment with the lesson in sin you gave them laid up before God against you. Some of them are still sinning here, and are prolonging your days in teaching a new generation to sin your sin. Sin yourself, if you will sin. But, as you would have a drop of water to cool your tongue in that torment, do not make other men to sin. Break the Sabbath law, neglect God's house, do despite to His means of grace, drink, bet, pollute yourself, scoff, blaspheme: your soul is your own. Make your bed in hell, if you will have it so; but, as God will smite you for it, let alone the young, and the innocent, and the pure, and the unsuspecting. So Jeroboam, who sinned and who made Israel to sin, though dead, yet speaketh.

LIII

THE DISOBEDIENT PROPHET

It was an high day of idolatry at Bethel. And, all the time, Bethel, of all the cities of Israel, was one of the most ancient and the most sacred. Bethel, as its name bears, was none other but the house of God, and it was the very gate of heaven. Bethel was built on that very spot on which their father Jacob had slept and dreamed when he was on his lonely way to Padan-aram; and it is that very heaven out of which the ladder was let down on Jacob's pillow that is to-day to be darkened by the unclean incense of Jeroboam's altar-fires. It was a brave step in Jeroboam to set up his false gods at Bethel, of all places in the land. And he needed a stout heart and a profane to support him as he stood up to kindle with his own hands the heathen fires of idolatry and impurity at Bethel.

Where angels down the lucid stair
  Came hovering to our sainted sires,
Now, in the twilight glare
  The heathen's wizard fires.

And, behold, there came a man of God out of Judah by the word of the Lord unto Bethel: and Jeroboam stood by the altar to burn incense. And the man of God cried against the altar of the Lord, and said, O altar, altar! And then he foretold the fall of the altar, and with it the fall of him who stood in his royal robes that day ministering to his unclean gods at that altar. And how Jeroboam's hand was withered that moment; how it was healed immediately at the intercession of the man of God; how Jeroboam invited the prophet to come home with him to eat and to drink and to get a reward; and how the prophet answered the king that he had the command of the Lord neither to eat bread nor to drink in that polluted land, but to return home to Judah as soon as he had delivered his prophetic burden—all that is to be read in the thirteenth chapter of First Kings. At the same time, we are not told so much as this great prophet's name. He was wholly worthy thus far to have his name held up aloft along with the names of Samuel and Elijah themselves, for he stood up alone against Jeroboam and against all Israel and nailed the curse of God to Jeroboam's altar under the king's own eyes. We would hold his name in more than royal honour if we knew it. But for some reason or other of her own the Bible holds his great name back. This great man of God comes out of a cloud, he shines for a splendid moment before all men's eyes, and then he dies under a cloud. Alas, my brother!

As the man of God from Judah so nobly refuses Jeroboam's royal hospitality, I am reminded of Lord Napier. On one occasion his lordship was sent down to Scotland by the Queen on a royal errand of review and arbitration between a great duke and his poor crofters. The duke, the administration of whose estate was to be inquired into, was good enough to offer his lordship his ducal hospitality for as long as the royal session of review lasted. But her Majesty's Deputy felt that neither his Royal Mistress nor himself could afford to be for one moment compromised, or even suspected, by her poorest subject; and therefore it was that his lordship excused himself from the duke's table, and took up his quarters in the little wayside inn. 'At any rate, you will come to the manse,' said the minister, who was on the crofters' side. 'Thank you,' said Napier. 'But in your college days you must have read Plutarch about Cæsar's wife.

No, thank you.' And his lordship lodged all his time in the little hotel, and went back to his Royal Mistress when his work was done, not only with clean hands, but without even a suspicion attaching to her or to him. 'Come home with me and refresh thyself.' But the man of God said to the king, 'If thou wilt give me half thine house, I will not go in with thee, neither will I eat bread nor drink water with thee.' So he went another way, and returned not by the way that he came to Bethel.

Just as the man of God is setting out to go back to Judah with a hungry belly indeed, but with a good conscience, we are taken by the hand and are led into the house of an old prophet who dwells at Bethel. Yes. There are prophets and prophets' sons all this time at Bethel. Only, they had their domiciles and their doles from Jeroboam's bounty on the strict condition that they kept at home and kept silence. Well, this old Bethelite prophet was keeping at home and was keeping silence when his sons burst in upon him with the great news of the day. Father, you should have come with us! We asked you to come. What a day it has been! And what a man of God we have seen! Till they told him all that we are told about Jeroboam, and his altar, and the man of God from Judah, and his cry that shook down the altar, and the king's withered hand, and the prayer of the man of God, and the king's hospitality, and the man of God's refusal of the king's hospitality. 'What way went he home?' demanded the old prophet of his excited sons. 'Saddle me the ass,' he instantly ordered. 'Art thou the man of God from Judah?' he asked, as he overtook the man of God sitting under an oak. 'Come home with me and eat bread.' 'I may not eat bread, nor drink water by the word of the Lord,' said the man of God. 'But I am a prophet also as thou art,' said the old Bethelite; 'and an angel bade me bring thee back.' But it was a lie, adds the sacred writer. So the man of God rose and went back and did eat bread and drink water. And so on; till a lion met him in the way home that night, and slew him because he had gone back. And when the old Bethelite prophet, who had deceived him, heard of it, he mourned over him, and said, 'Alas, my brother!' And he said to his sons, 'Bury me beside this man of God. Lay my bones beside his bones.'

What is it that makes the decrepit old prophet of Bethel post at such a pace after the man of God who is on his way home to Judah? Has his conscience at last been awakened? Have the tidings of his delighted sons filled the poor old time-server with bitter remorse for his fat table and for his dumb pulpit? Or, is it deadly envy and revenge at the man who has so stolen his sons' hearts that day till they are about to set off to Judah to go to school to this man of God? It is too late now for him to command his sons' reverence and love. And how can he ever forgive the man who has so taken from him his crown as a prophet and as a father? 'Saddle me the ass,' he shouted. And the decayed old creature rode down the Judean road at a pace he had not ridden since he used, as a godly youth, to be sent out on errands of life and death and mercy from Samuel's School of Mount Ephraim. If lies will do it; if flattery, flesh, and wine will do it; if there is man or woman in Bethel that will do it,—that Judean prophet's pride shall be brought down to-day! 'Saddle me the ass!' he thundered. So they saddled him the ass, and he rode after the man of God. 'I am a prophet as thou art!' But he lied unto him.

Let us all take care of the swift and sure collapse that always comes on us after every great excitement. As sure as we are made of flesh, and blood, and brains, and nerves, and feelings, a great reaction always takes place in body and mind after any unusually great effort of body and mind. And especially after any great preaching effort. After you have faced for hours a surging congregation, and have worked yourself and them up to heaven,—to see them scatter, and to be left worn out and alone,—then comes the hour of temptation: a temptation that has been fatal in more ways than one to some temperaments of men. Some temperaments are tempted at such times to eat and drink and smoke and talk all night to any listener if they have done well; and the same temperaments are just as much tempted to silence, and gloom, and bad temper if they have not done well: if they have not come up to themselves, and have not got the praise they worked for and expected. We are not told why this great man of God stopped short so soon on his way home from Bethel, and sat down so soon under one of the oaks of Bethel. He had done a splendid day's work. Never prophet of God did a more splendid day's work. But our hearts sink as we see him stop short, and then take his seat under that tempting tree. What was the matter? We are not told. He may have been very hungry by his time, and he may have begun to repent that he had not accepted the penitent king's hospitality. Who knows what good might have come of it had he, God's acknowledged prophet, been seen sitting in the place of honour at the royal table? Had he not been somewhat short, and sharp, and churlish after his great battle with Jeroboam's altar? Stern men have often been known to soften and secretly repent of their too-ascetical self-denial. They have felt it hard to have to pay the whole self-denying vow which they made when some great exaltation was upon them.

Some men have gone so far, indeed, as to call back in imagination the hour of temptation, and wish that they had not let it slip so soon. Well, then, if that was the case with the man of God from Judah,—here is the forbidden fruit of Bethel back and at his open mouth this moment: 'I am a prophet as thou art, and an angel spake unto me by the word of the Lord, saying: Bring him back to eat and to drink.' So he went back with him to his house.

As a rule let ministers sup at home on Sabbath nights; and let them sup alone. As a rule. It cannot always be acted on, but it is a good rule, nevertheless. Many a good sermon has been drowned dead in the supper, and in the supper-talk that followed it. Your people will not care one straw what you say to them from the pulpit if you sup heartily with them immediately after it. All the great awe of the morning went off the Bethelite prophet's sons and servants, as the man of God sat and ate and drank and laughed and talked over his supper that night. And the old Bethelite himself was quite at home, hail-fellow-well-met, with the terrible preacher of that awakening morning.

I was once spending a Sabbath in a well-known farm-house in Glenisla, and after church the old laird and I began to talk about John Duncan and his great sermons when he was a probationer in a chapel of ease in the neighbourhood. After supper and worship I was anxious to hear more about Dr. Duncan, and to hear more of his old sermons read. 'No,' said the old patriarch to me; 'No: no more to-night; we always take our candles immediately after family worship.' How often has that rebuke come back to me as another Sabbath night closed with all kinds of talk after public and family worship; talk that but too plainly had blotted out for ever all that had been said and heard that day. It is not possible that we should all spend the last hours of the Sabbath alone; but, most certainly, many a deep impression has been obliterated as the preacher ate and drank and talked and laughed after his solemn sermon.

And then this—follow your conscience to the end, let men and angels say what they will. A man is but a man: an angel is but an angel: and false prophets have come out into the world. But conscience is more than conscience. Conscience is God. Conscience is Immanuel, God in us. My conscience, accordingly, is more to me than all prophets and apostles and preachers, and very angels themselves. If that had been Paul sitting under that oak, and had the old Bethelite deceiver come riding on his ass, with his certificate of office, and with his story about an angel to Paul, we have Paul's answer to him in the Galatians: 'If an angel from heaven bids me go against God in my conscience, let him be accursed.' And the older receiver would have fallen down and would have reported at home that God was in the man of God from Judah of a truth. So would the secrets of his heart have been made manifest. 'Conscience,' says Sanderson, 'is a fast friend, and a fierce foe.' 'I take my ears,' said King Charles, 'to other preachers; but I take my conscience to Mr. Sanderson.' And go you to the preacher who speaks closest to your conscience, whatever denomination he preaches in, and then hold fast by your enlightened and awakened conscience against men and devils.

At the same time, to be slain by a lion on the way home was surely much too sharp a punishment for taking one's supper with a prophet and an angel; uneasy conscience and all. But then, 'some sins,' says that noble piece, the Westminster Larger Catechism, 'receive their aggravation from the persons offending; if they be of riper age, greater experience in grace, eminent for profession, gifts, place, office, and as such are guides to others, and whose example is likely to be followed by others. The very case, to the letter, of the man of God out of Judah. The sublimity of his public services that morning had henceforth set up a corresponding standard for his private life. And this is one of our best compensations for preaching the grace of God and the law of Christ. Our office quickens our conscience; it makes the law cut deeper and deeper into our hearts every day; and it compels us to a public and private life we would otherwise have escaped. Preaching recoils with terrible strokes on the preacher. It curtails his liberty in a most tyrannical way; it tracks him through all his life in a most remorseless manner. Think it out well, and count the cost, before you become a minister. For, it was surely a little sin, if ever there was a little sin, to sup that Sabbath night at an old prophet's table, and that, too, on the invitation of an angel. But the lion that met the disobedient prophet that night did not reason that way.

'Bury me,' said the remorseful old man to his sons standing in tears round his miserable deathbed, 'bury me in the same grave with the bones of the man of God out of Judah.' And the old prophet's sons so buried their father. And an awful grave that was in Bethel, with an awful epitaph upon it. Now, suppose this. Suppose that you were buried on the same awful principle,— in whose grave would your bones lie waiting together with his till the last trump to stand forth before God and man together? And what would your epitaph and his be? Would it be this: 'Here lie the liar and his victim'? Or would it be this: 'Here lie the seducer and the seduced'? Or would it be this! 'Here lie the hater and him he hated down to death'? Or would it be this: 'Here lie the tempting host and his too willing to be tempted guest'? Or, if you are a minister, would it be this: 'Here lies a dumb dog, and beside him one who was a crowded preacher in the morning of his days, but a castaway before night'? Alas, my brother!

LIV

REHOBOAM

JUST by one insolent and swaggering word King Rehoboam lost for ever the ten tribes of Israel. And all Rehoboam's insane and suicidal history is written in our Bibles for the admonition and instruction of all hot-blooded, ill-natured, and insolent-spoken men among ourselves.

The beginning of it all was the domestic disorders and the cancerous immoralities of David's house. And then it was the heathen idolatry and the heathen immorality and the reckless and exasperating extravagance of Solomon's declining years. Prophet after prophet had been sent of God to Solomon because of his shameful apostasies, but it was all in vain. Solomon's old advisers besought his son Rehoboam, as soon as he had sat down on the throne of his father Solomon, to attend to the complaints of the people, and to lighten their terrible burdens. But Rehoboam shut his ears to the wisdom of the elders of Israel, and answered the oppressed people in the insolent and insulting words that the young men about him had put in his mouth. 'My father made your yoke heavy, and I will add to your yoke; my father also chastised you with whips, but I will chastise you with scorpions.' At that the long-suppressed shout rose and rang through the angry land, 'To your tents, O Israel! Now see to thine own house, David!' So Israel rebelled, says the sacred writer, against the house of David to this day.

One might well be tempted to think that the sacred writer had told Rehoboam's history wholly in vain, so often has his insane folly been repeated east and west since his fatal day. And in no land has his folly been oftener repeated or better written about than just in our own England.

I am solicited [says Queen Katherine], not by a few,
And those of true condition, that your subjects
Are in great grievance; there have been commissions
Sent down among 'em, which have flaw'd the heart
Of all their loyalties; wherein, although,
My good lord cardinal, they vent reproaches
Most bitterly on you, as putter on
Of these exactions, yet the king our master—
Whose honour heaven shield from soil!—even he escapes not
Language unmannerly, yea, such which breaks
The sides of loyalty, and almost appears
In loud rebellion.—I would your highness
Would give it quick consideration, for
There is no primer business.

Our own Henrys, and Jameses, and Charleses, and Georges—the books of the kings of Israel were eminently written for their learning. But preaching like Bishop Hall's *Contemplation* on Rehoboam—if the light that is at our kings' courts be darkness, how great is that darkness. And such servile preaching as Joseph Hall's too often was, went on till the kings of England lost, not their kingdoms only, but their own heads to the bargain. Take Joseph Hall away from court, and there is not a racier or a more sagacious preacher in England; but put James's lawn sleeves on Bishop Hall, and there are few in their hour of temptation who are more contemptible. How much more true and just and wise is Dean Stanley: 'The demands of the nation were just. The old counsellors gave such advice as might have been found in the Book of Proverbs. Only the insolence of the younger courtiers imagined the possibility of coercing a great people. It was a doomed revolution.'

Every morning, all the last wet summer, my children and I read an hour in the best story-book in the world. And having Rehoboam in my mind, we came upon this about Coriolanus: 'But on the other side, for lack of education, he was so choleric, and so impatient, that he would yield to no living creature: which made him churlish, uncivil, and altogether unfit for any man's conversation. They could not be acquainted with him as one citizen careth to be with another in the city. His behaviour was so unpleasant to them by reason of a certain insolent and stern manner he had, which, because it was too lordly, was disliked. And, to say truly, the greatest benefit that learning bringeth men unto is this: that it teacheth them that be rude and rough of nature, by compass and rule of reason, to be civil and courteous, and to like better the mean state than the higher. But Martius was a man too full of passion and choler, and too much given over to self-will and opinion, and lacked the gravity and affability that is gotten with judgment of learning and reason. He remembered not how wilfulness is the thing of all the world which the governor of a state should shun. For a man that wishes to live in this world must needs have patience which lusty bloods [like Rehoboam's young counsellors] make but a mock at.' Reading the same charming book another wet morning we came on this: 'Now, Cæsar immediately won many men's goodwill at Rome through his eloquence in pleading their causes, and the people loved him marvellously also because of the courteous manner he had to speak with every man, and to use them gently, being more ceremonious therein than was looked for in one of his years. How little account Cæsar made of his diet, this example doth prove it. Supping one night in Milan with his friend Valerius Leo, there was served asparagus to his board and oil of perfume put into it instead of salad oil. Cæsar simply ate it and found no fault, but reproved his friends who were offended: and told them that it had been enough to have abstained to eat of that they misliked, and not to shame their friend, and how much he lacked good manners who found fault with his friend.' The whole chapter, indeed, is one of Plutarch's masterpieces. Though the great republican does not like Cæsar, yet his instinct as an author and his nobility as a man compel Plutarch to extol continually Cæsar's exquisite courtesy, his noble urbanity, and his unfailing good manners.

True, there are neither kings, nor kings' sons, nor kings' counsellors, nor kings' chaplains here, but there are plenty of hot-blooded, hectoring, insolent, and ill-natured men. There are husbands, and fathers, and masters, and many other kinds and classes of men to whom this Scripture comes direct from God. Husbands especially. You husbands, never, all your days, speak an impatient or an angry or an insolent word to your wife. And if you have already lost your fireside, which it is worse to lose than a kingdom; if you have spoken not one angry and cruel word, but many, which cannot now be unspoken, it is not too late even yet. Even if things have been said between you and your wife that neither of you can ever forget, your whole life is not lost. At the worst, if you both like, if you are both able, meat may yet come to you both out of the eater; that is to say, out of your angry, insolent, heart-cutting words to one another. You may gather quietness, and self-command, and a bridle for your mouth, and a balm for two sore hearts out of the carcass of your all-but-dead tenderness to one another. When the next debatable matter comes up between you, let it not come up. Put your foot upon it. Keep your foot firm down upon it.

> Prune thou thy words, the thoughts control
> That o'er thee swell and throng;
> They will condense within thy soul,
> And change to purpose strong.

All Scriptures are not written for all men alike. Some men are already strong men and wise masters of themselves. There are men from whom you will never hear one angry, sulky, insolent word all their days. But there are other men whose lips simply spit hell-fire as often as they open them upon your heart.

One would think that if there was any one of the near relationships of human life more than another that would of itself absolutely secure kindness, and tenderness, and affability, and love, it would be that of a father. But, as a matter of fact, it is often the very opposite. You never see more impatience, and harshness, and sullenness, and sourness than you see in some fathers. Why is that so, I wonder? It is very difficult to explain and account for it. Let every silent, sulky, churlish father watch and examine the working of his own heart till he understands and overcomes this monstrosity in himself. It is against nature. But it cannot be denied that it is very common. It is not for nothing, you may be very sure, that Paul gives to fathers this, at first reading, somewhat startling counsel, not to provoke their children to wrath. The apostle must often have seen it done. He must often have suffered from seeing it done. He must often have felt sore in his heart for such unhappy children, else he would never have said what he says in his Epistle to the Ephesians. He must often have sat at tables where the children were incessantly corrected and rebuked and exasperated. He must often have seen all-but-innocent children nagged and worried into answers and actions the whole blame of which he laid on their fathers and their mothers. Treat your children, he says to us, as your Father treats you. For His name is merciful, and gracious, and long-suffering, and slow to wrath. Study your children. Command your temper towards your children. Do not worry, and vex, and insult, and exasperate your children. 'When they do right, make a point of praising them openly,' says Cecil. 'And when they do wrong, reprehend them secretly.' A word of encouragement, a touch of the hand, a smile even; how easy to a wise and loving father it is to bring up his children in the nurture and admonition of the Lord, and how happy it makes him and them. But how hard and impossible all that is to a churl and a curmudgeon.

And King Rehoboam consulted with the old men that had stood before Solomon his father while he yet lived, and said, How do ye advise that I should answer this people? And they advised the king, saying, If thou wilt answer them, and speak good words unto them, then they will be thy servants for ever. But he forsook the counsel of the old men. The best sermon I know on that scene is to be read in a letter of Mr. Ruskin's to the editor of the *Daily Telegraph*. The editor had said in a leading article that it is the hardest thing in the world in these days to find a good servant. And that called out Mr. Ruskin the same day. I will not spoil his English. 'Sir,' he wrote, 'you so seldom write nonsense that you will, I am sure, pardon your friends for telling you when you do. Your article on servants to-day is sheer nonsense. It is just as easy and just as difficult now to get good servants as ever it was. You may have them, as you may have pines and peaches, for the growing; or you may even buy them good, if you can persuade the good growers to spare them off their walls; but you cannot get them by political economy and the law of supply and demand. Sir, there is only one way to have good servants, and that is to be worthy of being well served. All nature and all humanity will serve a good master, and will rebel against an ignoble one. There is no surer test of the quality of a nation than the quality of its servants. A wise nation will have philosophers in its servants' hall, a knavish nation will have knaves there, and a kindly nation will have friends there. Only let it be remembered that "kindness" means, as with your child, so with your servant, not indulgence, but care.' And then Mr. Ruskin winds up the whole correspondence with an apt and beautiful reference to Xenophon's *Economics*, and an advice to all his lady readers to get the old Greek book by heart, as the most perfect ideal of kingly character and kingly government ever given in literature, as also the ideal of domestic life.

No; there can be no manner of doubt that Mr. Ruskin is wholly right. Our servants would never leave us if we were sufficiently kind to them. Unless, indeed, it were to go to serve those who had sworn to be still kinder to them. And we would get two men's, two women's work out of each one of them while they are with us if we were only twice more kind to them. A word of recognition and appreciation; a word of trust and confidence and real respect now and then; a nod, a smile as you meet them in the passage or on the stair; once in a while to eat a meal or a part of a meal with them; to give them now and then the gift or the loan of a book that has done yourself real good to read, and to say so. O yes! the hearts and minds of men and women are neither better nor worse than ever they were. They live upon love, and esteem, and respect, and praise, just as much as ever they did. Just try them and see.

LV

JOSIAH

JOSIAH was born with a tender heart, says Huldah the prophetess. Josiah's father and grandfather were the two worst kings that had ever sold Israel into slavery. And Josiah inherited from his father and from his grandfather a name of shame, an undermined throne, a divided and a distracted kingdom, a national religion and a public worship debased, and, indeed, bestialised; and, over all, a fearful looking for of judgment. And all that broke and made tender Josiah's heart from the day of his birth. We are told nothing of Josiah's unhappy mother. But may we not be allowed to believe that her heart also was made tender within her by all that she had come through, till she bore and brought up her son Josiah to be the most tender-hearted man in all Israel, till Mary bore and brought up her child to be the most tender-hearted man in all the world?

If a boy has a good mother and a good minister he is all but independent of his father. And with Jedidah for his mother, and with Jeremiah for his minister, both Manasseh his grandfather and Amon his father taken together did not succeed in corrupting and destroying young Josiah. The tender heart of the young prince took all the good out of his so terribly untoward circumstances, and escaped all the evil, till Jeremiah was able to pronounce this noble panegyric over the too early grave of Josiah,—'That it is good for a man to bear the yoke in his youth; and that it is also good for such a man quietly to hope and to wait for the salvation of the Lord.' With Jeremiah every Sabbath-day among the ruins of the temple, and with Jedidah every week-day at home, notwithstanding all Josiah's drawbacks and heart-breaks,—or, rather, because of them,—I do not wonder that Josiah soon became the very best sovereign that had ever sat on the throne of David.

Early in the days of his youth Josiah began to seek after the

God of David his father. That is to say,—however well a boy may have been brought up; however good a mother he may have had, and however efficient and faithful a minister, the time soon comes when every young man must seek his own God for himself. Neither David's God, nor Jedidah's God, nor Jeremiah's God will suffice for Josiah. Josiah is an orphan and a prince with a terrible heritage of woe. And a second-hand and a merely educational and hereditary knowledge of God will not suffice for Josiah's singular and extraordinary case. Josiah cannot rest till he is able to say for himself—'Thou art my God. Early will I seek thee. O Lord, truly I am Thy servant, the son of Thine handmaid; Thou hast loosed my bonds.' And, all the time, while Josiah still sought the Lord, and till he found Him, the tenderness of Josiah's heart kept him safe and unspotted from all the corruptions of the world. A boy will be at a school where all kinds of evil are rampant. He will then enter a workshop or an office where so many young men go astray. But there has always been something about that boy that has kept him through it all both pure and pious. And it has been his tender heart that has done it. Augustine has his finest passage in point. Monica's son, like Jedidah's son, had drunk in the name of Jesus Christ with his mother's milk; and all the folly of philosophy, and all the sweetness of sensuality could never seduce nor satisfy Augustine's heart. God had made Augustine's great heart for Himself; and neither true nor false, neither sweet nor bitter, neither good nor bad, could solace or satiate that deep, predestinated heart. Nothing, and no one, but God Himself. So it was with Josiah. And so it was with ourselves. And so it has been, and so it will be, with thousands of the sons of mothers like Jedidah, and with thousands of the scholars and young communicants of ministers like Jeremiah and Zephaniah.

Josiah was only twenty years of age when he set about a national reformation of religion as radical and as complete as anything that Martin Luther or John Calvin or John Knox themselves ever undertook. But with this immense difference. Both Luther and Calvin and Knox had the whole Word of God in their hands both to inspire them and to guide them and to support them in their tremendous task. But Josiah had not one single book or chapter or verse even of the Word of God in his heathen day. The Five Books of Moses were as completely lost out of the whole land long before Josiah's day as much so as if Moses had never lifted a pen. And thus it was that Josiah's reformation had a creativeness, an originality, an enterprise, and boldness about it, such that in all these respects it has completely eclipsed all subsequent reformations and revivals, the greatest and the best. The truth is, the whole of that immense movement that resulted in the religious regeneration of Jerusalem and Judah in Josiah's day,—it all sprang originally and immediately out of nothing else but Josiah's extraordinary tenderness of heart. The Light that lighteth every man that cometh into the world shone with extraordinary clearness in Josiah's tender heart and open mind. And Josiah walked in that Light and obeyed it, till it became within him an overmastering sense of divine duty and an irresistible direction and drawing of the Divine Hand; and till he performed a work for God and for Israel second to no work that has ever been performed under the greatest and the best of the prophets and kings of Israel combined. It is a very noble spectacle. This royal youth of but about twenty years old, and the son and heir of Manasseh and Amon, having the intellectual boldness and the spiritual originality to take all his statesmanship, and all his churchmanship, and all his international politics, and all his righteous wars, as well as all his personal and household religion, all out of his own tender heart. There never was a nobler proof of our Lord's great New Testament principle that he that doeth the will of God shall know the doctrine. For it was in the progress of that reformation and revival of religion which his own tender heart had alone dictated to him that the long-lost law of Moses was recovered. And recovered in as many divine and commanding and rewarding words, so as to sanction and seal, as if from heaven itself, all the bold and believing task that Josiah had wholly of himself undertaken. We all profess to believe in special providences and in divine interpositions; but surely, the extraordinary providence that brought to the light of day and put into Josiah's hands the long-lost law of Moses concerning the worship and morals of Israel was an incomparable miracle of the Divine grace and goodness. Josiah was worthy; and God's recognition and reward of Josiah's worth came to Josiah at the very best moment, and in the very best way; for it came to him as the very law of the living God; and that, too, as good as if it had been written on the spot by God's own living hand. Humanly speaking, we should never have heard of the Five Books of Moses, as we have heard of them, but for Josiah's tender heart. Humanly speaking, and popularly speaking, our Old Testament would have begun with the Book of Joshua but for Josiah's tender heart. Had Josiah's heart not been tender toward the house of God, the temple would have been let lie in its utter ruin, till the buried Books of Moses would have been to this day the possession and the prey of the moles and the bats. Moses, says Matthew Henry, had a narrow turn for his life in Josiah's day. You do well to tremble at the thought of how near you were to the total loss of Moses and his law. And you are almost angry at Matthew Henry for telling you what you did not know before. But try your own hand on Moses and Josiah, and explain to me how you think you could have had Moses in your Bible but for Josiah; and, again, but for Josiah's tender heart. I defy you to do it. At any rate,—this is far more to your purpose—be sure of this, that both Moses, and David, and Paul, and John, and Jesus Christ Himself, are all as good as never written; they are as good as completely lost to you; till you take to them a tender heart, and out of that, a reformed and a repaired life. It will only be after your heart is tender and your life repaired that Hilkiah and Shaphan and Huldah the prophetess will be able to discover and to read to you either the law of Moses, or the grace and truth that has come by Jesus Christ. Till then, your Bible also is as good as buried under the ruin and rubbish of your fallen life. But when your heart is made tender by your father's sins and by your own; as also, by all God's providences towards you, and by all His grace in you; and when, in addition, your life has been made believing and obedient; then God's Word will more and more flash out continually upon you, a lamp to your feet and a light to your path.

When the law of the Lord, as it was written in the newly disinterred Books of Moses, was read for the first time to Josiah, and while Shaphan the scribe was still reading it, Josiah rose up and rent to pieces his royal robe. After having looked for it, I do not read that Shaphan the scribe rent his robe, nor Ahikam the son of Shaphan, nor Hilkiah the priest, nor Achbor, nor Asahiah the servant of Josiah, nor Huldah the prophetess. Josiah alone rent his robe as the law was read. Their hearts were not so tender as was Josiah's heart. They had not come through so much from their youth up. The iron of God had not entered their hearts, and the law of God after it. The finding of the law was, no doubt, a great event in sacred archæology, as well as in sacred letters, to Shaphan and Hilkiah; but it did not come home to their hearts as it all came home to Josiah's heart. It was Moses speaking to them: but it was God Himself speaking to Josiah. It was an old book to them: but it was the Word of the Living God to him. He felt—such was his tender heart—that all he had attained to, and all he had reformed and done, was just nothing at all while so much remained to be and to do. He felt, as Isaiah felt, that all his righteousnesses were but so much filthy rags. If you have any real interest in these things; if you care to go to the sources and are not indolently content with my poor paraphrase of these intensely interesting Scriptures: if you are a true student, a true sinner, and a true reformer of yourself and of the ruins that lie all around you—you will read 2 Kings and 2 Chronicles to yourselves, if only to see what a reformer both of himself and of his whole land Josiah was: and all that out of his own tender heart. And, best of all, how unsatisfied, and how tender-hearted he was with all he had done. All which, you must know, was the Holy Ghost in Josiah's tender heart before the Holy Ghost had yet been given. Has He even yet been given in that way to you? Do you rend your heart every day as you hear and read the Word of God? Or, are your clothes as whole, and your hearts, as were Hilkiah's and Shaphan's, and all the rest of the merely official and salaried servants of the palace and the temple? On the other hand, if all you have done only adds itself on to what you have not done: if your best works break your heart even more than your worst: if it is no rhetoric that all your righteousnesses are so much filthy rags: then, I wish much to assure you, that so it always is when the Holy Spirit accompanies the Word of God, either read or heard. Jeremiah—you all know the proverbial penitent, and the contrite heart, that Jeremiah was—but Jeremiah did not think that. He did not feel that. Oh that mine head were waters, and mine eyes a fountain of tears! wept that hard-hearted and dry-eyed prophet. 'I can sin much,' cries holy Lancelot Andrewes to God every night, 'but I cannot repent much. Woe is me for my hard and dry heart. Give me, O God, a molten heart. Give tears. Give the grace of tears. Give me, O Lord, this great grace. None were so welcome to me. Not all the good things of this life are to be coveted by me in comparison with tears. Tears such as Thou didst give to David, and to Jeremiah, and to Josiah, and to Peter, and to her out of whom were cast seven devils. O God, give the chief of sinners some tears for his great sin, and for Thy great salvation.' And the Word of God has never yet been aright read to you, or aright heard and believed by you, unless you feel like Josiah, and Jeremiah, and Peter, and Andrewes every day. Your religion is not worth one straw, as true religion, unless it is every day breaking and making more tender your hard heart. Woe unto you that laugh now, for ye shall mourn and weep. But blessed are ye that weep now, for ye shall laugh for it all when all tears shall have been wiped from your eyes.

Only, if you will have Josiah's tender heart in this hard-hearted world, you will have to pay a heavy price for it. Josiah paid a heavy price at the last for his tender heart. Josiah's tender heart, after it had done him all the good that we have seen, and more, at last it did him this terrible evil, that it lost him his life for this life. Josiah's tender heart was the cause of his too early death. The narrative is obscure and perplexed, and it lends itself to be read in more ways than one. But as I read Josiah's end it is something like this,—The king's tender heart led him out to do battle against the hereditary enemy of Israel and the oppressor and persecutor of the weak; in short, he went out against the Sultan of Turkey of that day. And the Judge of all the earth and the God of battles, for His own deep ends, let that battle go against Josiah, till Josiah said, Have me away, for I am wounded. Being unsuccessful, as we say, Josiah is almost universally blamed for letting his tender heart take up the sword. But I, for one, am quite content to leave Josiah's tender-hearted statesmanship to the arbitrament of the last day. I, for one, will applaud Josiah till my applause is reversed by Him whose tender heart took Him also to His death. And till Jesus Christ from the great white throne condemns and sentences Josiah for his too tender heart, I shall continue to read this to myself on his tombstone in the valley of Megiddo:—This,

THE REMEMBRANCE OF JOSIAH IS LIKE THE PERFUME OF THE APOTHECARY, AND HIS NAME IS LIKE MUSIC AT A BANQUET OF WINE. FOR HIS PURE AND HOLY YOUTH JEHOVAH WAS HIS SHIELD IN THE HOUR OF TEMPTATION, TILL HE BEHAVED HIMSELF RIGHTLY IN THE CONVERSION OF HIS PEOPLE, AND TILL HE TOOK AWAY ALL THEIR ABOMINATIONS OF INIQUITY. HE DIRECTED HIS HEART TO THE LORD, AND HE ESTABLISHED THE WORSHIP OF GOD: AND ALL BECAUSE HIS HEART WAS SO TENDER. THE REMEMBRANCE OF JOSIAH IN JUDAH AND IN JERUSALEM IS LIKE THE PERFUME OF THE APOTHECARY, AND LIKE MUSIC AT A BANQUET OF WINE.

LVI

ELIJAH

THE prophet Elijah towers up like a mountain in Gilead above all the other prophets. There is a solitary grandeur about Elijah that is all his own. There is a mystery and an unearthliness about Elijah that is all his own. There is a volcanic suddenness, and a volcanic violence, indeed, about all Elijah's descents upon us and all his disappearances from us. We call him Elijah the Tishbite, but we are no wiser of that. We do not even know where Tishbe is. Elijah has neither father nor mother. As Elijah never died, so he was never born, as we are born. Elijah came from God, and he went to God. Elijah stood before God till God could dispense with and spare Elijah out of His presence no longer. Elijah's very name will tell you all that, and more than all that, concerning both Elijah and his father and his mother, Eli-jah—my God is Jehovah. You may know the hearts of fathers and mothers to some extent, even among ourselves, by the names they give to their children. And I leave you to judge what kind of a father and mother they must have been who so boldly coined out of Moses, and out of their own hearts, this magnificent name for their circumcised child. Elijah had a heavenly name, but he had, to begin with, but an earthly nature. Elijah was a man, to begin with, subject to like passions as we are. Elijah was a man, indeed, of passions all compact. We never see Elijah that he is not subject to some passion or other. A passion of scorn and contempt; a passion of anger and revenge; a passion of sadness and dejection and despair; a passion of preaching; a passion of prayer. Elijah was a great man. There was a great mass of manhood in Elijah. He was a Mount-Sinai of a man, with a heart like a thunderstorm. That man among ourselves who has the most human nature in him and the most heart; the most heart and the most passion in his heart; the most love and the most hate; the most anger and the most meekness; the most scorn and the most sympathy; the most sunshine and the most melancholy; the most agony in prayer, and the most victorious assurance that, all the time, his prayer is already answered—that man is the likest of us all to the prophet Elijah; that man has Elijah's own mantle fallen upon him. Only, alas! there is no such man among us. There is no man among us fit, for one moment, to stand like Elijah before God.

Now, whatever is the matter with us that God has not an Elijah among us, or anything like an Elijah, it is not that we are wanting in passions. We have all plenty of passions; and too much, since we are all so subject to our passions. What an ocean of all kinds of passions all our hearts are; and lashed with what winds without rest. What dark depths of self-love are in all our hearts. And what a master-passion is that same self-love. Self-love is a serpent; and, like the famous serpent in Scripture, it swallows up and swells out on all the other serpents of which our hearts are full. Yes; we all have passions enough to make us not Elijahs and Ahabs only, but angels in heaven, or devils in hell. And our passions are every day doing that within us. All the difference between Elijah and Ahab was in the subjection of their passions. Elijah was a man of immensely stronger passions than poor Ahab ever was; only Elijah's powerful passions all swept him up to heaven, whereas all Ahab's contemptible passions shouldered and shovelled and sucked him down to hell. Queen Jezebel, also, Ahab's wife, when she was still a woman-child, her passions were as sweet and pure and good and subject as were the passions of the Virgin Mary herself. The whole difference between Elijah and Ahab, and between Jezebel and the mother of our Lord was in their hearts' desires, till their hearts' desires grew up into all-consuming passions.

> On life's vast ocean diversely we sail,
> Reason the card, but passion is the gale.
>
> May I govern my passions with absolute sway,
> And grow wiser and better as my strength wears away.

And what a passionate preacher Elijah was. You know the story of the play-actor who scouted the minister because he dawdled over his prayers and his sermons as if he was ashamed of his message. 'We act our parts in dead earnest,' he said; 'and that is the reason that you have to sell your empty churches to us to make our theatres out of them.'

> Yea,
> This man's brow, like to a title-page,
> Fortells the nature of a tragic volume.
> Thou tremblest, and the whiteness of thy cheek
> Is apter than thy tongue to tell thy errand.

'Hear, O Lord, and have mercy upon me in this matter of preaching. Lord, be Thou my helper. Turn my dreamings,' implores the passionate Andrewes, 'into earnestness, my follies into cleansings of myself, my guilt into indignation, my past sin into all the greater fear for the future, my sloth into passionate desire, and my pollution into revenge. And enable me, O my God, to bend all my passion of faith, and love, and hate, and fear, revenge, and remorse, and what not, in upon my own salvation, and the salvation of my people!'

And then in prayer. The translators of the New Testament

tell us that they have preserved the Apostle James's passionate idiom in the margin of the text, 'Elias with all his passions prayed in his prayer.' And I, for one, am for ever deep in their debt for their so doing, for the prophetic and apostolic idiom in the margin takes possession of my imagination. It touches my heart; it speaks to my conscience and that because, after all these years of prayer, how seldom it is that we really 'pray in our prayers,' as the apostle tells us that the prophet prayed. We repeat choice passages of scripture in our prayers. We recite with studied pathos classical paragraphs out of Isaiah and Ezekiel. We praise one man and we blame another man in our prayers. We pronounce appreciations and we pass judgments in our prayers. We do everything in our prayers but truly pray. The Bible naturally shows a preference for men of like passions with itself; and the more of his passions any man puts into his prayer, the more space and the more praise the Bible gives to that man. Jacob was a prince in the passionateness of his prayer all that night at the Jabbok. What a tempest of passion broke upon the throne of God all that night. What a tempest of fear, and despair and remorse, and self-accusation, of all indeed that was within Jacob's passionate heart. Jacob's raging passions really tore him to pieces that terrible night in his prayer. His very thigh-bones were twisted and torn out of their sockets, and his strongest sinews snapped like so many silly threads. There was not on the face of the earth another night of passion in prayer like that for the next two thousand years. Esau, also, often halted upon his thigh. But that was with hunting too hard; that was with running down venison, and leaping hedges and ditches after his quarry. Esau wrestled with wild beasts with all his passions, but Jacob wrestled with the angel. Now, let any man among ourselves henceforth pray in his prayers like Jacob and Elijah: let any man among ourselves determine to put his passions into his prayers like Jacob and Elijah, and it will make him a new man. His heart, and all the passions of his heart, will, in that way, more and more be drawn off the things of this life, and will be directed in upon the great world that is within him, and above him, and before him. The heat of his heart will begin to burn after heavenly things. His passions, that have made him so impossible for men to live with, will now all become subdued, and softened, and sweetened till he will be like a little child in your hands. He was at one time so hard, so harsh, so impossible to please, so full of his own opinions and prejudices, so loud, and so forward, and so wilful. But you never hear him now, he so despises himself, and so honours, and respects, and yields up to you. Nothing in the world so renews a man as putting his passions into his prayers. This, in time, will make a saint of the very chief of sinners. This, in time, will turn a heart of stone into a heart of flesh. O why do we ministers not preach more about prayer, and about the employment of our own and our people's passions in prayer! But if your ministers do not so preach, and do not know the way—you are independent of them. There is a great literature of prayer, and it would splendidly and immediately repay and reward you and your households to have it in your hands every day.

But Elijah would not be the great lesson to us that he is if he were always Elijah, with all his passions at all times at a flame in his prayers. That no man may glory before God, after all that Elijah has done, we see him before he dies just as weak, and as downcast, and as embittered, and as unhappy as if he had never known how to subdue and subject and sanctify his passions. No. It is no strange thing that is happening to us when we sit under our juniper-bush and say, 'It is enough. Now, O Lord, take away my life, and for I am no better than my fathers.' Elijah was getting old. He was feeling lonely. His work seemed to him to have all come to nothing. Till death was now his only desire, and the grave his true resting-place. All men have their own dejections, and defeats, and despairs. But ministers far more than all other men. Partly from themselves; partly from the peculiar nature of their work; and partly from the deadly opposition to it in the world, and in the hearts of their people. What have I been spending all my life for? an old minister asks himself. Who is any better of all my work? Who is any holier or any happier, or whose house? Who is any less selfish, any less proud, any less worldly-minded, any less envious, any less ill-natured, any less fault-finding, any less evil-spoken? So we despond. So we repine. So we despair. So we sit and say after the triumphs, and the praises, and the hopes of our youth are all past, and our early successes are all over. It is enough. And now, O Lord, take away my life. But it is our pride. It is our self-will. It is our passions coming out of our prayers and coming in between us and our despisers, opposers, and persecutors. How much better did Samuel behave himself when he was deprived and dismissed and his work all forgotten. Samuel's wisdom and sweetness and absolute heavenly-mindedness never came out more than in his solitary and superseded old age, when he counselled and comforted the people, and said, God forbid that I should sin against the Lord in ceasing to pray for you; but I will still teach you the good and the right way. In this way Samuel showed Elijah the way to keep his old heart young to the end, and his spirit quiet, and good, and sweet, and beautiful. And it was prayer that did it; and it was putting all his remaining passions still into his prayers to his very end; and it was in that way that Samuel did it, and that Elijah at last learned to do it also.

For Elijah's passions all came back to all their first obedience, and to all their former splendid service, as he stood by Jordan and waited for his signal from the Lord. For, what was the chariot of Israel to Elijah that day, but Elijah's heart already in heaven? And what were those horses of fire that day, but all Elijah's passions all harnessed, in all their heaven-bounding strength, to that heavenly chariot? His faith, his fearlessness, his scorn of evil, his prayerfulness, his devotion to Israel and to God. Those horses of heavenly fire all spurned the earth as they stood and champed by the Jordan. And when the Lord would take up Elijah to Himself. All those horses of fire sprang with one leap up to heaven. And when Elisha saw it he cried, My father, my father, the chariot of Israel, and the horsemen thereof! And he saw him no more.

LVII

ELISHA

Elisha, the servant and the successor of Elijah, was the son of a prosperous farmer in Israel. Shaphat, the father of Elisha, was a man of substance, but, like all true Israelites, rich and poor, he had brought up his son Elisha to a life of hard work. And thus it is that we come upon Elisha standing in the office of superior over his father's ploughmen, while he is, at the same time, one of those same ploughmen himself. One spring day, when all Shaphat's ploughs were at work in the spring-time meadow, and Elisha's plough the foremost among them, Elijah, the old prophet, came up suddenly behind Elisha and cast his rough mantle over Elisha's shoulder. In a moment the young ploughman saw and understood what it was that had happened to him. Elijah had not spoken a single word to Elisha. But Elijah's solemn silent act was sufficiently clear and eloquent to Elisha. 'When a great teacher dies,' says Sir John Malcolm in his *History of Persia,* 'he bequeaths his patched mantle to the disciple that he most esteems. And the moment the elect disciple puts on the holy mantle he is vested with the whole power and sanctity of his predecessor. The mantles which were used by ascetics and saints have always been the objects of religious veneration in the East. The holy man's power is founded upon his sacred character, and that rests upon his poverty and contempt of worldly goods. His mantle is his all, and its transfer marks out his heir. Some of these sacred mantles can be traced for several centuries, and their value increases with their age.' This is an old and superstitious tradition now; but in the ploughed field of Abel-Meholah we are back at its very beginning and first performance, when Elijah comes up behind Elisha and casts his cloak of camel's hair over the shoulders of Shaphat's son. And, as if to make it impossible for himself ever to turn back from following Elijah, Elisha made a fire of the wood of his familiar plough, and slew his favourite oxen and made a feast of the flesh, and thereby proclaimed openly to all men that he had put his hand to another plough than that plough of wood, from which he would never draw back. Elisha burned his ships that day, as the Romans would have said. Shaphat, Elisha's father, was growing old, and Elisha would soon have inherited the rich meadow he was then working in; but, in a moment, all that was for ever changed; and Shaphat may now cast his husbandman's mantle over what young farmer he will; his son Elisha is henceforth dead to all that Abel-Meholah has to hold out to him. For the next fifty years Elisha is to be a spiritual ploughman in the Lord's meadows, which are the hearts and lives of the men of Israel.

Elijah's mantle is one of our most expensive proverbs, and so is Elisha's request for a double portion of his departing master's spirit. 'Ask what I shall do for thee,' said Elijah 'before I be taken away from thee.' And Elisha said, 'I pray thee, let a double portion of thy spirit be upon me.' Not the double of all the gifts and all the graces that Elijah had possessed and had so well employed. That is an impossible explanation of Elisha's petition. I can easily imagine Elijah feeling now that life was over with him, that he had been an unprofitable servant. All true men so feel. I can easily imagine Elijah seeking of God in prayer that his successor should be twofold, should be tenfold, more gifted and more successful than he had been. But I cannot imagine a humble and loyal soul like Elisha so insulting his master on his deathbed as to say to him: 'I hope to have double thy success to show when I come to die.' No; the thing is inconceivable. What Elisha really asked for was simply the fulfilment of what had been already promised him when Elijah's mantle fell on his shoulders. That act of Elijah was the sign and the seal of Elisha's adoption. And the adopted son had always allotted to him the double portion that belonged to the first-born. Not the double of what the adopting father possessed himself; for no man can put into his testament the double of what he has of his own. But he can double the portion that would properly have belonged to one of his younger children. And thus it is that, when it is put to him, Elisha simply, and dutifully, and humbly asks that the divine law of adoption and primogeniture may immediately begin to hold and to take effect in his spiritual sonship to the departing prophet.

The world and the church live and thrive and grow from generation to generation under the guiding and upholding hand of God. All the time that Elijah was repining and meditating death under the juniper tree, God was preparing the young ploughman of Abel-Meholah to wear Elijah's mantle, and to carry forward Elijah's work. And when we are prognosticating the headlessness and the collapse of the church when this man and that man shall have fallen asleep, all the time God has His hidden servants, quite well known to Him, and quite ready to take up this man's and that man's great office when they shall demit it. There may be to be seen following the spring plough in Strathmore or in the Lothians at this moment, some young man who shall be as well known and as great in a few years in Scotland as Elisha was in Israel. There are certainly at school, at college, in the shop, in the office, on the hills, in the mine, young men who, five-and-twenty years after this, shall be as great preachers, as great writers, as great statesmen, as great administrators, and as great discoverers as any of those who are now in such fame, and far better suited for the time to come. Elisha was not Elijah. But he was the gift of the living God to the living Israel of his day. And I would have you all keep your dejected hearts in perfect peace, sure of this, that God will look after both the church and the world far better than the most anxious-minded and censorious-minded of His people.

And let all our prophets, and all the sons of our prophets, go to school in manners and in morals to those fifty sons of the prophets in that day in Israel. Look at them as they hail and bow down before a better man than themselves, though he is as young as themselves, and withal, has not had their schooling for his office. There is blessing in store for Israel, from such young ministers. Elisha had been a ploughman till he became Elijah's servant. And, yet, in a moment, and without a murmur, the fifty sons of the prophets at once accept Elisha as the true successor of Elijah, and as their young master. The old men who had not had great success themselves did not cast up Elisha's youth to him when his success began, nor did the sons of the prophets keep up against him his humble origin, or his lack of letters. There must have been good Divinity Halls in those days when there were fifty probationers just come out of them of such humility, and admiration, and belief in better men than themselves. These prophetical graces are beautiful to us to read about at a distance, but they are far more beautiful to God when they are seen in everyday men like ourselves. Those fifty students must have had good tutors and governors in ministerial morals and in pastoral theology.

About dead men's mantles. Elisha's first instinct was to bury and blot himself out under Elijah's coat of camel's hair and his leathern girdle. And he did actually begin his public life wearing those ancient coverings and austere accoutrements. But Elisha was far too simple and far too sincere a man to continue long wound up in such cerements. He set out, and I do not wonder at it, in Elijah's mantle, and he did his first prophetical work in it; but he wore it awkwardly, and he soon laid it aside. Elisha was an altogether smaller and more homely man than Elijah, and he wisely preferred before long to put on much less startling and outstanding clothes. Elisha was a gentle, homely, kindly lowland minister; as unlike Elijah as the green meadows of Abel-Meholah were unlike the savage solitudes of mountainous Gilead. And we must not demand of our young preachers that they shall all stride out with the same step, and pronounce just with the same accent as the Elijah of our youth. We had Elijah, and he fulfilled his day, and did his work. And no men among us need more to be men of to-day, and not of yesterday, than they who preach the Word of God to us and to our children. Even the Elijah you so often go back upon, were he here again, he would not be exactly the same man, with exactly the same mantle, the hem and the hair of which you were so wont to kiss.

Every ill-brought-up boy who calls names at old people and at odd people must be reminded of those miserable boys and girls of Bethel who called bad names at Elisha till two she-bears came out of the wood, and tore forty and two children of them. The Areopagus on one occasion sentenced a Greek boy to death only for plucking out a quail's eyes, because, they said, if that boy was let live, he would do widespread cruelty and mischief when he grew up, and he had better die at once; and so they sent him to the executioner. On December the 21st, 1719, Thomas Boston writes this in his journal: A poor boy came into the house begging, having such a defect in his speech that he pronounced the words father and mother *fao* and *moa,* at which my wife and others smiling, desired him to speak over again what he had said. In the meantime my little daughter stood looking on with tears in her eyes and in great distress, and at length she came up to her mother, and said, 'Mother, did God make that laddie?' 'Yes, my dear, He did.' 'Will He not then be angry at us all for laughing at the laddie, for my lesson says, "He that mocketh at the poor, reproacheth his Maker"?' She was in mighty concern also to let the boy have some old clothes.

With all that the sacred writer has given us about Elisha, I am not satisfied. I would have liked some more about Elisha's father and mother. I always regret hearing Elisha calling Elijah his father, and no more word of honest Shaphat. Fathers, come with me, and let no man run away with our best name from us! Let no man, no, not Elijah himself, take our crown. Let us determine to be the fathers of our children in the spirit also. Let us be specially jealous of our best ministers, lest our children pass us by, and claim any other man whatsoever as their spiritual father. Let our children be able all their days to say—it was my father; it was my mother. We feed them, we clothe them, we send them to school, and we work and lay up for them. O let no other man, the very best, cast the mantle of the Christian calling and the Christian spirit on the shoulders of our children. Let us do that ourselves; let us do it early; let us do it now. Here am I and the children which Thou hast given me!

LVIII

NAAMAN

THE instructive story of Naaman is known to all. His valiantness in battle, his greatness with his master, and the high honour in which he was held among his own people; and, with all that, his incurable leprosy—in two or three of his most eloquent strokes the sacred writer sets Naaman most impressively and most memorably before our eyes. The little captive maid also who whispered to Naaman's wife, 'Would God my lord were with the prophet that is in Samaria, for he would recover him of his leprosy.' And, then, how Naaman came to Samaria with his horses and his chariot; how Elisha sent out and told him to go and wash seven times in Jordan; how Naaman was wroth and would not wash in Jordan, but went away home in a rage: how his excellent servants reasoned with their angry master and how he repented and went and washed in Jordan till his flesh came again like the flesh of a little child—all that is told in fourteen as solid and as eloquent verses as ever were written. They have a miraculous talent of style, those Old Testament authors. Our very best authors cannot hold the candle to them. And those who are counted worthy to stand second to those Old Testament artists have come to their skill by reading nothing else but their Bible day and night. But we have opened our Bible this night—not to study the excellent art of writing, excellent art as it is; but to seek in our Bible the salvation of our souls; without which salvation, all our writing, and all our reading, and every other art and science of human life, is but whitewashing a sepulchre, which all the time is full within of dead men's bones and all uncleanness.

With all his valiantness, and with all his honours, Naaman was nothing better all the while than a dead man. For Naaman was a leper. Naaman had all that heart of man could wish; but what of that, when he was what he was? Leprosy was feared and fled from in Israel as the stroke of God. Leprosy was the most fearful and the most hateful disease known to man. Leprosy was so loathsome, and so utterly incurable and deadly, that it was not looked on as an ordinary disease at all: but, rather, as a special creation in His anger, and a direct curse of God, both to punish sin, and, at the same time, to teach His people something of what an accursed thing sin really is; till the whole nature of leprosy and all the laws laid down for its treatment, and the miraculous nature of its so seldom cure, all combined to work into the imagination, and into the conscience, and into the heart, and into the ritual, and into the literature of Israel, some of her deepest lessons about the terrible nature and the only proper treatment of sin.

For sin is like leprosy in this, that it is the most mysterious, stroke-like, malignant, loathsome, and mockingly incurable of all our incurable ills. Sin is like Naaman's leprosy in this also, that a man is great with men, and honourable, and a mighty deliverer—but all the time he is a sinner. And all a sinner's life, and all his greatness, and all his honour, and all his praise is but dressing a dead body with rich ornaments, and sprinkling a sepulchre with sweet smells. It needed no divine grace in Naaman to teach him that he was a leper. Day and night; in the council-chamber and in the field; eating and drinking; waking and sleeping, Naaman was a leper. But it needs a wisdom, and a truth, and an experience, and a stage of salvation that few men have attained to, before a sinner knows that he is a sinner; really and truly knows it, as Naaman knew his leprosy. Some men do: one here and another there. If you have made the discovery that you are a leprous sinner: if you have found no figure that so well describes you as Naaman's leprosy,—then you have made the greatest discovery a man can make in this world. 'What was your greatest discovery, Sir James?' asked an interviewer of the discoverer of chloroform. 'That I am a sinner,' answered the saintly man, 'and that Jesus Christ is my Saviour.' Yes, that was out of all sight Sir James's greatest and most fruitful discovery, for that made him a great man with his Master; and it made him full of love and honour among all the best people in the land. You will not yet believe it, but you also begin to belong to the race of the greatest men that have ever lived when you begin to make the deadly discovery that you are a leper at heart. Nay; not only is that the beginning of all your true greatness; but your knowledge of sin all along to the end of life—that is the best measure of your true greatness. All our true greatness has been lost to us through sin; and it is in sin, and through sin, and by escaping out of sin, that we shall not only recover all our lost greatness but shall attain to a far greater greatness than that we had lost. I do not care a straw to go to see the greatest scholar, or the greatest author, or the greatest preacher, or the greatest soldier, or the greatest statesman. But I would go a long way to see the greatest sinner; to see and to converse with that man still on this earth who has the deepest knowledge of his own heart. The man who has made that discovery, and who is daily and hourly making that discovery, and who is every hour of every day acting God and man on that discovery—that is the man of all men to me. The fifty-first Psalm is David's masterpiece to me. Isaiah's greatest chapters to me are his fifth and his fifty-third. Paul's greatest passage is his immortal morsel of autobiography in the seventh of the Romans. Augustine's best book is his *Confessions* and John Bunyan's his *Grace Abounding,* and Jacob Behmen's his *Way to Christ*. 'Sin?' exclaims even our own Carlyle in indignation; 'the deadliest sin of all is to be conscious of no sin.' And so it is.

But, leprosy and all, Naaman was still a very proud man; for all the leprosy in the world will not make a proud man meek and lowly in heart. When Naaman was told how he could be made clean, because the prophet's counsel did not fit in with Naaman's prejudices and his sense of his own importance, he was wroth at Elisha, and went home, leprosy and all, in a rage.

'Behold, I thought, he will surely come out, and stand, and will call on the name of the Lord his God, and strike his hand over the place, and recover the leper.' And there are men among ourselves who go home in the same rage as often as they are told their deadly disease and the only way of recovery from it. With all your prepossessions and prejudices, many of you must know that you are not one step nearer anything that could be called salvation than ever you were. There is as much leprosy in your heart to-night as ever there was. And in your best moments you would give ten talents of silver, and six thousand pieces of gold, and ten changes of raiment to be for ever rid of it. What do you say just to give a trial to the things that hitherto have most angered you to hear them spoken about? The real spiritual nature of salvation has always been an unwelcome subject to you. Preaching you greatly enjoy, and you are a great judge of it. Naaman went to the prophet's house to tell him how to preach, and because the prophet did not take his lesson from Naaman, Naaman went home in a rage. My brethren, salvation is not cut to your pattern. Leprosy is not cured on your prescription; its true and only cure has laws, and rules, and obediences, and submissions, and sacrifices of its own that may all anger you to be told them, but it can be had in no other way. What do you say to humble yourself for once, and to try the thing that has hitherto most exasperated you to be tied down to it? All the chances are that your salvation lies out in the direction of far more secret prayer, far more self-denial, far less eating and drinking, far less talking, and far more submission of your opinions and habits of life to other men. It may lie in putting away all your present reading, and giving up much more of your time and attention to books that treat of the soul, its diseases, its discipline, and its salvation. I advise you to get over your temper, and to try that very way that you have up till now been so hot and so loud against. It will humble you to do it, and you are not a humble man; but if you ever come back from Jordan with your flesh like the flesh of a little child, you will be the foremost to confess that you had almost been lost through your pride, and your prejudice, and your ill-nature.

What a fool that man Naaman must have been! everybody has exclaimed over his history ever since his day. He did not deserve to be healed! Surely he was not so ill after all! Either he had not much leprosy upon him, or else he was a perfect madman to do as he did. Yes; but madman with pride, and self-importance, and self-will as he was, Naaman will stand up in the day of judgment and will condemn some of us who have his history before us; for, like him at one time, we do not even yet feel the full curse and deadliness of our sin, else we would do very differently with it. Other men who see what the things are that stand between us and the salvation of our souls are astounded at us. Naaman's very heathen servants were astounded at him, till they broke through all their fear of him and told him so. We sell our souls every day for such contemptible things; such a small outlay would buy us eternal life. Jacob bought his birthright by denying himself just a single mess of pottage. And all that stood between Naaman and perfect health and long life was just to ascend his chariot, and let himself be driven to Jordan, when his servants would have undressed him and dipped him seven times; and, ere ever he was aware, he would have come up out of the water as sweet as a child. O son of Naaman, the suicidal leper! Day after day, year after year, you go on selling the health, the strength, the sweetness, and the whole salvation of your soul for a thing that I may not name; it is so impossible to be believed. It is so mad in you, so self-murderous. The devil, who so deceives you, laughs before God at the price you put upon the blood of His Son, and upon the grace of His Spirit, and upon your own soul. 'My father,' his servant came near and said to Naaman, 'if the prophet had bid thee do some great thing, wouldest thou not have done it? How much rather, then, when he saith to thee: Wash, and be clean?'

But, to speak still more face to face. To put away all types, and figures, and metaphors, however true and terrible. You all know, surely, what the true leprosy is. You all know what the leprosy of your own soul is. It is sin; yes, it is sin. Or, rather, to speak still more true and plain to you, it is yourself. Sin is self. Your true leprosy is yourself. There is no leprosy, there is no sin, but yourself. Get yourself killed in your heart; and God, and love, and heaven, and holiness, and eternal life are all, from that moment, in you. Self is an evil mother big with children tenfold more the children of hell than herself. And her firstborn is your pride, and your anger, and your envy, and your ill-will, and your hatred of so many men around you. O leper! leper! go out with thy loathsome and deadly heart from among living men. Go to thy charnel-house at once; or else, for thou art still a man, and not yet fully and finally a devil, go wash in Jordan.

Go in God's name. Go in God's strength. Go in God's pity, and patience, and mercy. Go on the spot. Go this moment, and go every day, and every hour of every day, and, blessed be God, every moment, as often as thy self-filled heart again stirs and sins in thee. There is a fountain filled with blood. Filled, that is, with the humiliation, and the obedience, and the submission, and the whole life and death of the Son of God. O son of sin and Satan, O child of wrath, wilt thou not submit thyself to be saved? Wilt thou not so much as wash thyself? Wilt thou not say there is a fountain opened for sin and for uncleanness like mine? And wilt thou not go down into it continually, saying without ceasing: O Holy God. O pure, and clean, and sweet, and blessed Son of God. Pity a man made of sin. Pity this leper of all lepers. Pity, if Thou hast such pity, the most miserable man on the face of the earth. A man who, as Thou seest, does nothing before Thee but sin. O pity and spare me, my God, for my sin is ever before me. Oh, able to save to the uttermost, wash me, Saviour, or I die! 'How,' asks the disciple in Jacob Behmen's *Supersensual Life,* 'How shall I be able to subsist in all this anxiety and tribulation so as not to lose the eternal peace?' And the Master answers: 'If thou dost once every hour throw thyself by faith beyond all creatures into the abysmal mercy of God, into the sufferings of our Lord, and into the fellowship of His intercession, and yieldest thyself fully and absolutely thereunto, then thou shalt receive grace from above to rule over death and the devil, and to subdue hell and the world under thee. And, then, thou mayest not only endure in all manner of temptation, but be actually the better and the brighter because of all thy temptations.' Then went he down and dipped himself seven times in Jordan, according to the saying of the man of God, and his flesh came again like the flesh of a little child, and he was clean.

LIX

JOB

THE greatest of all the men of the East, as Job afterwards became, he began his life with having nothing. In his own lowly-minded words, Job was at one time poor even to nakedness. When he was at the top of his shining prosperity, and when he suddenly lost it all in one day, his utter desolation threw his mind back on his absolutely destitute youth. The Lord gave, he said, with splendid thankfulness and with splendid submission, and the Lord hath taken away; blessed be the name of the Lord. But, far worse than all his early poverty, and far more difficult to escape and to surmount, were the long-lived sins of his youth. I have been in the same great trespass, says old Bishop Andrewes, from my youth up, and even to this day. Perfect and upright, and one that feared God and eschewed evil, as Job had now for such a long time been, at the same time he tells us that the heels of his feet still left an accusing and an arresting mark behind him, whatever he did, and wherever he dwelt. Job had been freely and fully forgiven of God, but vengeance was still being taken of God on all Job's inventions, as God's way has always been with His best saints, and always will be. My sins are ever before me, was Job's continual confession made toward God; while, all the time, he held fast his integrity toward all men, and in the face of all men. To his three friends, who so cruelly accused him of hypocrisy, and who kept insisting that there must be some cloked-up sin in Job's present life that was the cause of all his terrible troubles, he replied with a magnificent and a conclusive vindication of his absolute innocence and perfect integrity. But, all the time, we see Job turning from all men to God and confessing, with the most poignant shame and sorrow, both his past sins and his present sinfulness. 'How many are mine iniquities and my sins! For Thou writest bitter things against me, and makest me to possess the iniquities of my youth. Thou puttest my feet also into the stocks, and lookest narrowly to all my paths. Thou settest a print on the heels of my feet. If I wash myself with snow water, and make my hands never so clean, yet Thou wilt plunge me into the ditch, and mine own clothes shall abhor me.' The truth is: Job is both guilty and not guilty. Job is both unclean and vile. Job is absolutely innocent of all that Eliphaz and his fellows insinuate and impute to him. The Philistines understand me not, says John Bunyan in his *Grace Abounding*. But Job is not without much sin in his past life, and much sinfulness in his present heart. And it is this—with his unparalleled sufferings, and with the incessant insinuations and insults of his three friends—it is all this that so racks and tortures Job's tender conscience, and so darkens and crushes his pious heart, and so embitters and exasperates, sometimes almost to rank blasphemy, his far too many defences of himself.

'How long have I to live?' said Barzillai to David, when, at his restoration to the throne, David invited the loyal, hospitable, Highland chieftain to a thanksgiving feast in Jerusalem. 'I am this day fourscore years old. Can thy servant taste what I eat or what I drink? Can I hear any more the voice of singing men and women?' And in like manner, when Job's sons and daughters said to their old father, 'Come to our feasts with us!'

Job answered them thus: 'No, my children. There is a time for everything. I am no longer young as you are. Rejoice,' said the genial old man, 'in the days of your youth. Go your way; eat the fat and drink the sweet, and send portions unto them for whom nothing is prepared.' Only, all the time, Job had not forgotten his own early days. He knew to his lasting cost that folly is bound up in a young man's heart, and that eating and drinking and dancing, more than anything else, lets all that folly out. And thus it was that Job's sons and daughters had no sooner set out to the days of their feasting and the nights of their dancing, than their father set himself to his days and nights of prayer on behalf of his children. And every morning and every evening till the days of their feasting were all gone about Job never ceased his sacrifices and intercessions in his children's behalf. For each one of his sons and daughters their old father offered a special sacrifice, and set apart for each a special diet of intercession. So much so, that there is not a father or a mother among us to this day to whom God has not often said, Hast thou, in this matter of thy children, considered my servant Job? No. We confess with pain and shame and guilt concerning our children, that Job here condemns us to our face. But we feel to-night greatly drawn, if it is not too late, to imitate Job henceforth in behalf of our children. We have not wholly neglected them, nor the Great Sacrifice in their behalf. But we have not remembered it and them together at all with that regularity, and point, and perseverance, and watchfulness, that all combined to make Job such a good father to his children, and such a good servant to his God. But if our children are still about us, and if it is not yet too late, we shall vow before God to-night that whilst they are still with us we shall not again so forget them. When they set out to school we shall look out of our windows after them, and we shall imagine and picture to ourselves the life into which they must all enter and cannot escape. We shall remember the streets and the playgrounds of our own schooldays, and the older boys and their conversations. And we shall reflect that the games, and sports, and talks of the playground will bring things out of our children's hearts that we never see nor hear at home. And, then, when they come the length of taking walking and cycling tours, and fishing and shooting expeditions; and, still more, when they are invited out to eat and to drink and to dance, till they must now have a latch-key of their own—by that time it is more than time we had done with all our own late hours, and had taken ourselves to almost nothing in this world but intercessory prayer. We shall not go with them, but we shall not sleep till they have all come home and shut the door to our hearing behind them. And we shall every such night, and in as many words, plead before God the sacrifice of Jesus Christ, for each several one of our own and our neighbours' children. We shall go over their names, one after another. We shall spread out our fears and our hopes before God. We shall go over their ages, their temperaments, their inherited virtues and vices. We shall call up and remember where we were living, and what we were doing at their age; and that will make us fall on our face and plead with God that the heels of our son's feet shall leave no such marks behind them as our feet have left. It had been better they had never been born; it were better they died even now than that they should live to possess the iniquities of their youth, and to be put into those terrible stocks that God still keeps for young sinners. And, then, when they come home late at night, and see his candle still burning in their father's room, without any one pointing it out to them, or casting it up to them, they will understand their father's wistful ways, and that will bring them to their own knees also for the day past, and for the night past, and for their own souls, and for the souls of their companions. Thus did Job and his sons and his daughters continually.

The curse that always waits in this world on controversy and contradiction has never been clearer seen than it is seen in Job's case. For never was so much shrewd truth, and so many truly pious positions, and so much divine and human eloquence heard on both sides, and from any other five debating men, as was heard all round Job's ash-heap. The authorities on these things tell us that the debating in the Book of Job is the most wonderful piece of genius that has ever been heard or read since debating genius was. And, yet, such is the malignant and incurable curse of all controversy, even at its best, that Job and all his four friends seem sometimes as if they are to be consumed one of another—out of the same mouth so much blessing and so much cursing both proceed. If Job could have but endured to the end the near neighbourhood, and the suspicious looks, and the significant gestures, and the open broadsides of his four friends, 'that daily furnace of men's tongues,' as Augustine has it, Job would have been far too patient and far too perfect for an Old Testament saint. For, till Christ came, no soul was ever made such a battle-ground between heaven and hell, as Job's soul was made. Job's sorrows came not in single spies, but in battalions. Like the Captain of Salvation Himself, Job, His forerunner, took up successful arms against a whole sea of sorrows, and he would have won every battle of them all had he only been able to bear up under the suspicious looks and the reproving speeches of his four friends. But what Satan could not do with all his Sabeans, and all his Chaldeans, and all his winds from the wilderness to help him, that he soon did with the help of the debating approaches and the controversial assaults of Eliphaz, and Zophar, and Bildad, and Elihu. Oh, the unmitigable curse of controversy! Oh, the detestable passions that corrections and contradictions kindle up to fury in the proud heart of man! Eschew controversy, by brethren, as you would eschew the entrance to hell itself. Let them have it their own way. Let them talk. Let them write. Let them correct you. Let them traduce you. Let them judge and condemn you. Let them slay you. Rather let the truth of God itself suffer, than that love suffer. You have not enough of the divine nature in you to be a controversialist. He was oppressed, and He was afflicted, yet He opened not His mouth; He is brought as a lamb to the slaughter, and as a sheep before her shearers is dumb, so He opened not His mouth. Who, when He was reviled, reviled not again; when He suffered, He threatened not: by whose stripes ye were healed. Heal me, prays Augustine again and again, of this lust of mine of always vindicating myself. Read Santa Teresa's advice about self-excusing.

But, splendid, and, to this day, unapproached composition as the Book of Job is; and, magnificent victory of faith and patience as Job at last achieved; at the same time, the whole tragedy, down to its completion and coronation, is all displayed on an immensely lower stage of things than are a thousand far greater tragedies at present in progress among ourselves. For, after all, both Job's trials, and his triumphs of faith and patience also, savour somewhat too much of this present world. Job suffers first the loss of his oxen, and his asses, and his sheep, and his camels, and his servants; and then, with that, the loss of his sons and daughters; after which the patriarch is smitten in his own body with such a dreadful disease that he is more like a rotten carcass than a living man. All of which was surely tribulation enough for that day and that dispensation. But the fatal loss and the absolute despair of ever attaining to any true holiness of heart; to any true and spiritual love either to God or man; that is a trial of faith and patience to some men in our day that Job with all his battalions of trials knew nothing about. The Lord chastens some men among us with a heart so full of the blains, and boils, and elephantiasis of spiritual sin that a single day of it would have driven Job downright mad. Under it, in his day, Job would have cursed God, and died. But let those among us who are God's elect to the sanctification of the Spirit take comfort. And let them have patience; ay, and far more patience than all the patience of Job, even as they are called to endure far more than all the accumulated losses and all the intolerable diseases of Job. Let them be absolutely sure that when God has sufficiently tried them, they, too, shall come forth as gold. Behold, we count them happy which endure. Ye have heard of the patience of Job, and have seen the end of the Lord; that the Lord is very pitiful, and of tender mercy. The time is long; but the thing is true. Behold, I am vile; what shall I answer Thee? I shall lay my hand upon my mouth. I have heard of Thee by the hearing of the ear; but now mine eye seeth Thee. Therefore, I abhor myself, and repent in dust and ashes. It was when Job had been taught of God to see and to say all that, as never before; it was then that the Lord took pity and turned the captivity of Job. And it will just be when you both see and feel all that; and that a thousand times clearer and a thousand times keener than Job could either see it or feel it; it will just be then that the Lord will turn your captivity also till you will be like men that dream. For I know that my Redeemer liveth, and that He shall stand at the latter day upon the earth. And though after my skin worms destroy this body, yet in my flesh shall I see God. Whom I shall see for myself, and mine eyes shall behold, and not another; though my reins be consumed within me. For the which cause I also suffer these things; for I know in whom I have believed, and am persuaded that He is able to keep that which I have committed unto Him against that day. For I reckon that the sufferings of this present time are not worthy to be compared with the glory which shall be revealed in us. Be ye also patient, and stablish your hearts, for the coming of the Lord draweth nigh.

LX

JONAH

The Prophet Jonah was both the elder son and the unmerciful servant of the Old Testament. He was the elder son. For, as he came nigh to the house, he heard music and dancing. And he called one of the servants, and asked him what these things meant. And he said to him, Thy brother is come; and thy father hath killed the fatted calf, because he hath received him safe and sound. And he was angry, and would not go in; therefore, his father came out and entreated him. And the Lord entreated Jonah to leave his withered gourd and his sunbeaten booth, and to come in and share the joy of the spared city. Jonah was the unmerciful servant of that other New Testament parable also. O thou wicked servant, I forgave thee all that debt, because thou desiredst me: shouldest not thou also have had compassion on thy fellow-servant, even as I had pity on thee?

Everybody has the Book of Jonah by heart. How the word of the Lord came to Jonah, Arise, go to Nineveh, that great city, and cry against it, for their wickedness is come up before me. And how Jonah fled to Tarshish, and would not go to Nineveh; and how, on going down to Joppa, he found a ship going to Tarshish; so he paid the fare thereof, to go down to Tarshish from the presence of the Lord. The runaway prophet parted with far more than his proper passage-money that day. He paid the advertised fare in the current Joppa coin, with the image and superscription of Jeroboam II. stamped upon it. But no booking-clerk in Joppa could have counted up to Jonah all it would cost him all his future life on earth to have fled to Tarshish from his duty to Nineveh, and from the presence of the Lord his God.

Dr. Pusey tells us that the ships of Tarshish corresponded very much to the great East Indiamen of the days of his youth. And that to 'break the ships of Tarshish with an east wind' was a sailors' proverb for a terrible storm among the seafaring folk of those ancient days. But she would need to be a far more skilfully constructed, and a far more solidly built, and a far more scientifically navigated vessel than even an English East Indiaman that would engage to carry a disobedient prophet away from his post, and to land a guilty sinner in a harbour where God's hand would not hold him. As it was, the ship of Tarshish now in question soon began to give forth signs that she was not chartered to carry to Tarshish such a contraband cargo as that prophet of God was who now lay in her sides fast asleep. For no sooner was she well away to sea than the Lord sent out a mighty wind against that guilty ship, till every moment it seemed to all on board that she would go to the bottom. You may think the mariners to have been too superstitious, but you must judge gently of a screw of heathen men taken so suddenly between the jaws of death. Come, they said, this is no common storm. Come, therefore, and let us cast lots, that we may know for whose cause this evil is come upon us. Did you ever hold your breath while God and man were casting the discovering lots of life or death over you? What is thine occupation? And whence comest thou? What is thy country, and of what people art thou? I am an Hebrew; and I fear the Lord, the God of Heaven, which hath made the sea and the dry land. Why hast thou done this? And what shall we do unto thee? And he said unto them, Take me up, and cast me into the sea; so shall the sea be calm unto you; for I know that it is for my sake that this great tempest is come upon you. So they took up Jonah, and cast him forth into the sea; and the sea ceased from her raging.

Before we leave this remarkably-written chapter of this every way remarkable little book, let me again call your attention to the power and the piety of the Bible style. 'The Lord hurled out,' as old Coverdale excellently translates it, 'a great wind into the sea.' And Jonah himself says, speaking of that sea long after, 'Thou didst cast me into the deep; and all Thy waves and all Thy billows passed over me.' The science of storms was still in its first infancy in Jonah's day; but even if it had already attained a greater maturity and sure-footedness than it has come to down even to our own day, that would not have debased, or in any way undeified, this sacred writer's so strong and so splendid style. The advance of science does not involve the retreat of religion. Nor does the uniformity and harmony of Nature enable her to dispense with the sleepless oversight of her Creator. The heavens may become still more astronomical than they yet are, without that making them any the less conspicuously the immediate movement of the Divine Hand. And the sea herself will yet be found to ebb and flow, and toss and storm, according to fixed and foreseen laws, without thereby blotting out God's footprints in the deep, or causing any less praise to arise to Him from a smooth sea or any less prayer from a storm. Our meteorology has still a multitude of confused and restless phenomena to register, and a great mass of carefully-taken inductions to reduce to a rule: but, all the time, our Bible keeps impressing upon us that bad weather overtook Jonah for his bad behaviour; and that his disobedience before God had disturbed an equilibrium that was far too delicately poised for any earthly instrument of heat or cold, or dry or moist, to take account of.

That terrible storm arose because of quite open and quite easily ascertainable disturbances in the surrounding and overhanging atmosphere. Yes; most certainly and most indisputably it did. But it also arose,—the less reason does not deny the greater, nor does the proximate cause supersede the ultimate,—

it also, and much more, arose, says the word of God, because there was a controversy being carried on that day between God and His vagabond servant. Saints and sinners, prophets and mariners, are not made for the sake of the sea and the sky, but the sea and the sky are made for the sake of saints and sinners. Seas and skies and storms and fair weather all work together under the most complex and the most majestic laws for our good. Every disobedient sinner suddenly startled out of his sleep at midnight is wiser than all his teachers when he repents, and prays, and vows, and refuses to be comforted by the most correct barometric calculations. There is the making of a rare man of science in that young transgressor who wakens with a start, and cannot sleep for fear as the Great White Throne flashes into his prayerless room, and the last trump makes his sinful bed to shake.

After the terrible tempest, and the still more terrible outcome of the sin-discovering lots, and after his being taken up and cast out by the mariners into the raging sea, and by God into the belly of hell, and after his life was brought up from corruption, and his prayer came into God's holy temple; after all that you would have said that Jonah, so purified in such a furnace, would now be the best prophet that God had ever had. He will be the very best ambassador that could possibly be sent to the king of Nineveh. With a great joy in God Jonah will be an ambassador to beseech the king of Nineveh and all his nobles and all his people to be reconciled to the righteous God of Israel. He had so tasted the bitterness of death in his own soul; and, then, after that, he had so tasted that the Lord is gracious—Jonah will preach repentance with a will. Yes. He who had been three days and three nights in such remorse was surely the very preacher to be sent to a people who were, every man of them, within forty days of destruction. Come and see a man who has just come up out of hell, whispered the trembling people of Ravenna to one another, as Dante staggered through their streets. Come, said the men of Nineveh, and hear what the prophet from Israel has to say to our city, for he has just been vomited out of the fish's belly to preach repentance to us, and to our city.

Till the people of Nineveh believed God, and proclaimed a fast, and put on sackcloth, and turned every one from his evil way, and from the violence that was in their hands. And till God saw their works, that they turned from their evil way: and God repented of the evil that He had said He would do unto them: and He did it not.

But it displeased Jonah exceedingly, and he was very angry.

And he said, Therefore now, O Lord, take, I beseech Thee, my life from me; for it is better for me to die than to live. I do well to be angry, even unto death. What ails Jonah? Why is God's prophet in such a passion? Why is it better for Jonah to die than to live? Even Calvin confesses that he suspects some of his own explanations and apologies for Jonah to be but specious pretences, as they are. Jonah would thank no man for his specious apologies for him. Jonah did not write his noble book in an apologetic interest. He wrote his book in sackcloth and ashes. And, as it was written, so it must be read, if it is not to be read in vain: if it is not to be wholly misread, and its lessons wholly lost.

Biting my truant pen,
Beating myself for spite,
Fool, said my muse to me,
Look in thy heart and write.

Jonah was exceedingly displeased, and he was very angry at the repentance and deliverance of Nineveh, because, like all his people in the house of Israel, he both feared and hated Nineveh with his whole soul. Nineveh, as Jonah knew, was predestinated and prepared, and prophesied of God to be the fast-coming scourge and the cruel prison-house of the conquered and captive Israel. And, such was the power and the policy of Nineveh, and such was the sin and the weakness of Israel, that Jonah could look for not one atom of hope for his country unless it was in the great and insufferable wickedness of Nineveh, and in the swift and sure judgment of God against Nineveh. And thus it was that every report that came across the wilderness of the increasing wickedness of Nineveh, Jonah rejoiced in that, and took comfort out of that both for himself and for his people. It was the best thing that could happen to Jonah when the word of the Lord came to him and said, Arise, go to Nineveh, that great city, and cry against it, for their wickedness is come up before me. Jonah's heart beat high with hope that Nineveh was now so near her destruction. And if only all possibility of her repentance and reformation could be kept back from Nineveh for forty days, then all might yet be well with Jonah and with his foredoomed people. But, with such a God as his God was, Jonah had no security. With a God so given to mercy at the first sign of repentance in a sinner, Jonah felt that Israel was not safe till Nineveh was completely destroyed, and for ever blotted out. If I go and preach that preaching to them; if I go and warn and alarm them; and if they repent and turn them to God; then it were better I were dead. Perish my prophet's place: perish the presence of God and all, rather than that I should take a single step to preach repentance to Nineveh! And Jonah rose up to flee to Tarshish from the presence of the Lord, with the result that all the world knows. And, then, when he was shut up to choose between preaching in Nineveh, or making his bed in the belly of hell; and, then, when his compulsory preaching ended as he felt sure it would end—it displeased Jonah exceedingly, and he was very angry. 'Were it known to us,' says Dr. Pusey, 'that some European or Asiatic people were to carry our own people captive out of our land, more than would be willing to confess it of themselves, would still inwardly rejoice that such a calamity as the earthquake of Lisbon befell the capital of that people.' Ay, and far short of our captivity, let any Continental people, by the education and the industry of their workmen, threaten to take away some of our foreign markets from us, and what an outburst of scorn and indignation will immediately sweep over our land. What is that upstart Germany that she should make better merchandise and sell it cheaper than England! What is that volatile France that she should with such insistence demand what we intend to do in Egypt! And what is our secular rival Russia that she should seek an outlet to any ocean east or west! Does Britannia not rule the waves by Divine right and by her ironclad fleet! Let England expand and increase, and let all the other nations of the earth keep silence. It displeased Jonah exceedingly that the Lord had not destroyed Nineveh, and he was very angry. And not only between contending and competing nations, but much more so between contending and competing churches. With what Jonah-like displeasure do we Free Churchmen and Dissenters hear that an Established Church is prospering, and with what a like uneasiness do State Churchmen read that our Sustentation Funds stand firm. We hear much worse news than that a certain church is likely to have to withdraw from some of her mission-fields because her people will not support her work. We are not overwhelmed with sadness when we read of a morning how her greatest orators drew but a thin house on that subject last night. Better the heathen perish than that such prosperiy should attend the labours of our rival. Better that the whole city lapsed than that her communion-roll should so run over. How angry Jonah is still made—he never forgives you—if you have any good to say of any other church than his own, or of any party in his own church than his own party. Till you come down to this, —if you have any good to say of any man but himself. Poor

Jonah! who had to make his choice between the belly of hell and the possible repentance, and preservation, and prosperity of Nineveh. But far poorer, and far more to be both blamed and pitied, you and I who have to make our choice between that same arrest and imprisonment and a life of service and of continual prayer and good-will for all our enemies. Behold, I will move them to jealousy with those which are not a people. I will provoke them to anger with a foolish nation!

John Calvin is certainly correct when he says that Jonah had far more respect to his own reputation as a prophet of the divine judgment to Nineveh than he had either to the good of Nineveh or to the glory of God. And we are all like Jonah in that respect. Our reputation is our first and our chief regard in all that we do. At any rate, when I watch the working of my own heart in this matter, and then write honestly out of my own heart, this is what I am compelled to write: I am Jonah. In the matter of my own reputation as a preacher, that is. For I used to say, Let me die first before I am eclipsed by another in my pulpit, and among my people. I fought with a Jonah-like fierceness against the remotest thought of my reputation ever passing over, in my day at any rate, to another. I kept my eyes shut to the decay going on around my pulpit till I could shut my eyes to it no longer. And then, when the proper cure came for that decay, how unwelcome at heart all the time that cure was to me. Jonah was exceedingly displeased at the success of his mission to Nineveh, and I myself have taken a part in missions in my ministry also, the success of which sometimes makes me sick at heart. 'I beseech Thee now, O God'—they are Augustine's words—'to reveal me to myself still more than Thou hast yet done; so that I may confess myself to my brethren, who have promised to pray for me.' 'And those things, my brethren'—they are Paul's words—'I have in a figure transferred to myself for your sakes, that ye might learn in me not to think of men above that which is written. We are fools for Christ's sake, but ye are wise in Christ; we are weak, but ye are strong; ye are honourable, but we are despised'—and deserve to be.

But Jonah came to himself again during those five-and-twenty days or so, from the east gate of Nineveh back to Gath-hepher, his father's house. 'He travels the fastest who travels alone.' Week after week, Sabbath day after Sabbath day, alone with God and his own thoughts in that sacred wilderness made Jonah another man. So much so, that by the time that Jonah crossed the Jabbok, and spent the night at Peniel, Jonah was prepared not only to go to whatever work God sent him, but far more than that, and far better than that, Jonah was now prepared to pay his vow, and to write his book, and to say in every humiliating chapter of it—Come and hear, all ye that fear God; I will declare what He hath done for my soul. And, long before the first day of atonement after his flight to Tarshish came round, Jonah had his autobiography ready to bind it with cords to the horns of the altar. And thus it is that we have now lying open before us to this day the very identical psalm that Jonah sang every new morning on his way home from Nineveh to the land of Israel. And a splendid and a fruitful psalm it is for the use of all redeemed and restored sinners, and especially for the use of all redeemed and restored ministers of such sinners. I cried by reason of mine affliction to the Lord, and He heard me. Out of the belly of hell cried I, and Thou heardest me. I am cast out of Thy sight, yet will I look again toward Thy holy temple. I went down to the bottoms of the mountains; the earth with her bars was about me for ever; yet hast Thou brought up my life from corruption, O Lord my God. They that observe lying vanities—their own reputation, that is—forsake their own mercy. But I will pay that that I have vowed. Salvation is of the Lord.

LXI

ISAIAH

It was the day of atonement in the Temple. And a sadder day of atonement had never dawned on Jerusalem. For King Uzziah, one of the best kings Jerusalem had ever seen, had been struck of the Lord with leprosy but yesterday. For fifty years Uzziah had reigned in Jerusalem, and had done judgment and justice till he was accepted of his people as almost the promised Messiah Himself. But his great services, and his great successes, and his great honours had all exalted and intoxicated Uzziah's heart till he fell in his old age into what was the unpardonable sin of the Old Testament. And thus it was that on that atonement day he lay in a lazar-house waiting for his death and burial, a castaway from before both God and man. And thus it was that all Judah and Jerusalem were afflicting their souls that day because of the fall of their aged king, and because of his hopeless leprosy. And thus it was that Isaiah also, the son of Amoz, came up to the Temple that day clothed with sackcloth, and with ashes upon his head, and with the leper's rag upon his upper lip. You speak of your preachers, and you praise their power of imagination, and their eloquence, and their dramatic passion, and the way they sink and lose themselves in their work. But if you had lived in Israel in those days you would have seen imagination, and eloquence, and dramatic passion, and all else to astonish you. You would have seen Elijah running with girded-up loins before Ahab's chariot from Mount Carmel to the entrance of Jezreel, while the little cloud like a man's hand made the heavens black with wind and with a great rain. And then you would have seen the same prophet in his old age casting his mantle in silence on the shoulders of Elisha the son of Shaphat, as he ploughed in his father's field with the twelfth yoke of oxen. At another time, you would have seen the prophet Jeremiah hiding his girdle in the hole of a rock of Euphrates till it was marred so that it was profitable for nothing. Again, you would have seen the same sad prophet preparing a prophecy as he stood in the potter's house while the potter wrought a work on the wheels. Again, the same prophet at another time took a potter's earthen bottle, and taking with him of the ancients of the people, and of the ancients of the priests, he brake the bottle in the valley of Hinnom and said, This will I do to Jerusalem, saith the Lord. At another time Jeremiah made him bonds and yokes upon his neck, and even went up into his pulpit with the bonds and the yokes upon his neck. At another time he buys a field in Anathoth and weighs the money, and subscribes the evidence, and takes witnesses, and seals the purchase according to law and custom, and then takes that field in Anathoth for his text. And, then, toward the end of his ministry, this same prophet wrote in a book all he had ever said about Babylon, and bound a stone to the book, and cast it into the river Euphrates, and said, Thus shall Babylon sink, and shall not rise again from the evil that the Lord shall bring upon her. And you would have seen Ezekiel actually lying on his right side for three hundred and ninety days, while he ate his bread off the dunghill, and thus preached the hardness of the famine that the Lord would send upon his people for their sin. And again we read in Ezekiel: I did so as I was commanded; I brought forth my stuff by day, as stuff for captivity, and in the even I digged through the wall with my hands; I brought it forth in the twilight, and I bore it upon my shoulder in their sight. And, in like manner, with all the passion and sin and shame of the future foremost prophet of God, Isaiah, the son of Amoz, put the leper's filthy rag upon his lip, and took up all Uzziah's sin and misery upon his heart, and went and stood beside the altar that day of atonement in the Temple. Then said

I, Woe is me! for I am undone; because I am a man of unclean lips, and I dwell in the midst of a people of unclean lips; for mine eyes have seen the King, the LORD of hosts. Then flew one of the seraphim unto me, having a live coal in his hand, which he had taken with the tongs from off the altar: and he laid it upon my mouth, and said, Lo, this hath touched thy lips; and thine iniquity is taken away, and thy sin purged. Also I heard the voice of the Lord saying, Whom shall I send, and who will go for us? Then said I, Here am I: send me. And thus it was that that day of atonement for King Uzziah's leprosy was the day of Isaiah's call to be the prophet of the Lord to the leprous people of Jerusalem. The son of Amoz 'offered himself to great inspiration by means of great humiliation,' as Pascal so often repeats it, and so delights to repeat it.

'Whom shall I send? And who will go for us?' Why does the Lord ask that question with such anxiety when He has all these shining seraphs standing at His side, and each one of them with six wings? Why was Isaiah, the son of Amoz, a man of such unclean lips, and a man so woeful and undone, so accepted, and so sent? Seraphs, not sinners, should surely be the preachers of such holiness as that of the God of Israel, and the heralds of such a Saviour—that is what we would have expected. But God's thoughts in these things are not as our thoughts. It was not a seraph burning with heavenly love that was sent to preach to Jerusalem in Uzziah's day, but a young man who but a moment before had been full of leprosy to his lips, and laden to the earth with his own and his people's sin. It was Isaiah, the son of Amoz, who took boldness to say, Here am I, send me. And it was to that same Isaiah that the Lord said, Go and tell this people. And this has always been God's way in choosing and in ordaining and in sending both prophets, and psalmists, and priests, and preachers for His Church on earth. Only once did God choose a completely sinless preacher. Always, but that once, God has chosen sinful men; and, not seldom, the most sinful of men He could get to speak to their fellow-men about sin and salvation.

Gabriel might come with his six wings to announce to Mary that the fulness of time had come and that the Word was to be made flesh, but it was John, who was less than the least in the kingdom of heaven, who was sent to preach repentance to the vipers of his day, and to urge them to flee from the wrath to come. And, just as for the awakening and the warning of sinners, so for the edification and the comfort of saints. 'For every high priest is taken from among men, who can have compassion on the ignorant, and on them that are out of the way; for that he himself also is compassed with infirmity.' Isaiah, accordingly, of all men on the face of the earth at that moment, and of all angels in heaven, was the man chosen of God to preach repentance to Jerusalem, and to prophesy to her, as never before, the coming of her Messiah. And he preached on all these matters as no angel in all heaven could have preached. He preached as only a leper could preach to his brother lepers, and as only one undone man could preach to other undone men. Just hear him in his first sermon. 'The ox knoweth his owner, and the ass his master's crib. Ah! sinful nation, a people laden with iniquity, a seed of evil-doers. Why should ye be stricken any more? The whole head is sick, and the whole heart faint. From the sole of the foot even unto the head there is no soundness in it; but wounds and bruises and putrefying sores.' All God's seraphs taken together could not preach like that. It takes a great sinner to preach as well as to hear like that. You must call, and ordain, and inspire a leper if you would have passion in your pulpits like that. And you must be lepers yourselves to put up with passion in your pulpits like that. You cannot have preaching like that from your commonplace men, and from your commonplace sinners. You must have a man of men to see, and to feel, and to say things like that. And then, on the other hand, no seraph of them all, with all his eyes and with all his wings, had seen down so deep, and had come up so close to the holiness of God as Isaiah had seen and had come close. The seraphs cry Holy, Holy, Holy, to one another, but they do not know what they are saying. The seraphs are innocent children. And He whom they so innocently praise charges His seraphs with folly. But, 'Woe is me! for I am undone!' The Lord likes to hear that. He takes great pleasure in that. He bows down from His high throne at the sound of that. He sees what pleases Him in every syllable of that. With that young man will I dwell, He says to Himself, as He sees and hears Isaiah on that day of atonement. This young preacher, then, having seen both sin and holiness as no seraph ever saw these terrible things, proceeds in his sermon in this way: 'Wash you, make you clean; cease to do evil, learn to do well; judge the fatherless, plead for the widow. Come now, let us reason together, saith the Lord: though your sins be as scarlet, they shall be as white as snow: though they be red like crimson, they shall be as wool.' Every syllable of all that is out of Isaiah's own experience. Preaching like that never yet came out of the schools of the prophets, any more than it ever came out of the mouth of an angel. Isaiah had done it all to himself, and had had it all done to him of God. From unclean, he had washed him and made himself clean. From doing evil, he had put away the evil of his doings from before God's eyes. He had judged the fatherless, and he had pleaded for the widow. We hear him doing all that in tremendous words in this very sermon. And then the Lord had commanded His most evangelical seraph to take a live coal with the tongs from off the altar till Isaiah's iniquity was taken away and his sins purged, and till all Jerusalem knew that a prophet of the Lord had arisen among them.

Saint Jerome called Isaiah the evangelical prophet, and it was a very happy hit of the great translator. But we are entangled with a whole net-work of questions about the evangelical prophet that had not yet arisen in men's minds in Jerome's day. Are there *two* Isaiahs bound up together in this great evangelical book? Or is it the same son of Amoz we have here from the first chapter to the last? I do not know. I am like Mr. Spurgeon: my heart leans to one Isaiah, but the facts must be heard. And I shall resist to the death every attempt to keep the facts from being heard by those who are able to hear them. But I shall also claim for them and for myself that the common people shall be allowed to come to church to worship God without being teased and tormented about the age and authorship of this and that chapter of Holy Scripture. I shall take it for granted to-night, therefore, that the name of the son of Amoz may, with the utmost confidence and the very best propriety, be used here of the whole of his sixty-six bold and eloquent chapters. I shall always say 'Isaiah' here, just as the New Testament, and Jerome, and the universal Church of Christ has said 'Isaiah' about this book from the beginning down to our own day.

The now well-known name that Jerome first gave to Isaiah out of his cave at Bethlehem is a great name. There is no greater name that Old Testament prophet or New Testament preacher can bear. You will all think that you know quite well already how great a name Jerome's name to Isaiah was. But there is nothing that we know less than just those things that we think we know so well that we do not need to know any more about them. Feeling very sure that I did not know all that Jerome meant in his great name that he gave to Isaiah, I took down Dr. Murray's New English Dictionary, and turned to the part containing the word 'evangelical.' All who are able should order Dr. Murray's magnificent dictionary. It is a patriotic act to order it. It is to support the best scholarship of our land and our day to order it. And it is nothing less than a liberal education to have it delivered every three months at your door. You can have no idea what an ancient, what a noble, what a deeply-rooted, and what a far branching name that was that Jerome gave to Isaiah till you have read through the seven quarto columns that Dr. Murray, with such exact scholarship, and with such exquisite carefulness, gives to it. Beginning with Isaiah, the greatest preachers have all along been evangelical preachers. There is everything in the Evangel of the grace of God and of the work of Christ to make every man who preaches it a great preacher: and, besides the Evangel, there is nothing to inspire, or to uplift, or to empower and embolden any preacher. From Isaiah to Spurgeon the evangelical succession has run on through Paul, and Augustine, and Luther, and Calvin, and Knox, and Rutherford, and Baxter, and Bunyan, and Edwards, and Wesley, and Chalmers. And the great doctrines that have made all those great men such great preachers are all what we call the doctrines of grace. They are very bold doctrines; but then, they were all given by divine inspiration to Isaiah and to Paul, and they are all backed up in the preacher of our day by the authority of the Word of God, and by the testimony of the Spirit of God, and by the deepest and best and surest experiences of nineteen centuries both of the best preaching and the holiest life. They are such doctrines as—the image of God in the soul of man; the dreadful depravity and loathsome corruption of the soul of man by reason of original and indwelling sin; the spotless heart and life, and the sin-atoning death, of Jesus Christ; the mission and work of the Holy Ghost in the spiritual enlightenment of the soul, and its new birth to God and holiness; and the gradual but sure sanctification of the renewed soul to the fulness of eternal life for ever. Isaiah did not preach explicitly, and in as many words, all these evangelical doctrines, but they are all latent and involved in his preaching; and had he lived in our day he would have preached them all as boldly and as unceasingly as Wesley or Spurgeon preached them. The great evangelical books you all know, by name at least; the great evangelical hymns we sing in our families and in our own hearts every day; and the great evangelical hopes form great part of our evangelical preaching to you every Sabbath-day.

John Foster has one of his masterly Essays entitled, 'The Aversion of men of Taste to Evangelical Religion.' It is a piece of such great intellectual power on some of the besetting sins of evangelical preachers that all we who are evangelical preachers, and all you who are evangelical people, should read it till we have all laid it up in our hearts, as our evangelical catechism has it, and have practised it in our lives. John Foster was a preacher himself of such intellectual strength, and depth, and suggestiveness that I should have included his name in my too rapid enumeration of the great names of the evangelical succession. But many great names belong to that shining succession who would not by everybody be included in it. Law for one; Newman, one of Law's spiritual children, for another. I am bold to include Newman, for there is not a bolder sermon on substitution in the English language than Dr. Newman's post-Anglican sermon on 'The Mental Sufferings of our Lord in His Passion.' I was proceeding to say that Isaiah's style, so to call it, is one of the secrets of his so splendid and so abiding power. The Evangel of Salvation was his one goodly pearl, to buy which he had sold all; and then he always set that so goodly pearl in the shining casket of his superb style. 'In every kind of discourse,' says Dante in *The Banquet,* 'the speaker ought to think of what will be sure to charm his hearers'—a rhetorical rule that the eloquent author of the *Divine Comedy* never neglected to observe and obey. 'Because,' he says, 'if a hearer is not well disposed to us our best teaching will be but badly received.' Now, that is what the evangelical prophet always does. He always charms us with the music, and the melody, and the march of his style. Even when his message is the most accusing and condemning; even when there is no beauty in his doctrine that we should desire it, even then we are spellbound and held to the end in the great preacher's splendid hands. You will not have read or thought much about Isaiah's style. You have other things of more importance, and more worth your time and trouble to read in that prophet and to think about continually. But, for once, you will not grudge to hear a few words on that not irrelevant matter out of one who has given a long and a laborious lifetime to such subjects. 'Isaiah,' says Ewald, 'is not the especially lyrical prophet, or the especially elegiacal prophet, or the especially oratorical or the hortatory prophet—as we should describe a Joel, a Hosea, a Micah, with whom there is a greater prevalence of some particular colour. But just as the subject requires it, Isaiah has immediately at command every several kind and quality of style, and every several change and variety of delineation. And it is precisely this that, in point of language, establishes the prophet's personal greatness, as well as forms one of his most towering points of intellectual excellence. His discourse varies into every possible complexion: it is tender and stern, it is didactic and threatening; it is mourning and again exulting in divine joy; it is mocking and it is in earnest; but, ever, at the right time, Isaiah's style returns back to its original elevation and repose, and never loses the clear ground-colour of its divine seriousness.'

Yes; Esaias is very bold—

> With mouth of gold, and morning in his eyes.

LXII

JEREMIAH

THE most exquisite sensibility of soul was Jeremiah's singular and sovereign distinction above all the other Hebrew prophets. It was Jeremiah's life-long complaint to his mother that she had borne him, a man with such an unearthly sensibility of soul, into a world so out of joint for such souls. Such another child for sensibility of soul was not born of woman until the Virgin Mary brought forth the Man of Sorrows Himself. Those men of Cæsarea Philippi showed their own sensibility of soul when some said John the Baptist; some, Elias; but they would have it that Jesus of Nazareth was none other than Hilkiah's son, come back again with his broken heart. Woe is me, my mother, that thou hast borne me the man that I am! Is it nothing to you, all ye that pass by? Behold, and see if there be any sorrow like unto my sorrow.

Jeremiah was far and away the most spiritually-minded of all the prophets. Howbeit that was not first which is spiritual, but that which is natural; and afterward that which is spiritual. That is to say, it was the inborn, original, and unparalleled sensibility of Jeremiah's mind and heart that the Lord took up and turned to His own service both in the preaching of this prophet and in the production of this book, which stands to this day second only to the Psalms as the most spiritual book in the Old Testament. Some other prophets stand in time and in place nearer to the New Testament; but it is only in time and in place. No prophet of them all stands in reality so near to Jesus Christ. Jeremiah is the true forerunner of our Lord. Even Isaiah himself, evangelical as he is, still retains some of the shadowy and unspiritual elements of that imperfect economy in his prophecy. The restored kingdom of David and Solomon still haunts Isaiah's heart, and it still shapes and colours some of the finest pictures of his imperial imagination. But Jeremiah has nothing of that decayed economy either in himself or in his book. Jeremiah's extraordinary inwardness, and depth, and absolutely pure spirituality, have all combined to deliver both himself and his book from all those apocalyptic, secular, and unspiritual interpretations which have so infested the other prophets. Neither Peter nor the mother of Zebedee's children, could accuse Jeremiah of having misled them in one word of his, in any chapter of his, concerning the coming kingdom of the Messiah. And more and more as his ministry went on Jeremiah strove with all his might to draw both the hearts and the imaginations of his people not only off all alliance with the kingdoms that were around them, but also off the too pictorial Kingdom of the Messiah that had been hung up before them. And, for his pains, Jeremiah was cast into prison again and again, and was maltreated as only the offscourings of the city were maltreated. But his consolation and his hope always lay in that noble doctrine of the Kingdom of God, which he had been honoured to have revealed to him, and which he had preached for forty years at such a price. The depth, the purity, the beauty, the absolute heavenliness of his doctrine were the reward and the joy of his heart, let his fellow-citizens and his fellow-prophets and priests do to him what they pleased. Jeremiah was of all the prophets of the Old Testament the supreme prophet of the human heart. 'The heart is my haunt,' says Wordsworth. And again, 'My theme is no other than the heart of man.' But in an infinitely deeper sense than that, Jeremiah was the prophet of God to the human heart. Jeremiah would have nothing from his hearers and readers but their heart. Let other prophets negotiate and send embassies as they pleased; Jeremiah, in season and out of season, for a long life-time, laid siege to the hearts of his hearers. The cure of all your famines, he cried, and all your plagues, and all your defeats, and all your captivities—the cause and the cure of them all is in your own heart: in the heart of each inhabitant of Jerusalem and each captive in Babylon. And your prophets who say Peace, peace!—like Law, he called all such preachers so many dancing-masters; and, like Leighton, he called them so many mountebanks, till they smote him, and imprisoned him in the dungeon, and put his feet in the stocks.

And this is the true way still to preach, even at the same price; if only we had been born of our mothers to preach like Jeremiah. If only we had something of his sensibility, and spirituality, and knowledge of the heart. The salvation of our hearers must always begin with our own salvation: and it must go on to perfection with our perfection. And we cannot be the salvation to any perfection either of ourselves or of our people unless we have a pervading, and prevailing, and increasing sensibility of what salvation is, and what the want of it is. He who has—I will not say a full sensibility of the evil of sin, for he would go mad if he had—but a true beginning of such sensibility, he has the making of a true minister of Jesus Christ in him; otherwise he has not, and should at once go to make his bread in some more lawful calling. 'They will be thankful for your telling them the particular times when the gospels were writ: for explaining the word Euroclydon, or anathema maranatha; they will be glad of such useless instruction; but if you touch upon such subjects as really concern them in a high degree, such subjects as try the state and way of their lives, these religious people cannot bear to be thus instructed.' Yes, morning lectures on Euroclydon: evidences of Christianity; defences and debates round and round the subject: whole cartloads of Bampton, and all like lectures: they are all so much lost time and strength in the pulpit. They have their place elsewhere, and among those who get any good from them, but they would get all that good, and would not need it any more, if we had taught them some real sensibility for spiritual things. It is Jeremiah's sensibility and spirituality that both preachers and hearers need, and then we would both have the evidence in ourselves. Speak to your hearer's heart and you will soon undermine his head. All his lofty imaginations, with all his high thoughts, will lie all around him as soon as he lies in the dust himself; but not till then, with all your artillery. Young preachers, with your great life still before you, study your own heart day and night. Watch every beat, and flutter, and creep of your own heart day and night. Seek sensibility of heart above all Latin, and Greek, and Hebrew: above all logic, and style, and delivery. Add all these things, and everything else, to sensibility of heart: but one thing is needful if you would not be a castaway in the end. Were you spiritually-sensible preachers you would soon get inside your people's hearts, and you would hold your people's hearts to the end. Deep answers to deep. And if one here and another there should smite you as Pashur smote Jeremiah, say to him, 'The Lord hath not called thy name Pashur, but Magor-missabib,' and go on with your heart-searching and heart-sanctifying preaching to other people. And your sensibility of heart and mind once well begun will grow till your name is as famous as you could wish it to be where fame and name is alone worth working for. With ever-increasing sensibility preach every day to them the meekness, and the humility, and the spirituality, and the obedience, and the whole mind of Christ, and you will surely see Christ formed in your people before you are compelled to bequeath your pulpit to your successor. And oh, believe me, the shame and the remorse of having to hand over your pulpit, and you only beginning to preach! And it all lies in a true and a timely sensibility, and in saying, the heart is my haunt, till you know the heart, and can preach to it to some purpose. Return, thou backsliding Israel, saith the Lord, and I will give you pastors after mine own heart, which shall feed you with knowledge and understanding.

Nazianzen says somewhere that Jeremiah was both by nature and by grace the most inclined to pity of all the prophets. Which is just to say over again that he was the most sensitive and the most spiritual. Take natural sensibility and supernatural spirituality together, and you will have the most exquisite sympathy and the most perfect pity possible. There is nothing like the Lamentations of Jeremiah in the whole world again. There has been plenty of sorrow in every age, and in every land; but such another preacher and author as Jeremiah, with such a heart for sorrow, has never again been born. Dante comes next to Jeremiah, and we know that Jeremiah was that great exile's favourite prophet. Both prophet and poet were full to all the height and depth of their great hearts of the most thrilling sensibility; while, at the same time, they were both high towers, and brazen walls, and iron pillars against all unrighteousness of men. And they were alike in this also, that, just because of their combined strength, and sternness, and sensibility, no man in their day sympathised with them. They made all men's causes of suffering and sorrow their own, till all hated them, and put a price on their heads. 'There is nothing in all Scripture,' says Isaac Williams, 'so eloquent of love and sorrow and consolation as the 31st and 33rd chapters of Jeremiah. No words can be found in any language of such touching beauty as all that strain.' So surely does natural sensibility, when it is steeped in the Spirit of God, become the most perfect pity and the most exquisite sympathy.

In an unaccountably silly passage in his *Life of Erasmus,* Froude actually prints it that 'Erasmus, like all men of real genius, had a light and elastic nature.' That senseless and impossible passage came back to my mind as I read this melancholy book of this man of real genius. And this also came to my mind out of North's *Plutarch*: 'Aristotle has a place where he says that the wisest men be ever melancholy, as Socrates, Plato, and Hercules were.' And I have read somewhere also on this matter that 'merely to say man is to say melancholy.' I wish it were. At any rate, to say 'man endued by nature with sufficient sensibility, and then by grace with sufficient spiritual sympathy,' is to say the most profoundly melancholy of men. 'O hear me,' says the profoundly intellectual and equally spiritual Jacob Behmen in a comforting passage. 'Hear me, for I know well myself what melancholy is! I also have lodged all my days in the melancholy inn!' As Jeremiah lodged also. And how could it have been done otherwise? In such a land: in such a city: among such a people with such a past and with such a present, and doing their best to make their future as bad as their past and their present—it was enough to make the glorified on their thrones melancholy. Jeremiah's inconsolable melancholy was the mark and the measure of his greatness both as a man and as a prophet. It was a divine melancholy that made his head waters and his eyes a fountain of tears. 'Tears gain everything,' says Santa Teresa in her autobiography. No: not everything,—much; but not everything. Tears, when bitter enough, and in secret enough, always gain forgiveness indeed, which is almost everything, and is on the way to everything. But while such tears will always avail under grace to blot out the past, they have no power to bring back the past. Nor do they bring in the sure future so much as one day before its time. All Jeremiah's tears did not keep back the Chaldeans for a single day's march. But his tears softened his heart and bowed his head till he was able to go out to meet the Chaldeans, and almost to welcome them to Jerusalem in the name of God. Neither his tears, nor his prayers, nor his resignations, nor his submissions, shortened by a single hour the seventy years' captivity. But his tears did far better for himself at least. They perfected what both nature and grace had so well begun. For they made him not only an evangelical prophet, but an all but New Testament apostle. Jeremiah's tears were such that they gained the Holy Ghost for him before the Holy Ghost was given, and before Christ was glorified. Till Santa Teresa is amply justified when she says that tears gain every thing. And till I am justified in saying that Jeremiah at any rate was not a man of a light and elastic nature.

'Oh that I had in the wilderness a lodging-place of wayfaring men; that I might leave my people and go from them!' The loneliness of a man's heart among his own people is one of the heaviest crosses that any man has to take up. Jeremiah, to borrow one of his own bitter words, had plenty of 'familiars' among his own people, but he had very few friends. And his familiars watched for his halting and rejoiced over it, and said, Report, said they, and we will report it. Had Jeremiah had a friend among all his familiars, that solitary friend would have proved himself such by refusing to report it. 'He has fallen away to the Chaldeans,' was the report made among his familiars. But Jeremiah had no friend who would take the risk to understand and to defend his friend. And it was among such familiars, and in the lack of such friends, that Jeremiah sighed the sigh that has been taken up and sighed so often since that day: 'O that I might leave my people!' Jeremiah never was a married man. And it was as well that he was not. Men, and especially ministers, of such sensibility, and spirituality, and sympathy, and melancholy are not made to be married. A helpmeet for Jeremiah was not to be found in all the house of Israel. If his Master had seen it good for His servant to have a wife and children, He would have made Jeremiah's second self, and would have brought her to him till Jeremiah's melancholy would for the time have been somewhat abated. But whether it was that the Lord saw that His servant's sensibility was too exquisite, and his melancholy too extreme, or whatever it was, the Lord said to His servant, 'Thou shalt not take thee a wife, neither shalt thou have sons and daughters in this place.' And thus it was that what a sensitive and melancholy minister takes home and tells only to his wife, when he has a wife who is his friend, and not merely his familiar, all that Jeremiah took and told to God. Till his whole book before us is one long confidence, and conversation, and debate, and remonstrance; and, again, one long submission, and silence, and surrender, and service of God. And till he is home now where all men are friends, and where the familiars of Jerusalem, with their watching and their reporting, do not enter.

And, then, all that made Jeremiah the red-hot preacher that we still feel him to this day to have been. We see with what a fiery sensibility he both prepares and delivers his sermons. At one time we hear him groaning over his text as he stands beside the potter at his wheel, while the potter mars his vessel and casts it away. At another time he does not preach for many weeks. He is away at the Euphrates learning how to illustrate and enforce his next sermon, and he preaches it over and over to himself as he sees in the sand the footprints of his captive people. Another Sabbath morning he takes his elders out the valley beyond the city, and dashes an earthen vessel to pieces before their amazed and angry eyes, and that is all the sermon they get that morning. A preacher—like a great preacher of our own land

—to 'terrify even the godly.' A preacher for his familiars to take him and speak to him. And so they did, and almost succeeded. Pashur, the chief governor, was deputed on one occasion to tame, as we say, Jeremiah's pulpit. And of such sensibility and melancholy was the prophet at the visit of Pashur that the thing was almost done. Till the prophet appeared all of a sudden with a yoke of wood on his neck in his former pulpit next Sabbath, and with this apology to Pashur, and with this autobiographic introduction to his sermon that day: 'Then I said, I will not make mention of Him, or speak any more in His name. But His word was in my heart as a burning fire shut up in my bones, and I was weary with forbearing, and I could not stay.' I suppose every preacher with any fire in his bones has a Pashur or two among his governors. A familiar or two who say among themselves, Report, and we will report it. But I do not read that Jeremiah spake as he was moved by Pashur, the governor. Let Pashur preach himself if Jeremiah has too much sensibility, and spirituality, and sympathy, and melancholy for him. And let Jeremiah go on and preach out all the fire that God has kindled in his prophet's bones. 'I could have used a more adorned style,' says John Bunyan, in his *Grace Abounding*, 'but I dared not. God did not play in tempting me; neither did I play when the pangs of hell gat hold on me. Wherefore I may not play in relating those pangs, but be plain and simple, and lay down the thing just as it was.'

> Lo! this man's brow, like to a title-page,
> Foretells the nature of a tragic volume,
> Thou tremblest, and the whiteness in thy cheek
> Is apter than thy tongue to tell thine errand.

When Jesus came into the coasts of Cæsarea Philippi, He asked His disciples, saying, Whom do men say that I the Son of Man am? And they said, Some say that thou art John the Baptist; some, Elias; and others, Jeremiah.

LXIII

DANIEL

THERE is always a singular lustre, and nobility, and stately distinction about Daniel. There is a note of birth, and breeding, and aristocracy about Daniel's whole name and character. There is never at any time anything common or conventional in anything that Daniel says or does. Munro has gathered it all up in these three eloquent words: 'His refinement, his reserve, and the high sculpture of his character.'

The first thing in which Daniel's great qualities all come out is his so wise and so noble self-control and self-denial at the king's table. The narrative is a noble one. 'And the king appointed them a daily provision of the king's meat, and of the wines which he drank, so nourishing them three years, that at the end thereof they might stand before the king. But Daniel proposed not to defile himself with the portion of the king's meat, nor with the wine which he drank: therefore he requested of the prince of the eunuchs that he might not defile himself. Prove thy servants, I beseech thee, ten days; and let them give us pulse to eat and water to drink. Then let our countenances be looked upon before thee, and as thou then seest deal with thy servants. And at the end of the ten days their countenances appeared fairer and fatter in flesh than all the children that did eat of the king's meat.' 'I have remarked,' says an Eastern traveller, 'that their faces are in fact more rosy and smooth than those of others, and that those who fast much, I mean the Armenians and the Greeks, are very beautiful, sparkling with health, and of a clear and lively countenance.' At the same time, Daniel did not at all times and in all places live on bare pulse and water. Calvin says that when Daniel and his three companions got far enough away from the royal table they would both eat flesh with pleasant bread, and would drink wine also in the wayside inns of Babylon, just as they had done when they were at home in Jerusalem. It was the company at the king's table; it was the idolatry, and the self-indulgence, and the indecency, and the riot among the young men of the palace that made Daniel determine that it would be both far easier and far safer to abstain altogether and from the beginning. When he was far enough away at any time from those snares and temptations and associations, and when he was alone with his three virtuous and temperate companions, Daniel did not make a voluntary and an ostentatious virtue of pulse and water.

> A neat repast shall feast us, light and choice,
> Of Canaan's taste, with wine, whence we shall rise.
> He who of those delights can judge, and spare
> To interpose them oft, is not unwise—

Belteshazzar would say on occasion to Shadrach, Meshach, and Abed-nego, just as our English Daniel said in his fine sonnet to

> Lawrence, of virtuous father virtuous son.

At the same time, there was nothing morose or melancholy in Daniel's total abstinence. Daniel was not of a sad countenance over his pulse and water. Daniel did not disfigure his face at the royal feasts. Because of his abstinence Daniel all the more anointed his head and washed his face; till, unless you had watched him well, you would have thought that all that affability, and good humour, and merriment of his must come of the abundance of the king's wine that he drank. Unless you had been in the secret you would never have supposed that Daniel was not eating and drinking with the same self-indulgence as all the rest. In nothing was Daniel's fine character finer seen, not even when his window was set open towards Jerusalem, not even when he stepped down into the den of lions, than it was when he was the last to rise from the royal feasts, with such sweetness, and geniality, and simplicity did he converse with the men of Babylon. Daniel did not expect the young men of Chaldea to deny themselves like captive Hebrews. They had not either his Hebrew sorrow or his Hebrew hope in their hearts, and he did not look for those things in them. Now it is just here that so many of ourselves both injure ourselves and injure other people by our abstinence. We enter on our abstinence out of some constraint and compulsion. We are abstainers, many of us, against our own hearts; or, if our hearts are in our abstinence, then it is our hard and self-righteous hearts. We abstain with self-importance, and with self-righteousness, and with sourness, and soreness at those who still preserve their liberty. And this makes one man peevish and melancholy in his abstinence, and another man fierce and intolerant. And thus our latter end is worse than our beginning; and our self-denial than our self-indulgence. We must not only abstain, but we must make our abstinence genial and full of liberty and delight. 'Furthermore,' says Plutarch, 'Alexander was far less given to wine than men would have judged. He was thought to be a far greater bibber than he was because he sat long at the board, but it was rather to talk than to eat and drink. For even when he ate and drank he would propound some new and interesting subject, and yet but when he was at leisure. For, having matters to do, there was neither feast, nor banquet, nor marriage, nor any pastime that could stay him, as they had done other captains. He would ever sup late, and after his long day's work was done, and he was very curious to see that every man at his board was alike served, and would sit long at the table, because he ever loved to talk, as we have told you before. And in all other ways he was as gracious a prince and as noble to wait upon, and as pleasant as ever was.' One of Lord Ardmillan's daughters used to say of my dear old friend her father, that 'he breakfasted on the newspapers and dined on conversation.' And so he did; and thus it was that his step was the lightest, and his laugh the merriest, and his heart the most childlike of all the Parliament House men of his day. And in all other ways, like Plutarch's Alexander, Ardmillan was, I think, the most gracious and gentlemanly man I ever knew.

The Chaldean Schools: their literature, their true science and their pseudo-science, their architecture, their music, their political and military methods, their religion and the sacred arts connected with their religion—nothing of all that was at all foreign, or alien, or despicable to Daniel. The captive prince entered into all that with all the zest and with all the labour of what we would call a true student. Daniel foresaw that his whole life would have to be spent in Babylon, and he determined that his exile there should not be so much lost time either to his mind or to his heart. The Chaldean astrology has long since given way before the modern science of astronomy, and with it the so-called Magi, the star-gazers, and the soothsayers, and the sorcerers. But the truly philosophic temper that Daniel exhibited among the wise men of Babylon is still the true and wise temper for us all among the studies and the speculations and the scepticisms of our more learned, more scientific, and more speculative day. Daniel, by God's mercy, possessed the truth that the Chaldeans sought after in sun and moon and stars: in dreams and in incantations. And when he was cast among the speculations and superstitions of Chaldea he was able to study all he saw and all he heard with an interest, with an intelligence, and with a sympathy that are only to be found in a truly religious and a truly cultivated mind. In his birth, in his upbringing, in his breeding, and in his books, Daniel possessed a knowledge of God and of man that no sage of Chaldea could possibly approach: but, at the same time, Daniel was student enough to see that Chaldea had attained to a learning and to a religion of her own that well deserved his best attention. Till Daniel at last came to be acknowledged as more than the equal of the king's most learned and most consulted men. It was the largeness, and the expansiveness, and the hospitality of Daniel's fine mind, all combined with his extraordinary nobility and beauty of character, that gave Daniel such an unparalleled position in the court of Chaldea, and which has gained for Daniel such a famous and such a proverbial name in all subsequent literature. Ezekiel, a contemporary prophet, has heard so much of the wisdom of Daniel, that, to a proud enemy of Israel, he exclaims in irony: Thou art wiser than Daniel! We see the popular belief about Daniel strikingly illustrated also in the Apocryphal addition that was made to the Book of Daniel by its Greek translater and editor, and which was called the story of Susannah and the judgment of Daniel. And we are gratified to read in our own tongue a tribute to the same noble tradition in Shylock's exclamation:—

> A Daniel come to judgment! yea, a Daniel!
> O wise young judge, how do I honour thee!

The prophet Daniel became a great proficient both in penitential and in intercessory prayer also as the years went on. And he came to that great proficiency just as a great proficiency is come to in any other science or art: that is to say, by constant, and unremitting, and enterprising practice. Lord, teach us to pray, said a disciple on one occasion to our Lord. But not even our Lord with all His willingness, and with all His ability, can teach any of us off-hand to pray. Every man must teach himself, every day he lives, this most personal, most secret, and most experimental of all the arts. Every man must find out the best ways of prayer for himself. There is no royal road; there is no short or easy road to proficiency in prayer. It is like all the other arts that you have ever mastered; it must be early begun and assiduously practised, else you will be but a bungler at it all your days. You must also have special and extraordinary seasons of prayer, as Daniel had, over and above his daily habit of prayer. Special and extraordinary, original and unparalleled seasons of prayer, when you literally do nothing else day nor night but pray. You must pray in your very dreams. Till you will come at last to live, and move, and have your whole being in prayer. Now, it is plain that you cannot teach a lifetime of experiment and attainment like that to any chance man: and, especially, you cannot teach it to a man who still detests the very thought of such prayer. It was his yoke in his youth that first taught Daniel to pray. And Babylon taught Daniel and his three friends all to pray, and to pray together in their chambers, as we read. To be arrested in their fathers' houses by Nebuchadnezzar's soldiers; to have Babylonian chains put on their hands and their feet: to see the towers of Zion for the last time: to be asked to sing some of the songs of Zion to amuse their masters as they toiled over the Assyrian sands—you would have become experts yourselves in a school of prayer like that. You would have held little prayer-meetings with your class-fellows and your companions, if you had come through the half that Daniel and his three companions came through. It is because you are not being emptied from vessel to vessel all the week that we never see you at the prayer-meeting. Jeremiah, a great authority on why some men pray, and why other men never pray, has this about you in his book: 'Moab hath been at his ease from his youth up: he hath settled on his lees: he hath not been emptied from vessel to vessel: neither hath he gone into captivity; and, therefore, his taste remaineth in him, and his scent is not changed.'

'Why,' asks Pascal, 'has God established prayer?' And the first answer out of the three that Pascal gives to himself is this,—'To communicate to His creatures the dignity of causality.' And Daniel was of Pascal's deep and original mind. For Daniel, just because he read in Jeremiah that deliverance was at the door, all the more set himself to pray as if his prayer was to be the alone and predestinated cause of the coming deliverance. Daniel put on sackcloth, and fasted, and prayed, and went back upon all his own and all his people's sins in a way that confounds us to our face. We cannot understand Daniel. We are not deep enough. He prayed, and fasted, and returned to an agony of prayer, as if he had never heard of the near deliverance: he prayed in its very presence as if he despaired of ever seeing it. He fasted and prayed as he had not done all those seventy fasting and praying years. Read, all you experts in prayer, with all your mind, and with all your heart, and with all your experience, and with all your imagination this great causality chapter. It is written by a proficient for proficients. It is written by a great saint of God for all such. Read it and think about it. Read it with your Pascal open before you. Read it and sink down into the deep things of God and the soul. Read it and practise it till you know by experiment and by experience that decree, and covenant, and prophecy, and promise, and all, however sure, and however near, are only fulfilled in immediate and dependent answer to penitential and importunate prayer. Read it and pray as never before after the answer has actually begun. See the answer out to the last syllable before you begin to restrain penitence and prayer. And after the answer is all fulfilled, still read it and the still deeper chapters that follow, till you learn new fastings, and new sackcloth, and new ashes, and new repentance, away out to your saintliest old age. Read Daniel's greatest prayer and

> Know thy dread power—a creature, yet a cause.

LXIV

NEBUCHADNEZZAR

I FRANKLY confess myself a convert to Nebuchadnezzar. I frankly acknowledge my great debt to Nebuchadnezzar. I frankly confess that I had wholly misunderstood Nebuchadnezzar, and both the design and the end of God's ways with Nebuchadnezzar. And I would like to share with you to-night the great lesson in humility and in obedience that I have been led to learn out of Nebuchadnezzar.

Nebuchadnezzar was by far the most famous of all the kings of the East. In his early years, and before he came to his great throne, Nebuchadnezzar had won victory after victory over all the surrounding nations. Jerusalem fell before his army after eighteen months' siege, and Tyre, the proudest of ancient cities, succumbed to him after an investiture of thirteen years. The proud position of the king of Babylon among all the kings of that day will best be seen from the words of Daniel who assuredly was no flatterer of great men. 'Thou, O king, art a king of kings, for the God of heaven hath given thee a kingdom, and strength, and glory. The tree which thou sawest, which grew, and was strong, whose height reached to heaven, and the sight thereof to all the earth: whose leaves were fair and the fruit thereof much, and in it was meat for all: under which the beasts of the field dwelt, and upon whose branches the fowls of the heavens had their habitation: It is thou, O king, that art grown, and become strong: for thy greatness is grown, and reached unto heaven, and thy dominion to the end of the earth.' It could have been no ordinary greatness that drew from a man like Daniel an estimate and an eulogium like that.

But the fame of this magnificent monarch has rested even more on his unparalleled works of peace than on his great successes in war. Great as Nebuchadnezzar was as a warrior, he was still greater as a statesman and an administrator. The vast public works that he planned and executed for his capital and his kingdom in walls and in water-works: in parks and in gardens: in palaces and in temples—all these things, in their vastness, in their usefulness, in their beauty, and in their immense cost make Nebuchadnezzar to stand out absolutely unapproached among the great builder-kings of the ancient East. After we have read all that the historians and the travellers have to tell us about ancient Babylon, no wonder, we say to ourselves, that Nebuchadnezzar's dreams were the dreams of a magnificent imagination. No wonder that his heart swelled within him with pride: and no wonder that it took a stroke such as God has seldom struck before or since to humble and to abase Nebuchadnezzar, this great king of Babylon. 'This is the interpretation, O king, and this is the decree of the Most High: that they shall drive thee from men, and thy dwelling shall be with the beasts of the field, and they shall make thee to eat grass like an ox, and they shall wet thee with the dew of heaven, and seven times shall pass over thee, till thou know that the Most High ruleth in the kingdom of men, and giveth it to whomsoever He will.' All this came to Nebuchadnezzar the king, till at the end of it all he said—'I thought it good to show the signs and wonders the high God hath wrought toward me. Those that walk in pride the King of heaven is able to abase.' Though long dead, King Nebuchadnezzar still speaks in the Book of Daniel, and on a thousand cylinders in the British Museum; and, as on every page of Daniel, so on every brick of Babylon, he that runs may read this evening's text:—'Those that walk in pride the King of heaven is able to abase.'

But Nebuchadnezzar's pride, after all is said, was but the petty pride of a puffed-up and self-important child. If you have eyes in your hearts you will see all Nebuchadnezzar's pride in your own nursery every day. Nebuchadnezzar's bricks were made of clay; whereas the bricks of your nursery-Nebuchadnezzar are made of wood. That, and their ages, is all the difference. Look! your little Nebuchadnezzar cries after you as he pulls your gown, and will not give you peace till you lift up your hands in wonder over his great Babylon with its wonderful doors, and windows, and bridges, and portcullises. Is not this a great house that I have built? he demands of you. Is my house not far bigger, and far better every way, than my brother's house that he has built? Look, father! Look, mother! Look, nurse! Look, visitor! All wise-hearted mothers see and hear all that with tears behind their eyes, till they are at their wits' end how to deal with their so boastful and so imperious little emperor. The ancient Areopagus sentenced an Athenian boy to death because he had plucked out the eyes of a captive quail. For, said the wise and prescient judges, if that little savage does that to a tame bird when he is still young, what will he not do to the men who are in his power when he is hardened in vice? And they put him to death, and paid no attention to the prayers of his mother. Let all fathers and mothers give their best heed to their little Nebuchadnezzar and to his little Babylon which he has built for the honour of his majesty. This is the beginning. And you know what a great fire sometimes a little spark, if it is let fall and let burn, kindleth. You know the prophetic proverb also about the letting out of water. Let every father, and mother, and nurse, and tutor, and school-master read and lay to heart, as they shall answer for it, William Law's eighteenth chapter, in which he shows 'How the education which men receive in their youth makes the doctrine of humility so difficult to be practised all their after-days.'

But, with all that, I see in my own children every day a far worse kind of pride than any that the big child Nebuchadnezzar shows either in the Book of Daniel, or on the bricks of Babylon. Nebuchadnezzar never, that I have read of, got one single lesson from God or man that he did not instantly lay it to heart. As I read of Nebuchadnezzar's humility, and makeableness, and teachableness in Daniel's hands I am amazed at the boldness of the young Belteshazzar, and still more at the behaviour of his mighty master. When I put myself into Nebuchadnezzar's place, when I recall my own temper and my own conduct, I honour Nebuchadnezzar, and I cannot cease from wondering that the king of Babylon has not been far more made of as a pattern of humility and meekness both under the dispensations of God and under the doctrines of Daniel. After his orders had been disobeyed—in his own palace, remember, and at his own table—in the matter of the meat that Daniel and his three companions were to eat, and the wine they were to drink: and after he was compelled publicly to admit that the prince of the eunuchs had acted on far better advice than the king's commandment,—instead of Melzar's head being endangered to the king, Nebuchadnezzar communed with Daniel, and Daniel stood before the king. Then, again, after his great dream, and its interpretation to the destruction of his kingdom, 'King Nebuchadnezzar fell upon his face, and worshipped Daniel, and commanded that they should offer an oblation and sweet odours unto Daniel.' And, then, after his abominably despotic edict about the image of gold in the plain of Dura, and the furnace seven times heated, when the intoxicated king came to himself he said, Lo! I see four men loose, walking in the midst of the fire, and they have no hurt; and the form of the fourth is like the Son of God. Then Nebuchadnezzar spake and said, Blessed be the God of Shadrach, Meshach, and Abed-nego, who hath sent His angels, and delivered His servants that trusted in Him, and have changed the king's word and yielded their bodies that they might not serve nor worship any god except their own God. And, then, at the end of his life, the king not only let Daniel say this to him, 'Wherefore, O king, break off thy sins by righteousness, and thine iniquities by showing mercy to the poor, if it may be a lengthening of thy tranquillity, but he bowed his head and did it. A nobler state paper was never sent out even by the most Christian of kings than is that great document that we have in the fourth chapter of the Book of Daniel. Nebuchadnezzar is another illustration how we go on traditionally calling good men by bad names without looking at what is written out plain before our eyes. I cannot conceive where I got my bad opinion about Nebuchadnezzar. At any rate, I cannot entertain it any longer after I have read that magnificent chapter. I have read nothing nobler about the best kings of Judah, or Israel, or Scotland, or England. I do not know where among them all to look for its equal. But it was not great and ancient kings, but our own little children I was speaking about; and about our proud-blooded little children inevitably growing up into proud-blooded and bad men. And the hopeless unteachableness of the proud child and the proud man was the all-important point in hand. The proud man holds you henceforth to be his mortal enemy if you tell him the truth as Daniel told Nebuchadnezzar, and as Daniel was honoured and rewarded for telling it. Try to teach, try to correct a proud man, and you will not readily do it a second time. It may now be many years since some one found a true and notorious fault with some of us; but we cannot hide from ourselves the state of our heart after all these years at the mere mention of that insolent man's name. But Daniel's counsel was acceptable to Nebuchadnezzar, till that king broke off all the sins and all the iniquities that Daniel so boldly named to him. Can it be said about any of our living preachers of righteousness that his counsels have been acceptable to us, and that we have forgiven and obeyed him to the tranquillity of our conscience to this day?

> Rather than bear the pain of truth, fools stray;
> The proud will rather lose than ask their way.

It is true Nebuchadnezzar got a tremendous lesson. It was a lesson, as we would have thought, away out of all proportion to the king's transgression. It was one of those tremendous lessons that God only gives to His own sons whom He loves, and whom He is to chasten till they are made partakers of His holiness. To any man who is not a chastened son and a true saint of God it must look a small sin, if it is a sin at all, for a great king to walk in his own palace and to say to himself the simple truth. For Babylon was undoubtedly great. No greater city has ever been seen on the face of the earth than Babylon. And if Nebuchadnezzar had not built every single street of it, this, at any rate, he could say, that he had found Babylon a city of brick and had made it a city of marble. We hear of baptized kings every day walking in their palaces in Christendom at the end of the nineteenth century, and speaking far more proudly than heathen Nebuchadnezzar spake, and no Daniel dares to stand up and tell them that their feet are partly iron mixed with miry clay. It is as if God had predestinated Nebuchadnezzar to come out of that heathen dispensation, and to sit down in the kingdom of heaven, while the emperors of our modern Christendom are to be cast out. It would look like that; God took such unheard-of vengeance on Nebuchadnezzar's inventions. Did you ever read the fourth chapter of the Book of Daniel?—that splendid autobiographic chapter which king Nebuchadnezzar wrote out of his own inkhorn, and gave the document to Daniel to embody in his book? 'Come, all ye that fear God,' Nebuchadnezzar begins, 'and I will tell you what He did for my soul. I have thought it good to show the signs and wonders that the high God had wrought towards me. For how great are His signs, and how mighty are His wonders! I was walking proudly in my palace in the kingdom of Babylon, and I said, Is not this great Babylon, that I have built for the house of the kingdom by the might of my power, and for the honour of my majesty? And while the word was yet in my mouth, there fell a Voice from heaven, saying, O King Nebuchadnezzar, to thee it is spoken; The kingdom is departed from thee. And they shall drive thee from among men, and thy dwelling shall be with the beasts of the field; they shall make thee to eat grass as oxen, and seven times shall pass over thee until thou know that the Most High ruleth in the kingdom of men, and giveth it to whomsoever He will. The same hour was the thing fulfilled upon Nebuchadnezzar, and he was driven from men, and did eat grass as oxen, and his body was wet with the dew of heaven, till his hairs were grown as eagles' feathers, and his nails like birds' claws. And at the end of the days I, Nebuchadnezzar, lifted up mine eyes to heaven, and mine understanding returned to me, and I blessed the Most High, and I praised and honoured Him who liveth for ever, whose dominion is an everlasting dominion, and His kingdom is from generation to generation: and all the inhabitants of the earth are reputed as nothing: and He doeth according to His will in the army of heaven, and among the inhabitants of the earth: and none can stay His hand, or say to Him, What doest Thou? Now I, Nebuchadnezzar, praise and extol and honour the King of heaven, all whose works are truth, and His ways judgment; and those that walk in pride He is able to abase.' Has our own Christendom another royal edict anywhere to show like that chapter? If it has, I do not know where to find it.

To be driven out among the oxen made Nebuchadnezzar a new man. Asaph in Israel also, for his humiliation and his sanctification, was as a beast before God. The blessed Behmen, as his disciples all call him, teaches his disciples the same doctrine. 'Listen to my own process,' says that great spiritual genius. 'My soul will sometimes be all of a sudden turned into a wolf within me. Again, I am a dog at home; churlish, snappish, malicious, envious; my heart hides its bone that it cannot eat, lest another dog should get it. Then there is a lion within me; not in his nobility, but in his strong and proud cruelty. At another time, and at the proper provocation, I am a viper, as John preached to his hearers from Jerusalem, venomous, poisonous, and with a stealthy sting. At another time I am loathsome as a toad: at another time timorous as a hare.' Yes; our souls are now this beast within us, and now that,—when the law enters. Only, the law has not entered one in a hundred of us to that depth: and thus it is that we are all still so proud and so disputatious at the hearing of all these things. But when we see and feel ourselves to be oxen in our stupidity, and dogs in our selfishness, and swine in our miryness, and vipers in our poisonousness—then we have got the key within ourselves to God's great dispensation of humiliation with Nebuchadnezzar. Then we say to Belteshazzar, and to Behmen, Thou art able: and the spirit of the God of holiness is in thee. And then we leave it like Nebuchadnezzar to be read on our tombstone by all that pass by—

Those that walk in pride He is able to abase.

But Nebuchadnezzar would not have needed to be made to eat grass as an ox if he had early enough and often enough asked Daniel to teach him to pray. Prayer would have done it to Nebuchadnezzar also. Daniel himself was mightily tempted to pride; far more than Nebuchadnezzar ever was with all his wars and with all his palaces. For, was not Nebuchadnezzar, with all his power and with all his pride, prostrate again and again at Daniel's feet? Did not king Nebuchadnezzar fall upon his face, and worship Daniel, and command that they should offer an oblation and sweet odours to Daniel? What could it have been, then, that kept Daniel's heart so sweetly humble through all that, till Daniel was a man greatly beloved of Him who resisteth the proud and giveth grace to the humble? It was prayer that did it. It was secret prayer that did it. It was his place of secret prayer three times a day every day he lived that did it. Look in at that window in Babylon that stands open toward Jerusalem, and you will see Daniel on his knees and on the palms of his hands till all his comeliness is turned to corruption. It was that that did it. Seneca says somewhere that nothing is bought so dear as that which is bought with prayer—that is to say, you must sell all if you would truly pray. You must begin with selling all your pride, and everything else as you proceed in prayer, down to your whole soul. I am dust and ashes, said Abraham, not at the beginning, but as he went on in prayer. We are dust and ashes, and far worse than that, says Hooker also, as he went on in prayer. Count the cost, then, before you propose to be a man of prayer. But, then, on the other hand, if any man has come to this, that he would fain, if it were possible, put on humility before both God and man, then let that man pray without ceasing. Enough prayer will work all possible humility into the proudest heart. Prayer every day, and many times every day, and all the day, would bring down and would abase into the very dust very Lucifer himself.

LXV

BELSHAZZAR

NEVER did a military commander attempt a more impossible task than Cyrus atempted when he sat down before Babylon to blockade it. For Babylon was indeed 'Babylon the Great.' Babylon was great in size, in fortified strength, in wide dominion, in wealth, in every kind of resource, and in her proud defiance of all her enemies. But then, to set over against all that, Cyrus was a soldier of the foremost military genius: and, besides that, Almighty God was with Cyrus, and was against Belshazzar.

That was an high day in all the temples and palaces of Babylon. It was the day that Bel had made, and all Babylon was in public worship before Bel their god. And as an evening's sacrifice to Bel, a great feast was to be held in Belshazzar's palace that night. But before the sunset, and to prepare his proud heart for his great banquet, Belshazzar rode out in his royal chariot that afternoon on that splendid chariot-drive that his famous father, Nebuchadnezzar, had built round about Babylon. The wall of Babylon was the wonder of the world. The wall of Babylon reached unto heaven; and such a mighty rampart was that wall round the city, that no less than four royal chariots were driven abreast on the top of the wall that afternoon, and all in the sight of Cyrus lying below. And as Belshazzar saw Cyrus and his thin red line lying round the mighty fortress, he mocked at Cyrus, and all Belshazzar's princes laughed with him at that spider's thread laid round a sleeping lion. It was a dazzling spectacle at Belshazzar's supper-table that night. All the grandeur, all the wealth, all the princely blood, and all the beauty of Babylon, drank wine at the king's table, and praised the gods of Babylon. When, just as Belshazzar lifted to his lips that cup of the Lord, which had been carried captive out of the temple of Jerusalem, a man's hand suddenly came out and wrote a writing on the wall over against the king's candlestick. But what is that writing on the wall? Neither the king nor any of his Chaldeans can either read the writing or understand the interpretation thereof. Till Daniel is brought in,—'Let thy gifts be to thyself, and give thy rewards to another; yet will I read the writing to the king, and make known to him the interpretation. Mene, Mene, Tekel, Upharsin. God hath numbered thy kingdom. Thou art weighed in the balances. And thy kingdom is given to the Medes and Persians.' And while Daniel was yet speaking to Belshazzar, Jehovah was at that same moment saying to Cyrus, 'Thou art Mine anointed, and I will loose the loins of kings, and will open before thee the two-leaved gates. I will break in pieces the gates of brass, and cut in sunder the bars of iron. I will say to the deep, Be dry, and I will dry up the rivers. I am the Lord, and there is none else.' And Cyrus arose, and lifted up the great sluices that he had made in secret, and the Euphrates flowed away into the new bed that Cyrus had dug for it, till the former bed of the river became the broad and open way by which Cyrus led his men into the revelling city. And that night was Belshazzar, the king of Babylon slain.

Belshazzar's grave is made,
　His kingdom's passed away,
He, in his balance laid,
　Is light and worthless clay.
The shroud his robe of state,
　His canopy the stone;
The Mede is at his gate,
　The Persian on his throne!

But come back and look at this. Did you ever think of this? How do you account for this? If King Belshazzar does not know what the words are that are written on the wall, why do his knees smite so, the one against the other, and why is his countenance so changed? Is this not a banquet to Bel to-night? And are not all these princes and lords and queens and concubines all Bel's worshippers to-night? Why, then, is Belshazzar in such a terror? Why does he not salute with joy and assurance that divine hand? That must be Bel's hand. Rise up, Belshazzar, and kiss the great hand of thy god. Rise up and command more wine. Rise up and call for music and dancing. For that must be the mighty arm of thy god denouncing destruction to Cyrus, and sealing down thy victory to thee. What a cold welcome to give to thy god! O unbelieving and unthankful king Belshazzar! But Belshazzar knew better. Belshazzar's conscience had already interpreted the words before they were all written. You can all sympathise with Belshazzar's state of mind as that hand went on with its awful writing over against the candlestick. You have all come through the same thing yourselves. When something shot in upon you without warning. Something when you were at your ungodly feast with your ungodly companions, or when you had just said, Surely the darkness shall cover me. Something sudden and unaccountable. When your heart suddenly stood still, and did not beat again for a moment. When you were in some sudden accident so that your hair has been white ever since. THAT IS GOD! your conscience whispered to you. That is God come in anger at last. No wonder your knees shook. No wonder you were as cold as a corpse. If a hand came out on the plaster of the wall opposite the pulpit lamp at this moment you would all swoon in your seats. You would know that that hand had come to write your sentence on that wall. Sitting there in your own soft seats you would all, in a moment, be Belshazzar over again.

Belshazzar was as good as dead and at the judgment-seat already. And this was the sentence of the last day upon Belshazzar: 'Thou art weighed in the balances, and art found wanting.' What balances! What tremendous balances! Balances with all Belshazzar's power, and riches, and opportunities, and responsibilities in the one scale, and then Belshazzar himself, naked and open, in the other scale. Belshazzar was weighed that night with weights of the most absolute truth and justice. Belshazzar was not weighed with King Saul's weights, nor with King David's weights, nor with King Solomon's. Belshazzar was weighed with weights of his own, that no man, before nor since, has ever been weighed with but Belshazzar himself. And you will be weighed, you are being weighed at this moment, with your own proper weights also. God Almighty has a special pair of balances beside Him, waiting and filling up till your life also is numbered and finished. Look up, sinner, at the awful instrument. Forecast the awful scene. All that God has done for you in your birth, in your godly upbringing, in your means of grace, in providences, in all privileges, in divine calls to a better life; all such warnings and all such instructions are collecting into one scale, and your soul—your naked and shivering soul—into the other scale with the whole universe looking on. Well may your knees knock! Well may your thoughts trouble you! How wilt thou do in the swelling of Jordan?

'The Lord is a God of knowledge,' says a solemn Scripture, 'and by Him actions are weighed.' That is to say, you will be weighed in those scales of God by means of which He gets at the very heart's blood of all your actions. Till He has got at the very heart's blood, till He has got at the thoughts and intent of an action, at its most secret motive, He is not yet a God of knowledge. But after that He is. You deceive us, you and your actions both pass with us for what at your heart you are not. But God is not mocked. He knows your exact weight and worth; and the exact weight and worth of all your words and all your deeds. He knows down to the bottom why you did this; and down to the bottom why you did not do that. He has known it all the time, only He has numbered your kingdom, and He lets you go on, deceiving and being deceived, till the Persian is at your gate.

> For I am 'ware it is the seed of act
> God holds appraising in His hollow palm,
> Not act grown great thence in the world below—
> Leafage and branchage vulgar eyes admire.

O my soul, what a day that will be for thee when the God of truth, and not any more of lies, brings forth His great balances! His balances, so awful in their burning truth and holiness! What a reversal of reputations! What a stain and overthrow of great names! What a dreadful trumpet-blowing upon the housetops! What nakedness! What shame! What everlasting contempt! Rocks, fall on us and hide us. O ministers! O people! But O ministers, above all, on that day! your people will gnash their teeth at you on that day unless your preach to them now the terrible balances of that day. Be sure you preach for one whole sermon every Sabbath the terrors of the Lord. To have even one of your people saved as by fire on that terrible day will be your salvation. For your God is a God of knowledge, and by Him every minister's motive and aims and ends will be weighed before the whole assembled world that day. Rock of Ages, cleft for me!

As you go about in this city you will see great scales sometimes at the street corner, sometimes in a shop for loungers, sometimes at a railway station, strong scales, in which, for a penny, you will see people amusing themselves by weighing themselves and one another, some for pure sport and just to kill time, and some in fear and anxiety lest they should turn out lighter and less in health than they were yesterday. Seek out the places where the scales of the soul are kept open, and seat thy soul in them every day. And, especially, never pass a Sabbath day without comparing your light soul with last Sabbath. God hangs out His scales in the heavens every Sabbath morning. And, above all, He weighs ministers, and their pulpits, and their people on that day. Choose your church, then, above all your choices, choose well your church. The city is before you. Choose a church with God's scales in it at any price. Call a minister who, when he is a probationer, and preaches two trial sermons, at one of the diets hangs God's great balances out of his pulpit and over your pew. And if there is no such probationer in all the poor leet, and no such preacher in all the besotted parish, then, all the more, and better for you, learn how to weigh yourself without a minister. Weigh and weigh, and weigh yourself till, in all you think, and all you say, and all you do, you find yourself wanting. Be sure there is something wrong with the balances; all the weights are not in, or there is some hidden rust in the hinges, or you have not read the index right, or something, if you do not find yourself wanting. If you are satisfied with yourself any one day, be sure there is a fatal mistake somewhere. Be sure that a dreadful awakening awaits you if you think that all things are fairly well with you. Never go up into your bed till you have been back in the balance; you and your past day. Never sleep till you know how you weigh, well or ill to-night. Weigh, and weigh, and weigh yourself every day, every night,—till there is no more left for the last day to do. Weigh yourself till you have relieved that terrible day of some of its pressure of business on God's hand. He will be pleased, amid much displeasure, on that day, to be lightened of His strange work even in one sinner. When the book comes to your name, He will say: 'Pass by that man, I know all about him; he is weighed and settled up with Me already.' It will be in that case as the Catechism, which is in your other scale, has it; you will be 'openly acknowledged and acquitted in the day of judgment.' Weigh yourself, and find yourself ever more and more wanting, till, in pure pity, God will put away His balance behind His back, and will bring forward His touchstone. I got that out of Thomas Goodwin's fine book, *A Child of Light Walking in Darkness*. 'For God brings not a pair of scales to weigh your graces with, and if they be too light refuseth them. No: but He brings a touchstone to try your graces. And, if they be true gold, though never so little of it, that gold will pass current with Him. Though it be but smoke, and not yet flame; though it be but as a wick in the socket, Matt. xii. 20 (as it is there in the original), likelier to die and to go out than to continue, and which we use to throw away; yet He will not quench it, but will accept it. These things you are to recall and to consider in times of distress.' That is to say, as often as you every day and every hour weigh yourselves, and find yourselves wanting, after the balance make use of the touchstone. And then, as King Brennus, in the old history book, cast his heavy sword into the too-light scale when the gold was being weighed; so will Christ cast in His cross into your too-light scale where His gold is being weighed on that day in you.

LXVI

ESTHER

THE Ahasuerus of the Book of Esther was the same sovereign as the Xerxes of Herodotus and Plutarch and Thirlwall and Grote. The Ahasuerus of Holy Scripture was the Xerxes who, after he had subdued Egypt, set out to invade Greece with an army and a navy of absolutely fabulous size and strength. He was the madman who beheaded his chief military engineers, and bastinadoed the Hellespont, and laid fetters of iron upon its waves, because a terrible storm had risen on its waters and had destroyed his great bridge of pontoon boats. He was that incubus of carnage who seated himself on a throne of gold on a hill-top of Greece to see his vast fleet of ships sweep off the sea the sea-forces of Athens.

A king sat on a rocky brow,
  Which looks o'er sea-born Salamis:
And ships by thousands lay below,
  And men in nations all were his.
He counted them at break of day,
But when the sun set, where were they?

'That Ahasuerus,' says an old Hebrew treatise called the Second Targum of Esther, 'whose counsels were perverse, and whose orders were not right: who commanded Queen Vashti to appear unveiled before him, but she would not appear. That Ahasuerus in whose time the house of Israel was sold for nought, and in whose time Israel's face became black like the side of a pot. That Ahasuerus in whose days was fulfilled the threatening that in the morning thou shalt say, Would God it were evening! and in the evening, Would God it were morning!'

The sacred writer makes us respect Queen Vashti amid all her disgusting surroundings. Whether or no the drunken despot actually sent to her the whole cruel order that the Targumist reports, the sacred writer does not in as many words say. But, whatever the royal order that came to her out of the banqueting-hall exactly was, the brave queen refused to obey it. Her beauty was her own and her husband's: it was not for open show among hundreds of half-drunk men. And in the long-run, the result of that night's evil work was that Vashti was dismissed into disgrace and banishment, and Esther, the Hebrew orphan, was promoted into her place. The whole story of Vashti's fall and Esther's rise would take us into too many miry places for us to-night to wade through. I shall leave this part of the unsavoury story veiled up in all the restrained and dignified language of the sacred writer. Only, let us take heed to note that the sacred writer's whole point is this, that the Divine Hand was, all the time, overruling Ahesuerus's brutality, and Vashti's brave womanliness, and Esther's beauty, and her elevation into Vashti's vacant seat, all this, and more than all this, to work together for the deliverance and the well-being of the remnant of Israel that still lay dispersed in the vast empire of Persia.

Mordecai was the uncle and the foster-father of the orphaned Esther. He had brought Esther up, and his one love in his whole life, after his love for Israel and for the God of Israel, was his love for his little adopted daughter. You may be sure that the devout old man had many thoughts in his heart that he could not get to the bottom of, as he stood by and watched his sister's child lifted up in a moment from her exile and poverty, and actually made the queen of the greatest empire then standing on the face of the earth; and, what was to him still more full of faith and hope, and love, the favourite queen of the absolute earthly master of all Mordecai's brethren of the house of Israel both at home in Jerusalem, and still scattered abroad over the whole of the Persian empire. I leave you to imagine what were the prayers and psalms that Mordecai offered up with his window open toward Jerusalem, as he saw all Esther's election, and promotion, and coronation, and all her splendour and all her power. And Mordecai walked every day before the court of the women's house, to know how Esther did, and what should become of her.

You would need to transport yourselves away east to the Constantinople of our day at all to understand Haman, and all his diabolical plots against Esther, and against Mordecai, and against all the people of Israel. Diabolically wicked as our own hearts often are with jealousy and with revenge, at the same time, our hearts are so held down and covered over by religion and civilisation that we do not know ourselves. There is no difference, says Paul. All vices are in us all, says Seneca; only, all vices are not equally extant in us all. But you will see all but all the vices extant in Haman, the favourite, for the time, of Ahasuerus. How Haman rose, and how he fell: how his seat was set above all the other princes of the empire at the beginning, and how his face was covered at the end; how he and Ahasuerus arranged it between themselves that Israel should be exterminated on a set day by a universal slaughter: how Haman had a gallows of fifty cubits high built for Mordecai yesterday, only to be hanged himself on that same gallows to-day: how Israel was sold to Haman by the seal of Ahasuerus, and was delivered by the perilous but successful interposition of Esther, all that is told as only a sacred writer could tell it. He that diggeth a pit shall fall into it. And he that rolleth a stone, it shall return upon his own head.

Such, then, was Esther's circle, so to call it. But what, exactly, was her opportunity? What was Esther's great opportunity that put her watchful uncle Mordecai into such sleepless anxiety lest she should either miss it, or betray it? Esther's splendid opportunity rose out of that extraordinary combination and concentration of circumstances in the very heart of which she had been so providentially placed. Haman, as we have seen, was the very devil himself. Haman, the son of Hammedatha the Agagite, was seven devils rolled into one. He was a very devil of pride, and jealousy, and of revenge, and of an insatiable thirst for Hebrew blood. How almighty God should have let so many devils loose in one devil-possessed man is another mystery of His power, and wisdom, and judgment, and love. But there it is, as plain as inspired words can write it. Only, when the end comes, we see that all the time the God of righteousness had His rope round Haman's neck. And when Haman got to the end of his rope, God said over Haman also: Hitherto thou shalt go in thy diabolical wickedness, but no farther. And, then, as another stepping-stone up to Esther's incomparable opportunity, Ahasuerus, Haman's master, was a fit master, as we have seen, for such a servant of Satan as Haman was. Till, between them, the children of Israel of that day were on the very point of being exterminated all over the land by a universal and prearranged assassination. But, as God's providence would have it, step after step, Esther was on the throne, and was in all the fulness of her first influence with Ahasuerus just at that critical moment for the Church of God in the empire of Persia. The great war with Greece; the great national feast consequent on that great war; the absolute intoxication of the king's mind with pride, and with ambition, and with wine; the brutal summons to Vashti; her brave refusal of her master's brutal demand; her fall and her banishment; the election and elevation of Esther, and her immense influence with the despot; all these things were so many stepping-stones on which Esther had so providentially risen to her splendid opportunity. And, then, to complete and finish it all, there was added to it all, Mordecai's so watchful solicitude over the wickedness of Haman, and over the caprice of Ahasuerus, and over the safety of Israel, and over the miraculous opportunity of Esther. What a long, and complex, and shining chain, link after link, till Mordecai fashioned its last link and bound it with his strong but tender hands upon both the imagination, and the conscience, and the heart of Esther in these noble words: 'Think not with thyself that thou shalt escape in the king's house, more than all the Jews. For if thou altogether holdest thy peace at this time, then shall there enlargement and deliverance arise to the Jews from another place; but both thou and thy father's house shall be destroyed; and who knoweth whether thou art come to the kingdom for such a time as this?' Then Esther bade them return to Mordecai this answer: 'I will go in unto the king, and if I perish, I perish.' But she did not perish. For she obtained favour in the sight of the king; and the king held out to her the golden sceptre that was in his hand, and said to her, 'What wilt thou, Queen Esther? And what is thy request? For it shall be given thee to the half of the kingdom.' And the end was that Haman and all his murderous plots fell, and Mordecai was promoted to sit in Haman's seat, and Israel was saved. And all because, under God, Esther had her opportunity pointed out to her till she saw it and seized it.

The Book of Esther is surely a very clear prophecy and a very impressive parable of the plots, and the persecutions, and the politics of our own day. Armenia under the Sultan is Israel over again under Haman and Ahasuerus. Western Christendom, and England especially, is Esther with her opportunity and her responsibility over again, and the voice of warning by whomsoever spoken is the summons of Mordecai to Esther over again. It is three hundred years of God's long-suffering since Bacon wrote his *Holy War*. 'There cannot but ensue a dissolution of the State of the Turk,' said Bacon, 'whereof the time seemeth to approach. The events of the times do seem to invite Christian kings to a war in respect of the great corruption and relaxation of discipline in the empire of the enemy of Christendom.' So wrote Bacon in 1622. But our Christian kings, if not our Christian people, are still, at the end of the nineteenth century, keeping Haman in his seat, and holding up his hands. In a very fine sermon on my present text, Mr. Spurgeon, in the very spirit and power of Mordecai, has warned England that the God of all the earth has raised her up to her supreme position among the nations of the earth, not for her own aggrandisement, and power, and glory—but for the glory of God, and for the good of mankind. And, that there is no respect or immunity of nations, any more than of men, with the Judge of all the earth. And that if England, for fear, or for favour, or for ease, or for herself only, flinches and fails God and man in the hour of her opportunity, deliverance will come somehow to the cause of God and man; and,—one holds back his tongue from saying it, and his pen from writing it—'Thou and thy father's house shall be destroyed.' As I read Captain Mahan's masterly and noble *Life of Nelson* the other day with Esther in my mind, I could not but mark such things as these in that great sea-captain who had such a hand in setting England up on her high opportunity. 'Opportunity,' says the excellent biographer, 'flitted by, but Nelson was always ready and grasped it.' Again, and again, and again the same thing is said of Nelson. Till it shines out above all his other great gifts, and becomes the best description of his great genius. Opportunity, opportunity, opportunity! And, again, 'duty, not ease; honour, not gain; the ideal, not the material—such, not indeed without frailty and blemish, were ever Nelson's motives.' This new *Nelson* is a noble book for sailors and for all men to read. It is a noble book to be written and read at any time time, but especially at this present time of gain with dishonour, and of ease at the sacrifice of duty.

But we are not great queens like Esther, with the deliverance of Israel in our hands; nor are we great sea-captains like Lord Nelson, with the making of modern England in our hands. No. But we are what we are; and what God has made us to be and to do. We all have our own circle set round us of God, and out of our own circle our own opportunities continually arise. Our opportunities may not be so far-reaching or so high-sounding as some other men's are; but they are our opportunities, and they are far-reaching enough for us. Our opportunities are life or death to us and to others; they are salvation or condemnation to our immortal souls; and is that not circle and opportunity enough? We are all tempted every day to say: If I only were Esther! If I only had a great opportunity, Would I not rise to it! Would I not speak out at any risk! Would I not do a work, and win a name, and deliver Israel, and glorify God! Did you ever read of Clemens, and Fervidus, and Eugenia, and their imaginary piety? Clemens had his head full of all manner of hypothetical liberalities. He kept proposing to himself continually what he would do if he only had a great estate. Come to thy senses, Clemens. Do not talk what thou wouldst be sure to do if thou wast an angel, but think what thou canst do as a man. Remember what the poor widow did with her two mites, and go and do likewise. Fervidus, again, is only sorry he is not a minister. What a reformation he would have worked in his own life by this time, and in his whole parish, if only God had made him a minister! He would have saved his own soul, and the souls of his people, in season and out of season. Do not believe yourself, Fervidus. You are deceiving yourself. You hire a cabman to drive you to church, and he sits in the wet street waiting for you, and you never ask him how he manages to live with no Sabbath. It is not asked of you, Fervidus, to live and die a martyr; but just to visit your cabman's wife and children, and have family worship with them on a Sabbath night as you would have done if you had been a minister. Eugenia, again, is a young lady full of the most devout dispositions. If she ever has a family she will let you see family religion. She is more scandalised than she can tell you at the way that some of her schoolfellows have married heathens, and at the life they lead without God's worship in their newly-married houses. But, Eugenia, you may never be married so as to show married people how to live. At the same time, you have a maid already, all to yourself. She dresses you for church, and then you leave her to have as little religion as a Hottentot. You turn her away when she displeases you, and you hire another, and so on, till you will die unmarried, and without a godly household, and your circle will be dissolved and your opportunity for ever lost. Your maid, and her sister, and her widowed mother, and her ill-doing brother, and her lover, all are your circle at present, and your opportunity is fast flitting by; and, because it is so near you every day, you do not discover it. Oh, Eugenia, full to the eyes of so many vain imaginations!

You never heard of Eugenia, and Fervidus, and Clemens before, and do not know where to find them. But, no matter. You and I are Fervidus and Eugenia ourselves. You and I are Mordecai and Esther ourselves. We are in that circle, and we are amid those opportunities, the very best that all the power, and all the wisdom, and all the love of God can provide for us. If it had been better for you and me that we had been born in Jerusalem, and had been exiles in Shushan, and subjects of King Ahasuerus, instead of the free-men of Queen Victoria, Almighty God could as easily have ordered it so when He was ordering all such matters. But, according to His best judgment, you are in the very best place for you in all the world. He could as easily have made you rich as poor. He could have made you successful in life, and married, and at the head of a house of your own, as easily as He has made you what you are. He could have made you a captain as easily as a common sailor. A queen, also, is as easy to God, as a kitchen-maid. But we are all talented of God, each according to our several ability. And the servant-maid has as good an opportunity, in the long-run, as her mistress. And the cabin-boy as the captain. A cabin-boy saved Nelson's life at Teneriffe, and thus won the Nile, and Copenhagen, and Trafalgar, for England. And he who with love and prayer and sweet civility keeps a door in God's house, has a far easier and a far safer life of it; he has his salvation at far less risk than he who has to work out his own salvation, and the salvation of so many others, on the slippery floor of a popular pulpit. All God's very best wisdom, and all His very deepest counsel, and all His very greatest love, have all been laid out in collecting and concentrating our circle round us, and in evoking our opportunities out of our surroundings, and we pay Him back with grumblings, and with neglect, and with the loss of our own souls and the souls of all who have anything to do with us.

Only open your eyes, and you will see all around you your circle set of God, and all dazzling you with its endless and splendid opportunities. Your most commonplace, most monotonous, most uninteresting, and most every-day circle so shines, if you only saw it aright. What a magnificent and unparalleled opportunity—you dare not deny it—is yours, for your self-control, for the reducing of your pride, for the extermination of your temper, for your humility and your patience, for the forgiving of your injuries, and for hiding your hungry, broken, bleeding heart with God! And what more would have? Yours is a circle with opportunities in it that an elect angel might well envy. Look, O my soul! how many, and what manner of people, are in thy very family and all around thee, and every one in his evil, even more than in his good, a divine stepping-stone laid there of God for thee whereon to climb up to the place that He has prepared for thee in His heavenly kingdom. What an antipathy you feel, and cannot get over, at that pestilential man. What an ever-gnawing envy at that other man. What an everlasting resentment and retaliation at such and such a man. What a genius has that fourth man for finding out for you the most corrupt places in your so corrupt and so deceitful heart. And so on, till there is nobody on earth, or in hell, like you. What a circle for a soul like your soul to be set in! What a sin-discovering and sin-exasperating circle! What a seven-fold furnace you walk in every day! There is nobody like you. There never was. O, man, what a chance you have! They know nothing about it sitting there in their soft seats. But what is the chaff to the wheat, if only you will let God cleanse you? These are they—the elders in heaven look down and say over you—who come up hither out of great tribulation! The chaff think that I am describing a monstrosity and an impossibility in my poor description of you. Never mind them. They and their thoughts are nothing to you. You know that the half of your temptations, and exasperations, and mortifications, and humiliations, and harassments of God, and men, and devils, has not been told. There is no tongue to tell it in, and no ear on earth to hear it with. Never mind them. All the deeper, then, is God's so deep plot for thee. All the more secret and unfathomable are His judgments for thee. All the richer set about thee is thy circle. All the more a miracle of grace are thy endless opportunities. All the more incomparable will be thy salvation, and all the more lustrous and weighty thy crown. Let neither man nor devil take it. Have it on thy head, all shining with pearls out of thy seas of sorrow, to cast at thy Saviour's feet on that day.

There is just one circle in the whole universe better than yours for a sinful man's most superb sanctification and salvation, and that is the pulpit, and the pastorate round about the pulpit. I do not wonder that Fervidus never forgave his father for not having made him a minister. For the divine subtlety has surpassed itself in the circle and in the opportunity it has set round every pulpit. O, all you who are our very best young men, all you, our ablest, foremost at college, most gifted, most many-sided, most original, most speculative, most intellectually pioneering and enterprising young men, I beseech you with all my might, do not miss the magnificent opportunity that the pulpit offers to him who can fill it as you could. Even we who will never now fill it—unless it is with tears and prayers night and day—we see, when it is too late, the incomparable life it at one time held out to us, and now holds out to you. There is no circle anywhere under heaven for individual interest; for all kinds of influence, the most immediate and the most lasting; and for the ever-deepening discipline of your own mind, and heart, and life, like the evangelical pulpit. O young men of Scotland, our choicest and our best young men, why stand ye so long hesitating? Open your eyes. Look around. Look within. Look at the church. Look at the world. Look forward to death and to the last day. And then look at the everlasting reward. They that be wise shall shine as the brightness of the firmament; and they that turn many to righteousness as the stars for ever and ever. Then Esther bade them return to Modecai this answer: Fast ye, and pray for me, and so will I go in unto the king.

LXVII

EZRA

Ezra was a great student, he was a great statesman, he was a great reformer, and he was a great preacher. Ezra was born in Babylon. Ezra was a child of the Captivity. But all that only made his heart break all the more for the longing he had to see the land of his fathers, and to do what in him lay fully to turn back again the captivity of Judah and completely to rebuild and restore Jerusalem. Ezra was as near as possibie Daniel over again, only in other circumstances. For Ezra also was a youth in whom was no blemish, but well-favoured, and skilful in all wisdom, and cunning in knowledge, and understanding science. But Ezra was all the time essentially himself. He was the slavish copy of no man over again—no, not even of Daniel. Ezra was what no man had ever been before him. He was the first scribe in Israel, whatever that was, and he was the first Scriptural preacher, as we say, and his original principle in preaching lasts on to this day, as it will last on and will grow in power and in fruitfulness till the last day. Ezra was full of originality and of distinction of mind, and his originality and his distinction of mind had their roots deep down in a heart and in a character of the very foremost and the very rarest order. For he was 'a ready scribe in the law of Moses, which the Lord God of Israel had given. Because Ezra had prepared his heart to seek the law of the Lord, and to do it, and to teach in Israel the divine statutes and the divine judgments'—a noble introduction, truly, to a noble life.

We are not told why it was that Ezra had not gone up out of Babylon along with the first body of returning exiles. 'The chaff came out of Babylon, but the wheat remained behind,' is a pungent saying of the Jews to this day about the first return of their forefathers from the Babylonian captivity. But, just as our own forefathers had a reformation in Scotland, and then a second reformation, so there was a return and a second return of the children of Judah from their captivity in Babylon. For when the new Jerusalem was in the very greatest straits from her enemies round about, and still more from the slackened faith and the corrupt life of her first return, Ezra rose up and came from Babylon, and was the salvation of Jerusalem. Happily for us, Ezra has embodied in his autobiography the remarkable letter that King Artaxerxes gave to him, and by which the Chaldean scribe was made nothing less than the king's viceroy in Jerusalem. Here are some sentences out of that royal edict: 'Artaxerxes, king of kings, unto Ezra the priest, a scribe of the law of the God of heaven, perfect peace, and at such a time. I make a decree, that all they of the people of Israel, and of the priests and Levites, in my realm, which are minded of their own free will to go up to Jerusalem, go with thee. And I, even I, Artaxerxes the king, do make a decree to all the treasurers that are beyond the river, that whatever Ezra the priest, the scribe of the law of the God of heaven, shall require of you, it be done speedily. And thou, Ezra, after the wisdom of thy God that is in thine hand, set magistrates and judges, which may judge all the people that are beyond the river, all such as know the law of thy God; and teach ye them that know them not.' And so on. A remarkable glimpse into the mind and heart of Artaxerxes, and a remarkable tribute, from a remarkable quarter, to the ability, and to the worth, and to the immense influence of Ezra.

Before Ezra had time to rest himself from the fatigue of his long journey, he was plunged into a perfect sea of trouble in Jerusalem. Ever since the death of the two great leaders of the first return, the social and the religious life of the new Jerusalem had been fast going down to moral corruption and death. And had Ezra not come to her deliverance, Jerusalem would soon have become again what she had so often been before—as Sodom, and like unto Gomorrah. The complete and even scrupulous separation of Israel from the absolute brutishness of the nations round about her,—this was the first law of Israel's life as a nation and as a church. There was no reason why Jehovah, at such a cost, so to speak, should continue to preserve Israel alive on the earth, unless she was to be a people pure and holy, and separated to the Lord, till the time should come when she would be able to be the salt of the whole earth and the light of the whole world. How Jerusalem could have fallen so suddenly and so low the history does not tell us; it leaves us to read all that in our own hearts. But, to his absolute consternation, Ezra found that already every wall of separation had been broken down between Israel and the Canaanites round about, till both the domestic life and the public life of Jerusalem was in nothing but in name to be distinguished from the abominations of the nations that their fathers had been brought out of Egypt to avenge and to root out. It was only then that Ezra saw how good the providence of God had been to him in having provided him with an instrument of such absolute authority as the king's letter was. For it needed all the authority of this autograph letter, and all the courage and resolution of Ezra to boot, in order to deal with the terrible disorders that everywhere faced him as he went about in Jerusalem. Those who are well enough read to remember how John Calvin ruled Geneva, and how John Knox and his colleagues did their best to rule Edinburgh—they will best understand and appreciate the rule of Ezra in Jerusalem. So far as those great men could do it, Jerusalem and Geneva and Edinburgh were for the time true theocracies: cities of God, that is; governed as Artaxerxes decreed that Jerusalem should be governed, by the law of the God of heaven. Not perfectly; not without many mistakes and infirmities of temper, and even crimes. But withal, both Ezra and Calvin and Knox made most able and most fearless efforts to set up the Kingdom of God in those three famous cities. So like, indeed, were those three statesmen and churchmen to one another that the modern historians of Israel are fain to come to Edinburgh for their best parallels and illustrations when they are engaged in writing about the Jerusalem of Ezra's day. Our Reformation, our Congregation, our First and Second Books of Discipline, our Solemn League and Covenant, and our Edinburgh pulpit—without those illustrations, taken from our own city, some of the most brilliant pages of Ewald, and Milman, and Stanley, and Plumptre, and our own Robertson Smith, would never have been written.

Ezra, while yet a young man in Babylon, had become 'a ready scribe in the law of Moses; in that law which the Lord God of Israel had given.' In the words of the 45th Psalm, Ezra's was already the 'pen of a ready writer.' By his high birth Ezra was by office a priest; when he cared to do it he could trace his unbroken and unblemished descent back to Aaron himself. But what of that, when there was neither temple, nor altar, nor mercy-seat, nor anything else of all the temple apparatus in Babylon? And had Ezra not discovered other and better work for himself: had Ezra not adapted himself to his new circumstances, and fitted himself into his new world, his would have been an idle and a lost and an embittered life in Babylon. But Ezra had the humility and the insight, the genius and the grace, to see that the future seat of spiritual worship, and the true source of spiritual life on earth was not to be a building any more, but a book. Ages and ages before books became what they are, Ezra was a believer in books, and in the Book of books. You who make a truly evangelical use of your Bible, and thus have a truly evangelical and a truly intelligent love for your Bible, must not forget what you owe to Ezra; for it was in Babylon, and it was under Ezra's so scholarly and so spiritual hands, that your Bible first began to take its shape and solidity. When all the other priests and Levites were moping about, not knowing what to do with themselves because they had no traditional altar at which to minister, Ezra struck out a new kind of priesthood and ministry in Israel which has outlasted all the temples and priesthoods in Israel, and which will last till the end of time. We can easily see what a splendid time the young priest-scribe must have spent in Babylon when we imaginatively construct to ourselves those eloquent and epoch-making words: 'Ezra prepared his heart to seek the law of the Lord, and to do it; and to teach in Israel statutes and judgments.' Ezra's true successors among ourselves; and, especially, those who, like Ezra, are still in their opportune youth and with their life in Jerusalem all before them—they will not fail to take note that Ezra's studies began and were carried on in his own heart. Having no temple precincts made with hands in which to dwell with God, Ezra dwelt all the more with God in the New Testament temple of his own heart. All other studies may more or less prosper independently of the state of the student's heart—language, law, medicine, science, philosophy even,—but not divinity. Divinity, and the great Ezrahite text-book of divinity, absolutely demand a devout, a humble, a penitent and a clean heart. And Ezra, the father of all our expository and experimental preachers, has this testimany, that he prepared his heart to seek the law of the Lord, and to do it. Ezra was of Luther's mind, so long before Luther's day, that it is the clean heart even more than the clear head that makes the theologian. Let all our intending preachers examine themselves, and so let them enter on their ever venerable, ever fresh, and ever vacant office.

A distinguished critic has claimed for Jonathan Edwards that his favourite and most frequently recurring word is 'sweetness.' At the same time, I see that a truly Catholic and Episcopal Professor holds that the word 'light,' even more than sweetness, is Edwards's characteristic word. Had I been suddenly asked that about Edwards, I would have said 'beauty.' You are safe to take all the three. John's favourite utterance is 'love,' as all the world knows; while Paul's peculiar mark and sure token in every epistle of his is 'grace.' Now, what is Ezra's most frequent and most often recurring utterance in his autobiography? Well, it is not taxes nor tithes, though he was a great civil and ecclesiastical administrator. It is nothing technical to masons or carpenters, though he has armies of such workmen engaged in the temple and on the walls of Jerusalem. It is not even the words that we would look for in a ready writer. Ezra's peculiar and characteristic expression is 'The hand of the Lord,' 'The hand of the Lord,' 'The hand of the Lord.' The hand of the Lord is constantly upon Ezra. When anything prospers with Ezra it is again, not Artaxerxes, nor himself, but 'The hand of the Lord.' He introduces himself to his readers as a man in all things under the hand of the Lord. The king granted him all his requests according to the hand of the Lord his God upon him. And upon the first day of the first month began he to go up out of Babylon, and on the first day of the fifth month came he to Jerusalem according to the good hand of his God upon him. And I was strengthened as the hand of the Lord my God was upon me, and I gathered together out of Israel chief men to go with me. And as soon as he secured a suitable colleague to assist him in his immense work, 'by the good hand of God upon us, they brought me a man of understanding.' Just as he had refused an armed convoy with these same words, The hand of our God is upon all them that seek Him. 'And from the river Ahava to Jerusalem the hand of our God was upon us to deliver us out of the hand of the enemy.' Our learned men are able to trace and detect the authorship and the authenticity of anonymous and pseudonymous books and manuscripts by the peculiar words and phrases and constructions that occur in them. I think we might almost let the higher critics assert that if there is any page of personal narrative, and no acknowledgment of the hand of God in it, whoever may have written that self-sufficient page it cannot have been Ezra.

Have you discovered and appropriated to yourself Ezra's great prayer was in the temple of the new, but already backsliding, For that, as you know, was Andrewes's famous and fruitful way with himself. Whenever he came in his reading on any prayer, or psalm, or verse, or even a single word that first spoke to his heart from God, and then uttered his heart to God, he straightway took it down till his *Private Devotions* became the extraordinary treasure-house that it is. I do not remember another such intercession and suretyship prayer in all the Bible as Ezra's prayer? Bishop Andrewes discovered and appropriated it bodily. Jerusalem. How this true priest makes himself one with the great transgressors for whom he prays! As you listen you would think that Ezra had been a very ringleader in all those utter abominations that he blushes to have to name. Ezra confesses Jerusalem's sin with an agony such as if all that sin had all been his own. Ezra's spirit in public prayer, his attitude, and his utterances are enough to scandalise all hard and dry and meagre-hearted men. But Ezra's prayer, whether in his own book, or borrowed into another book, or assimilated into another praying heart, will always carry captive all tender, and generous, and deep, and holy hearts around it. And thus it was that day that a kindred spirit in that congregation named Shechaniah broke in upon Ezra's prayer and declared that he and his fellow-elders could stand such praying no longer. If Ezra would only stop they would do anything he was pleased to command them. It is always so. If you would move me with your preaching, or with your praying, or with your singing, first be moved yourself. Only, where have we the chance of such commanding and contagious prayer as that was which made all Jerusalem take such sudden fire that day? There had been a long-laid and a daily-built-up altar-fire in Ezra's own heart ever since that early day in Babylon when he first began to prepare his heart to seek the law of the Lord. A life like Ezra's life, first in Babylon and then in Jerusalem,—that is the real secret of every sudden and all-prevailing outburst of prayer both with God and with man.

But, with all that, such is my immense and evergrowing appreciation of the pulpit that I look on all that—Ezra's birth in Babylon, his suspension from his priesthood, his great and original work upon the law of Moses, his summons to Jerusalem, his hourly and unceasing experience under the hand of the Lord, his extraordinary exercises both in personal and in intercessory prayer,—as but so much providential preparation for Ezra's expository and experimental pulpit. It is a grand picture —who will worthily paint it?—and it is only the first of a multitude of such grand pictures. Ezra, standing in his pulpit of wood, with his thirteen elders standing supporting him, six on his right hand and seven on his left. And Ezra opened the book in the sight of all the people, and he and his colleagues caused the people to understand the law and the people stood in their place. So Ezra read in the book in the law of God distinctly, and gave the sense, and caused the people to understand the reading. That is delightfully described, is it not? And that is the very first original and most ancient type and pattern of our best pulpit work to this day. And that type and that pattern has been kept up with splendid success down to this day. To name some of the very masters of pulpit exposition—we have Chrysostom.

and Augustine, and Calvin, and Matthew Henry, and, the richest of them all to me, that masterly exegete of the Puritan pulpit, an interpreter, one of a thousand, Thomas Goodwin. And, because he is still alive, and not two hundred years dead, is that a right reason why I should not here name Goodwin's direct successor in his incomparable pulpit—Dr. Joseph Parker? An expositor and a commentator quite worthy to be written in that shining roll. If you have not enough brotherly love to believe that, just borrow, if you will not buy, say the tenth volume of the People's Bible, and read what Dr. Parker says about Ezra, and then be honest enough to agree with me and to thank me. All those men laid out their pulpit life on Ezra's exact plan. That is to say, not so much preaching trite and hackneyed sermons, on trite and hackneyed texts; but reading in the law of God consecutively, giving the sense, and causing the people to understand the reading. That exactly describes our own Scottish habit of 'lecturing,' as we call it. And it was to that pulpit practice, in no small degree, that our forefathers owed it that they came to know the Bible so well, till they were, and are, so ill to please with the pulpit work of their preachers. It is a noble tradition and perfect method; only, to do it well demands very hard labour, and very wide reading, and very deep thinking, as well as an early and a life-long preparation of the preacher's heart. But he who sets to himself this noblest of all possible tasks, and perseveres to the end in it, ever learning in it, ever improving in it, ever adding to his treasures of exposition and illustration, ever putting himself into his lecture, and ever keeping himself out of it, he will never grow old, he will never become worked out, he will never weary out his people, but he will to old age bring forth his fruit in his season, and his leaf will not wither. And, then, both to him and to his happy people, will be fulfilled every new Sabbath morning some of the most blessed promises in all the Word of God. 'For I will bring you to Zion, saith the Lord, and I will give you pastors after mine own heart, which shall feed you with knowledge and understanding, till we all come in the unity of the faith, and of the knowledge of the Son of God, unto a perfect man, unto the measure of the stature of the fulness of Christ.'

LXVIII

SANBALLAT

You must clearly understand, to begin with, that Samaria was already, even in that early year, the deadly enemy of Jerusalem, and also that Sanballat was the governor of Samaria. And Sanballat was a man of this kind, that he was not content with doing his very best to make Samaria both prosperous and powerful, but he must also do his very best to keep Jerusalem downtrodden and destroyed. And thus it was that, when Sanballat heard that Nehemiah had come from Shushan with a commission from Artaxerxes to rebuild the walls of Jerusalem, the exasperating news drove Sanballat absolutely beside himself. And thus it is that such a large part of Nehemiah's autobiography is taken up with Sanballat's diabolical plots and conspiracies both to murder Nehemiah and to destroy the new Jerusalem.

The Book of Nehemiah, you must know, is the last written of all the historical books of the Old Testament. We have nothing in our Bible between Nehemiah and Matthew. Nehemiah, among the historical books of the Old Testament, is just what Malachi is among the prophetical books. Nehemiah is not much read, but his book is full of information and instruction and impression of the most interesting and fruitful kind. And as we work our way through Nehemiah's memoirs of himself. we see in Sanballat an outstanding instance of the sleepless malice and the diabolical wickedness of all unprincipled party spirit and besotted partisanship.

Now, in the first place, diabolically wicked as party spirit too often becomes, this must be clearly understood about party spirit, that, after all, it is but the excess, and the perversion, and the depravity of an originally natural, and a perfectly proper principle in our hearts. It was of God, and it was of human nature as God had made it, that Sanballat should love and serve Samaria best, and that Nehemiah should love and serve Jerusalem best. And all party spirit among ourselves also, at its beginning, is but our natural and dutiful love for our own land, and for our own city, and for our own Church, and for those who think with us, and work with us, and love us. And as long as this world lasts, and as long as human nature remains what it is, there will always be predilections, and preferences, and parties both in the family, and in the city, and in the State, and in the very Church of Christ itself. As long as there is such a rich variety and diversity of talents, and capacities, and dispositions, and tastes, and interests among men, there will always be bodies of men thinking together, and working together, and living together, and loving one another, more than they can live with, and work with, and love other men who see their duties and pursue their interests in another light. Now, this natural principle of mutual attraction is not planted in human nature for no reason. But all the discoverable final causes of this principle are too many for me to enter on now; to enter on them at all would lead me far away from far more important and urgent work to-night. Suffice it to say then, that party spirit, at its very worst, is but another case and illustration of the corruption and the depravity of the very best.

But, then, when it comes to its worst, as it too often does come, party spirit is the complete destruction of both of truth and of love. The truth is hateful to the out-and-out and thoroughgoing partisan. We all know that in ourselves. When we have, at any time, become abandoned partisans in anything, then, farewell the truth. We will not have it. As many lies as you like, but not the truth. We hate and detest both you and your truth. It exasperates us to hear it. You are henceforth our enemy if you will insist on speaking it. We cast it, and all its organs, out of doors. We shut our eyes to the truth, and we stop our ears. It is not truth that divides us up into such opposed parties as we see all around us in Church and State; it is far more lies. It is not principle once in ten times. Nine times out of ten it is pure party spirit. And I cling to that bad spirit, and to all its works, as if it were my life. I feel unhappy when you tell me the truth, if it is good truth, about my rival. I feel the sore pain of concession. I feel as if all my foundations were being taken away from under me. How fierce you always make me when you so rejoice in the truth and go about spreading it! I am a Jew, and I want no dealings with the Samaritans. All I want is to hear that fire has fallen from heaven to consume them. I am a Protestant, and a Presbyterian, and a Free Churchman, and I want to stand aloof all my life from all who differ from me. I do not want to hear what they have to say for their fathers and for themselves. I hate like poison all your proposed fraternisings and unions. I hope that the old walls of separation will hold together all my time.

And where truth is hated in that way love can have no possible home. Truth is love in the mind, just as love is truth in the heart. Trample on the one, and you crush the other to death. Cherish and be tender with the one, and you will eat the fruits and drink the sweets of the other. Now the full-blown party spirit is utter poison to the spirit of love as well as to the spirit of truth. 'Love suffereth long, and is kind: love rejoiceth not in inquity, but rejoiceth in the truth; beareth all things, believeth all things, endureth all things.' But party spirit is the clean contradiction of all that. 'No assurances,' says Thucydides, 'no pledges of either party could gain credit with the other. The most reasonable proposals, coming from an opponent, were received not with candour, but with suspicion. No artifice was reckoned dishonourable by which a point could be carried. Every recommendation of moderate measures was reckoned either a mark of cowardice, or of insincerity. He only was considered a completely safe man whose violence was blind and boundless; and those who endeavoured to steer a middle course were spared by neither side.' That might have been written yesterday, so true to our own public life also is every syllable of it. Archbishop Whately's Bampton Lecture, for the year 1822, has for its subject, 'The Use and the Abuse of Party Spirit in matters of Religion,' and a very able piece of work it is. Whately was one of the ablest men in a very able day in the Church of England. His strong Saxon sense, supported by wide reading, and by clear and disciplined habits of thought, rose almost to the level of genius. Could Whately and Newman have been mixed together we should have had a perfect English theologian. Whately's third lecture is entitled 'A Carnal Mind the Cause of Divisions,' and at the foot of a page in which he shows 'how self-interest may chance to be the first mover of discord,' this footnote stands, which I repeat to you with both pain, and shame, and indignation: 'It happens but too often, it is to be feared,' so the note runs, 'that a dissenting chapel is regarded as a profitable speculation by persons of corrupt minds, and destitute of the truth, looking upon religion as a gainful occupation.' Why, I wonder, should it be so much feared that a dissenting chapel is a profitable speculation to persons of corrupt minds, more than a cathedral stall or an Episcopal palace? What an indecent blot is that on such an able book! And what an illustration it supplies of that very vice the Archbishop is so ably exposing—the blinding and perverting influences of party positions and of a party spirit! Those five lines of prejudice and partisanship made far more impression on me than all the rest of the Archbishop's so masterly and so impressive volume. With my own ears I once heard the late Canon Liddon, when preaching in St. Paul's Cathedral, class Oliver Cromwell with Alexander the Sixth and Richard the Third! To such lengths will a malevolent party spirit go even in the Christian pulpit!

By the just and righteous ordination of Almighty God all our sins carry their own punishment immediately and inseparably with them. And party spirit, being such a wicked spirit, infallibly inflicts a very swift and a very severe punishment on the man who entertains it. You know yourselves how party spirit hardens your heart, and narrows and imprisons and impoverishes your mind. You must all know how party spirit poisons your feelings, and fills you with antipathy to men you never saw, as well as to men all around you who have never hurt a hair of your head, and would not if they could. We read in the *Apologia* how Newman's imagination was stained by his prejudices and his passions. And every man who labours to keep his imagination and his heart open and clean and unstained, will have to confess what a tremendous task he has undertaken. You must either be a great saint, or a great fool, if your imagination and your heart are not stained to absolute wickedness against men, and against churches, and against this and that party in the Church and in the State. It humiliates my head to the dust of death, and it breaks my heart before God and before myself every day I live, to discover such stains in my heart against men who have hurt me in nothing but in this—that they have given their great talents and their shining services to another church than my church, and to another party than my party. I cannot meet such men on the streets but they scowl at me, and I at them back again. Or if we must stop and speak for a moment, we put on Sanballat's face to one another, and take hold of Sanballat's hand, while all the time our hearts are as full as they can hold of Sanballat's mischief that he thought to do to Nehemiah. What a terrible punishment all that is, let him tell us who, before God, is keeping his heart clean of all that. Unless it is casting pearls before swine to attempt to tell such things to us. No! Do not attempt to tell such things to us lest we turn again and rend you.

Another divine punishment of party spirit is seen in the way that it provokes retaliation, and thus reproduces and perpetuates itself till the iniquity of the fathers is visited upon the children to the third and fourth generation of them that hate the truth and murder love. Sanballat hated Nehemiah and plotted against him; and Nehemiah, not yet being Jesus Christ, nor one of His disciples, retaliated on Sanballat and on Samaria in a way that sadly stains the otherwise spotless pages of his noble book. And between them, Sanballat and Nehemiah kindled that intense and unnatural hatred that is still burning in every heart in Jerusalem and Samaria, when the woman at the well refuses a cup of cold water to our Lord, and when the Samaritans will not make ready for Him nor receive Him, because His face is as though He would go to Jerusalem; and till He pays the woman back with a well of water springing up to everlasting life, and the men of Samaria with the parable of the Good Samaritan. As you know, it takes two to make a complete and a lasting quarrel; so it takes many more than two to make party spirit perfect. And if Nehemiah, and the other builders of Jerusalem, had but had our New Testament truth and love, long centuries of ill-will, and insult, and injury, would have been escaped, and a welcome given to the Lord of truth and love that He did not get. And, inheriting no little good from our contending forefathers, we have inherited too many of their injuries, and retaliations, and antipathies, and alienations also. And the worst of it is, that we look on it as true patriotism, and the perfection of religious principle, to keep up and perpetuate all those ancient misunderstandings, and injuries, and recriminations, and alienations. 'Ye know not what spirit ye are of,' said our Lord to His disciples when they wished Him to consume the Samaritans off the face of the earth, 'for the Son of Man is not come to destroy men's lives, but to save them.' To save them, that is, from all their inherited hurts, and hatreds, and antipathies, and animosities, and suspicions. Who, then, is a wise man, and endued with knowledge among you? Let him shew, out of a good conversation, his works with meekness of wisdom. But if ye have bitter envyings and strife in your hearts, glory not, and lie not against the truth. This wisdom descendeth not from above, but is earthly, sensual, devilish; for where envying and strife is, there is confusion and every evil work.

Who, then, is a wise man, and endued with wisdom among you? Who would fain be such a man? Who would fain at once and for ever extinguish out of his heart this fire from hell? Who would behave to his rivals and enemies, not as Nehemiah, good man though he was, behaved to the Samaritans, but as Jesus Christ behaved to them? Who, in one word, would escape the sin, and the misery, and the long-lasting mischief of party spirit? Butler has an inimitable way of saying some of his very best and very deepest things. Our master-moralist seems to be saying nothing at all, when all the time what he is saying is everything. And here is one of his great sayings that has helped me more in this matter than I can tell you. 'Let us remember,' he says, 'that we differ as much from other men as they differ from us.' What a lamp to our feet is that sentence as we go through this world! As we travel from home and go abroad; as we see other nations with their own habits and their own manners; as we see other churches at their worship; as we read other men's books, and speeches, and newspapers, and they ours; as we encounter other men's principles, and prejudices, and habits of mind, and life and heart—what a light to our path are Butler's wise words! And till we come, in God's spirit of truth, and humility, and love, to take every other man's place and point of view, till we look at all things, and especially at ourselves, with all other men's eyes, and ears, and hearts. But why multiply many words about this plain matter? It is all contained long ago in the two old Commandments—to love our neighbour as ourselves, and to love God with all our mind, and heart, and strength, and will.

And, then, when at any time, and towards any party, or towards any person whatsoever, you find in yourself that you are growing in love, and in peace, and in patience, and in toleration, and in goodwill, and in good wishes, acknowledge it to yourself; see it, understand it, and confess it. Do not be afraid to admit it, for that is God within your heart. That is the Divine Nature, that is the Holy Ghost. Just go on in that Spirit, and ere ever you are aware you will be caught up and taken home to that Holy Land where there is neither Jerusalem nor Samaria. There will be no party spirit there. There will be no controversy there. There will be no corruption of motive there, and no imputation of it. No ignorance will be found there, and no prejudice, no partiality, no antipathy, no malignity, and no delight in doing mischief. The envy also of Ephraim shall depart, and the adversaries of Judah shall be cut off. Ephraim shall not envy Judah, and Judah shall not vex Ephraim. Violence shall no more be heard in thy land, wasting nor destruction within thy borders; but shalt call thy walls Salvation, and thy gates Praise. Thy sun shall no more go down, neither shall thy moon withdraw itself; for the Lord shall be thine everlasting light, and the days of thy mourning shall be ended.

LXIX

NEHEMIAH

For a long time I was not much drawn to Nehemiah. I did not aright understand Nehemiah, and I did not love him. He was not my kind, as we say: the kind, that is, that I like best to read about, and to think about, and to imitate and to preach. I thought him, if a patriotic, at the same time, an outside, a surface, a hard, and an austere man. And, worst of all, a man who was always pleased with himself; the first of Pharisees, in short, as Ezra was the first of Scribes. I should have remembered what Canon Gore puts so well in *Lux Mundi*: 'At starting, each of us, according to our disposition, is conscious of liking some books of Scripture better than others. This, however, should lead us to recognise that, in some way, we specially need the teaching that is less attractive to us. We should set ourselves to study what we less like, till that, too, has had its proper effect in moulding our conscience and shaping our character.' 'If I met a man from New England,' said Dr. Duncan. 'I would say to him, "Read the Marrow Men." If I met a Marrow Man, I would say, "Read the New Englanders."'

Like Daniel and his three companions, and like Ezra his own colleague, Nehemiah was a child of the Captivity. They had all been born and brought up in the furnace of affliction. And they were all children in whom was no blemish, but well favoured, and skilful in all wisdom, and cunning in knowledge, and understanding science, and such as had ability in them to stand in the king's palace. Like Ezra also, Nehemiah has written his own biography, and like Ezra also, he both begins and ends his autobiography with great abruptness. We have neither Nehemiah's youth nor his old age in his autobiography. His whole memoir of himself is taken up with his leave of absence from Shushan the palace, and with what he was able to do for Jerusalem during his furlough from Shushan. By the time that Nehemiah's fragment of autobiography opens, the first return from the captivity has for some time taken place. Jerusalem, in a way, has been largely rebuilt. The temple also, after a fashion, has been restored, and the daily services of the temple are in full operation. But the walls and the gates and the towers and the battlements of the new Jerusalem still lie in ruins all round the city;

and while that is the case, the whole city stands open to the inroads and the ravages of their enemies round about. Nor is all that the worst. It is a weariness and a despair to read it,—but the returned captives themselves were living in far greater poverty and bondage in Jerusalem than in all their seventy years in Babylon itself. Those of you who have ever read and at all understand the two sad little books of Ezra and Nehemiah, and the still more sad little book of Malachi,—that saddened and despairing reader will have seen in those three books what a hopeless people God had to do with. And, with still more self-disgust and self-despair, he will have seen what an Old Testament type and example the Jews always are of ourselves.

The schoolboys who have read the *Cyropædia* can best picture Nehemiah to themselves when he says that he was the King of Persia's cupbearer. The amusing episode of Cyrus and his grandfather's cupbearer is the best commentary we possess on the position of Nehemiah in Shushan the palace. The Persian cupbearer was far more than a cupbearer. He was a kind of prime minister, and master of the ceremonies, both in one. He was the royal favourite above all the rest of the palace, till his privileges and his powers and his wealth were all a proverb. He was able to keep a table and set up an equipage at his own expense like a prince. Daniel's youthful beauty, his graces of character and manner, his shining talents, and his high state-services may all be borrowed and set down as the opening pages of Nehemiah's memoirs of himself. Where Josephus got it he does not tell us, but he gives us a most picturesque and pathetic account of the way in which the terrible state of Jerusalem came to the cupbearer's ears. Nehemiah was taking the air one evening outside the walls of Persepolis when some travel-stained men passed him on their way into the gate of the city. As they passed him he overheard them conversing together in the Hebrew tongue. You know how your mother-tongue would go to your heart if you were an exile in a far country, however prosperous outwardly you were. And Nehemiah forgot all about Artaxerxes' supper as he talked with the travellers, till he said to them as he bade them farewell, 'If I forget thee, O Jerusalem, let my right hand forget her cunning; if I do not remember thee, let my tongue cleave to the roof of my mouth; if I prefer not Jerusalem above my chief joy!' Young John Milton, you will remember, could not enjoy the skies, or the art, or the letters of Italy, while England at home was as she was. And it came to pass in the month Nisan, in the twentieth year of Artaxerxes the king, that wine was before him: and I took the wine and gave it to the king. Now I had not been sad in his presence heretofore. Wherefore the king said unto me, Why is thy countenance sad, seeing thou art not sick? This is nothing else but sorrow of heart. Then I was very sore afraid, and said unto the king, Let the king live for ever! Why should not my countenance be sad, when the city, the place of my fathers' sepulchres, lieth waste, and the gates thereof are consumed with fire? Then the king said to me, For what dost thou make request? So I prayed to the God of heaven, says the cupbearer. How he was heard, and how the king's heart was moved, and how Nehemiah got leave of absence to go and build the walls of Jerusalem, and the letters that he carried to the king's foresters, and to those that kept the royal quarries, and how he set out to the city of his fathers to finish it—all that is to be read in Nehemiah's own memoirs written out for us to this day by his own graphic hand.

If the style is the man in the Scriptures also, then we see Nehemiah to the very life in the whole of his book; but, especially, in his second and third chapters. We see him as well as if we had carried the candle before him all those three nights in which he went round the ruins of Jerusalem. So I came to Jerusalem, and was there three days. And I arose in the night, I and some few men with me: neither told I any man what my God had put in my heart to do at Jerusalem: neither was there any beast with me, save the beast that I rode upon. And I went out by night by the gate of the valley, even before the dragon well, and to the dungport, and viewed the walls of Jerusalem, which were broken down, and the gates thereof were consumed with fire. Then went I up in the night by the brook, and viewed the wall, and turned back, and entered by the gate of the valley, and so returned. And the rulers knew not whither I went, or what I did: neither had I as yet told it to the Jews, nor to the priests, nor to the nobles, nor to the rulers, nor to the rest that did the work. A self-contained man. A man of his own counsel. A man with the counsel of God alone in his mind and in his heart. A reserved and a resolute man. A man to take the command of other men. A man who will see things with his own eyes, and that without all eyes seeing him. A man in no haste or hurry. He will not begin till he has counted the cost. And then he will not stop till he has finished the work. The way that Nehemiah took to build and complete the whole wall round about Jerusalem was this: Every trade, and profession, and corporation, and outstanding city family took a portion, and undertook either to build that portion with their own hands or to see it built. And, to begin with, as was but natural and seemly,

Eliashib the high priest began first to build; and, as was to be expected, he held a special sacrifice and spiritual service both at the beginning and at the end of his portion of the wall. A volunteer party from the neighbouring city of Jericho took up the portion of the wall adjoining Eliashib; and next to them a man whose name we do not know. 'I will take the fish gate,' said Hassenaah. 'I and my sons will lay the beams thereof, and set up the doors thereof, the locks thereof, and the bars thereof.' Then came three men,—but we have never heard their strange names before nor since: their names are only written in heaven, and in the third chapter of Nehemiah. And next unto them the Tekoites repaired; 'but their nobles,' Nehemiah takes this note on his tablets, 'put not their necks to the work of the Lord.' 'Let me have the old gate to repair,' said Jehoiada, the son of Paseah. 'My heart warms to the old gate.' And he and Meshullam divided the old gate between them. Then the guild of the goldsmiths did a large piece, and next to them the apothecaries. These last fortified a strong and a broad portion of the wall, as I have known apothecaries do among ourselves. And, then, after some unknown but noble men: look here at the ruler of the half of Jerusalem and his daughters. I opened Matthew Henry in a hurry here, so sure was I that he would have something specially shrewd on the daughters of Shallum. But even Homer sometimes nods. To my great disappointment I found nothing in the unfailing annotator worth repeating to you. But he wakens up when he comes to the thirtieth verse. Meshullam Matthew Henry holds to have been a lodger who undertook a piece of the wall the size of his own rented room. So that you see our adherents here, and our seat-holders, and those not yet full members, may take their part in all our work till the time comes when they shall have sons and daughters to help them. Thus, at any rate, did Berechiah's lodger, if he was not also his son. That is not the half of Nehemiah's roll of noble names; but you can go round the whole wall for yourselves, and see the rest of the builders at their work for yourselves, till you come to the goldsmith's son at the going up of the corner.

And let it not be overlooked, to their praise, that all the builders builded every man with his sword by his side because of the deadly envy and ill-will of their enemies round about. The enemies of Jerusalem 'took it heinously,' says Josephus, that the wall of Jerusalem was in the way to be rebuilt. They so laboured, Nehemiah proudly writes it about them, from the rising of the morning till the stars appeared. And all the time Artaxerxes' cupbearer had his eye on everything. He was everywhere, and he was the power and the success of everything. The young cupbearer has now become a great statesman and an experienced administrator, till he has left his mark on Jerusalem as long as one stone shall stand upon another. But you must really take time and read the whole of this inimitable little book for yourselves at a downsitting. And that, if only to see how Ezra and Nehemiah worked together, the old scribe and the young cupbearer. How the priests' pulpit of wood was set up, how the support of the altar and the pulpit was seen to, how the public sanctification of the Sabbath was secured, and other reforms instituted with a firmness of hand that there was no resisting. Altogether, this little book is full of Nehemiah's absolute mastery in Jerusalem, and his determination that Jerusalem shall be both a safe, a happy, and a holy city to dwell in. Speaking of the preachers of Jerusalem and their support, just as we get our Presbytery, and our Kirk-Session, and our Expository Pulpit, and our Puritan Sabbath from the new Jerusalem of that day, so we get our Deacons' Court and our Sustentation Fund from Ezra and Nehemiah. Ezra was an old preacher, full of years, full of learning, and full of an experienced piety, giving himself continually to prayer and to the ministry of the Word, while young Nehemiah, like Stephen in the Acts, served tables in the new Jerusalem. That is to say, he looked after the walls of Jerusalem, and the whole temple furniture, and the support of the temple ministry. If our pulpit of wood and its method of work on the Word of God is ancient and honourable, so also is our Deacons' Court. And neither in the new Jerusalem of Nehemiah's day, nor in the same Jerusalem in Peter's day, was the prophetic and apostolic and diaconate compact better observed, on the deacons' side at any rate, than it is in our own congregations at the present moment. And because of all this, says Nehemiah, we make a sure covenant and write it out, and our princes, Levites, and priests all seal unto it, that we will not forsake nor forget the house of our God.

Nehemiah was such a worker in and around the house of God that he would have satisfied James the Just himself. James, the brother of the Lord, was always insisting on work in all the twelve tribes scattered abroad. 'Even faith, if it hath not works, is dead, being alone. Wilt thou know, O vain man, that faith without works is dead? For as the body without the spirit is dead, so faith without works is dead also.' But for his love of work, Nehemiah again and again would have been a dead man. Again and again Sanballat would have had Nehemiah in his clutches, but that Nehemiah would not come down. 'Come out to a conference in the plains of Ono, at any rate,' said Sanballat. 'No,' answered Nehemiah, 'I have no time for conferences. I am doing such a great work on the wall up here that I cannot for one moment leave it.' Yes, it was the cupbearer's quenchless love of work that both saved his life on several occasions, as well as built and finished the wall of Jerusalem. Cupid, in the old fable, complained bitterly to Jupiter that he could never debauch the Muses, because he never could come on them sitting idle. If work is not worship, then it is surely the next thing to it, so much so that, just bring up your son in idleness, and your grey hairs are as good as in their grave already. Whereas, give your son something to do, from making tables to serving them, and you have as good as saved his soul. He has no time so much as to speak to Sanballat. Let every young man then begin early to do something. Let him be a student and a lover of good books. Let him teach a class. Let him be honoured, and trusted, and elected like Stephen to be a deacon. Let him do his noble duties with the understanding and the heart. Let him know what he is doing every time he does it, and he will thus purchase for himself a good degree; that is to say, good work, and a real love for the good work, and step after step, he will escape all the Sanballats of the city, and will go on from work to work, through a youth and a manhood of interest and usefulness, occupation and protection, to an old age of the best love among us and the highest honours.

And if any young minister should be ordained, like Nehemiah, over such a congregation as Jerusalem was in that day; if he finds the gates thereof burned with fire, and the walls laid waste, and the whole house of God in reproach round about; let him read the Book of Nehemiah till he has it by heart. Let him view the wreck and ruin on his arrival as the young cupbearer did. Let him say nothing to any man. Only let him rise up in the King's name and build. Let him come to the King's quarries for stone, and to the King's forests for timber. The good hand of his God being upon him. Let him preach his very best to his long-starved people every Sabbath morning; and better and better every year he lives. Let him visit his long-neglected people night and day. Let him be like Samuel Rutherford in as small a church as was in Scotland in that day, and now and for ever as famous. Let him be his people's boast. Let him be always in his study, always at their sickbeds, always preaching, always praying. So neither I, nor my brethren, nor my servants, nor the men of the guard that followed me, none of us put off our clothes, saving that every one put them off for the washing. And at the dedication of the wall there was great gladness, both with thanksgivings and with singing, with cymbals, with psalteries, and with harps. For God had made them to rejoice with great joy; the wives also and the children rejoiced. So that the joy of Jerusalem was heard even afar off. And it was Nehemiah's faith in God, his love of Jerusalem, and his hard work for Jerusalem that did it.